D0987214

THE WAR CAME TO US

For Bri, my love and partner through everything.
For my parents, whose guidance and support mean the world.
For my brave Ukrainian friends, who welcomed and inspired me.

"Hell is empty and all the devils are here."
—William Shakespeare, *"The Tempest"*

"Boritesya—poborete." — "Fight on and you shall prevail."
—Taras Shevchenko, *The Caucasus*

THE WAR CAME TO US

LIFE AND DEATH IN UKRAINE

CHRISTOPHER MILLER

BLOOMSBURY CONTINUUM
LONDON • OXFORD • NEW YORK • NEW DELHI • SYDNEY

BLOOMSBURY CONTINUUM
Bloomsbury Publishing Plc
50 Bedford Square, London, WC1B 3DP, UK
29 Earlsfort Terrace, Dublin 2, Ireland

BLOOMSBURY, BLOOMSBURY CONTINUUM and the Diana logo are trademarks
of Bloomsbury Publishing Plc

First published in Great Britain 2023

Copyright © Christopher Miller 2023

Christopher Miller has asserted his right under the Copyright, Designs and Patents Act, 1988, to be
identified as Author of this work

Map credits: Ukraine © PeterHermesFurian/Getty Images; The Donbas © Goran_tek-en,
CC BY-SA 4.0 <https://creativecommons.org/licenses/by-sa/4.0>, via Wikimedia Commons;
Crimea © PeterHermesFurian/Getty Images

All rights reserved. No part of this publication may be reproduced or transmitted in any form or by
any means, electronic or mechanical, including photocopying, recording, or any information storage
or retrieval system, without prior permission in writing from the publishers

Bloomsbury Publishing Plc does not have any control over, or responsibility for, any third-party
websites referred to or in this book. All internet addresses given in this book were correct at the
time of going to press. The author and publisher regret any inconvenience caused if addresses have
changed or sites have ceased to exist, but can accept no responsibility for any such changes

A catalogue record for this book is available from the British Library

Library of Congress Cataloguing-in-Publication data has been applied for

ISBN: HB: 978-1-3994-0685-7; eBook: 978-1-3994-0681-9; ePDF: 978-1-3994-0682-6

2 4 6 8 10 9 7 5 3

Typeset by Deanta Global Publishing Services, Chennai, India
Printed and bound in the U.S.A. by Berryville Graphics Inc., Berryville, Virginia

To find out more about our authors and books visit www.bloomsbury.com
and sign up for our newsletters

Contents

Author's Note

In many ways, this is the book I always wanted to write about Ukraine. In other ways, it's the book I never wanted to write about Ukraine. After reading it, I think you'll understand what I mean.

This is not a history book, but I've provided a brief timeline of important historical events that will provide useful context. It is a collection of stories about people and events that have altered the course of Ukrainian and even world history. It is also a story of my experiences in Ukraine. It is all true. Only a few people's names have been changed or omitted in cases where the subject matter is especially sensitive or at their request, for security reasons.

I made some stylistic choices that are important to point out. I used Ukrainian transliteration in most cases when referring to Ukrainian people and places. For example, Oleksiy is a Ukrainian man's first name in Ukrainian, while Alexei is the same name in Russian. Vladimir is the first name of the Russian leader; Volodymyr is the first name of Ukraine's president. I only used Russian transliteration or another alternative spelling of a person's name when the person preferred it, or when mentioning the Ukrainian warlords and figureheads who served as Russia's separatist proxies in Crimea or eastern Ukraine. Ukraine's capital is Kyiv, not Kiev; Odesa has replaced the previously accepted spelling, Odessa. Ukraine's de-communization push since 2014, has seen hundreds, if not thousands, of cities, towns, and villages across the country renamed. I mostly used names as they appeared at the time of the events described in the book. For instance, Artemivsk is what the city of Bakhmut used to be called and what I and the residents there referred to it as before 2016 when its name was legally changed. The same goes for the nearby village of Krasne, which is now known as Ivanivske. There are a few more instances like this throughout the book but these places are notable because several of the chapters and scenes take place in those locations.

You'll notice there's a gap in events between 2015 and 2022. This was a transformative period for Ukraine, during which it did much to set itself on a European path and shake Russia's grip, even as the Kremlin continued to try to destabilize the country. But it would have taken dozens if not hundreds more pages to detail the many complex events of that period, and I didn't have the space they deserve to tell you about them here.

Maps

Ukraine, administrative divisions and centers, political map.

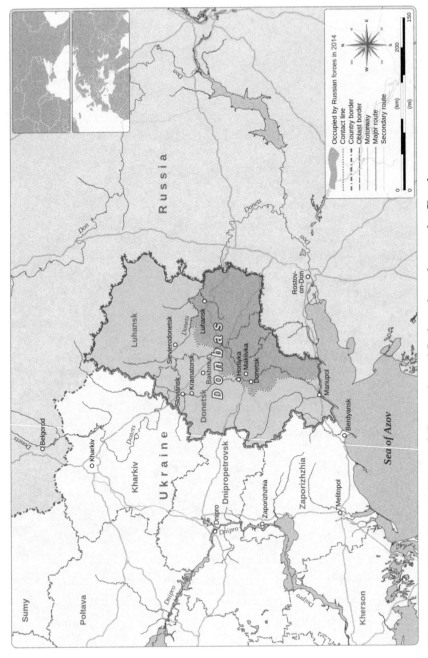

The eastern Ukrainian oblasts of Donetsk and Luhansk make up the Donbas.

Ukraine's Crimean Peninsula, illegally annexed and under Russian
occupation since March 2014.

A Brief History Of Ukraine

9th–11th century: Kyivan Rus, the first major Eastern Slavonic state, is founded and develops. Its center is located on the Dnipro river in Kyiv. Neither Ukraine nor Russia exist at this point. Moscow is a forest.

11th century: Kyivan Rus reaches its peak under Yaroslav the Wise, and Kyiv becomes a political and cultural center within Europe.

12th–18th century: Various foreign powers invade and conquer the region. Kyivan Rus is destroyed.

17th–18th century: The idea of a Ukrainian nation and a Ukrainian nationality emerges.

18th–19th century: The Russian Empire under the rule of Catherine the Great seizes control of much of Ukraine. Ukrainian intellectuals emerge to oppose their imperial leader. Russia suppresses the Ukrainian language and culture.

1917: Ukraine fights to break free from Russian rule amid the Russian Revolution and subsequent collapse of the Russian Empire.

1918–19: Ukraine declares independence but chaos reigns. Various breakaway entities vie for control of swathes or all of Ukraine.

1919: Ukraine becomes the Ukrainian Soviet Socialist Republic, part of the Soviet Union.

1932–33: Millions of Ukrainians die from the artificial famine, known in Ukraine as the Holodomor, imposed by Joseph Stalin during his collectivization campaign.

1941–44: Nazi forces invade and occupy Ukraine, which suffers horrific devastation and atrocities. Millions die fighting Adolf Hitler's troops; some 1.5 million Jews are murdered.

1954: Soviet leader Nikita Khrushchev gifts Crimea to Ukraine in a goodwill gesture.

1990: The Revolution on Granite erupts in Kyiv in October, with young Ukrainians protesting to prevent Ukraine from remaining part of the Soviet Union.

24 August 1991: Ukraine declares independence as the Soviet Union collapses. The dissolution of the USSR would be completed by December.

June–July 1994: First presidential election of the new Ukrainian government. Former prime minister Leonid Kuchma defeats incumbent President Leonid Kravchuk. The first peaceful transfer of political power in independent Ukraine.

5 December 1994: Budapest Memorandum on Security Assurances. The memorandum prohibited the Russian Federation, the United Kingdom, and the United States from threatening or using military force or economic coercion against Ukraine, Belarus, and Kazakhstan, "except in self-defense or otherwise in accordance with the Charter of the United Nations."

November 2004–January 2005: Ukrainians flood Kyiv's Independence Square, the Maidan, to protest corruption and a presidential election said to be rigged in favor of the Russia-friendly Viktor Yanukovych. The protests transform into the Orange Revolution. The election is overturned and Viktor Yushchenko becomes president.

January–February 2010: Disappointed by a lack of progress made and years of infighting, Ukrainians vote out Yushchenko, who is trounced in the first round of presidential elections. Yanukovych wins and becomes president after a free and fair second-round vote.

November 2013–February 2014: Ukrainians spill onto the Maidan to protest Yanukovych's refusal to sign a free-trade agreement with the European Union, demanding that Ukraine join the European Union and claim its place as part of Europe. They reject Russian pressure to form closer ties with the Russian Federation. Yanukovych unleashes his security forces on peaceful demonstrators, sparking a bloodbath that would lead to the deaths of more than a hundred protestors, known as The Heavenly Hundred.

21 February 2014: Yanukovych flees Kyiv to Russia, and Ukraine's parliament officially deposes him.

Late February–March 2014: Vladimir Putin orders a covert military invasion of Ukraine's Crimean Peninsula. Russian troops in unmarked uniforms, known as "little green men", storm Ukrainian bases, seize the peninsula's government buildings and airports, and detain pro-Ukrainian activists.

16 March 2014: Russia holds a sham "referendum" in Crimea, claiming 97 per cent of voters chose to join the Russian Federation. Ukraine and its Western allies condemn the illegitimate vote.

17 March 2014: Putin signs a decree recognizing Crimea as "a sovereign and independent state."

21 March 2014: Putin signs a treaty to recognize Crimea as part of the Russian Federation, and his forced annexation of Crimea is complete. Ukraine and the international community condemn the move.

April 2014: Russian forces covertly invade eastern Ukraine's Donetsk and Luhansk oblast, collectively known as the Donbas, using troops, special forces, and intelligence operatives to foment a faux, pro-Russia separatist uprising. Thousands of disaffected locals who did not support the Euromaidan and Revolution of Dignity join in, giving the impression of a Maidan-style grassroots uprising.

11 May 2014: Russian puppet authorities hold sham referendums and declare Donetsk and Luhansk "people's republics" to be independent, solidifying Russia's control and occupation of the region.

June 2014: The Normandy Format Group is established to negotiate a settlement to end the conflict. It includes leaders from Ukraine, France,

Germany, and Russia, who first meet during the events marking the 70th anniversary of the Allied landings in Normandy on D-Day. Five meetings occur between 2014 and 2016.

8 June 2014: The Trilateral Contact Group on Ukraine, a group of representatives from Ukraine, Russia, and the Organization for Security and Co-operation in Europe, is established as a means to facilitate a diplomatic resolution to the war in the Donbas.

September 2014: The Minsk Protocol, or Minsk I, significantly reduces fighting in the conflict zone of the Donbas. The negotiations to achieve this agreement are held in Minsk, the capital of Belarus.

February 2015: The Package of Measures for the Implementation of the Minsk Agreements, commonly called Minsk II, is signed, but never enforced by Russia.

2016–21: Russia's war in Ukraine grinds on in the east. Talks between the leaders of Ukraine, Russia, France, and Germany fail to secure a peace deal. The United States ramps up support for Ukraine and its military. Russia ramps up attacks on Ukraine in other ways throughout the country – in cyberwarfare, economic war, and targeting traitors and enemies in a wave of assassinations. Meanwhile, Ukraine's pro-Western government struggles to reform and stamp out corruption. But Ukrainian society moves farther from Russia, Ukrainian culture begins to flourish, and a new generation of Ukrainians comes of age.

April 2021–January 2022: Russia masses troops and military equipment around the Ukrainian border in the north, south, and east, as well as inside Belarus and occupied Crimea. US intelligence estimates a total military force of 150,000 to 200,000 and warns of an "imminent" invasion. Ukraine's President Zelensky downplays the threat and warns President Joe Biden that such words may cause panic in Ukraine.

21 February 2022: Putin recognizes the "independence" of the so-called Donetsk and Luhansk "people's republics" that Russia has propped up since 2014 – and not only the areas in the eponymous oblasts it occupies, but the entirety of the regions, including Ukrainian-controlled territory.

24 February 2022: Putin launches a full-scale invasion of Ukraine. The multi-pronged assault includes cruise missile attacks and ground forces storming through border crossings from Russia, Belarus, and Crimea. The attack triggers Europe's largest refugee crisis since the Second World War, with roughly six million Ukrainians fleeing the country and more than seven million others internally displaced.

Prologue

"Special Military Operation"

Kramatorsk, Eastern Ukraine, 24 February 2022

The text message landed with a piercing *ding* in the silent darkness. It was 4:36 a.m., but I was lying wide awake and fully dressed on the bed in my kitschy fifth-floor room inside Hotel Kramatorsk, situated in the northern portion of Donetsk oblast, eastern Ukraine. The eyes of an oil-painted, voluptuous nude bathing in the surf of some tranquil beach gazed down at me.

"You OK?" the text read.

The sender was Alexander Vindman, retired US Army lieutenant colonel and former director of European Affairs for the National Security Council, and he was checking in from Washington. Like the rest of the world, the Kyiv-born military man who had recently served on the White House National Security Council was waiting with bated breath to see what Russian President Vladimir Putin's military was about to do.

"Yeah. Quiet here in Kramatorsk," I replied with false confidence. "But don't think many people are sleeping."

"Glad that's the case," Vindman texted back. "As an infantryman, we sleep when we can. Get rest. I fear you'll need it."

It was impossible to sleep, though. My heart was pounding through my chest. Over the course of the last three days, a feeling of impending doom had swept over the country.

In an unusual move, the United States had gone to unusually great lengths in the weeks before to declassify and publicly share intelligence that showed Russia would soon launch a full-scale military invasion of Ukraine, and that it had formalized lists of enemies in the country to capture or kill. Ukrainians received the news with skepticism, especially as their president, Volodymyr Zelensky, was calling for the Biden administration to pipe down, as this could cause panic and hurt the country's economy.

"What, exactly, is news? Hasn't this been a reality for eight years? Didn't the invasion begin in 2014? Did the threat of a large-scale war appear only now?" Zelensky told Ukrainians in a 19 January address.

He assured them that they'd be barbecuing kebabs in the spring, not fighting a new war.

"In May, as always, there is sun, weekends, barbecues, and, of course, Victory Day," he said.

But then on 21 February, Putin recognized the "independence" of the Donetsk and Luhansk oblasts – the two areas that belonged to Ukraine but saw large swathes seized by Russian troops and their separatist puppets during the war that started in 2014. And those puppet leaders had sent hastily orchestrated requests to the Kremlin "to assist in repelling aggression from the Armed Forces of Ukraine in order to avoid civilian casualties and prevent a humanitarian catastrophe" in the Donbas, as the eastern regions are collectively known.

It was an ominous sign. Having covered Russia's war in Ukraine since the start in 2014, I sensed that we were on the brink of a bigger, bloodier phase of the conflict that would erupt at any moment – and very likely right outside my window.

Any lingering doubts were dashed just minutes before Alexander sent his text. Putin, sitting at a desk in the Kremlin and flanked by the white, blue, and red Russian tricolor, had addressed the nation on state television, telling them about his aims in Ukraine. He was giving the military a green light for a "special military operation" on the bogus grounds that "the demilitarization and denazification of Ukraine," which had become an "anti-Russia" state supplied with "the most modern weapons" from NATO, was needed to ensure the security of Russia and its people. He urged Zelensky and his army to surrender.

The moment I heard that I jumped in the shower. With shit about to hit the fan, I knew it might be my last chance for one in a while. Then I packed my bags and placed them by the door. I took a quick glance out of the window, which I had earlier taped in a criss-cross pattern so that it wouldn't explode and send shards of glass flying everywhere if we were bombed. Lights were on in kitchens and bedrooms in the apartment building across the way and I could see people sitting and scanning their phones, the blue screens illuminating their faces. The streets were empty and the sky was pitch black. Then I took my position on the bed and waited:

Shwooo … BOOM! Shwooo … BOOM!

Then a few seconds' pause:

Shwooo … BOOM! Shwooo … BOOM!

Sixteen agonizing minutes after my exchange with Alexander, four successive explosions from Russian cruise missiles struck the Kramatorsk airbase just 2,000 feet away.

The blasts illuminated the sky with such an intense glow that it penetrated the thick curtains on my windows and shot out of the cracks at their sides like lasers. Each shockwave from the blast hit the hotel with a massive thud and shook it violently.

Adrenaline coursed through my veins. I rolled from the bed onto the ground, scrambling on all fours to the door. When I opened it and looked down the hallway, a pair of foreign journalists were spinning confusingly around in just their underwear.

"What the fuck just happened?" one of them shouted at me, totally dazed.

"We're being attacked," I said.

"What?" the man replied.

"Russia's invading Ukraine," I told him.

"Yeah?" the other man said.

"Yeah, man!" I shouted back.

The door of the room across the hall from me opened and the front-desk receptionist strolled calmly out, tying her hair up. She'd been getting a few winks before the morning shift.

"Boys!" she hollered to the journalists in Russian. "Stay calm. Go to the bomb shelter."

The men stood there squinting at her with their arms at their sides.

"She said to get down to the bomb shelter," I told them.

They darted back into their rooms to dress and gather their things.

"*Yolky palky*," the receptionist muttered, using a Russian expression that translates literally as "pine trees and sticks" but is used to express bewilderment much like we might say in English, "Jesus Christ!" or even "For fuck's sake!"

"We will be fine," she assured me, speaking in Russian. "Get to the basement."

I appreciated her assurance and confidence in that moment but everything definitely *did not* feel fine. These were cruise missiles being fired at us, not mortar rounds or even tank shells. War on a terrifying new level had just broken out.

But she had lived in a war zone for eight long years.

"You worked here in 2014, right?" I asked her as we walked to the twist of stairs. I had recognized her from the last time I had stayed at the hotel and found myself caught up in a Russian invasion, with soldiers spilling into the streets from atop tanks and armored personnel carriers.

"Yes," she answered. "We've been through this before."

Journalists were filing into the bomb shelter and strapping on their body armor. That's where I found Pete Kiehart, an American photographer, and Isobel Koshiw, a British reporter. Both were part of my team covering the tense lead-up to this morning for BuzzFeed News. They had been staying on lower floors of Hotel Kramatorsk and were quick to collect their gear and get underground.

"Welp, things are looking pretty bad, huh?" said Pete, a master of understatement. "That was really fucking loud."

Isobel was less composed. She was visibly shaken and had a terrified look in her eyes. She was worried about Anatoliy, a family friend in his fifties who we'd hired as our driver.

"Have you seen Anatoliy?" she asked, checking her phone for a text. "He was here and then just disappeared."

"I'll go look for him," I said.

The hotel lobby was in chaos. Staff and security were trying to keep order in a room full of journalists who were simultaneously filled with dread and exhilarated by the promise of a huge story they were smack in the middle of. They fumbled around with their gear and spun in circles trying to locate their Ukrainian fixers. Several journalists paced back and forth outside the entrance, chain smoking while calling their editors in London, Paris, Berlin, and other European hubs.

Among the few calm foreigners was Lindsey Hilsum, a veteran war correspondent for Britain's Channel 4. Like everyone else, she wasn't sure what to do or where to go exactly. But she kept her cool and settled into the well-worn sofa in the hotel foyer, where she began typing up notes on her laptop.

"I'm in the right place if you're here," she said to me.

"That all depends on what you're looking for," I said.

"A war story," she replied.

By and large the Ukrainian journalists among us were the most composed. Like the receptionist, they carried themselves with the stoicism of veterans who had been at war for the better part of a decade. Looking for Anatoliy outside, I spotted Anastasia Vlasova, a Ukrainian photographer with whom I had covered the first Russian invasion eight years earlier. Her body armor hung from her arm and she was smoking at the bottom of the stairs.

"Oh, hello!" she said to me with a wide smile as she took a deep puff and exhaled into the winter air. "Look who is here!"

Around us, foreign TV reporters clambered over tangles of wires and camera equipment as they set up their live shots.

"Here we go again!" Anastasia quipped, rattling off an anecdote about a previous time we were someplace nearby during a gun battle and narrowly made it out unscathed.

I found Anatoliy cleaning the windshield of our Honda SUV, taping the letters "PRESS" to the hood and sides, and filling the washer fluid reserve. As he turned to wave at me, two fighter jets came screaming overhead. They were so low they almost scraped the rooftops of the surrounding buildings. The TV reporters dropped their microphones and sprinted inside the hotel, screaming, "Jets! Jets! Jets!" A crowd of them stumbled down the stairs to the bomb shelter.

"It's OK!" Anatoliy yelled with excitement and a deep chortle. "*Nashi*" – ours – "Ukrainian Su-27s!"

He had served in the Soviet Army and was well acquainted with Ukraine's Armed Forces. He recognized the blue color scheme and markings on the bellies of the jets. Gazing at them as they roared toward the eastern horizon, he clicked his tongue in astonishment.

I was surprised to see that the hotel canteen was opening. Journalists spilled in to fill up on coffee and breakfast. Anatoliy piled milk sausages and sunny-side-up eggs onto his plate with a side of sliced tomatoes. As I ate a banana and sipped an Americano, he asked if he could tell me a joke. He had a way of choosing the worst possible moments to share his favorite anecdotes, most of which didn't translate well from Russian to English. I told him that it wasn't really the time and we should think about getting back to Kyiv, a nine-hour drive west. He said he was up for driving and could get us there quickly.

Reports were coming in that battles were unfolding in Kyiv Oblast. Certainly that would be the story, if the country's center of power were attacked, encircled, or worse – captured. Plus, in those first hours, it felt entirely possible that the might of the Russian Army could come barreling through Ukrainian lines in the Donbas and show up on our street. After all, we were only 40 miles west of where they had been dug in for the past eight years, and where for the past several months they had been massing fresh troops and armor.

A dozen journalists banged away on their laptops and phones in the musty bomb shelter. Pete and Isobel were contacting sources and scanning social media for news of attacks elsewhere. Twitter was flooded with images of destruction from Russian cruise missile strikes in every corner of the country. Black plumes of smoke filled the skies. Ukraine was burning.

Security camera footage shared by Ukrainian Border Guards captured hundreds of Russian tanks and military trucks rolling through border crossings from Belarus in the north, Russia in the east, and Moscow-controlled Crimea in the south. They even came barreling through the radioactive Chornobyl exclusion zone.

More videos showed dozens of Russian military helicopters swooping south through the Dnipro river valley toward the Hostomel airbase outside Kyiv. And rumors swirled that a gun battle was underway in the government quarter near the presidential administration. *Were the Russians about to nab Zelensky?* I wondered.

The shape and scale of Putin's invasion was becoming terrifyingly clear. This was not a "special operation" focused on the Donbas – this was an all-out assault meant to destroy Ukraine. A Second World War-style blitzkrieg was unfolding before our eyes.

In that moment, seeing Pete and Isobel hiding underground and dressed in their 20 pounds of body armor, wondering whether a bomb was going to fall on our heads and kill us all, everything seemed unreal. Just hours earlier we had been celebrating a strong reporting week with cocktails and steaks around the corner at RIA Pizza, the local journalists' haunt. Then, because I had used up all my reporter's notebooks, I visited a stationery shop, where I watched a young girl plead with her mother to buy her a pen with a teddy bear on it. I thought about them at that moment, possibly the last truly normal one before the bombs started falling.

The world had been turned upside down overnight.

Dressed in a black suit and tie, President Zelensky went on TV to address the nation. He hadn't been captured. We watched on our phones as he spoke directly into the camera.

"Today I initiated a phone call with the president of the Russian Federation," he began. "The result was silence."

Putin didn't want to talk – he wanted Zelensky's complete and unconditional surrender.

Zelensky announced he was imposing martial law and had ordered Ukraine's armories to open their doors and stocks to "all patriots" willing to defend freedom and democracy against Russian tyranny and terrorism.

I had no idea what would happen at that point. But rushing back to Kyiv made sense, since it was possible that the Ukrainian authorities could lock down the city. I told Pete, Isobel, and Anatoliy to get ready.

Anatoliy sped through the streets as I navigated from the passenger seat. On the way out of Kramatorsk, heading west, Ukrainian tanks and armored personnel carriers rumbled past us, heading east and carrying soldiers on top. It reminded me of similar scenes in May 2014, when I witnessed Russians and Ukrainians fighting on the very same Kramatorsk roads. Trolley buses and checkpoints were in flames, a tanker truck sat idle in the road, ripped open like the top of a sardine tin after a massive blast, and troops ran around shooting anti-tank rockets wildly between apartment blocks. *Were the Russians already on the ground and close by?* I wondered.

The city was in a frenzy. Long queues had formed at ATMs, pharmacies, and gas stations. People were dashing in and out of supermarkets, stocking up on goods. The roads were jammed with cars carrying anyone with the means to flee and the few possessions they had managed to scrape together in a hurry. So many people were staring toward the sky, fearful of what the Russians might unleash on them from above.

We were nearly running on fumes a few hours later when we found a gas station with a line of vehicles just 300 meters long. It took an hour to get to the pump. Anatoliy filled the tank while Isobel and I chatted with a group of local men on the roadside. They were discussing setting up their own defense force to protect their homes from the Russian Army. They had no weapons but were prepared to hurl Molotov cocktails at the invaders if they had to.

As we continued our journey in the direction of Kyiv, I made calls to Ukrainian sources. One of the first to answer was Ukraine's deputy minister of foreign affairs, Emine Dzhaparova. She described seeing a Russian missile fly overhead and then crash into a building in Kyiv. She was shaken up and worried about whether the country's Western allies would move quickly enough to help Ukraine. She had been on the phone all morning with her interlocutors in Europe, trying to mobilize them.

Two officials in Zelensky's office responded ominously to my text messages.

"Do not quote me. We don't want to cause panic," one replied. "But it is very bad. Total war."

"God help us!" wrote another from inside the fortified presidential bunker.

Traffic was at a standstill when we reached Boryspil, a suburb on the eastern edge of Kyiv that is home to the country's biggest international airport. Stopped at a light, I looked to my left and noticed that the local government building had already been barricaded with concrete blocks and sandbags and was being guarded by armed troops.

Police and military forces had set up a checkpoint at the entrance to Kyiv just beyond that and vehicles were backed up for miles waiting to get through. Everyone was trying to get to the west of the country, as close to the EU border as possible.

Anatoliy zipped around the line of vehicles, nearly scraping our SUV against the metal guardrail until we reached the front.

"Press!" he shouted at the Kalashnikov-wielding police officer even before fully rolling down his window. We quickly flashed our passports and press badges and were waved through.

It was 6:30 p.m. when we pulled into Kyiv and the sun had set. Crossing the bridge over the Dnipro river, the city was darker than usual. I couldn't make out the towering Motherland monument or the golden domes of the historic Pechersk Lavra Eastern Orthodox Christian monastery that stand on the hillside.

When we arrived at the Radisson Blu hotel in Kyiv's city center, we pulled into the underground parking garage to find that hotel staff had transformed it into a bomb shelter. There were chairs and boxes of bedding, tables with water and sandwiches. Guests were trying to make themselves comfortable between elevator rooms, furnaces, and Škodas.

I went up to my room on the fourth floor to get some clean clothes and extra power banks to charge my phone and laptop. Waiting for me on the table beside the bed was a small, round cake topped with a drizzle of chocolate, fresh berries, and gold leaf. My birthday had been one week earlier. Despite everything, the staff had placed it there in anticipation of my return. A handwritten note accompanying the cake read, "Welcome back to Kyiv!"

I looked at my phone and saw more than 100 missed calls and unanswered text messages. Family and friends in the United States wanted to know if I was safe. My Ukrainian friends wanted information and advice.

In Bakhmut, eastern Ukraine, the mother of my friend Vika was terrified and unsure of what to do. She had worked for years in Moscow and refused to believe her daughter, now living in Munich with her partner, when she warned her mother days in advance that a new Russian invasion was likely imminent.

"I just don't know what to tell her. She's totally brainwashed," Vika had told me in one of our many calls leading up to the invasion. "I'm desperate to get her out but she won't listen. She's in denial."

Now the missiles had started falling and she wanted out.

"*Now* she wants to go!" Vika screamed into the phone when I called her. "Chris, tell me, is it possible? How can she leave now?"

"Vika, I really don't know," I said. "She needs to find a friend with a car or else hunker down in a basement tonight."

Others had similar questions. Should they stay where they were? Or take their chance in the open, with jets and missiles flying overhead and stuck in traffic jams with hundreds of thousands of cars, maybe never to return home?

Being unable to offer much help in that moment was hard.

I tried sleeping inside our SUV in the car park that night, partly to keep warm, partly because it was more comfortable than lying atop a couple of thin blankets on a concrete floor. But again, I struggled to calm my mind enough to get any real shut-eye. I pulled my hat over my eyes and attempted to conjure memories of myself with Ukrainian friends before the war came to us, as if to return briefly to a Ukraine I knew was gone forever.

PART ONE

PEACE

1

American Boy

Artemivsk, eastern Ukraine, May–September 2010

The United States Peace Corps recruiter showed me a world map separated into seven color-coded regions and asked me where I would like to go. I pointed to sub-Saharan Africa.

It was spring of 2009, I was 25 years old, and had been working for about four years as a local reporter in Portland, Oregon, where I wrote about the city's indie music scene, craft beer, city politics, and, naturally, all things *weird* – like naked bike rides, NyQuil-laced donuts, and weddings at the 24-hour Church of Elvis. Portland was a hipster's paradise and a fun, comfortable place where it felt like you could live and work without ever really having to grow up. But I *was* outgrowing it. Plus, things were beginning to feel grim and opportunities slim. The economy was in a tailspin. The impact from the Great Recession had caused an economic tsunami that stretched from Wall Street to my home on SW Main Street in Downtown Portland. Many of my favorite haunts closed their doors. And work was getting hard to come by, especially journalism jobs, which were already hard to find in the small city. Now the seemingly few that existed were being axed left and right.

One afternoon that May, I walked into a Peace Corps recruiting office and filled out an application. A foreign adventure sounded like a great way to escape. The organization quickly invited me to spend 27 months abroad with them. But there was a slight hitch: instead of going to Africa, as I had hoped, the recruiter told me that I would be sent to Ukraine. The Peace Corps was known for doing that. It was one of the many ways in which it weeded out the less serious applicants.

I knew almost nothing about Ukraine, had no familial ties to the country, and didn't speak Russian or Ukrainian, the two main languages spoken there. I hadn't even traveled beyond Western Europe at the time. I just knew that Ukraine was vast, it had been a republic of the Soviet Union, it was the site of the world's worst nuclear disaster, and it bordered Russia – details gleaned from geography and history lessons in school, and my childhood obsession with Risk, the board game of world domination. On the Risk board, as in real life, Ukraine held a key place on the world map, a borderland straddling east and west.

I was pleased with the choice. And when I found a blog online by a Peace Corps volunteer, referring to the Ukraine posting as "Posh Corps", a pleasant lifestyle that volunteers could enjoy compared to other places where they lived in huts without running water, I thought I might even have a good, leisurely time. The pages of a Lonely Planet guidebook on Ukraine seemed to lend credence to that belief. I visualized myself on the pebbled shores of Crimea, swimming in the Black Sea and tossing back vodka with sailors. Or maybe I'd end up living in a traditional Hutsul house high up in the western Carpathian Mountains, surrounded by ancient castles and lush forests, where I would hike and learn to make goat's cheese. Perhaps I'd be based in historic Lviv, surrounded by its mix of stunning Baroque, Renaissance, and Classical architecture, using the evenings to explore the city, its cobbled streets romantically illuminated by dim lamps.

In late March 2010, I duly got on a plane heading for Kyiv with 76 other American volunteers who comprised the Peace Corps group 38. We were to be teachers, small-business developers, and healthcare educators. After three months of hasty language and cultural trainings around Kyiv and Chernihiv in north-central Ukraine, we would be dispatched to far-flung towns and villages across the country to work in schools, libraries, local government offices, and nongovernmental organizations.

But as I would discover upon arrival, I had lost the group lottery to go to the Carpathian Mountains or the Crimean Peninsula. Lviv? Another regional capital? Nope.

Instead, I was assigned to a landlocked city deep in Ukraine's hard-knuckled industrial east, within a short bus ride to the Russian border.

My first glimpse of the Donbas, an abbreviated name for the Donets Coal Basin – a region in Ukraine's east about the size of Slovakia or the American state of West Virginia and shaped like a bone-in ribeye steak – came through the steamy, sealed windows of a clattering overnight train from the capital. It was a hot, stuffy morning in early June 2010, four years before war would erupt here and 12 years before it would be the hottest spot in Russia's all-out war against Ukraine. The rising summer sun heated the train carriage I shared with dozens of half-naked Ukrainians. The sweet, pungent odor of our unbathed bodies, and the boiled eggs that my bunkmates had eaten for dinner the night before at the tiny communal table, hung heavy in the still air.

Watching everyone casually wipe sweat from their skinfolds with yellow-stained handkerchiefs and just carry on chatting, I was baffled by how they were able to remain seemingly undeterred while trapped for so long inside this baking, airless box. Lying on my back on a top bunk, my face inches from the paint-chipped ceiling where condensation had accumulated and was dripping onto the pillow, I fantasized about reaching for the red emergency hammer to shatter a window for a single breath of something that didn't feel like someone else's exhalation.

At least once every 40 minutes of the 13-hour journey, the train would whistle and lurch to a stop to pack in more passengers. The one time I came close to falling asleep, someone passing through the aisle bumped their shoulder into my dangling feet and roused me.

So it came as a huge relief when dawn broke and I knew I'd soon reach my destination. Then I wiped the window clean with my palm and peered outside. The scenes of charming country homes with their brightly painted gates and shutters, surrounded by fields of sunflowers, sorghum, and wheat so green and gold that they looked electrified as the train rushed through central Ukraine, had vanished. Visible now was a disconcerting panorama of crumbling factories belching black smoke into the sky, concrete apartment blocks adorned with chipped Soviet-era mosaics, and mountainous slag heaps.

What is this post-apocalyptic-looking wasteland? I pondered the idea that maybe we had made a wrong turn in the night and ended up in Chornobyl.

Accompanying me was Nikolai Georgievich Sokolov, a 68-year-old Russian-speaking physical education teacher with the interminable energy and curiosity of a teenage boy. He had been assigned to be what the Peace Corps called a "counterpart." Put another way, Nikolai was to be my chaperone for the duration of my 24 months at "site" – the Peace Corps term for volunteers' temporary homes and workplaces. But he soon came to refer to me as *moy malchik*, my boy.

His first task was to get me and my absurd amount of luggage from Kyiv to Artemivsk and set me up in an apartment. He wasn't bothered by the train ride at all. But when he saw the look on my face as I glanced out of the train window, he grew worried about me.

"It's nothing, everything is normal," he assured me, unconvincingly. "This is Kostyantynivka. Artemivsk is beautiful."

Kostyantynivka had once been home to some of the most successful factories in all of the Soviet Union. Glass production was its specialty and it was famous for having made the ruby glass stars that top the spires of the Kremlin. But it took a massive hit with the collapse of the Soviet Union in the 1990s. Lucrative state contracts that kept its 20 or so factories running had been ripped up overnight, tens of thousands of people were made redundant. The population fell from over 100,000 to less than 70,000 in the decades that followed. Time and the elements had led the former glass factory to literally collapse. All that was left when I saw it with friends months later were the crumbling facades of two former administrative buildings adorned with Soviet propaganda. One faded message read, "Our goal is Communism!" The other: "Lenin's ideas are immortal!"

A train attendant brought around our ticket stubs and offered us glasses of hot black tea in *podstakanniki*, or tea glass holders, adorned with an ornate train-engine design. I kept the stub as a souvenir but declined the tea; Nikolai and all the other passengers took both. I followed their leads in folding our bedsheets and taking them to the attendant. We had just two minutes to disembark from the train in Kostyantynivka before it continued south for another 90 kilometers to Donetsk, the regional capital. It was a rush to get off, but the state railway company's punctuality was something I would eventually come to greatly respect and appreciate.

The station was situated between several fast-food kiosks and an unfinished Orthodox Church, and it was a hive of activity. Flocks of taxi drivers swarmed around passengers to offer rides and they haggled over prices. Men with outrageously large bouquets of roses greeted their wives and girlfriends. Police pulled people aside for random document checks, looking for any little infraction that could land them a bribe to cover lunch. And people returning from Kyiv carried famous *Kyivski* cakes in little box-like hat containers.

Nikolai and I were met by a paunchy man dressed in a denim fishing vest worn over a fitted white tank top that he tucked into khaki trousers. He carried a small gray man purse over his shoulder and a Winston cigarette behind his left ear. The two of them shoved my things into the trunk of a battered blue Lada, a Soviet-era car that was little more than a tin can on wheels but ubiquitous because of its simplicity and affordability, and we were off.

Once we had left the Kostyantynivka city limits the area opened up and I began to see the Donbas as it truly was. The landscape changed drastically at every turn. It was wide and flat and seemingly boundless. Then all of a sudden there were verdant valleys and rolling hills. A mile-long stretch saw us zip through a tunnel of poplar trees so dense that the light barely shone through. There were quarries with large machines digging out white rock, and around the next bend sprawling fields of sunflowers, their golden heads bowing toward the sunrise. The sky was vast and a vivid cobalt color. The scene was the living embodiment of the Ukrainian flag.

But the road itself was rough and it felt like driving over a giant cheese grater. The man weaved around potholes big enough to swallow a car. It got so bad at one point he just drove off-road to avoid potholes entirely. It was common for the authorities to skim money off the top of funds set aside for infrastructure projects, leaving little for road repairs. Instead of redoing an entire stretch of highway, they'd fill in the potholes with gravel and cover it with a thin layer of asphalt that would quickly get chewed up. Every time we accelerated the Lada would backfire. I rolled down the window because I was feeling carsick, but instead of fresh air I was hit with a cloud of exhaust from a passing truck.

The driver seemed undeterred by all of this. He rolled down his window, pulled the cigarette from his ear and lit it while singing along with the radio. He had a decent voice, a rich baritone. But he struggled to hold a note for long and a couple of times he gasped for air and launched into coughing fits. The radio station played some Russian chanson ditty, a lyric-forward romance genre performed by singer-songwriters crooning about love over the sounds of electronic keyboards and tinny beat machines. The genre was popular among the post-Soviet working class, particularly those nostalgic for the *good old days*, and soon I'd hear it everywhere – at discotheques, on trolleybuses, *marshrutkas* – minibuses – and yes, blaring from the radios of most of the taxi rides I would endure over the next years.

To me, Russian chanson sounded like an Eastern European imitation of Leonard Cohen tunes. If you've ever listened to "Dance Me to the End of Love" then you have an idea of what it sounds like. Maybe that's why I would learn to appreciate chanson. It was familiar and inviting. And nobody needed to have rhythm to dance to it – you just sort of stepped, swayed and twirled. The drunker you were while doing it, the better it felt.

When the song ended, the driver switched to a pop station and "American Boy," the seminal hit by the Russian female pop group *Kombinaciya* – a word meaning "combination" but also a Russian term for a slip dress – blared from the speaker. Released in 1990, as a demoralized Russia saw the Soviet Union crumbling, the song tapped into the zeitgeist of the moment. "American boy, American joy / American boy for always time . . ." the chorus repeated between verses that told the story of a Russian woman dreaming of finding an American boy who would whisk her away to the US and a life of luxury. The song remained popular 20 years later, when life in this part of the world should have been drastically different than it was when the song had been written, but hadn't changed all that much for most people.

"*Oho! Ameriken boi!*" the driver howled in heavily accented English.

He took a drag on his cigarette and turned up the volume. In the rear-view mirror, I could see his eyes tighten and then lock onto mine. Shouting over the music, he said in deep Russian that there were no Americans where I was going.

"You are alone," he told me.

I would come to find out there was in fact one other American, a young woman named Sarah, a Fulbright scholar, who worked at an orphanage and overlapped with me in the city for a short period of time before returning to the US. But otherwise, the driver was right. For most of the next two years, I would be the one and only American in Artemivsk.

Fitting In

Artemivsk was home to around 70,000 people, a majority of whom identified as Ukrainians; less than a third were ethnic Russians. There was also a smattering of other ethnicities mostly from areas in the former USSR. Many of the Russians were descendants of those who had arrived during the Soviet Union's industrialization between the late 1920s and 1940. These figures were roughly equal to many cities in the rest of the Donetsk and Luhansk oblasts.

The predominant language was Russian but it was spoken by many people with a softer accent and a blend of Ukrainian words that confused my untrained ears. I had studied Russian while in Kyiv during my first three months in the country. But here, I struggled at first to understand the words coming out of people's mouths.

Nikolai was a good example of this. His speech was 90–95 per cent Russian but he peppered it with Ukrainian words and softer pronunciation. Eventually I'd come to learn that many residents of Ukraine's eastern Donbas region spoke *surzhyk*; besides being a Ukrainian word for a mix of wheat and rye flour, *surzhyk* was what people called the mashup of the Russian and Ukrainian languages they spoke. Nikolai liked to joke about the language barrier between us in my first months in Artemivsk. He said that he'd learn

English so we could communicate better and asked me to teach him several phrases. Among the first he wanted to know how to say was, "I love you."

The Artemivsk I had arrived in was an archetypically post-Soviet-style city. It featured a handful of buildings still standing from the pre-Russian Revolution period, surrounded by the usual gray, pre-fab concrete apartment buildings that most residents now lived in. The flag of independent Ukraine flew atop government buildings, but many streets were still named after Red Army and Communist heroes.

My street was an outlier. It had been named for Oleksandr Sybirtsev, a lieutenant colonel in the Artemivsk branch of the Security Service of Ukraine, or the SBU, the successor of the Soviets' notorious KGB. He had become a local hero in 1996, when he exchanged himself for a hostage during a bank heist in town and was shot by an armed robber who then turned the gun on himself.

My one-bedroom apartment was on the top floor of a four-story *Khrushchyovka* building erected in the 1960s, when its namesake Nikita Khrushchev was the Soviet premier. There was nothing particularly attractive about it. It was all concrete but didn't feel solid. Time and the elements had caused cracks in its facade, and the foundation chipped away with ease when I rubbed my finger across it. Inside, dust and plaster fell from the ceilings every time someone slammed a door, which was a dozen times an hour. Instead of replacing things that broke, a "master" would come and patch it. How the place remained standing I have no idea. It seemed to be held together with tape, twine, and glue.

Nikolai owned the apartment, which meant that besides working together he was also my landlord. The place had recently undergone a *Yevro remont* – a term derived from a combination of the Russian words for "Europe" and "repair" or "modification" – which meant it was now supposed to be a European-style flat. While clean, the place was mostly empty and colorless except for the living room's pink puff-painted floral wallpaper laden with flecks of glitter that transferred to whatever or whomever rubbed against it. The kitchen also had puffy wallpaper – it was coffee-themed and embellished with images of steaming brown mugs beside the words "cafe," "latte," "cappuccino," and "espresso" spelled in English. Nikolai took pride in the fact that he had chosen the wallpaper himself.

The linoleum floors were full of bubbles that shifted under my feet. And the few furniture pieces in the living room were things Nikolai had taken from storage at the Krasne village school where he taught PE and where I would soon work alongside him. There was a school desk and chair combo with etchings of past students' names on top and old gum stuck underneath. And a credenza with a mirror that had a sticker of the Virgin Mary affixed in the top left corner that I would later learn had been nicked from the teachers' lounge.

The bedroom was sparse and narrow. Two single beds stood end to end in what was a space three times as long as it was wide. The mattresses bowed terribly. They were also stained yellow and reeked of mold and mildew, but I wouldn't notice that until my third week in the apartment, when I awoke after feeling something crawl across by face to find the mattresses were infested with mites. Dozens of red bites marked my body. I hadn't thought to check the mattresses at first because the bedding covering them was new. Most notably absent was a washing machine, meaning I had to do my laundry by hand in the tub, a painstaking task that I would eventually come to enjoy if for no other reason than to have something to help pass the time.

The apartment walls were thin. A middle-aged woman, Natalia, and her adult son, Vadym, lived in one adjacent apartment. They argued non-stop, often about Vadym not contributing enough to the family and instead doing little more than drinking and chasing girls. He had dropped out of the engineering college years earlier and started working as a taxi driver, sharing a car owned by a friend. That was, until he crashed the car during one of his benders. Most times I saw him chewing sunflower seeds and squatting outside the building with another man, open bottles of cheap beer tucked between their legs, Eminem's *The Marshall Mathers LP* blaring from a portable speaker he carried everywhere. I could hear them rapping.

"*Ai yem Sleem Sheddy, yes ai yem zee rrreel Sheddy . . .*"

Vadym loved to curse at me in English for no reason other than to prove he could.

"*Beech! Mazzer facker! Sheet!*" he shouted in my face more than once as we passed in the hall or courtyard, before breaking out into laughter.

Running water was always something to be thankful for in the building. The ration schedule was running water for roughly three hours every morning and again for about three hours every evening. I had to schedule my entire life around those blocks of time. Miss the window and you didn't get to shower until hours later, didn't get to wash those dishes or clothes. There would be times when utility workers would have to repair broken water pipes and the whole neighborhood would have to go without water for days. In those cases, I made multiple trips to the well across the street to fill buckets and plastic jugs that I kept stored all around my apartment like some sort of prepper worried about the end of the world.

When I did have running water, it wasn't always hot. I can't tell you how many times I had to heat water on the stove and then carry it to the tub in order to have a warm bath.

My sanctuary was the balcony that overlooked the courtyard and had a view of the upper part of Artemivsk where a Ferris wheel stood. There I could sit, read, smoke, and eavesdrop on my gossiping neighbors on the benches below. For the first few weeks I was there, the topic of conversation was, of course, me.

My neighbors, especially the babushkas in their baggy, floral-patterned dressing gowns and slippers, wondered aloud why I was here and discussed whether I might be an American spy sent to gather intelligence about them. They narrowed their eyes and stared at me each time I came and went from the building, sitting on the benches outside with their arms crossed, not uttering a word until I rounded the corner. Then I would hear them start up again. I didn't get so much as a nod from the courtyard babushkas gang until late June, when I had finally tired of the glares and approached a bench occupied by four of the women. In my rudimentary but ever-evolving Russian, I explained that I had come here to help in the community by teaching in schools and working at the central library, among other places. I quoted from the Peace Corps mission statement and repeated a line that volunteers were told to memorize early on in case someone asked about the organization.

"Peace Corps is a non-profit, non-religious, non-political government agency," I said.

"*Shpyon*," one snapped. "I think you're a spy."

"No, I'm not a spy," I insisted with a slight grin.

That smile didn't help my case, though. Older Ukrainians thought foreigners were idiots for smiling all the time. Or else spies. A friend's mother would tell me later, "You smile too much. People here will know you're a foreigner or think you are a spy. Or they will believe you're both."

The babushkas eventually came around to me and by the end of June I was getting knocks on my door from almost all of my neighbors, many of whom brought gifts in the form of pickled vegetables and homemade *vareneky*, savory boiled dumplings filled with combinations of meat, potatoes, mushrooms, and cabbage. My favorites were the sweet *vareneky* stuffed with cherries. It was summer, so the cherries were ripe and perfect.

The babushkas came with food to be neighborly but also because they began to worry that I couldn't cook for myself and would eventually starve, and then my death would be on their hands.

"What would America think of us then?" my neighbor Lyudmila pondered aloud, lifting her hand to her forehead. Whatever she imagined the consequences would be, they seemed to be so horrific she couldn't even utter them. I repeatedly told Lyudmila and the other women (it was mostly women who dropped by to bring things, except for one older man and one younger man, who came by to drink beer and try to teach me to play chess every once in a while) that I'd be fine, that I'd actually lived alone for years as a college student. I even went so far as to try to prove to them that I was self-sufficient by cooking *holubtsi* – cabbage rolls filled with meat, rice, and onions and baked in tomato sauce – and steaming pots of borsch that I would take to them in Tupperware containers I'd purchased at the bazaar. They all went through the same motions when they saw my food: they lifted the lid, studied it for a second, let out a curious "*O!*", and give it a sniff. Then it was time to taste it. They gave it a careful stir and pulled a spoonful of the red-purple soup up to their mouth. There was just a slight hesitation before swallowing and then the finish – always a nod.

"It's not bad," one said.

I respected that. "Not bad" was truthful. There was no way she'd tell me that I had gotten it just right.

Others simply thanked me and said it was "tasty," but in a way I could tell they probably didn't mean it, though they seemed to appreciate the effort.

The gifts and the food exchange, as nice as they were, came with lots of questions – sometimes they felt like interrogations – and other offerings. Several of the older women began coming over with their daughters and granddaughters, inviting me for walks in the park together. I would chat for a few moments and politely decline, excusing myself by saying that I had some work to finish, which they knew was a fib since it was summer and school was out. The conversations were always similar.

"Are you married?" they'd ask.

"No," I'd say. "But I have a girlfriend."

That never stopped them, it just forced them to rephrase their questioning.

"Is she here?"

"No."

"Where is she?"

"She's in the US."

"So she's not Ukrainian?"

"No, she's American."

"So, you need a Ukrainian girlfriend here."

"No, I think I'm fine. But thank you."

They always threw me a frustrating look at this point.

"How are you fine? Look at you."

To be fair, my appearance had changed since I arrived. I had lost 15 pounds in about two months and was the thinnest and lightest I'd been since high school at just 130 pounds. At five feet nine inches tall and usually around 145 pounds, I was never big. Years of playing basketball and training for track and field made me strong and healthy, and gave me an athletic physique that I maintained through college and my mid-twenties without much effort.

But I had definitely slimmed down in Ukraine. My clothes were hanging off of my frame and I had to poke a new hole farther up my belt to keep my trousers from slipping down.

I wasn't unhealthy or starved. I just consumed almost exclusively bread and produce from the market, and much less meat than in the States. I was eating like a local. There were no more Portland happy-hour burgers and fries, no processed foods. Moreover, I was walking or riding a bike several miles each day. I actually felt great.

The married couple I shared a floor with, however, were concerned. Oleksandr and Olesya were kind people who were happiest on the days when their young granddaughter came to visit them. They spoiled her with ice-cream bars and let her watch cartoons. Olesya knocked on my door a few times a week with leftover borsch or *varenyky*. Because it was summer she had home-made jams. Later, in winter, she would bring me cold medicine and vitamins. If she suspected I wasn't taking the vitamins, she'd invite herself into my apartment to check how many were left in the bottles by giving them a shake. Sometimes she would just come over with a bag of potatoes or milk. Eggs were a regular gift. She said she bought too many and Oleksandr would never eat them all, but I knew she bought too many on purpose.

"You're too thin, you need to be like Oleksandr," she told me one day, puffing her cheeks and patting her belly.

Another reason my eating habits changed was because I couldn't afford to dine out or buy expensive imported food at the supermarket. The Peace Corps paid its volunteers salaries that were right around the local average. Nationally, that came to a little over $300 a month. In Artemivsk, it was about $200, and pensions ranged from around $70 to $175. I was lucky in that I made $260 a month – $100 of which went to Nikolai for rent.

People did all sorts of things to supplement their meager incomes and pensions. If folks had a private house and a backyard, or a *dacha* – a summer home – they gardened and stocked up their cellars with vegetables and pickled foods for the winter. Men, in particular, moonlighted as taxi drivers in private cars. I never told the Peace Corps, but I did some freelance writing for travel and culture magazines that brought in a couple of hundred extra bucks every few months, helping to pay for the occasional pizza or weekend visit to another volunteer's site.

But the extra money-making venture that stood out to me was the local hair game. On nearly every lamppost and public announcement board were flyers from hair buyers soliciting women for their long blonde locks.

"Pokupayem volosy!" – "We buy hair!" announced the flyers, always printed in all caps and on bright sheets of paper. Each had pull tabs at the bottom with a number to call. Rarely did I see one that still had tabs attached.

Slavic blonde hair is known around the world as "white gold" and Ukraine's buyer sold it for hundreds or even thousands of dollars to foreign clients who used it for luxurious hair extensions and wigs. The Ukrainian women who opted to part with their long tresses were often college-aged and had been growing it since childhood. They would call the number and go into a salon chosen by the buyer, get their hair chopped off in one cut, and leave crying with $50 to $100 in their skinny-jean pocket.

As I settled into Artemivsk and got to know the place and its people, much of the fear and doubt that had come over me on the train ride disappeared and the place quickly began to feel like a second home.

Nikolai was a big reason for that. He seemed to know everyone and everything in the city. In my first days and weeks there, he took me to see various landmarks and notable places. There were the decommissioned MiG-15 with its nose sticking up toward the sky, the green battle tank atop its plinth positioned like it's about to fire, and the sculpture of the soldier picking up a comrade who'd been wounded in battle – all monuments to the Great Patriotic War, as the Soviets called the Second World War, and the Red Army's victory over fascism. Of course, there were the statues of Lenin and Artyom, always used as meeting locations. "See you at Artyom at 10 o'clock," we'd say to each other, or "Under Lenin at seven."

Nikolai showed me City Hall, a hulking, unremarkable building adorned with a blue and yellow Ukrainian trident, the country's coat of arms, and said he didn't like the government much and wasn't political. Up the hill was the main bus station and the train station, places I would come to know very well. He also pointed out a nursing school where he said young women could be found in the evenings singing in the windows and standing outside waiting for their cigarettes to be lit by potential suitors.

His favorite places, though, were the sports stadium, which had both indoor and outdoor tracks and a workout facility that was used by some members of the Ukrainian Olympic team; and the central bazaar, a sprawling maze of produce stalls, home supplies, and clothing shops featuring counterfeit Western brands.

On our first visit to the bazaar, he introduced me to dozens of people, including many I would visit weekly for the next two years. One of them was Valeriy, a mustachioed man who was nearly as wide as he was tall. Like many other middle-aged men around, he wore a fishing vest with several pockets. In his case, they served an important purpose. He was one of several money-exchange guys who operated outside the official banking systems and offered an exchange rate just slightly better than the city banks. The pockets were filled with cash in various currencies and he always occupied the same spot near the bazaar's entrance.

I also met Leonid, who preferred to go by his diminutive, Lyonya. He sold bicycles and gave me a good price on a no-frills, single-speed blue bike made in Kharkiv. It cost me $100, or a little less than half of my monthly Peace Corps salary. I ate little for the next month because of it.

Artemivsk didn't look half bad from what I could tell. Red and pink and yellow roses lined the streets and parks, which were mostly paved and flat. Many of the buildings were painted in pastel blues, greens, yellows, and pinks – or maybe they had been painted brighter colors and faded over the years, but they weren't all drab. Children splashed around in a fountain on Artyom Square as their mothers posed for photos on a small decorative bridge, always with a leg lifted behind them or standing on their toes to elongate their legs. Older kids zipped around on bicycles and stuffed their faces with *plombir* ice-cream cones. City workers in fluorescent orange vests were always sweeping the central squares and sidewalks, and for reasons I would never come to understand painting the trunks of every tree in the city white. Every few weeks in the summer, the workers would dig up and replace the flowers in front of City Hall and in the beds running through the central park that connected the lower and upper parts of town.

On the second week I was there, Nikolai took me inside to meet Artemivsk's mayor Oleksiy Reva, whose term had begun in 1990, a year before Ukraine gained independence from the Soviet Union, making him the longest-serving elected leader on any government level in the country. Reva was a hulking man with thick gray-white hair, caterpillar eyebrows with strays that sprung out like worn mattress coils, and a neatly trimmed mustache. His hands were as big and thick as baseball catchers' mitts and his handshake had the power of a vice grip. Reva wore a white button-up shirt with the collar open under a dark blue sharkskin suit that looked expensive but clearly hadn't been tailored to fit him; the shoulders were a couple of inches too long and jutted out like the pads of a linebacker in American football, and the sleeves fell below the cuffs of his shirt. He told his assistant to make us two Americanos before taking a seat in a large cushioned chair behind his desk.

Reva was a busy man and he got straight to the point of the meeting. Could I come to an event with him the following week where city and regional education officials would be hosting big shots from the Ministry of Education in Kyiv to discuss the upcoming school year? I would need to shake some hands and deliver a short speech in Russian to his guests. There had been one Peace Corps volunteer in Artemivsk a couple of years earlier and Reva had liked the attention that she brought to the city. Having a Western volunteer in your town seemed to mean something. This was the first request of many of its kind.

The next week I arrived at the event dressed in a blazer and tie, but Nikolai was displeased that I hadn't shaved off my beard completely and had only trimmed it a bit. At that time, young men in Ukraine didn't wear facial hair. Scruff and full-on beards were worn exclusively by old men and scoundrels, and Ukrainians had a tendency to pass swift judgment on strangers. In my first weeks in Kyiv a security guard at a supermarket followed me around and asked me to leave because he thought I was a "bum" – *bomzh*. He allowed me to stay when I showed him my American passport. And I had weirded out the seven-year-old daughter of a Ukrainian friend with my bushy face when I first met her. She asked why I looked like her uncle. But by the end of my visit, she had given me a friendly nickname: *Dyadya Yozhyk*, or Uncle Hedgehog. Nobody at the school conference seemed to care about my appearance except Nikolai.

The event was held at school in the village of Opytne, just a five-minute drive south of Bakhmut. A pair of young students opened the event by singing the national anthem. And then state and regional education officials got up and spoke about budgets and curriculums. For official events like this, Ukrainian was almost always used. So as they spoke, I followed along as best I could, nodding along with those around me and clapping with the group. But I understood less than half of what was being said. As Reva concluded his speech, he introduced several new teachers who would be working in schools in the Artemivsk area. I was the last to be introduced.

"This year we have one very special new teacher," he told the audience. "This young man came all the way from America because he heard about how beautiful our city is."

That wasn't exactly true, but I understood that Reva was doing his thing to build up the city in the eyes of superiors.

"Christopher, please come up here and say a few words."

The crowd applauded as I walked to the podium. With the help of a few notecards on which I had hand-written what I wanted to say in Russian, I delivered a mistake-free speech.

"Dear ladies and gentlemen and new friends. Thank you very much for your attention," I began. "When I came to Artemivsk I didn't know what to expect. I knew it would be very different than my home in the United States. But I feel very welcome in your beautiful city. I know that this school year will be great and we will work together very well. I wish you all great happiness and success in the new year!" I concluded.

When it was over, Nikolai patted me on the back and told me I did well. *"Moy malchik!"*

"What's next?" I asked him.

"Now you rest," he said. "I'll see you in September."

Salt, Champagne, and a Soviet Hangover

Artemivsk in Ukrainian, or Artyomovsk in Russian, had originally been named Bakhmut and founded in 1571. That name was derived from the Bakhmutka river that ran through the city, but nobody I asked seemed to know exactly what it means or where the river's name came from. The name Bakhmut was changed to Artemivsk in 1924, in honor of the Bolshevik revolutionary Fyodor "Artyom" Sergeyev, a close friend of Joseph Stalin. Sergeyev had been killed three years earlier during a test ride of a high-speed railcar fitted with a plane engine, called an Aerowagon. Stalin adopted Artyom's son after his father's death. A monument to Artyom, with his right arm reaching into the sky and his left hand squeezing a cap, towered above the central square on a stone pedestal when I arrived. The monument would come down in 2016, and the city would see its historic name of Bakhmut restored – six years before Bakhmut would become synonymous with brutal military tactics and the site of the longest-running battle of Russia's full-scale war against Ukraine, and decades after it had been occupied by another invading army.

17

Adolf Hitler's Nazi army occupied Artemivsk between 1941 and 1943, during which time they de-Sovietized the city and briefly returned it to its original name of Bakhmut. The Germans carried out atrocities while they were there. In 1942 they marched some 3,000 Jews to the underground tunnels of an old gypsum mine, shot and killed several of them, then forced the rest of the group into one of the dead-end tunnels and stoned up the only way out, leaving them to suffocate. Dozens of Nazis themselves were killed during their occupation, and I would eventually learn that some of the bodies of Hitler's troops had been buried behind Artemivsk's Palace of Culture in unmarked graves. In the years following the war, after the Germans were long gone, a public square was built overtop the makeshift cemetery and a statue of Lenin was erected. I came to know about all this after a stroll past Lenin Square one day. There, a group of men were exhuming the Nazis' remains. They said the German government had asked local authorities to help repatriate them. One of the workers lifted a plastic flap for me to see the piles of decomposed bones before they were packed and shipped off.

Artemivsk wasn't unique in that sense. It seemed that every city and town in eastern Ukraine was steeped in history and haunted by a dark past. Little did I or anyone else know then that my new adopted home would see so much more darkness in the very near future.

Artemivsk was long known for its salt mines, which were first excavated by Cossacks under orders from Peter the Great in the early eighteenth century. It later became famous in the Soviet Union for its sparkling wine, which was produced inside the labyrinth of underground, climate-controlled tunnels of the same former gypsum mine where the Nazis murdered those thousands of Jews. A "wailing wall" memorialized them inside and tour guides always paused there to cross themselves and say a little prayer. The Artemivsk Winery, now known as Artwinery, opened in celebration of Joseph Stalin's birthday in December 1950, and made "Soviet champagne" in the French style, with a lengthy and tedious aging process that meant workers had to monitor and constantly turn the bottles as they gathered dust for months. But the bubbly certainly didn't taste French. It was so sweet that it made my mouth pucker. And it caused absolutely brutal hangovers. The one bottle that was particularly drinkable – and truly different from the rest – was the sparkling red brut made with grapes from vineyards in Crimea. The winery loved to boast to visitors that the British Royal Family and Queen Elizabeth II herself served it to guests at banquets. Trying to fact-check this claim, however, proved impossible. I would make several trips to the winery, including three times with visiting friends and family from Portland, and a few more trips with other foreign guests. Artwinery's managers would call me on occasion to ask if I could come and help with translation for guests who didn't speak Russian or Ukrainian. By my fifth visit, I knew by memory many of the stories that its caves held and came to understand the reason why its white-gray tunnel walls were painted the rainbow colors that first intrigued me: to warm up the otherwise dark and drab chambers that reached a depth of 262 feet below Ukraine's famous black earth. "It lifts their spirits," Viktoria Malyovana, Artwinery's deputy general manager, told me about the color scheme. "We want everyone to be happy here."

The salt mines, formed by an ancient sea that had dried up, were in Soledar, a suburb on the northern edge of Artemivsk. With 125 miles of mazes 945 feet below the surface, they composed a sort of underground city run by some 3,000 people. Their main use, of course, was the production of salt by the Artemsil company. Mined with massive combines that drilled swirly holes into the walls, Artemsil supplied 95 per cent of Ukraine – and huge swathes of the former Soviet Union – with the stuff.

Artemsil also served as a recreation and health center. Each autumn, a Salt Symphony was held for Ukraine's political and business elite inside a six-story-high chamber within the mine. It was famous for its acoustics. Down the salt hall was a speleological sanatorium, where people with respiratory problems and body aches could come for a day or even weeks. My friends spoke of the mines in an almost mystical way, always touting their rejuvenation capabilities. The salt in the air, they said, helped suppress wheezing and joint pain. I visited twice, spending four hours each time inside the speleological sanatorium and wandering the dark, seemingly endless tunnels of the mines. My guides took me down in a large, open elevator. The temperature was a cool and controlled 57 degrees Fahrenheit. When we reached the bottom, I saw that everything was salt – the walls, the ground, and light fixtures. Statues carved from salt lined the tunnels. There were several shaped as palm trees. A church stood at one end, with bas-reliefs of religious icons and an altar of salt. While I can't be certain it was the salt air that did it, or merely the relaxing atmosphere, I left each time feeling better than I had before.

Hiding somewhere farther south in the salt tunnel system there was also a massive weapons depot – one of the largest in Eastern Europe. Accessible only through a heavily guarded underground entrance or an elevator at the surface in the neighboring village of Paraskoviivka, the depot housed millions of weapons and masses of ammunition dating as far back as the

First World War. The stable climatic conditions were perfect for storage, and the materiel being held at such a depth was great for security.

———————

In 2022, more than a decade later and ten months into Putin's all-out invasion of Ukraine, these underground cities in Bakhmut and Soledar would be targeted by Russian forces and particularly by the bloodthirsty mercenaries fighting for the Wagner Group, a private military company founded by Evgeny Prigozhin, a close Putin ally. Looking like a villain from a James Bond film with his melon-like bald head, beady eyes, and perma-scowl, and with a backstory to match (he had been dubbed "Putin's chef" by the Russian media because he owned a catering company that served the Kremlin), Prigozhin would recruit murderers from prison colonies in far-flung Russian regions to fight in Ukraine. On the battlefields around Bakhmut and Soledar, Wagner commanders would send them in waves across a no man's land in an attempt to overwhelm Ukrainian troops, who would fire on as many as possible with machine guns.

Prigozhin's intent there was clear. On his Telegram account, he'd write: "The cherry on the cake is the system of Soledar and Bakhmut mines, which is actually a network of underground cities. It not only has the ability to hold a big group of people at a depth of 80–100 meters, but tanks and infantry fighting vehicles can also move about. And stockpiles of weapons have been stored there since the First World War."

I would see and hear the fierce fighting for myself and witness the waves of men being sent to their slaughter. I counted the dozens of wounded Ukrainian troops streaming into the hospital that sat across from my apartment on Peace Street.

———————

The politics of Artemivsk were complicated. I met more people who had traveled to, had family in, or did business in Rostov or Moscow than Kyiv. Russian television was watched more than Ukrainian programming. Yet to simply assume that Artemivsk was pro-Russian because of those things and its obvious proximity to Russia was to ignore its many underlying complexities.

People here, generally, had long harbored a cynical view of politicians and the government. Most voters had helped to elect in February 2010 the new president, Viktor Yanukovych, and members of his Russia-friendly Party of Regions to represent them in the Verkhovna Rada, Ukraine's national parliament, just months before I arrived. But few seemed enthusiastic about having done so and openly acknowledged that they believed Yanukovych was a crook and his party was corrupt. They were seen as the least bad option in a race where the alternatives included leaders of the 2004 pro-democracy Orange Revolution and government that followed. The Donbas was still sour from what it felt was a raw deal after the previous national elections in December 2004, when Yanukovych had lost to the more Western-friendly Viktor Yushchenko in a re-vote after it was found that the Party of Regions camp had rigged the vote in their party leader's favor. And there was a sense that Kyiv didn't care much about people in the east or see them as true Ukrainians. Their view of Moscow was similar. In fact, when I asked people about their identities, many said they identified first as people of the Donbas. That was interesting to me but was hardly surprising to people I discussed it with, given that the Donbas, a vast, wild steppe land once controlled by Cossacks, had a long history of rebelling against rulers in both Moscow and Kyiv.

People here valued freedom and independence above all else; they didn't want anyone telling them what to do. But that wasn't to be confused with a desire to separate from Ukraine. Only once did I hear someone speak of their desire to form an independent "republic." It happened during my second summer in Artemivsk, in 2011, during a picnic in the woods with the family of a student I taught at Krasne school. A fire was crackling and skewered meat was barbecuing over the small open flame when Ilya, the father of the student, pulled me aside. He had a bottle of *samohon*, Ukrainian moonshine, and poured small shots for us in little tin cups. Then he started rambling on about something called the Donetsk–Krivoy Rog Soviet Republic, which I later looked up and discovered was an unrecognized, self-declared entity in the Donbas that had existed for only 37 days in February and March 1918. Ilya said he dreamed of it being resurrected – not as a totally independent state, but as an autonomous republic in the way that modern Crimea existed, part of Ukraine but with its own parliament.

Ilya poured me another shot and walked me to his yellow Lada. Inside the trunk he pulled out a black, blue, and red flag he claimed was that of the Donetsk–Krivoy Rog Soviet Republic – though I never found evidence to support this – and held it up for me to see.

"The flag of our republic," he said proudly. "With God's help, one day it will return."

He said a man named Andrei Purgin was the leader of a movement to bring it back. In fact, Purgin had founded "Donetsk Republic" in 2005, as a civic movement. But local authorities quickly banned it. The movement was barely a blip on anyone's political radar. It consisted of just a few dozen people, Ilya said. But he claimed that some of them were deeply motivated and not afraid to fight if the government came after them.

He tucked the flag back in a box and reached for something deeper in the trunk of his car. I stumbled a few steps backward when I saw him pull out an old AK-47. There was no magazine in it, but I saw one in the trunk.

"Let's hope we don't need to use this," he said, taking aim at an imagined foe someplace beyond the treeline and pulling the trigger. We drank another shot of *samohon* and he raised a toast.

"To freedom!" he said.

2

Friends

I had a lot of free time on my hands until the school year began. Luckily, my new Ukrainian friends were eager to help me fill it. The first friend I made was Igor Moroz. I sometimes called him Mr Frost, as his surname in both Russian and Ukrainian translates to "frost" in English. But Igor was anything but cold. Gregarious and funny, he was popular with people around town and knew all the best places to go and things to do. We became fast friends.

Igor seemed almost like a Ukrainian version of myself. We were born three weeks apart in 1984. We both preferred old-school rock to new pop music. We had questionable taste in hats – I liked my newsboy cap which in Ukraine was typically worn by old, working-class men; Igor often donned a fedora. We were brown-haired and brown-eyed with short, scruffy facial hair. We were both restless when left alone and preferred being in the company of friends most of the time.

We liked to stroll through the park with a bottle of beer in hand. Igor called them "walking beers." Four nights a week at least, we'd meet at a kiosk to buy a cold *pivo* and then sip on it as we circled Artemivsk's rose-lined central park. Igor smoked Chesterfield cigarettes and sometimes I bummed one from him.

We got to know each other on those strolls. Igor had studied international relations at a university in Kyiv, where he lived in a small apartment with two other students. They had little money. Igor worked as a bartender at a bar that had been built as a bomb shelter in a building erected after the Second World War – or the Great Patriotic War. The memory of the war still lingered, but the thought of another like it was nowhere in people's minds. The shelters were transformed into businesses, usually pubs, cafes, and strip clubs. Igor worked at Art Club 44, just off Khreshchatyk Street, Kyiv's main drag. It was hard to find and that was the point. If you were there, you were cool. Ukraine's best underground bands performed there nightly as the capital's hipsters smoked and sipped on Johnnie Walker and Jack Daniels.

Igor had studied English and political science and was interested in international human rights. His dream after graduation was to work with the United Nations. But it didn't pan out and he lacked enough money to remain in Kyiv. So he returned to Artemivsk to be close to his mother, a doctor, and his father, who ran a seasonal tourism business that transported Ukrainians from Donetsk Oblast to Crimea. Igor quickly landed a job with the city government.

Igor had an office inside city hall, one floor below the Artemivsk mayor, Oleksiy Reva, where he worked as an elections official. He liked it because it was an easy job with little to do except in the months ahead of an election. Even then, he just needed to make sure voter lists were up to date and the voting went smoothly. But at the same time he didn't enjoy being a part of the government because many people mistrusted government officials and believed them all to be corrupt. Igor wasn't a political person. Like many young Ukrainians at the time, he was politically apathetic. Whenever I brought up politics he scowled and quickly changed the subject. Despite being an elections official, he said he didn't vote.

"There are no good choices," he explained. "I'm not sure I like any of them."

On days when he had very little to do – and there were many such days – Igor would call me to chat or make plans for the evening. Sometimes he invited me over to hang out for the last few hours of the day. He always met me in the lobby and walked me upstairs, sometimes introducing me to people around the office. Many of them knew who I was but hadn't yet interacted with me. Igor would put on a serious face and make it seem as though we had some sort of business to discuss. When he closed his office door behind us, he relaxed. Under his desk he kept bottles of Ukrainian "cognac" and a set of *ryumki*, shot glasses with short stems, which he would fill to the brim.

"To work!" we toasted and laughed.

"To us!" we toasted again.

"To girls!" Igor always added.

We kept going after he finished work.

Two or three times a week that summer we went to an outdoor cafe and discotheque called Paradise. The kitchen served tall beers and *shashlik*, meat barbecued over an open flame. A disco ball and colored lights illuminated the dance floor. The DJ played a bizarre mix of Russian, Ukrainian, and

American pop. But the hit of the summer that got everyone on their feet was "We Speak No Americano" by the Australian electronic duo Yolanda Be Cool. It played once an hour and as soon as the crowd heard the opening horns they slammed down their glasses and leapt up. Slim women with the longest hair I'd ever seen teetered atop their six-inch stilettos as men with plump bellies gyrated awkwardly beside them.

We would sometimes dance, too, making great fools of ourselves bouncing around to a dance song that was completely undanceable.

Igor was the life of any party, never knew when to go home, and always had one more drink in him. He could also never remember the word "hangover" and it was just as well that he didn't because the words he used to describe how incredibly bad he felt after a night of drinking were much better.

"Kreees," he cried into the phone to me one morning after a long night that saw us bounce from Club Bananas to Paradise to another discotheque I could never remember the name of. "I feel . . . my head . . . it's like a Brontosaurus Rex."

"How late were you out?" I asked.

"Four in the morning. No, I think five."

"Good time?"

"Yes, of course! But now I must go to my job. And I feel myself really terrible."

Igor was far from the only person living it up. Ukrainians loved a good party and seemed to take advantage of every opportunity to partake of one. There seemed to be a celebration every week, maybe even twice a week – a birthday or a public holiday or a professional holiday. There were so many holidays I couldn't keep track of them all. On top of the usual ones, like Independence Day, Christmas, New Year, and Easter, there were Women's Day, Men's Day, and Victory Day, and holidays for every profession — Miners' Day, Journalists' Day, Airborne Forces' Day, Metal Workers' Day, Food Industry Workers' Day, Architects' Day . . . It went on and on.

The dozens of professional holidays were a holdover from Soviet times, when the state recognized the work of its specialist workers. Some people didn't celebrate them but many did – often with stiff spirits and tables covered with food, flowers, and cakes.

Igor explained it to me like this: "We can't know what will come tomorrow. So we live for today. Why not celebrate and have a party? Maybe there will be no tomorrow."

It was at many of those parties that I honed my toasting skills. Everyone wanted to teach the American a new one and the proper way to say it. Sometimes I practiced my Russian with Igor but he didn't have the patience to listen to me struggle with it, so I sought out others with whom I could hold more intense Russian conversations.

Konstantin, a short man with a handsome face and a gruff voice, was an early acquaintance and my first Russian tutor. Originally from St Petersburg, Russia's former imperial capital, he told me he would teach me to speak "real Russian."

"Whatever this is that you were taught and you are speaking," he told me during our first lesson, waving his hand in my face, "it is not *Russian*."

Konstantin gave me old, worn Russian-language books and novels by Chekhov, Gogol, Tolstoy, and others that were way above my Russian reading and comprehension level. He asked me to translate lengthy passages and to come prepared to discuss them. It took me hours and I rarely completed the tasks.

He never told me how he had ended up in Artemivsk, but it was clear Konstantin didn't think much of it or of Ukrainians generally. He spoke about them as if they were second-class people and on more than one occasion claimed that the Donbas was actually Russian land. I didn't yet have the experience and knowledge – let alone the vocabulary – that I would later acquire to strongly argue with him otherwise. So I listened and tried to get the most out of our language lessons. Before long, Konstantin went back to St Petersburg and I never heard from him again.

I picked up my Russian studies with Vika, a hilarious university student in her early twenties with a contagious laugh. She tutored me until the school year began, when she moved an hour south to Horlivka to finish her last year at one of the country's top language institutes. Vika was a polyglot who besides her native Russian and Ukrainian spoke nearly fluent English and was proficient in German and French. I was incredibly envious of her abilities. Our deal was that she'd help me get past speaking basic Russian and I would help her with her accent. One of the few things she struggled with was figuring out how and when to pronounce and differentiate between the short "i" in itch and the long "e" in each. I noticed this one day when she was telling me about her dreams to travel to Mexico.

"I really, really want to see the bitches of Mexico," she seemed to say.

"The bitches of Mexico?" I asked to confirm.

"Yes! Chris! Oh, beautiful bitches!"

"Vika? I think you mean beaches."

"Yes. Bitches."

"*Be*aches."

"*Bi*tches."

"Vika, you're saying *suki*," I told her, using the Russian word for "bitches." Swear words were, of course, among the first words I had learned.

Her face went red and she laughed so hard she gasped for air.

Mostly I helped Vika to speak more colloquial American English. Sometimes we would watch TV shows like the American sitcom "How I Met Your Mother," which was wildly popular in Ukraine and dubbed in Ukrainian. We would practice some of the catchphrases in both English and Russian.

"*Legen* – wait for it – *dary*!" Vika would say.

"*Legen – podozhdite – darniy!*" I'd mimic in Russian.

Vika lived alone in a fairly old but large apartment in Artemivsk's upper district. Her father was estranged from the family and her mother worked as a maid in Moscow, where she earned a salary several times higher than what she could make in Artemivsk, even in jobs that many would deem to be much better. It helped Vika to afford a good education and later an opportunity to study abroad in Germany. She didn't see many opportunities in Ukraine, let alone Artemivsk, and she was right. For people her age in eastern Ukraine's smaller cities, there wasn't much enlightening work. Those who stuck around worked in mines or factories or operated small businesses. They made enough to live on but not enough to afford many – or any – real luxuries.

Through Igor and Vika I met Rostislav, who I knew simply as Slava. He worked at his family's housewares business in an Artemivsk market in the upper part of the city. He was lanky, kind, and soft-spoken. He fancied himself as an amateur historian. He led me around the city on our bicycles, pointing out some of the older buildings in the city.

On hot days, we rode beyond the city limits, through fields of sunflowers, until we found a pond to swim in. A favorite was in Chasiv Yar, where young women donned skimpy thong bikinis and lay out on the sand. The place had a volleyball court and a cafe on a dock where we could get cold beers and *sukharyky* (biscotti) in flavors like green onion, sour cream, and crab. There were a lot of hot days that summer. July and August saw a record-breaking heatwave come through with temperatures reaching as high as 104 degrees Fahrenheit (40 Celsius). The central government in Kyiv put out an official notice urging Ukrainians to take three- to four-hour-long lunch breaks at home to stay out of the heat.

Slava introduced me to Natasha. She was smart, tall, and matter-of-fact with glasses and thick hair. She wrote articles about local news and culture for the *Sobytiya* newspaper. (She didn't like the other paper, *Vpered* (Forward), because she thought it was too close to the city government and wrote fawning articles about the mayor and his son, a local developer, and his cronies.) She also spoke English better than everyone else in town and moonlighted as an English-language tutor for school-age children. Among her many hobbies was tracking down historic photographs of Artemivsk that she would donate to the city's museum of local lore.

Natasha was much more political than the others and considered herself a Ukrainian nationalist and patriot. She was interested in the nationalist party *Svoboda*, meaning Freedom. Founded in 1995 as the Social–National Party of Ukraine (SNPU), it leaned politically to the right and was rooted in the nationalist ideology of Second World War-era western Ukrainian figures and groups like Stepan Bandera and the Ukrainian Insurgent Army (UPA), who were much vaunted for their efforts in fighting for an independent Ukraine but controversial due to their methods, including at least some collaboration with the Germans in the fight against the Soviet Union, and murderous campaigns against Poles and Jews. The SNPU party used a modified Wolfsangel that resembled one used by the Nazis. But the party claimed the symbol was an "N" with a vertical "I" through its center and stood for the phrase "Idea of the nation."

SNPU and Svoboda was led by Oleh Tyahnybok, a thickset man with a permanent shit-eating grin on his face. He often wore a black-and-red uniform that alluded to the UPA flag of the same colors and symbolized red Ukrainian blood spilled on its famous black earth. In an attempt to turn SNPU into a moderate, mainstream party in 2004, he changed its symbol from the Wolfsangel to a three-fingered hand redolent of the *tryzub* – Ukraine's coat of arms and a popular pro-independence gesture. But that same year, Tyahnybok gave a speech in western Ukraine in which he lauded the UPA for fighting against Russians, Germans, Jews, and "other scum who wanted to take away our Ukrainian state." Svoboda didn't have popular support and operated on the political fringe. But it managed to garner more interest in the wake of Yanukovych's victory in February 2010.

Natasha lived in the east but her soul seemed to be in the west, a region that I had yet to visit but was interested in learning more about. So I joined her a few times at local Svoboda meetings where nationalist-minded people met to speak in Ukrainian and discuss politics and Ukrainian literature. It was a very different side of the country's politics and history than I had seen and heard about up to that point. I mostly knew about the two mainstream parties – the Moscow-friendly Party of Regions that rose up here in the east and was led by Yanukovych; and the *Batkivshchyna*, or Fatherland, party of Yulia Tymoshenko, one of the political leaders of the 2004 Orange Revolution and a former prime minister. She was also known by some as "The Gas Princess" because she rose up through Ukraine's murky and cut-throat gas industry in south-central Dnipropetrovsk. But she had hired an image consultant to make her more appealing and more patriotic to everyday Ukrainians by speaking Ukrainian in her public speeches and donning a golden crown of folky braids.

They began their Svoboda meetings by singing the Ukrainian national anthem, which I was surprised and impressed by, as it was called "Ukraine has not yet perished." They stood and placed their hands over their hearts. Then someone pressed the play button on a little boombox and the song began:

Ukraine is not yet dead, nor its glory and freedom,
Still upon us, young brothers, fate shall smile.
Our enemies shall vanish, like dew in the sun.
And we too, brothers, shall rule our country.
Soul and body we shall lay down for our freedom,
And we will show, brothers, that we are of the Cossack nation!

I loved the sound of Ukrainian, though I didn't understand much of it then. Unlike Russian, which I thought sounded harsh and as if everyone was angry at each other when they spoke, Ukrainian was soft and lyrical. I hadn't heard much of it spoken since arriving in the east.

Some of my Ukrainian friends asked why I was learning Russian instead of Ukrainian. The answer wasn't always satisfactory but it was simple: the Peace Corps had assigned Russian-language training to the half of our group of 77 volunteers who were being deployed to the east and the south, where Russian was the dominant language. Only a few times was I ever scolded for not speaking Ukrainian, the official state language. Most people didn't mind.

Language policy had always been a fraught issue among politicians, but ordinary folks didn't seem to care much about it. I met plenty of people who communicated with each other in both languages simultaneously, as I would eventually come to do. And some spoke a mixture of both, making it seem as though the languages were one and the same at times – and when people spoke in *surzhyk*, they could be.

My friends were always taking me around and introducing me to more people. Natasha and Slava introduced me to the main librarians at the Artemivsk library. This was one of the only places in town with internet access. A computer room held five or six desktop computers with what was essentially dial-up internet. The speed was almost never enough to do anything but send emails, access Facebook, and read news sites. I spent a couple of hours there each day, partly to read the news and touch base with family and friends, and partly to avoid the heat; the library was one of the few places where the local government had installed an air conditioner.

The librarians asked if I would host a weekly English club for some of the students who were in town and hadn't gone away to summer camps. We held the club once a week. I devised various word games and simple lessons for the group of ten people who usually came. Most were young children, but Slava and Igor joined in sometimes, as well as a couple of curious adults in town who had picked up some English from pirated DVDs sold at the market. By the third lesson, more than 20 people were coming, and the librarians had to bring in extra chairs. I also began getting noticed more on the street and stopped for chats.

One of the women who came to English club worked at the maternity hospital and asked me whether I would like to come meet the head doctor there. The doctor and her nurses were curious about the new American in town and also wanted to inquire whether I might be able to help them from time to time. Eastern Ukraine's poorer cities and towns were popular places for American missionaries to come and work and for adoption agencies to operate. Prospective parents, usually very religious ones, showed up several times a year at the maternity ward to see about adopting babies who needed homes.

On the day I arrived, it was Dr Halyna's birthday. I brought her pink roses and a box of chocolates and she kissed me on the cheek. Halyna set up a light lunch of *buterbrodi* – open-faced sandwiches topped with sausage, cheese, green onions, tomatoes, and cucumbers.

"Just a second," she said, reaching into a cabinet door to grab a bottle of Ukrainian brandy. "Let's celebrate."

She handed me the bottle and I poured small shots into little glasses for us all. We ate and drank together with several nurses in Halyna's office while discussing all the babies they had delivered and some of the adoptions. The doctor spoke about all the newborns as if they were her own. She said it was the joy of her life to see many get adopted and live in the United States who would otherwise have been orphans.

"American boys," the doctor said in accented English, gesturing at me and shaking her head in astonishment of what they would become. At the same time, she lamented the fact that there were fewer young families in Artemivsk, fewer babies being born. "So many of our young people leave after they graduate from school," she said. "It's a pity."

Halyna told me that she had delivered two babies not long before we'd arrived. Both were born to happy young local families.

"I hope they will stay and make a new future for us here," she said.

Over the next hour, we drank and toasted several more times.

To Halyna! — Happy birthday!

To friendship!

To love!

To women!

To the babies!

To the future!

We were silly drunk with booze-flushed faces when the doctor glanced at her watch and said it was time to get back to the delivery room.

"We have work to do," she said to my great surprise. "There are two more babies who want to meet us."

I stumbled slightly as I stood, the blood rushing from my head to my legs. Halyna thanked me for my company and then excused herself.

"Mr Chris"

Krasne village, September 2010–May 2011

The phone rang at dawn and startled me from my sleep. Nikolai's voice boomed on the other end of the line, making sure I wouldn't be late for the first day of school. September 1st always marks the first day of autumn and the start of a new school year in Ukraine.

"Wear a tie," he said, "and shave your beard."

When the *marshrutka* dropped me off outside the Krasne village school shortly before 7 a.m., I could see that many of its 100 students and their parents had already arrived and were waiting for the festivities to begin.

Krasne, meaning Red, as in the Soviets' Red Army red or Communist red, was the name of the village on the western edge of Artemivsk. Just

31

over 1,000 people lived there and many of them were *surzhyk* speakers like Nikolai. The Peace Corps had made teaching at the Krasne school my primary assignment.

Nikolai took me inside to the teachers' lounge where the staff were milling around. A few of the men were sitting in a corner sipping coffee and chatting. A group of women were crowded around a tiny wall mirror, touching up their make-up. They nodded and said good morning. A few doors down, we found the school director, Olga Yevgenyevna Kazachenko, curling her hair at her desk. A buxom woman with fluffy, curled bangs and a shiny gold tooth, she was pleasant and professional.

"Welcome! We are very pleased to have you here, Christopher," she said. "Do you have a speech prepared?"

"Yes, I do," I told her. It would be the same one I'd given a week earlier to a room full of national and regional educators. But none of the students or their parents would know that.

Nikolai asked for help setting up the sound system in the front of the school. While testing the microphone he asked me to say something in English. He thought it would impress the crowd.

"Hello," I said. "I'm very happy to be here. We will begin soon."

The crowd just stared. I saw a few of the youngest children furrow their brows, grab their parents' legs, and whisper something up to them.

Olga Yevgenyevna gathered everyone outside and announced the start of the ceremony. I always called her by her first name and patronymic, as a sign of respect but also because Nikolai had asked me to do so, even while he said it was fine to simply refer to him by his first name because we were "friends." Apparently, I could not be friends with Olga Yevgenyevna, just an acquaintance and colleague.

All the girls wore black skirts with white blouses and tall white socks. Their hair was pulled back into long ponytails or pigtails and topped with large white bows. They looked a little like maids in their formal attire. The boys wore boxy suits that were either a little too big or a little too small (they were growing out of their last school year's suit or had purchased a new one to grow into in the new year). The eleventh-form class had red sashes draped over their shoulders to indicate their seniority.

One by one, the teachers stood up to speak, some of them visibly nervous and reading from prepared notes. Many of their speeches were delivered in Tennyson-style verse, with stanzas about knowledge and friendship, dreams and victories, and the start of autumn. Olga Yevgenyevna delivered her own speech to rapturous applause, punctuated by the Ukrainian national anthem that blared from the speakers.

Then it was my turn.

"Dear ladies and gentlemen and new friends," I began again, this time in Russian. "I know that this school year will be great and we will work together very well. I wish you all great happiness and success in the new year!"

The applause started slowly but quickly picked up steam. It was clear the crowd was surprised – maybe impressed? – by my speaking Russian and simply by my even being there.

A series of songs and dances followed, with Nikolai acting as emcee. The students linked arms and spun in circles as the crowd of parents clapped along slightly out of rhythm.

The celebration culminated with the oldest student – a young woman in the eleventh form – and the youngest student – a small boy from the first form – walking together in a circle and ringing the first bells of the new school year.

A blue-and-yellow Ukrainian flag jutted from the wall and a painting of a walrus-mustachioed Taras Shevchenko, the country's foremost poet and artist, loomed over the class of youngsters who were the first to endure an English lesson with me.

"Good morning, good morning, good morning to you! Good morning, good morning, I'm glad to see you!" they greeted me cheerily in stiff, robotic English that day and every day for the next nine months.

"Good morning! I'm very glad to see all of you, too," I told them. "My name is Christopher, but you can call me Mr Chris."

The students giggled at my shortened name, which sounded similar to the Russian word for rat, *krisa*.

"Maybe it's better to call you Mr Christopher," Olha, a teacher who was assisting me, suggested.

The students objected.

"No! No! *Meester Krees*!"

My English lessons with all of the younger classes consisted mainly of games designed for them to recognize words, phrases, and numbers, and get used to speaking and hearing English. With the older students, my task was much more challenging: I needed to get them to be able to communicate in what was their third language after Russian and Ukrainian.

From the very start, my eleventh-form class of 16- and 17-year-olds weren't interested in learning English. There were ten of them and just three were boys. Many boys left school after 9th form, when they are allowed to go off and study a trade, like plumbing, carpentry, auto repair, or mining. So the tenth and eleventh forms were mostly composed of female students.

The eleventh formers had a serious case of senioritis and little patience for an American teacher with limited local language skills and no experience in the classroom. Their knowledge of English was rudimentary at best and their previous teachers had done little more than assign them memorization tasks that would get them through exams with passing marks.

Indeed, they were great at memorizing speeches and passages from books. But they almost never knew what they were saying and did not understand the fundamentals of the English language. Asking them the simplest of questions in English elicited blank stares and awkward smiles.

We quickly developed a running-joke reply for when I asked a question and the students didn't comprehend the request. "Can you please read from the top of the page?" I would ask, for instance. And when they didn't know what had been said, they would reply, "London is the capital of Great Britain," and the class would explode with laughter.

So I set out with the very basic goal of teaching them to hold simple conversations in English, not dissimilar to how I was communicating in Russian with people around town.

"Let's make a deal," I told them during the first week. "I'll teach you to speak and understand English. And you will help me with my Russian. Agreed?"

They stared at me, unsure of what I was saying until I translated my offer into Russian.

"*Da!* Yes, yes, okay," said Sofia, an energetic blonde who sat in the front of the class and had impeccable posture. The others nodded apprehensively.

But to appease Olga Yevgenyevna, we also had to use the textbook assigned to the class from time to time. Aptly titled English 11, it was rigid and filled with lectures as much as language lessons. On our first day together, I asked Sofia to read the opening page aloud. It began:

Now you are eleventh-formers. It means that this is your last school year. You will pass your school-leaving examinations and have to decide how to use the knowledge you have received at school.

The end of the school is the beginning of your independent life, the beginning of a far more serious examination connected with your further study and labor activity. To pass that examination you must choose the road in life which will open before you. You must choose the occupation in which you can best develop your talents and work with the best results for you personally and for your Motherland, Ukraine. A wide road lies open before you. And you must think very hard and ask advice of your parents, your teachers and your friends to be sure that you have chosen the right occupation in which you will be able to satisfy your own tastes and the needs of your country.

I used the textbook as the basis for my lessons, but I rarely assigned my students the tasks within it, unless a teaching assistant was present or another teacher would come in to observe, as was sometimes the case. Instead, we found our way around much of the instruction and within weeks their English had improved significantly and we were able to talk about our hobbies, favorite films, favorite foods, travel, and a topic of great interest to them – celebrities.

Every student was under the impression that, as an American, I personally must know and even be friends with people like Eminem, Lady Gaga, and Justin Bieber.

"How often do you see them?" one student inquired.

"I've never actually seen any of *those* people in person," I said, to their great dissatisfaction. I listed some other musicians with whom I'd hobnobbed in Portland, but the names meant nothing to my students. The internet hadn't penetrated their lives very deeply yet, and only the names of the biggest stars reached this corner of the world.

While Olga Yevgenyevna wanted to use me mostly as an English teacher, I was actually meant to teach about what the Peace Corps called "healthy lifestyles" issues. Those included everything from lessons on the importance of personal hygiene, such as regularly brushing one's teeth and bathing, to HIV and AIDS awareness and prevention. Of course, the older students, the pimple-faced teenagers entering puberty or already well into young adulthood and sexually active, were the target audience for the heavier topics. But HIV and AIDS weren't completely foreign subjects to the younger students.

An angry kid named Dima sat in the back of my fifth-form class. Short and stocky with messy blonde hair, he always had a grumpy look on his face and would often get into arguments and shoving matches with other students. Many classmates poked fun at him and when they did he would sometimes smack them up the side of their head. At first I didn't know what the deal was with him and why he was being ridiculed. It was only after

I inquired about him with the school psychologist that I understood what was going on.

Dima's mother had passed away a year earlier from an HIV-related illness, and without a father in the picture he was now being raised by his elderly grandmother. In the Krasne community, Dima's family was kept at a distance but was sometimes the object of harsh condemnation and criticism because of the mother's HIV-positive status.

She had contracted HIV from a man she had dated – not through intravenous drug use, which is how most people in the community assumed it was spread. A teacher at the school once told me that "only bad people" were infected with HIV, which obviously wasn't true. Dima's mother, so I learned, was a kind woman who loved her son dearly and would play in their yard with him until she became too ill and fragile to do so. It was no wonder why he was so angry – he had not only lost someone who loved him and whom he loved deeply, but the village believed she was "bad" because she had unwittingly been infected with a virus.

HIV and AIDS were ravaging eastern Ukraine, and after years of being transmitted predominantly through drug use, more Ukrainians were now contracting HIV through heterosexual sex. A note that was given to us Peace Corps volunteers described the seriousness of the situation:

> The HIV/AIDS epidemic in Ukraine started in 1987 and has accelerated dramatically since then. At present, Ukraine's HIV/AIDS epidemic is among the fastest growing in Europe, with officially registered new HIV cases having doubled over 2000–2004. Data suggest Ukraine may be on the brink of the generalized epidemic phase.
>
> The epidemic is shifting from high-risk groups to the general population. The young and women are hit hardest. The data indicate that in 2006 every fifth HIV-infected person is in the 18–24 age group. The share of women among the new cases reached 42 per cent.
>
> By 2014, the total number of HIV-positive people could range from 500,000 to 800,000 people. The southern and eastern regions of Ukraine are the most affected – including the oblasts of Dnipropetrovsk, Donetsk, Odesa, Mykolaiv, and the Crimean Republic. While only a third of the country's population lives in these regions, they constitute two-thirds of all officially registered HIV cases.

Part of my lessons included teaching about HIV and AIDS, using plans provided, designed, and honed by the Peace Corps and other volunteers over the years. A lesson plan for eighth-formers that I adapted for my tenth-and eleventh-form classes in Krasne looked in part like this:

Lesson Plan Outline

1 Title: HIV/AIDS for the 8th Form
2 Objectives: Students will be able to tell the difference between fact and fiction about HIV and AIDS and will know the impact of HIV in Ukraine. Participants will be able to explain the myths and facts of how HIV is transmitted, identify factors that increase the risk of HIV infection, and explain how to prevent transmission of HIV. Students will be able to discriminate between safe and unsafe sexual behavior. Students will confront stigma surrounding HIV.
3 Materials: Tape; Signs placed on the wall with the words True and False; Bowl with pieces of paper in it describing myths and facts; HIV in Ukraine information sheet; HIV Quiz and Answer Sheet in Russian or English (attached); Transmission Methods word cards (attached).
4 Procedures:

   1 Using the "Facts and Myths About HIV and AIDS" sheet, write individual true and false statements and place them in a bowl. Have students one-by-one each take a piece of paper from the bowl.
   2 Using "Who Gets HIV in Ukraine?" information sheet, quiz students to see their preconceptions about who gets HIV in Ukraine. Areas often full of misinformation include: . . .
   3 Hand out the HIV/AIDS Quiz
   4 Teacher begins discussion of what is needed to become infected by HIV. HIV can be contracted only in very specific ways.

Summary: Invite students to share their experience of the activity with the group. Use the conversation to underscore the nature of loss – that, ultimately, we don't get to control what happens to us, even if it concerns something important.

I only taught these lessons a few times, mainly because Olga Yevgenyevna and Krasne teachers weren't enthusiastic about them and said they made the students "feel bad." The one day I was allowed to teach on the topic of HIV and AIDS was on 1 December, World AIDS Day.

On that day in 2010, I taught several lessons to a collective class of eighth to eleventh-form students. But the lessons were highly modified. We kept the segment in which we discussed "Facts and Myths About HIV and AIDS."

Statements under the "True" section included: "Africa has been more affected by AIDS than any other part of the world, but HIV infection rates are rising in many other regions" and "In Ukraine about 5 per cent of adults are infected with HIV."

Under "False" there were: "AIDS is a disease that mostly affects black people", "Since everyone dies of AIDS, it is better not to know if you have it", "You can be cured of AIDS by having sex with a virgin", "No one has AIDS in our country", and "AIDS is a disease of immoral people, such as prostitutes."

Students drew the statements from a box and taped them to the chalkboard under "True" or "False."

Instead of the other parts of the lesson, the teachers decided that the rest of the time should be spent drawing posters promoting a healthy lifestyle – which they said amounted to eating well, exercising regularly, and obeying your parents and teachers – and encouraging HIV awareness.

"We are for a future without AIDS," read a poster drawn by one group of tenth-formers. It had a large red ribbon placed over the image of a blue Earth.

As I got to know Dima and understand his home life better, he confided in me about his frustrations with kids at school. He said he was sad and just wanted a friend. I moved him to the front of the class and called on him often to read and answer questions. He was smart and picked up new things quickly. We practiced simple English phrases on our short walks from the school to the bus stop, where his grandmother would meet him and I could catch a ride into Artemivsk.

The teasing didn't stop completely, but it happened less and less as months passed. Eventually, Dima made a friend and our walks stopped. Instead, the two of them ran down the road together.

One day I was waiting at the bus stop when his grandmother approached me. She hadn't come to meet Dima, who was off playing somewhere. She was there to deliver a gift.

"Thank you for giving Dima your attention," she said, handing me a crumpled shopping bag. Inside were jars of pickled tomatoes from her garden, a jar of *adjika* – a sauce made with red peppers, onions, garlic, herbs and spices – and a single orange. I told her I couldn't accept it but she insisted. Then she pulled my face to her level and kissed my cheek.

It was in the third month of teaching when I was summoned to the office for a word. There had been some complaints from teachers and students who felt I was taking the responsibility of assigning grades for tasks and exams too seriously.

Apparently, my assigning marks of 0 and 1 to two boys – one of whom refused to even write his name atop an exam – and a 6 to a girl who only completed half of a test – and got only half of the questions she answered correct – crossed the line.

I was told I wouldn't be giving the students marks anymore.

It was explained to me that all students should not receive anything lower than marks of 7, but that 8s or higher were preferred.

Everyone needed to pass and move onto the next grade. Nobody would be held back. Passing them with good scores would also earn the school more money from the government if the average student marks at year's end were shown to have improved upon the previous year.

On the upper end of the grading scale, I also needed to be careful. "We never give 12s. Or very rarely do we give 12s," it was explained.

"Why not?" I asked, stupidly. "If they complete their work and get a perfect test score it's not a 12?"

"We can't tell students they are perfect," the staff said. "They need to know that they always must do better."

To be certain the students were treated fairly, I would be unburdened from having to deal with grades.

I was to continue with my lessons but another teacher would assign the marks from then on, as they knew the students better.

At first the decision frustrated me and I thought about how shady the situation seemed. But then I realized that the move had actually freed me from having to stick so tightly to the curriculum. From then on, teaching for me became more fun, and I got the sense from the students that the learning did, too.

A big part of Peace Corps work was writing grants, and there was a term for those who wrote several of them and received funding: Super Volunteers. By grant-writing standards, I was not a super volunteer. But it wasn't for a lack of trying. Olga Yevgenyevna and Nikolai were never very interested in my proposals for grant projects, many of which were related to health education or small infrastructure improvements.

I managed to get a small grant to send the school psychologist to Kyiv for various trainings, which she used as a shopping trip during what was her first visit to the Ukrainian capital. I also wrote one to build a new, updated washroom and toilet for the Krasne school, whose facilities were old and dirty and sometimes didn't work. The plumbing needed to be completely overhauled. It was always getting clogged with toilet paper and other objects the students would try to flush down bowls not meant to receive anything other than human waste.

When the bathrooms inside the school were out of order – which was a frequent occurrence – everyone had to walk outside, across the soccer field, past the playground to the edge of the property line, where there stood a wooden outhouse with a square hole cut into the floorboards. In winter, when the temperature fell well below freezing and everyone wore parkas with hats and gloves in class, it was an especially terrible trek to make just to relieve oneself.

But the grant was turned down – not by the grantees, but by Krasne school. What they wanted and what they thought I had come with was money – cold hard American dollars. They asked how much Peace Corps paid me and they had a large five-digit number in mind. Much to their surprise, I told them that I was being paid around the same as they made, and that this was so I would learn to live like everyone else in town and be treated as an equal. They didn't believe me and continued to press me.

"Really," I insisted. "I get paid like you."

One day I gave in and told them I was paid $260 a month – $100 of which was going straight to Nikolai for renting his apartment. Olga Yevgenyevna said that that was more than any other teacher was paid. Nikolai inquired as to whether I would be able to donate and/or raise $25,000 to construct a new gymnasium with a wing to showcase the awards of his student athletes.

I bumbled along and by the second semester I had settled into a comfortable groove. Each week I taught a few English lessons at the Krasne school, held an American culture club, a journalism club, and was assisting Nikolai with his PE classes, during which I often played basketball, soccer, and volleyball along with the students. I also had an English club at the Artemivsk central library, where the librarians were enthusiastic about a grant I had secured for English-language books and news magazines to add to a small English section of the library that had been started by a previous Peace Corps volunteer.

I celebrated my first birthday in Ukraine with my fellow teachers at the Krasne school and learned that it's customary to provide all the trappings of a birthday party yourself. I brought in cake and tea and coffee and cognac – and was scolded for taking the latter into the school. But after school hours, a small group of teachers and Olga Yevgenyevna drank some of the booze with me, toasting to a successful, if not slightly awkward, school year.

My birthday coincided with one of Nikolai's favorite days: Men's Day. A holdover from the Soviet Union and officially called Defender of the Fatherland Day, it was a war holiday and was once a relatively big deal. Coming two weeks before Women's Day – another very important Soviet holiday – it was previously known as Red Army Day and meant to celebrate the triumphs of the men who fought for the USSR, which is partly why Ukraine didn't recognize it as an official state holiday and Ukrainians in the west of the country often dismissed it. Yet many people in the east of Ukraine still celebrated the holiday. However, it had been transformed into a celebration not of the military but of male dominance and masculinity, hence Men's Day.

Nikolai served as the master of ceremonies for a competition between the Krasne schoolboys of the ninth, tenth, and eleventh forms to decide who would be Man of the Year. And I was called up to help him organize it. The boys partook in various tests of physical strength and endurance. The one who performed best in competitions of pull-ups and push-ups, and finally a challenge to see who could keep their legs outstretched in front of them the longest, would be crowned the winner.

All 100 students and the dozen or so teachers crowded into the school's small auditorium to watch. A shy boy from the tenth form won a trophy adorned with a parrot.

In stark contrast to Men's Day, Women's Day passed off with little celebration. The teaching staff were showered with bouquets of roses, chocolates, and Artemivsk sparkling wine. Male students recited poems to female students during classes. I used the opportunity in my upper-form classes to discuss the history of International Women's Day, women's rights in America and elsewhere, and asked the girls to talk about their hopes and dreams, trying to put a progressive spin on things. Many of them said they wanted to marry young and have children. But some said they wanted to become doctors or teachers, while one hoped to join the military. Two of the boys blurted something out, saying that girls couldn't be soldiers, at which all the girls in the class walked over and took turns swatting them up the side of the head. I didn't do much to stop them.

In addition to Men's Day, each spring, boy students from schools in Artemivsk, including the surrounding village schools, held a physical fitness day to decide which school was the most athletically accomplished. It was never much of a competition – the boys from School No. 11, the city's premier secondary school, with serious sports programs, were always victorious. The boys were built like young men in their twenties, muscular and tall, and their facial hair had started to grow in. My students from Krasne and those from most other schools were scrawny, with a hint of light peach fuzz visible on their pimply faces. Their elbows and knees were the thickest parts of their limbs.

The competition included various relay races, strength and endurance challenges. In one, the teams had to dress in firemen's outfits, carry a hose up four flights of stairs, and run back down before taking off their outfits and tagging a teammate, who would then run back up the stairs and carry a dummy meant to be an incapacitated person back down. The second leg of the competition saw them rush to put on hazmat suits that were too big for their little frames and then place Soviet-era gas masks on their faces before racing across a field carrying a stretcher loaded with sandbags. They looked like little Chornobyl liquidators.

I asked one of my students about the class where they were timed in putting on gas masks, had to learn how to shoot guns and throw grenades, and he said simply "Our country must be prepared."

The school year ended a lot like it had begun: with a ceremony and celebration. Last Bell was maybe a bigger deal than First Bell, since it meant that eleventh-form students were graduating and heading out into the world. Some of my eleventh-formers were off to universities and technical colleges in Horlivka, Donetsk, and Kharkiv. None of them were going as far west as Kyiv, either because it was too expensive or they wanted to stay relatively close to home.

We gathered again in front of the Krasne village school, in the time-honored tradition of students and parents standing around as teachers delivered their time-practiced speeches. Huge bouquets of roses were given to the graduating girls. After some singing and dancing, the oldest girl and the youngest boy rang the last bell of the year, then summer break in Artemivsk and across Ukraine began.

I was as excited about this as the students. I made plans to travel across the Donbas, crashing at homes of friends in every city along the way to Mariupol and then Crimea. My girlfriend, Bri, had come over from

Prague, where she had been living and teaching English, and spent the second half of the summer with me before moving to Kyiv to take another teaching job. We took an overnight train to Crimea and met friends there, touring the defunct Soviet-era submarine base in Balaclava, wandering around the Greek ruins of Khersones, and relaxing on the beaches of Sevastopol and Yalta, the historic seaside city where Franklin Roosevelt, Winston Churchill, and Joseph Stalin met in February 1945 to decide on the post-war reorganization of Europe.

In Artemivsk, we strolled through the markets in the morning and rode our bikes through the fields in the afternoon. In the evening we wandered over to the park and watched tipsy locals gyrate on the dance floor at Club Paradise until the early morning.

There was something magical about that summer, how everyone seemed to be so content, how the city's roses were so fragrant, how time passed so slowly and the days were so long.

3

A Darker Side of the Donbas

Donetsk Oblast, Eastern Ukraine, September 2011–September 2012

By the time the new school year began in September 2011, my desire to delve deeper into Ukraine's complexities and write more about them had largely overtaken my interest in my Peace Corps tasks.

The Krasne school wasn't interested in many of the grant programs available to them, and Nikolai had gotten into his mind that I could somehow secure tens of thousands of dollars to build them an entirely new sports facility with a museum to display the achievements of their alumni. When I explained that that wasn't really what I was there to do and that the budget for the project was well over what Peace Corps could fund, I was all but sidelined. My class load dropped to just a few weekly English lessons and PE classes where I mostly played basketball or soccer with the students. The various health lessons I had been trained to conduct were scrapped after parents complained that the subject encouraged students to have more sex and because, as one administrator put it to me, the topic of HIV/AIDS was "boring" and "sad."

I filled some of my new free time teaching American history lessons to English-language students at Artemivsk's School No. 11, and helping the budding young journalists working at the school newspaper to shape their articles about dances, sporting events, and exams.

Sometimes on weekends I snuck back to Kyiv on the overnight train to stay with Bri and spend time together in the Ukrainian capital. There, we went to museums, monasteries and parks, walking the streets of Kyiv for hours and well into the night. We went to festivals and drank at its pubs and ate *shashlik* on the sandy banks of Trukhanov Island, watching the bikini-clad locals plunge into the Dnipro river, framed by the glimmering golden domes of the Pechersk Lavra and the towering Motherland monument positioned atop the opposite hillside.

44

But most of my new free time was spent exploring more of the Donbas region, cashing in on the many invitations extended to me over the years from fellow Peace Corps volunteers and Ukrainian friends to visit them in their hometowns. I rode my bike or took buses to cities and towns across Donetsk and Luhansk oblasts. Within a few months, the map that hung on my apartment wall had pins stuck into dozens of locations, including Dobropillya, Kharkiv, Kostyantynivka, Krasnoarmiisk, Makiivka, Mariupol, Novoazovsk, Siedove, Severodonetsk, Soledar, Snezhnoe, Stakhanov, and Svyatohirsk. In each place I met pensioners who told me stories of life under Nazi occupation, veterans of the Soviet Union's failed invasion of Afghanistan, university professors who outlined how Moscow had "Russified" Ukraine's east, farmers sowing Ukraine's famous black earth that had earned their country the name of the "breadbasket of Europe."

I also began spending time with a group of Ukrainian investigative reporters. Among them was Oleksiy Matsuka, the editor-in-chief of the Donetsk-based news site *Novosti Donbassa* – News of the Donbas – who was fast becoming one of Ukraine's top independent journalists. We had been introduced during a tour of Kostyantynivka's industrial ruins by a mutual journalist acquaintance who described Oleksiy to me as that rare type of Ukrainian reporter who didn't pander to the agendas of politicians and oligarchs. Oleksiy didn't take money from officials to turn the other cheek or provide positive coverage of them, a common pay-for-play type of journalism known as *jeansa* because the money would end up in reporters' jeans pockets. He was working to expose their corrupt activities.

Oleksiy was athletic-looking with a serious face, close-cropped hair, and piercing blue eyes that widened when discussing his work. His voice was soft and his demeanor exceedingly polite, but he also gave off an air of confidence and was full of curiosity. He was 28, I was 27. We hit it off immediately, sharing stories about journalism, traveling and growing up as millennials on opposite sides of the world and under vastly different circumstances – me in a middle-class American family bubble where my world rarely extended beyond the boundaries of the state of Oregon, and him a Soviet-born Ukrainian living through the growing pains of a newly independent country struggling to find its identity in the long shadow of Russia and torn between east and west.

There was one pressing question he needed an answer to when we met: "Are parties in America really like we see in the movies?"

"Maybe some of them but, honestly, most of them aren't anything like that," I said. "That's just Hollywood."

45

He seemed to like that answer, nodding as if it had confirmed a suspicion that at least some things in the West were also greatly exaggerated. He would soon get a chance to see for himself during a weeks-long trip to Southern California that included a dispiriting visit to Universal Studios.

One October morning shortly after Oleksiy returned from his trip, I hopped on a bus from Artemivsk to Donetsk to see him and get a sense of what life and work were like for an independent Ukrainian journalist. It was chilly and gray. Wind whipped through the city's broad avenues and sent the first fallen leaves of autumn swirling around the towering Lenin statue that loomed over the main square. Women waiting for trolleybuses plunged their chins into the tops of their padded coats and men tugged at the front of their flat caps to shield their faces.

Donetsk was covered in political ads promoting the home-town, Russia-friendly Party of Regions – Ukraine's current ruling party. One billboard, in particular, featured the party's leader, local boy turned president, Viktor Yanukovych, who was positioned in front of a blue and yellow flag background. He had carefully coiffed, dyed hair, glassy eyes, and wore a shiny suit and a smirk. A message beside him read, "One Ukraine. One story." It was an image and message skillfully burnished by a crafty American political consultant by the name of Paul Manafort at the behest of a Ukrainian oligarch and Party of Regions donor, Rinat Akhmetov. But Yanukovych's election victory, which came just six weeks before my arrival in Ukraine, had done more to divide – not unite – the country. Eastern Ukrainians with whom I spoke weren't thrilled about him and believed him to be a thug and a crook – but he was *their* thug and *their* crook, at least. After feeling abandoned by Kyiv and ignored by the Orange Revolutionaries who viewed residents of the Donbas as un-Ukrainian or even pro-Russian, many here felt they were being heard. But in central Ukraine and the west of the country, Yanukovych was despised for being too friendly with Russia.

Many of Yanukovych's party members and business associates had been the subjects of Oleksiy's reporting, and that had led to him being regularly followed and threatened. Two months before my visit, arsonists had set ablaze the front door of Oleksiy's Donetsk apartment. He said it was retaliation for articles he'd published about Yanukovych's clan, which journalists and anti-corruption activists referred to as "The Family." It sounded like something out of *The Sopranos* and many of Yanukovych's people even resembled Eastern European versions of the show's characters, with their garish clothes, greasy hair, and absurdly expensive wristwatches.

Yanukovych himself was a brawler in his early life. Growing up poor in the Donetsk Oblast town of Yenakiieve without a mother, who died when he was two, he became streetwise in order to survive. In 1967, aged 17, he was convicted of assault and robbery and sentenced to three years in prison. He did seven months but was convicted again of assault in 1970, and given a two-year sentence. When he got out he married Lyudmyla, the niece of a local judge, and a few years later got a job as a truck driver for a coal-mining company. He rose to top management positions quickly and eventually executive roles in Donetsk. By the mid-1990s, he was a known entity, and in 1996 was appointed as vice-head of the Donetsk Oblast Administration. A year later, he was made governor of the region.

As a kleptocratic president, Yanukovych had allegedly amassed a fortune worth billions and had taken over a 340-acre palatial estate outside of Kyiv the size of Monaco, where he built an ostentatious log cabin-style mansion he named "Honka," a faux display of Egyptian ruins, a museum for a car collection numbering in the many dozens, a model pirate ship anchored in a small inlet of the Kyiv sea where he dined with guests, and an ostrich farm.

Through his tenacious reporting, Oleksiy was working to reveal his investigations into the systemic corruption inside Yanukovych's "family," the Party of Regions, and their representatives in Donetsk's regional government. On *Novosti Donbassa*'s website he published photographs of their multimillion-dollar homes and imported luxury cars, and documents that proved the real salaries of government officials to be outrageously higher than the amounts they had publicly disclosed. Officially, civil servants in Ukraine made well under $75,000 a year. Unofficially, even the low-level bureaucrats were raking in millions. Yanukovych and his top lieutenants were allegedly stealing billions from the state and lining their own Italian silk pockets. "This money was stolen from the Ukrainian people," Petro Poroshenko, the man who would later be elected president would say, as quoted by the Interfax news agency. "It was pulled out of the pocket of every Ukrainian."

When Oleksiy and I communicated by phone and email, the exchanges were brief and often coded because he was worried that Yanukovych's security services were listening to his calls. Instead of using words like "attack," "assault," and "threat," he used "incident," "visit," and "message." Once when he described being tailed, he said that his "friends had come to watch me work." We never spoke in detail about his work or about politics. We could only speak openly about those things, Yanukovych's "family," and the attacks against Oleksiy when we met in person, in the relative safety of the *Novosti Donbassa* office, a darkened pub, or his Hyundai sedan. So I had to go to Donetsk.

Ukrainians were under no illusions that the collapse of the Soviet Union and their subsequent declaration of independence from Russia would usher in a Western-style democratic system in which human rights and freedoms, including press freedom, would flourish. But they did believe things would get better – eventually. In Ukraine's "wild '90s" – an era of economic depression, high inflation, and privatization that saw gangsters become entrepreneurs and entrepreneurs become gangsters – many rights and freedoms remained out of reach and some were even rolled back. The media sphere was dominated by Ukraine's wealthy elite, known as oligarchs, who bought up mainstream TV and print news outlets to use for their own personal instrument with which they could attack political or business opponents and shape public opinion in their favor. State-censorship and self-censorship worsened during Leonid Kuchma's presidency from 1994 to 2004, a decade associated with lawlessness and corruption. Kuchma didn't take criticism well and forced the closure of many opposition newspapers that had sprung up in the years following Ukraine's independence.

The most widely known and talked-about example in Ukraine of violence against a journalist was the horrific murder of Georgiy Gongadze, a Ukrainian of Georgian descent. Gongadze was a complex man and a true muckraker, and in the months before his death he had set out to investigate corruption within the Kuchma administration for his fledgling online news site *Ukrayinska Pravda* – Ukrainian Truth – in Kyiv. Just after 10 p.m. on the night of 16 September 2000, Gongadze left the home of a colleague to meet his wife and two young daughters. But he never arrived. Weeks later his headless corpse was found in a forest south of Kyiv. An autopsy revealed that he had been beaten and strangled, doused in gasoline and torched. It would be years before his skull turned up.

Later, leaked tapes secretly recorded by a bodyguard appeared to implicate Kuchma and several of his underlings in Gongadze's murder. Kuchma denied involvement, but a voice closely resembling the president's was heard on tape saying the journalist should be dealt with and suggesting he be "kidnapped by Chechens."

Gongadze's murder sent a chill across Ukraine and made international headlines. Western governments and organizations condemned the Ukrainian government's bad handling of his case, which it said was a litmus test for the Ukrainian judicial system. But in the years after Gongadze's gruesome murder, only the killer would be held accountable.

The man who confessed to the murder, Oleksiy Pukach, was a former top police officer in the external surveillance department of Ukraine's Ministry of the Interior. He was arrested in 2009, along with three henchmen, and tried for the murder. Pukach said in court that he personally had strangled and beheaded Gongadze, and that he did so at the behest of Kuchma and other top officials, including the minister of the interior, Yuriy Kravchenko.

Kravchenko never got the chance to tell his side of the story. He was found dead in his home in March 2005. Authorities ruled his death a suicide, but reporters found it suspicious. He had been shot twice in the head.

In March 2011, more than ten years after Gongadze's death, a criminal case was finally opened against Kuchma on charges that he exceeded his authority, leading to the journalist's killing. The tape was to be the most damaging evidence against the former president. But in October that year Ukraine's constitutional court decided the recording was inadmissible on the grounds that it was made without Kuchma's consent. An appeal failed and the case against Kuchma was dismissed.

Pukach and his henchmen were convicted and sentenced to lengthy prison terms. For Pukach it was a life sentence. Years later he would appeal for early release and be denied.

Meanwhile, several journalists were killed without a culprit being found, or died in mysterious circumstances, many in ways fit for Hollywood thrillers, which may be why some Ukrainians believed what they saw in American blockbuster films.

On 14 April 1995 a remote-detonated bomb placed in a garbage can exploded outside the home of Volodymyr Ivanov, editor-in-chief of the Crimean newspaper *The Glory of Sevastopol*, fatally wounding him. In the previous weeks he'd published stories denouncing the Crimean mafia as well as others critical of a Ukrainian–Swedish company's plan to construct an oil refinery on the peninsula.

Petro Shevchenko, a reporter for *Kyivskiye Vedomosti*, was found hanged in an abandoned building in Kyiv on 13 March 1997. The authorities said he'd killed himself, but his colleagues believed he had been murdered over a series of stories about disputes between the mayor of Luhansk and the local branch of the Ukrainian Security Service, the successor of the Ukrainian SSR's branch of the KGB. Usually referred to by its Ukrainian acronym, the SBU, it was the country's main counter-espionage and domestic security agency.

On 11 August 1997 a hitman shot Borys Derevyanko, editor-in-chief of *Vechernyaya Odesa*, at point-blank range on his way to work. His paper claimed he was snuffed out because of its vocal opposition to the policies of Odesa's mayor.

Oleksiy and I especially liked discussing the messy and murky world of Ukrainian politics in which he was deeply immersed. At that time one of the biggest political issues was the jailing of the firebrand and former prime minister, Yulia Tymoshenko, on charges that she had abused her power while in office when she brokered a gas deal with Russia. The deal, cut back in 2009, was certainly controversial, but her jailing was widely viewed by Ukrainians as a move by Yanukovych to eliminate his chief political opponent – later the European Court of Human Rights would state her detention was "arbitrary and unlawful".

I had gone to observe the protests in support of Tymoshenko outside the Kyiv courthouse where she was tried. An encampment that resembled the Orange Revolution's camp in miniature had sprung up on the corner of Khreshchatyk and Bohdan Khmelnytsky streets, and crowds of mostly older, provincial Ukrainians – Tymoshenko's core support network – were there holding signs adorned with heavily photoshopped images of her wearing her trademark crown of golden braids. Some posters showed her as a Slavic Joan of Arc, donning armor and balancing birds on her fingertips, or staring longingly through prison bars. Others depicted Yanukovych as a swine on a spit ready for roasting. Demonstrators chanted slogans like "Down with the criminal band!" and "Yanukovych, out! Bandits, out!"

Sometimes rival protests would pop up across the street but would disappear as quickly as they appeared. In fact, they were Potemkin demonstrations, fake rallies meant to give the impression of real grassroots opposition. The people who took part were never enthusiastic. Many confessed that they had come because they were promised by some mysterious man or woman on the other end of a phone call 200 *hryvnia* (about $25 at the time, or what would be about a fifth of their pensions) to stand opposite the Tymoshenko camp and wave pro-Yanukovych and pro-Party of Regions banners. Some of them were professionals and came equipped with hot soup in thermoses and fold-out stools to sit on.

Protests like these, I would come to find out, were known as rent-a-crowds – and they were common. On any given day a crowd of people would emerge from buses and stand in a public square or in front of a ministry or the home of a government official or anti-government activist, and then disappear as quickly as they appeared. The rent-a-crowd could never really explain what the purpose of their protest was beyond a line or two they were told to memorize in case any pesky reporters approached them. Sometimes they would simply tell reporters that they didn't really back whatever cause it was – they just saw it as a way of making an easy *hryvnia*.

Like many in the West, the European Union and American government included, Oleksiy condemned Tymoshenko's arrest and subsequent conviction as politically motivated. But many Ukrainians had long lost faith in Tymoshenko, whose social and political capital was wasted during her time serving as prime minister in the post-Orange Revolution, lame-duck government.

In late 2004, with Kuchma's second and last term as president coming to a close, it seemed for a moment that Ukraine had turned the page on the authoritarianism and repression endured during the past decade. The democratic opposition led by Tymoshenko and Viktor Yushchenko was on the rise. Polls showed a tight presidential race between Yushchenko and Yanukovych, who had served as prime minister under Kuchma and was hand-picked to succeed him. But Yushchenko had a slight advantage. In an apparent attempt to gain the upper hand, Yanukovych's camp is believed to have poisoned Yushchenko, who survived after ingesting a heavy dose of dioxin, a chemical found in Agent Orange, but emerged with a disfigured, pockmarked face and stayed in the race. Yanukovych and his security services denied any involvement in the poisoning.

Ukrainians turned out in record numbers that Fall to vote. Exit polls showed Yushchenko with a commanding 11 per cent lead over Yanukovych. But when the official results were announced, Yanukovych had miraculously come out on top. It didn't take long for evidence to surface that showed the election had been rigged in favor of Yanukovych. Ukraine's Supreme Court overturned the results, citing "systemic and massive violations," state news agencies reported. Almost instantly, hundreds of thousands of Ukrainians – on some days their numbers reached more than a million – clad in opposition-party orange descended upon Kyiv's Independence Square to protest the result.

The protest quickly evolved into the Orange Revolution. Demonstrators endured freezing temperatures, rain, and snow for two months, during which time Ukraine's Supreme Court ordered a new vote. This time the result came out in favor of Yushchenko, and on 23 January 2005 he was inaugurated, bringing the protests to an end.

As president, however, Yushchenko would disappoint. Infighting between members of his cabinet, and the dismissal of Tymoshenko and other Orange Revolution leaders with whom he fought, led what was then Ukraine's most pro-democracy government to squander its chance to clean up the country, stamp out rampant corruption, and improve basic rights and freedoms for its people.

By the Fall of 2009 many Ukrainians had decided they'd had enough of Yushchenko's empty promises, and the Party of Regions was seeing a resurgence. In a race decided by just a few points, Ukraine re-elected Yanukovych – and this time international observers ruled the vote free and fair.

With Yanukovych in office, Ukraine began backsliding again. Despite multiple promises during his incumbency to improve civil rights, they grew worse. In the media sphere, things were especially grim, with numerous cases of censorship and "multiple press freedom violations," according to a 2010 report by the media watchdog Reporters Without Borders. Among them were attacks like the one on Oleksiy.

"Yanukovych wants to get rid of all his political opponents," Oleksiy had told me. And those opponents ranged from top political rivals to muckraking reporters like Oleksiy himself. A year earlier, another independent journalist doing work similar to his had gone missing in a case that felt familiar to many Ukrainians. In August of 2010, Vasyl Klymentyev, editor-in-chief of the Kharkiv newspaper *Novy Stil*, known for publishing stories critical of Party of Regions officials, vanished. He was last seen getting into a car with an unknown man. His mobile phone and keys were discovered a week later inside an empty boat floating ominously in a nearby reservoir. His body was never found.

Personal security was the biggest reason for all of the precautions Oleksiy took. This included the need for us to meet in person if I wanted to discuss anything sensitive with him, especially his reporting.

Through email, we had agreed to meet outside a McDonald's near the center of Donetsk. Ukrainians, I had come to learn, adored the Golden Arches. While I dismissed McDonald's in America as cheap, grimy fast food, in Ukraine it was seen as almost fine dining. Couples rendezvoused there to share a romantic meal of Big Macs and McNuggets, businessmen and women cut deals over Big N' Tastys with fries. In our case, we were meeting there to talk about corruption and a possible attempted murder.

Oleksiy rolled up in his black Hyundai and parked out front. We quickly grabbed a couple of cheeseburger and fries combos and devoured them. Then we got back on the road to the *Novosti Donbassa* office. He had a meeting with a local police detective soon.

Oleksiy fought his way through the traffic, passing shimmering skyscrapers and opulent business centers built and owned by members of Yanukovych's "family," and the state-of-the-art soccer stadium built by

Akhmetov, the billionaire who had made Yanukovych into the politician he had become. Akhmetov had flown in Beyoncé two years earlier and, rumor had it, paid her a cool million bucks to perform at the arena's official opening. As we passed it, crossing the river to the east side of the city, Oleksiy told me the details of what had happened at his place.

It was just after dawn on 31 July 2011. The attackers entered the building and barricaded Oleksiy's apartment door with bags of cement and placed a colorful funeral wreath up against them. A handwritten note that was left with the wreath read: "To Oleksiy Vitaliyovych" – his patronymic – "From grieving friends." Then they doused the door with an accelerant and set it on fire. Oleksiy believed the point was to send a message but that if he'd been there the attackers would have been happy to see him "burn alive." He said it in a serious tone but also with a sort of shrug, like he'd accepted that it was the cost of doing journalism in Ukraine. The attack hadn't surprised him, but it did rattle him. I was worried for him, too, and as we drove I thought about my own security and what the people who were after him might think of the two of us together – a muckraking journalist and an American volunteer with the Peace Corps, an organization that some in this part of the world still viewed with suspicion and through the lens of the Cold War. It was common for people in eastern Ukraine to ask whether the organization was part of the CIA – and most didn't do so jokingly like the babushkas in Artemivsk. In 2002, during Vladimir Putin's second year in office, Russia had kicked out the Peace Corps, and the Federal Security Service, or FSB – the successor to the Soviet-era notorious KGB – had accused volunteers of spying. "Among them are persons who were collecting information on the social, political and economic situation in Russian regions, on officials of governmental bodies and departments, on the course of elections and so on," Nikolai Patrushev, head of the FSB, was quoted by CNN as saying about the decision at the time.

Oleksiy was lucky not to be home when the attack occurred. He had left early to go to work. His apartment was only saved because a neighbor smelled smoke coming from the hall and peeked out her door, where she saw the fire. She tried to put it out with water and when that didn't work called the fire department and then Oleksiy. He rushed home.

"I knew right away why this happened," he told me. "I have a conflict with very major people in the city that don't like me writing about their luxurious lifestyles."

One of those "very major people" was the Donetsk mayor, Oleksandr Lukyanchenko. Lukyanchenko had publicly condemned it and ordered a police investigation into the attack, but only after pressure from media rights groups. He also assigned police protection to Oleksiy, but just for a day.

Oleksiy was meeting with police detectives on the morning I met him, to discuss what progress had been made in the case. But he wasn't holding his breath for answers.

"I'm thinking [the police] will not have any new information for me. I don't think they want this case to be solved," he said.

Oleksiy led me into a narrow and dimly lit elevator, which took us up nine terrifyingly shaky floors before we had to exit and climb three flights of stairs to reach the *Novosti Donbassa* office. It was neat and bright but sparsely furnished. The Ukrainian flag hung on one wall. On another were cutouts of news articles and a map with districts of Donetsk outlined in red marker. A small table with packets of instant coffee, teabags, and a kettle atop it stood against the west-facing wall. Windows made up the entire eastern side of the office and from that height I was able to get my best view yet of the Donbas landscape: pre-fab concrete apartment buildings stood puzzled together like Tetris pieces and rose above clusters of pine and ash trees; slag heaps poked up unnaturally from the steppe like an alligator's back. And the road from Donetsk stretched for miles toward the Russian border, disappearing in the haze created by all the factories on the horizon.

Two casually dressed young men with short hair and serious faces pecked at their laptops. Vitaliy Sizov had started *Novosti Donbassa* with Oleksiy; the other was Denis Kazansky, a popular blogger who published under the pseudonym Frankensstein to avoid detection from the authorities. Kazansky made me a cup of coffee and told me about how he enjoyed rankling Donetsk's political elite with his scathing and snakily written LiveJournal posts about their corruption and gaudy clothes and home decor they spent their money on. Oleksiy left me to chat with them while he went to meet with the police investigators.

When he returned two hours later, I asked him how it went.

"The police have no new information," he shrugged.

He wasn't surprised or disappointed. He knew the mayor's word meant nothing and that the police had no interest in actually solving his case. Oleksiy leaned against the wall and wondered aloud whether the police were in on it. After all, he had written critically of them, too. And it was no secret that Yanukovych's clan had the police in their pockets.

Oleksiy's interest in becoming a fly in the ink-stained ointment evolved while studying political science at Donetsk National University. There, he and several colleagues began publishing their own student newspaper, which riled the academic leadership immediately.

"The university faculty didn't like how outspoken we were," Oleksiy told me. "In teaching journalism at the university, our teachers still used *Pravda* [the official newspaper of the Soviet Union's Communist Party] as an example of proper journalism. It was propaganda."

The dean of the university threatened Oleksiy and his colleagues with expulsion unless they halted publication. The threat was enough for his team to abandon him. But Oleksiy continued to put out the paper on his own, printing about 400 copies of each issue – enough for every faculty member and student in his department.

"I handed all of the newspapers out myself," he said.

He was never expelled.

"There was no formal ground for expulsion."

In 2003, Oleksiy founded *Novosti Donbassa* with the intent to expose the crooked dealings of a government rife with corruption. It quickly became a go-to source of information and was widely respected by independent journalists and opposition politicians, even if it was so glaringly anti-Party of Regions that it couldn't be considered objective. But that didn't bother Oleksiy, who often referred to himself as an opposition journalist, which was the closest in Ukraine one could get to doing Western-style journalism.

"It is generally accepted that the government is corrupt here," he said, justifying his stance. Essentially what Oleksiy was saying was, if everyone believes the government is corrupt, if you've grown up in a society so rife with it, how could you remain impartial when reporting on it? Impartiality was complicity.

Novosti Donbassa published stories about the mysterious and growing Yanukovych family fortune; about illegal coal-mining operations with ties to Party of Regions officials in government; and about the multimillion-dollar mansion of Donetsk's regional governor and his 2010 tax return, which stated his primary residence to be a meager apartment in the city center. Oleksiy's investigation concluded that the governor was using a tried-and-true method long favored by Ukraine's elite: he had transferred ownership of many of his expensive assets over to his wife, thus avoiding scrutiny.

Novosti Donbassa also exposed a regional vote-rigging scandal; and a city council whose members were recorded having voted for resolutions while not in attendance.

Publishing these stories and many others like them led to Oleksiy and other *Novosti Donbassa* journalists being followed, intimidated, and threatened with violence. In one instance, the mayor of nearby Kramatorsk got in Oleksiy's face, bumped chests with him, and slammed his forearm into his chest after Oleksiy confronted him in a public parking lot to ask for an interview. The tense encounter was filmed by another journalist and posted to YouTube, where it went viral.

As *Novosti Donbassa* gained notoriety and readers, and intimidation tactics failed to stop Oleksiy and his colleagues, the regional and city officials targeted by the outlet decided on a different tactic: they offered what they said could be a lucrative partnership. Oleksiy described the deal to me: he would stop publishing critical articles about Yanukovych-linked officials, and in return he'd receive cash, perhaps even a job in government if he so desired.

Of course, he didn't indulge them. And when they came back to him every so often with more offers, he turned those down, too. And so Oleksiy and *Novosti Donbassa* cemented their reputation as an opposition news organization or, using a term uttered by one of Yanukovych's cronies, "improper" journalists.

Oleksiy farther described the "improper" label in a post on his LiveJournal blog, which later was translated and republished by openDemocracy:

> Here journalists are perceived as support staff by the regional authorities, and journalism itself as a medium for communicating only news the authorities find it necessary to broadcast. In the opinion of the elite, this is "proper" journalism.
>
> "Proper" journalists wind up on the list of regional deputies for the ruling Party of Regions – like the chief editors of prominent newspapers *Donetskie Novosti* (Donetsk News) and *Priazovskii rabochii* (The Priazovsky Worker). In the past week the new governor of the region has appointed Rima Fil, chief editor of *Donetskie Novosti*, as his personal press secretary.
>
> "Improper" journalism, in their understanding, is that which dares to mention the double standards of local authorities.
>
> It follows that "improper" journalism is conducted by "improper" journalists. I and a few of my colleagues belong to precisely this category. They burn the flats of "improper" journalists in Donetsk, and they confiscate servers in editorial offices which house the databases of independent mass media.

The sun was setting behind the Donetsk skyline, turning the sky a deep pinkish-orange. It was time for me to get back to Artemivsk, so Oleksiy drove me to the bus station. He was quiet in the car. We listened to a radio news program and I tried to make out everything that was being said but didn't catch much of what the fast-talking Russian host was saying. My mind locked onto the harsh consonants, the rolling of "Rs," as if I could glean something from them alone. A radio reporter was speed-reading a report that mentioned something about Yanukovych, so Oleksiy glanced over at me and rolled his eyes.

"You must understand," he told me, breaking our silence. "Here freedom of speech exists only on paper. In real life there is no free speech in Ukraine. They want journalists to tell only one story – their story."

This is what Yanukovych meant by "One Ukraine, one story" – the story was the one he allowed to be told. Anything else was sedition, even treason.

"This makes it dangerous to be an independent journalist here, especially coming after the election victory of Yanukovych – the journalists disappear," Oleksiy said.

"I know the goal of journalism is telling the truth, leveling double standards. But [the government] doesn't want this. Our society is passive. People do not trust government, do not trust each other, do not trust anyone at all.

"Without us, without independent free press the people will not see the real picture. It must be shown to them. This is why the importance of our job and independent journalism cannot be overstated," he continued. "But the authorities think another way. To powerful people I am an improper journalist."

Oleksiy took a deep breath, let out a slow, heavy sigh, tightened his grip on the steering wheel, and accelerated through a blinking light.

Outside the bus station he turned to me and I saw his face had lightened up.

"You know, when we were children, me and my friends, we painted over the road signs here in Donetsk that were named for Soviet heroes," he said, smirking and gesturing to a placard across the street. "We painted them Ukraine's colors, blue and yellow."

We both laughed. It was the first time all day we had allowed ourselves a moment of levity.

A few years later, the Hyundai we had ridden in would also be torched. Black-and-white footage filmed by a security camera caught someone dressed in disguise approaching the vehicle, dumping a flammable liquid on the hood, striking a match and tossing it on the car. Flames shot into the air, and the person disappeared into the darkness, never to be caught.

Rubbing shoulders with oligarchs

I returned to Donetsk soon after my previous visit to get my first in-person glimpse into the world of Ukraine's political and business elite at the Russian-Ukrainian Interregional Economic Forum in Donetsk. There, Dmitry Medvedev, the man keeping Vladimir Putin's seat warm in the Kremlin as stand-in president for one term, was appearing alongside Yanukovych and top Ukrainian oligarchs.

Oleksiy had helped me with accreditation to the event by signing me up as a photographer for *Novosti Donbassa*, a move that my Peace Corps managers would have very much not allowed, and maybe even have booted me out of the country for had they known about it. I arrived early with my camera in tow, passing through a series of metal detectors and pat-downs by neckless toughs before entering the summit. Inside, Ukraine's and Russia's political elite mingled freely with oligarchs, economists, analysts, and journalists. I wandered cautiously around the room, trying to blend in by shadowing the movements of the real photojournalists there.

The irony was, of course, that Yanukovych had allegedly amassed billions of dollars from Ukraine's coffers, according to anticorruption journalists and activists at the time and later the post-revolution authorities investigating his crimes, while seeking billions more from both the West and Russia to keep Ukraine's economy afloat. Russia didn't want to see Kyiv turn westward and was offering financial support to keep it in its perceived sphere of influence. The oligarchs were pleased to see deals cut with Russia and relations to remain cozy, since many of them had businesses across the border.

Among those I recognized at the summit were Akhmetov, the coal and metals magnate whose wealth was then estimated to be around $10 billion, and Viktor Pinchuk, a steel and media tycoon who was married to former president Kuchma's daughter. In an attempt to shed some of the public's criticism of him and shape a more appealing image of himself, he had spent millions of dollars acquiring high-profile works of Western modern art, including pieces by Damien Hirst, and opened a gallery to display them beside Kyiv's historic Bessarabska Square. I snapped photographs of Akhmetov and Pinchuk and followed them to a cafeteria. Their security detail stopped me from following them farther into a VIP room.

It was in these smoke-filled rooms where Ukrainians and Russians compared their riches and hashed schemes to grow their fortunes, Oleksiy had said, and we journalists watched cigar smoke swirl in the air as a couple of heavies closed the door behind the tycoons.

After they emerged, I took a seat directly behind them and settled in for the speeches of Yanukovych and Medvedev. The Russian leader was there to discuss "regional cooperation," "integration," and "plans for the future" as they related to Russia and Ukraine, he told the audience. In other words – and what appeared to be the true reason for his visit – he was continuing a Moscow pressure campaign for Ukraine to join a Russian-led customs union and get Yanukovych to quit flirting with the West, and particularly the idea of signing a far-reaching pact with the European Union that would significantly deepen political and economic cooperation with the bloc, shifting Kyiv away from Moscow's orbit.

Yanukovych and his Party of Regions hadn't made any decisions on the matter and, thinking of their own personal interests, actually seemed uninterested in Medvedev's proposals. Indeed, Ukraine's oligarchs and corrupt political elite didn't want to hear about deeper integration with Russia, which many believed would likely lead to them being at the mercy of the Kremlin, weaken their standing, and cut into their wealth. The schemes they had devised to rob the Ukrainian state, line their own pockets, and grow their power and influence would almost certainly be taken over by the Russians.

For this reason, the event was fraught with tension. I watched it all between the heads of Akhmetov and Pinchuk, who did not applaud the Russian president but shared side-eye glances with each other.

Kopanki

A few days after the summit, I went to see for myself how one of the most lucrative schemes devised by the Yanukovych clan worked, and at whose expense, joining Oleksiy and Denis Kazansky on what would be my first field-reporting adventure in Ukraine.

The three of us rode in Oleksiy's Hyundai down the fume-choked H21 highway east from Donetsk to the mining city of Torez. I watched from the back seat as Oleksiy overtook large trucks filled with coal, or what locals here in this area referred to as "black gold." Denis rode shotgun and every few minutes or so he pointed out things along the highway as we passed by. There was the lavish estate of Rinat Akhmetov – Ukraine's richest person – built on the grounds of the local botanical garden. The childhood home of the country's finance minister, who had recently renamed the street on which it was located after himself. And Denis's reporting showed that there was an unfinished home that Yanukovych was said to be building with the money he was allegedly stealing from the state, as also reported by *Novosti Donbassa*.

The opulence of those places was starkly juxtaposed with drab apartment blocks, shabby cottages, and roadside kiosks where pensioners living on $100 a month sold potatoes, onions, eggs, and myriad pickled items to make ends meet. Large factories and coal elevators jutted out of the sprawling steppe every few miles or so. Slag heaps, or *terykony*, from all the mining refuse rose like pyramids all around.

Oleksiy, Denis and I were on our way to visit a group of men working at one of the area's hundreds of illegal mines, called *kopanki*.

Torez sits deep in the black heart of the Donbas. And if you think its name sounds strange for a Ukrainian city, you'd be right. Originally founded by serfs in the late eighteenth century as Oleksiyivka and renamed Chystyakove nearly a century later, the Soviets renamed it a third time in 1964, in honor of the French Communist Party leader Maurice Thorez shortly after his death that year.

Most notably, it was here in August 1935 that the Donbas' most famous miner, Aleksey Stakhanov, is said to have mined a record 102 tons of coal in under six hours, igniting an industrial boom known as the Stakhanovite movement that over the next 40 years brought a flood of mining and manufacturing jobs to the region. His face even graced the cover of *Time* magazine in December that year and was profiled in a story titled "Stakhanovism's Great Stakhanov."

Coal forged the Donbas into an industrial Mecca in the decades that followed, with Torez at its center. A Soviet propaganda poster from the time called the Donbas "The heart of Russia" and showed an anatomical red heart positioned over the Donbas on a map with arteries flowing to cities across the Soviet Union. Record amounts of coal were extracted at mind-blowing speeds – even if much of the data was inflated for propaganda purposes. Apartment homes couldn't be built quickly enough to accommodate a growing population flooding in from Russia. Near the end of the coal boom in 1978, some 100,000 people lived in Torez, with even more residing in neighboring Makiivka and Donetsk. Torez, which still flies a flag emblazoned with a piece of black coal, once had more than a dozen large-scale mines, employing tens of thousands of workers.

By the time we rolled into Torez, the city was a decrepit shell of its former self. Stakhanovism was long gone, along with many of the jobs it had created. The development of coal, oil, and gas in resource-rich Siberia, which began after the 1917 revolution and accelerated in the 1960s, came at huge expense to the Donbas. Independence from the Soviet Union in 1991 all but finished off the mining industry. The 12 large-scale mining operations that once dotted the area had been reduced to just four. In their place, an uncountable number of tiny, illegal mining operations had sprung up.

As an independent country, Ukraine didn't have the money to invest what it needed in the industry and was forced to close many of its mines. Others were sold in a fire sale during the privatization in the 1990s to the country's oligarchs, who invested little in them. Interested only in squeezing out what they could to line their own pockets, most of the mines ended up unprofitable and insolvent. Thousands of workers were laid off and families left the area in search of remunerative work elsewhere. Torez's population plummeted to 72,000, according to a 2001 census, and then to 60,000 by the time I had arrived in 2011, government figures showed.

Driving through town that Fall morning, it was apparent that the trend had continued. I noticed the faded pastel-colored paint peeling off walls, shutters dangling from window frames. Across the road two men covered in dirt drank beers at a bus stop. It wasn't even 10 a.m.

Oleksiy pulled over and asked a young man on a rickety bicycle with a bag of potatoes slung over his shoulder for directions to a quarry, and he pointed us toward a right turn two blocks back. We drove down flooded dirt roads speckled with glimmering coal dust and littered with empty mayonnaise packets, until we eventually arrived at a large pit filled with water.

As our car neared the edge of the quarry, a man with wild red hair springing out from under a Rasta-colored knit beanie, and a thick beard matted from months of untamed growth, emerged from the bushes. Oleksiy motioned to me to open the rear passenger door and let him in. We shook hands and I noticed his skin was cracked and callused.

For reasons I failed to understand, Nikolai had given up his apartment in Donetsk and moved into a shack at the edge of the quarry, which he shared with another man. Nikolai had been a journalist once, too, but now ran a Donetsk-based NGO called Cohort of Light that focused on helping recovering alcoholics and drug addicts. Many of the people he helped were miners who worked in the *kopanki*.

Through his connections we were going to get access to men of the illegal mines who were often cagey toward outsiders, especially journalists. But before we were to meet them, Nikolai suggested we stop at a shop to pick up a few things. It would have been un-Ukrainian of us to drop in unannounced and empty handed.

Oleksiy and Denis waited outside while I ran in with Nikolai. With a glint of gold in her teeth, a woman behind the counter wearing a blue apron asked what we wanted.

"Ten beers will be enough, I think," Nikolai told her. "Let's also get cigarettes and two salted fish."

The car bounced back and forth and bottles clanked in the space between Nikolai and me as we made our way down a gravel road. We came to a stop 20 minutes later and trudged through the forest, kicking aside fallen tree limbs in our way and crossing a rickety wooden footbridge over a narrow creek. Spindly, naked branches of the canopy disappeared into the fog. Crows cawed around us. Approaching a clearing in a small ravine, I could hear the clinks and hisses of something mechanical. The noises grew louder as we got closer. And then at an opening in the brush a crude mining operation appeared in plain view.

"We're here," Nikolai said. "I will do the talking first."

In the days of the Soviet Union, miners were treated as celebrities and given their own holiday, Miners' Day, the last Sunday of August. They even had a football team named for them, Shakhtar Donetsk, which was owned by Akhmetov. Akhat Bragin, Shakhtar Donetsk's previous owner, known among the area's various business clans at the time as "Alik the Greek," had survived several attempts on his life. But it was a bombing at the Shakhtar stadium that finally killed him.

An historian at the Artemivsk museum of local lore once told me over a conversation about the history of Donetsk Oblast that to be a miner was to be a "hero."

"We celebrated them. They gave us everything," she said.

Until the mid-1970s, one-third of every household in Ukraine was dependent on coal for power. And miners were once some of the highest paid workers in the USSR. Now their wages were in line with the nation's average – about $300 a month. Those working in the *kopanki*, however, pocketed a meager $200 each month – if they were lucky.

Much like the miners did, Nikolai believed Torez itself was descending into a black hole. Each year there were more empty houses, fewer people, and much less coal. Independent analysis at the time estimated that just ten years of reserves remained. People saw little or no chance for Torez to transform itself into anything other than a mining town, so nobody invested in it. It was dying a slow death.

"*Poyekhali!*" – Let's go!

A stout middle-aged man named Viktor announced a shift turnover with the switch of a generator which powered a four-cylinder engine that had been taken from a rusted, Soviet-era Lada sedan. Smoke puffed out as the engine bellowed and rattled. A winch began to turn. A few minutes passed, and then a porcelain bathtub appeared from a black opening in the earth. Inside was a heap of coal with some pieces as large as a shoebox. The winch pulled the tub to level ground and lifted one end in the air, dumping its contents into a pile at our feet.

"There it is – our black gold!" Viktor shouted at me over the noise, wiping his forehead with his forearm.

The tub came from deep below ground, inside what he and the other miners there referred to simply as "the hole." This was one of hundreds of hastily cut *kopanki* in eastern Ukraine where men work off any official book to carve out coal with little or no safety mechanism, and no support from the government or companies.

Viktor had mined for so long he couldn't remember when he began. But he recalled how he didn't always work in the *kopanki*. Like many older unofficial miners in the Donbas, at one point he worked at a legal, state-operated facility. It wasn't until he lost his job there after the collapse of the Soviet Union that he resorted to mining illegally. Without a higher education or other professional experience, he said, "I wasn't able to do anything else."

The hole looked terrifying. Its opening was only slightly larger than a car's hatchback and supported by medium-sized fir trunks and old fence boards nailed together; its shaft was nearly as deep as a football pitch. Tubs attached to a rusted cable carried men, equipment, and coal up and down an earthen track compacted from years of use to form a sort of slide. Powering the entire operation was a shoddy engine more than 20 years old. I thought it was perhaps the most dangerous situation I'd ever encountered.

Another miner, Oleksiy, said that six men worked the hole. His skin and clothes appeared mostly clean, except for a few black swipe-mark stains on the thighs of his pants. While speaking to me he sharpened the head of a jackhammer bit on a grinder. Despite sparks shooting off in every direction, he wore no protection of any kind.

As we spoke, three men were inside the shaft, carving away at the walls, filling the tub with coal and sending it back to the surface, all the while trying not to breathe in too much black dust, cause a cave-in, or ignite a methane pocket. That day, the miner Oleksiy had chosen to remain above ground with two other men, though it meant taking home a little less cash at the end of the day.

"They've got the difficult jobs," he said of the men underground and explaining that those who did the digging took a larger cut of the day's wages. In the time I was at the hole, from late morning to evening, none of the miners in the shaft surfaced.

"If you want to see them, you will have to go down," Oleksiy told me.

I glanced at the tub and the hole, and told him I'd be staying above ground.

Viktor shouted again. Another porcelain bathtub was being hauled up with the winch. I watched as Ruslan, a well-built 25-year-old miner, dumped its rocky contents onto the ground and scooped the coal with a large, flat shovel into the bed of a truck. A dusty cloud formed around him and clung to his sweaty face, hands, and forearms, one of which was covered with a flame tattoo.

Afterward he lit a cigarette and drew from it slowly.

"Why do you do this? Why not something else?" I asked him. He was young and strong and handsome. I couldn't imagine there was much to do in Torez.

"The money is good and studies are a waste of time," he said.

Ruslan said he had been working the *kopanki* for almost a decade after dropping out of school to work and help support his family.

"And this is Torez," he added, with a heavy dose of resignation in his voice.

Indeed, this was Torez. What else was there?

The miner Oleksiy heard us talking and sauntered over. His story was similar to Ruslan's. He finished school but started working the illegal mines right after, at 18. He was now 32 and admitted he'd probably be digging out coal for the rest of his life.

"Or until it's all gone," he quipped.

"When the coal is gone there will be nothing here. Torez will be dead," he said. "We can only wish this will happen after our time."

His reasons were much the same as Ruslan's.

"I didn't like school," he said. "And I didn't want to leave [Torez] and my family."

They made good money mining the hole, though they didn't say exactly how much. In any case, it had been enough for Oleksiy to buy a car, a house, and support a beautiful young wife and child. He was proud that he made enough not only to afford to buy his family the things they needed but could take them on vacation each year to Mariupol and the Sea of Azov, or Crimea and the Black Sea.

I wondered aloud how much a truck load of coal was worth, and he began doing the math on his fingers.

"Maybe $1,000 a day," Oleksiy said.

But this was before expenses such as gas and repairs, and the payoffs to local police, government officials, and the coal companies that would launder the illicit coal. After all that, the six men would split the couple hundred bucks left over.

Once the truck reached capacity, the load would be taken to a nearby storage center. From there, it would be mixed with locally mined coal and get shipped across the country. The great irony, Oleksiy said, was that hardly any of it would stay in the region and residents in Torez would likely not have enough to stay warm in the winter. A popular local anecdote, he told me, went like this: A miner works all day extracting fuel to heat the houses in the rest of the country, only to come home to find his own family freezing.

Ruslan chuckled, tossed his cigarette butt to the ground and pulled on his gloves. A third bathtub was on its way up from the mine. The winch lurched to a halt, the tub spilled the coal, and he began shoveling again.

Oleksiy, meanwhile, went to a shack and took one of the salted fish we had brought out of its white paper wrapping and laid it atop a stump. With a large knife he pulled from his pocket he cut off the head and tossed it on the ground. Then he chopped the body into pieces to share with the other miners and us.

I asked Oleksiy about the police and whether or not there was a chance any of the *kopanki* could be closed. He explained they were protected by the police, politicians, and government officials who took a cut of the profits from them. He didn't expect that the *kopanki* would ever be shut down, at least not entirely.

"There are just too many of them," he said.

But there were instances when some were closed.

The authorities had to at least appear as though they were abiding by the laws on Ukraine's books and shut *kopanki* down if there were major accidents – and there certainly were. Not long before I visited Torez, a *kopanka* not far away had collapsed and killed six men. Police came and closed it, arresting surviving miners involved in the operation.

Oleksiy said whenever a *kopanka* collapsed or someone was reported killed by a methane leak or explosion underground, for instance, police would come and close it. Sometimes it would remain closed, at other times it would be opened again when the dust settled.

To keep from being shut down, he told me, the miners often didn't report deadly accidents at the illegal mines. Instead, they'd report a person missing and pay off their family. Or they would dig out the body, clean it up and re-dress it, and move it to a quarry or stream. There, they would pump the person's lungs full of water to make it look like they had gotten drunk and accidentally drowned. By doing so, the mine would stay open. They would pay the family its lost loved one's share of profits for some time. The drunk drowning was also believable because of the heavy alcohol consumption in the region. *Samogon*, or moonshine, was a big part of the miners' culture.

But with Yanukovych leading the country, the miners weren't worried about the *kopanki* being closed – especially since his "family" was so deeply involved in the illicit business.

However, Yanukovych's predecessor and fervent political opponent, Viktor Yushchenko, as part of his fight against corruption and lawlessness, had attempted to shut down the illegal mines, filling some of them with water, rock, or other materials. But the task was too great – there were just too many of them to track down – and he became distracted by political troubles in Kyiv to see the plan through.

Not long after, the defiant miners of the *kopanki* dug out their holes.

"It's not difficult to pull out rocks or pump out water," the miner Oleksiy said.

Even as the daylight faded, the Lada engine thundered on. The winch kept turning, bathtubs continued to be hauled up and emptied, and Ruslan kept shoveling.

Oleksiy, Denis, Nikolai, and I said our goodbyes and headed back through the forest and over the footbridge to the road, with the autumn leaves crunching beneath our feet.

On the highway we passed more trucks filled to the brim with coal. On the horizon, framed by the faded light, I watched the massive refineries spew smoke from their chimneys and I thought about the miners going home that night, scraping the coal dust out from under their fingernails and washing up for dinner with their families. The next day would be another grueling one for them, scraping and shoveling and cranking up bathtubs full of black gold for their oligarch overlords.

Close of Service

The next several months were a grind. Nikolai sold the apartment I rented from him, giving me just a week's notice to move out. So I shacked up with Igor and his girlfriend, Ira, which was fun but felt like being back in college at times. I had introduced them months earlier and they hit it off immediately. She was an English teacher and had invited me to help with a few lessons. Igor eagerly came along after seeing a photograph of Ira and me together.

The apartment was a century old and had withstood the Russian Revolution and Nazi occupation. It was smack in the city center, 50 feet from Artem Square and right across the street from School No. 11 and the library, meaning I could simply roll out of bed and be at work in minutes.

We had fun cooking and drinking together. On Ira's birthday, her family came over to celebrate. In traditional style, there were tables covered in food and plenty of vodka. Her uncle took a special liking to me, an American, and he proclaimed at the start of the festivities that it would be his mission to get me plastered. He proceeded to do so, despite my attempt to hide in my room.

It was no surprise then that I struggled to focus on work as I closed out my Peace Corps service in Artemivsk in May 2012. What I really wanted was to get back into the journalism game.

First, I flew to Shanghai over the summer for a change of scenery. It was just as the 2012 UEFA European Football Championship was about to kick off in Ukraine, which shared hosting duties with neighboring Poland. The championship was Ukraine's moment to show the world it wasn't just some post-Soviet, uncivilized backwater, like much of the Western press had made it out to be. The British tabloids were especially brutal, smearing Ukraine as "violent" and "racist," with former England defender Sol Campbell warning supporters in a BBC Panorama segment that if you went to Ukraine, "you could end up coming back in a coffin."

But the championship went off without any hitches and scandals. England fans who flooded Donetsk to see their team defeat Ukraine 1-0 even paraded through the city's streets with a coffin adorned with the words "You're wrong Campbell" and chanting "Rubbish!"

After years without seeing any other foreigners besides Peace Corps volunteers in the Donbas, it felt strange knowing that so many were arriving in the east all at once and that I wouldn't be there to experience that moment of change. At the same time, I was immensely glad that Ukrainians had been such great hosts, as I knew they would be.

I wouldn't stay away from Ukraine for long. I was hooked on the place, its complexities, idiosyncrasies, and especially its people. I felt a closeness with Ukraine that I hadn't felt in America, and my adopted home country stirred an excitement in me like never before.

I met Bri in Shanghai, a stunning and electric metropolis but where we struggled to navigate China's dense bureaucracy and find remunerative and rewarding employment that wasn't English teaching. Our frustration boiled over with the oppressive summer humidity and deafening screeches of cicadas.

In September 2012, we returned home to Portland briefly to consider our options. I weighed up several unusual and uninteresting job opportunities – editor of a yachting magazine in the Caribbean, reporter for a travel magazine in Dubai, scribe covering courts for a local newspaper – and turned them all down. Then an opportunity in Kyiv arose, after I was offered a job as a reporter for the English-language *Kyiv Post*. Weeks later, we were married and on our way back to Ukraine.

4

Acts of Journalism

Kyiv, January–November 2013

We settled into Kyiv just after New Year in January 2013. The Ukrainian capital was rough and gritty but also beautiful. With seemingly endless places to explore, it was the most mysterious place I had been. I immediately fell in love with its patchwork of architectural styles – baroque, constructivism, neo-Gothic, neo-modernism, and so on – punctuated with its golden-domed monasteries that marked its hilltops. People filled Kyiv's medieval streets that led to large public squares and untamed gardens. The capital's metro system – one of the deepest in the world with stations hundreds of feet underground and reachable only by long escalators – was cheap and reliable. Built in the wake of the Second World War, the metro's stations doubled as bomb shelters, with heavy, hermetically sealed doors that would close in case of nuclear attacks or floods.

I made a point also to get to know the city behind its facades, wandering through its courtyards, or *dvory*, which felt like little neighborhoods within neighborhoods. Step through a gate and suddenly you were transported to another little world. One of the first and most magical courtyards that I discovered after moving to the city was shown to me by a Ukrainian friend. A stone's throw from Golden Gate, or *Zoloti Vorota*, the eleventh-century entrance to Kyiv erected during the time of Yaroslav the Wise, the Grand Prince of Kyiv, it was home to a large cage housing three ravens named Korbin, Karlusha, and Kyrylo. They were rumored to have been put there by a local gangster who rescued them from injuries, but the residents of the buildings surrounding the courtyard were now taking care of them.

Bri and I rented a one-bedroom apartment in a 110-year-old building on Volodymyrska Street. It was just a block south of the bright red Taras Shevchenko National University and Shevchenko Park, where old men in oversized coats puffed cigarettes as they played chess for hours near young lovers who kissed on the park benches.

The landlord was a young woman roughly our age, in her late twenties, and she had inherited the apartment from her parents, to whom it had been assigned during the Soviet Union, when her mother worked for the state intelligence service, the KGB. They had then inherited the apartment when the USSR collapsed, and eventually passed it on to their daughter. She kept up the place and, naturally, gave it a *Yevro-remont*, updating it with pink wallpaper. It wasn't fancy. The real benefits were the affordable price – $500 a month – and its proximity to Kyiv's city center, where we spent most of our social time with friends and where I walked to work each morning.

The *Kyiv Post* printed a weekly newspaper and published daily articles on its buggy and outdated website. It had been founded by an American in 1995, at a time when English-language newspapers were opening up in cities across the former Soviet space. There was *The Moscow Times, The St. Petersburg Times*, as well as many others in Central and Eastern Europe that didn't do so well. The papers mostly catered to the English-speaking travelers and expats who had flocked to Eastern Europe when the Iron Curtain fell and made a killing exploiting the chaos of privatization that followed. For years their pages included ads for escort services that targeted many of those same Western men, often referred to as "sexpats."

In 2009 the *Post*'s American founder sold the paper to the Pakistan-born British citizen and self-made billionaire Mohammad Zahoor, who had made a fortune in Ukrainian steel production in the 1990s. Zahoor didn't know much about news and rarely stopped by the office. To his credit, he only once attempted to interfere with the news operation. And when the *Post* staff went on strike, he backed down.

He liked the paper because all the powerful business and political elite in the country owned at least one newspaper and it gave him bragging rights and an air of prestige. But he also liked the favorable publicity it brought him and because it promoted his singer wife, Kamaliya, a former Miss World who he claimed was destined to be the next Lady Gaga. But if the price for doing real journalism was to write about the sputtering pop music career of Kamaliya, who the newsroom called Lady Haha, the staff seemed willing to pay it.

Unsurprisingly, the *Post* employed some colorful people. At the helm was a middle-aged Minnesota native by the name of Brian Bonner. His glasses balanced on the end of his nose as he pounded away at his keyboard. Bonner had wanted to be a star foreign correspondent in his youth but regretfully missed his chance. Over a "business lunch special" at a Czech restaurant one day, he lamented that fact while telling me about his path to Ukraine.

Back in the early 1990s, he had been working at Minnesota's *St. Paul Pioneer Press*. It was an era in which even state and regional newspapers had foreign correspondents spread across the globe. Maybe they didn't have them everywhere, but many operated bureaus in Beijing, Moscow, London, and Paris, the big hubs. And they dispatched foreign correspondents to conflicts and crises in far-flung corners of the world to report on big stories.

When the Gulf War broke out, the *Pioneer Press* offered several young reporters the chance to go and cover it as correspondents. Those who raised their hands would go on to work for major national newspapers and TV channels. But Brian didn't volunteer and instead stayed behind in Minnesota. It was something he regretted, he told me, describing how he watched his colleagues go on to work for major American newspapers after the war. And he offered a piece of advice that would turn out to be very useful: if I was serious about making it as a foreign correspondent, then working at the *Kyiv Post* was a good start, but if I could find a way into a story of great international significance – maybe even a war – I should do it.

Indeed, the *Post* could be a great place for young, budding foreign correspondents to hone their skills. Several Western and Ukrainian reporters at the paper had gone on to work for major Western news operations, and more would later do so too.

While Brian managed the *Post*'s daily operations and set the agenda for the weekly edition, Katya Gorchinskaya, the news editor, was the brains of the newsroom. Nobody was better sourced than Katya. She would open her mouth to speak in her oddly accented British English, and story ideas would spill out. She rarely spent more than a couple of hours at a time at her desk. And she almost never came into the office before lunch because she was always out meeting with sources – the energy minister, the foreign minister, the majority leader in parliament, an oligarch, a CEO, a spymaster. She would storm into the office in a near-frenzied state saying we would never believe who she saw and what they told her. She would stand in the middle of the room and assign stories for us as she scribbled them on a big white board. Nobody argued with her. If Katya said it was a story, then it was a story. I learned a lot about reporting, but especially about Ukraine, from sticking close to her.

Katya had cut her teeth in the take-no-prisoners Ukrainian TV news scene of the late 1990s. She was around 20 years old when she confronted Ukraine's then-president Leonid Kuchma on live television. Kuchma, having rarely been questioned in such a way, especially by a young female reporter, was taken aback. The interaction won her serious credibility and she would go on to become one of the country's top political reporters and even host her own news program while in her twenties.

The rest of the *Post* team was composed of young Ukrainian journalists, a Pole, and two Americans – myself included. The Ukrainians were young, hip, smart and ambitious. We held conversations and debated story ideas in a mix of Russian, Ukrainian, and English. Everyone jockeyed to get their stories onto the front page of the newspaper. And we religiously drank beer and wine on Thursday evenings, as we pieced the paper together. By the time it was sent to the printers – sometimes close to midnight – we were all sauced.

The *Post* was also a tumultuous place. We operated knowing that we could be shut down at any moment, that funding could dry up, that we might not get paid on time, or ever, that the authorities could storm in and seize our servers. We faced several Distributed Denial of Service (DDoS) attacks, and at least one break-in. There were times after publishing controversial investigative stories when we hired security guards to watch over the office. It was as nerve-wracking as it was thrilling.

We were all paid horrendously low salaries and partly under the table. The expats like myself were paid three times more than the Ukrainians. When someone threatened to quit over money, Brian would appear with an offer of a 25 per cent raise. We never knew where that extra money came from. Still, the pay was never enough to keep people – Westerners in particular – on staff for long. The *Post* was a revolving door.

The *Post* was one of the few news outlets in the country that was truly independent and much of the focus of our reporting consisted of political and hard-hitting investigations into government corruption. In other words, stories that many of the Ukrainian newspapers wouldn't or couldn't touch for fear of harassment from Yanukovych and his Party of Regions, or bogus criminal charges from the judges they were said to have controlled, or even physical attacks from the thugs they were accused by political opponents and journalists of hiring to keep critics and competition in line.

In the Yanukovych era, scandals were a dime a dozen. Crooked gas contracts, secret political pacts made behind closed doors, company takeovers aided by hired thugs, and much more were reported on by Ukraine's independent news outlets, including *Ukrainska Pravda* and *Forbes Ukraine*, among others. We published investigative stories every week on a given top government official or oligarch who was running elaborate schemes to rob money from state coffers, secure lucrative state contracts, or muscle their way into power.

Graft, embezzlement, and extortion weren't just products of rampant corruption. They were so deeply ingrained in Ukrainian politics and business at that time that the country could barely run without them. Of course, it all came at the expense of ordinary Ukrainians. Education and healthcare, for instance, were technically free to all Ukrainians. But to get into a good school or a quality medical facility, high grades and good performance weren't enough – bribes needed to be paid to directors. To obtain a new business license, one "fee" needed to be paid to inspectors and another to landowners. To do or acquire anything required some form of payoff.

I made a point never to pay a bribe. As a Western foreigner and a journalist writing about politics and corruption, I couldn't, as doing so would undermine my credibility. But one day I got a glimpse into how at least part of the system worked.

The caller ID showed a number I didn't recognize but I answered anyway. The man on the other line identified himself in Russian as Vladimir, no last name or patronymic, which was odd I thought. He said he was someone representing Energoatom, the Ukrainian state-run National Nuclear Energy Generating Company. And he wanted to meet in person.

"We have a lot to discuss," he said cryptically.

The mysterious nature of the offer piqued my interest. Days earlier I had reported one of my first big scoops as a reporter in Kyiv. The front-page story was about a fight happening behind the scenes between the United States and Russia over who would be the main supplier of nuclear fuel to Ukraine's four nuclear power plants and 16 nuclear reactors, a deal worth more than half a billion dollars.

The front-page splash read "Fuel Duel" and showed two thermal images of nuclear power-plant cooling towers with steam rising from them. Katya had been tipped off by one of her sources that reports in Russian and pro-Russian Ukrainian media, about fuel rods provided by the American company Westinghouse being faulty, were wrong. She connected me with the source, who invited me to meet him and others. They then provided me with documents and photographs that showed the Westinghouse fuel rods were just fine. In fact, it was the Russian fuel rods that were the problem. They were flimsy and would jiggle around in the tubes where they were stuck beside Westinghouse's fuel rods as part of a test to see if Ukraine could use them together to power its nuclear reactors. Some in the Ukrainian government wanted to see Russia's monopoly on nuclear fuel broken, which would happen if Kyiv began buying more of it from

America. Others simply wanted to use the test as leverage to negotiate a better price with Moscow for the fuel.

I didn't think my report would ruffle many feathers or garner much attention, but I was wrong. It spread like wildfire through Russian and Ukrainian media, and the local correspondent for Russia's state-run RIA Novosti called to interview me about the story. There were statements put out by various officials taking one side or the other of the report. I was excited by the fact that I had sparked a debate and my work was being talked about in the halls of power in Kyiv, and likely Moscow and Washington. But the scoop and the ripples from it – especially this mysterious phone call – made me anxious.

I agreed to meet Vladimir inside a coffee shop behind the National Opera in central Kyiv the next afternoon. This all seemed shady so I didn't want to go alone in case something should happen. I wanted a witness, at least, if not a bodyguard. I took Jakub, our young business editor who had become editor-in-chief for a period of months after Brian had been fired by Zahoor.

Vladimir, wearing a dark suit and button-up shirt without a tie, was sitting at the farthest table in the back corner of the back room. He stood up and shook our hands and waved over the waitress to take our coffee orders. Then he got straight down to business.

"It was an interesting article you wrote, Christopher. It's a shame that you wrote it because you have the story all wrong," he said. "I want to offer you a chance to fix it and be a part of something very important. And you both can make a lot of money at the same time."

He offered us $50,000 if we were willing to help him.

Jakub, never one to be able to mask his emotions, screwed up his face and threw his head back.

"Very interesting!" Jakub said, turning toward me with a wide grin.

"I'm sorry," I said, "but we don't take bribes."

"Oh, Christopher, this isn't a bribe," Vladimir said. "It's payment for your work."

"That is not what it sounds like," I continued. "However, knowing there is a black PR campaign is very interesting and if you would like to tell us more about that, we would be happy to write an article about this."

"Who did you say you were working with?" Jakub asked. "And who is behind this black PR campaign?"

"What campaign are you talking about?" Vladimir said, looking us straight in the eyes. "Christopher," he said with a little chuckle, "I'm worried you're confused. You must have misunderstood something."

With that, he put a 100-*hryvnia* note on the table, stood up, shook our hands, and walked out. But before he left he had one last message: "Be careful what you write."

Jakub and I were stunned. We laughed for a whole minute before the fear of potentially becoming targets of the pro-Russian government – or perhaps the Russians themselves – set in.

"Holy shit!" Jakub exclaimed.

We had heard reports of what Yanukovych's government did to enemies. In our cases, we were Western foreigners, so whatever might happen to us would likely be less severe than what Yanukovych is said to have done to one of his own, a Ukrainian.

Still, it was exhilarating to feel like we were really onto something and that we had obviously ruffled some seriously rich and corrupt feathers.

"Wow! Fucking hell!" Katya exclaimed back in the newsroom.

I kept on the story and wrote two follow-ups. Westinghouse kept its fuel rods in Ukrainian reactors. The Russians would still provide most of the fuel but would see its monopoly crack.

Years later, I would meet American representatives from Westinghouse and US diplomats in Kyiv and we'd reminisce about that story. And they would tell me how the Westinghouse people had been followed on the streets by bulky goons in black cars and were threatened with physical violence unless they leave Ukraine and take their American fuel rods with them.

"Maybe we should have warned you," one of them would tell me. "Because these guys were always talking about you, too."

"I would have appreciated that," I said.

PART TWO

REVOLUTION AND ANNEXATION

5

Euromaidan

Kyiv, November 2013

Tensions between Moscow, Kyiv, and the West were escalating now. Much of the talk in Kyiv that summer centered around Ukraine's future and whether it should work toward closer ties with the democratic West or authoritarian Russia. Yanukovych seemed to be leaning toward the idea of signing a much-anticipated deal with the European Union to integrate Ukraine politically and economically with the West, to appease his critics who worried he had grown too authoritarian and corrupt, and, of course, to legitimize his fortune. The deal was called an "association agreement" and it would create a "Deep and Comprehensive Free Trade Area" between Ukraine and the EU. It wasn't an application for EU membership, a move that would infuriate Putin, who regretted Ukraine's break from Russia at the collapse of the Soviet Union and believed it still to be a part of Russia. But it would mark a big step away from Moscow and the Customs Union that Putin wanted Kyiv to sign up to. At the time, independent polls showed more than 45 per cent of Ukrainians supported integration with the West. A big reason for that was to see the systemic corruption, which had plagued Ukraine for so long, stamped out.

Yanukovych would soon be heading to the Lithuanian capital, Vilnius, where he was expected to sign the deal and meet with EU leaders. But in the run-up to the highly anticipated Eastern Partnership Summit, there were very few public rallies or events showing support for the move to integrate with the West. It was as though Ukrainians thought it was already a done deal. I wrote an article about how grassroots movements and mass public demonstrations had been noticeably absent.

More visible were the anti-EU billboards of pro-Russian *Ukrainskiy Vybor*, or Ukrainian Choice, an organization headed by Viktor Medvedchuk, a close friend of Putin's and the former head of ex-president Leonid Kuchma's administration in the early 2000s. The group's billboards, which its advertising director Artem Bidenko told me cost roughly $1.4 million, included those with such messages as "association with the EU leads to growing prices," "association with the EU will lead to job losses," and "association with the EU means gay marriages." In the case of the latter, the message was displayed beside an image of same-sex couples holding hands. The anti-LGBT and anti-Western propaganda mirrored that which was used in Russia that summer to promote Putin's gay propaganda law.

Olena Markosian, one of Medvedchuk's associates, claimed the EU association agreement was a "scam." "It will be a sharp break of two economies," she told me. "At least 20 million people will lose their jobs." She didn't have any statistics to back up her claims, which went against most economic studies about the potential impact of EU association.

For my part, I didn't have scientific proof that the *Ukrainskiy Vybor* campaign was having an impact on the Ukrainian population. But as the Vilnius summit approached, I heard more and more concerns from Yanukovych's people that echoed Medvedchuk's propaganda.

I kept one eye on the summit that November, as I headed to the western city of Kalush, a sleepy town of 64,000 residents at the foot of the Carpathian Mountains in western Ivano-Frankivsk Oblast, with Anastasia Vlasova, a photojournalist for the *Kyiv Post*. We were there to investigate a corrupt industrial site clean-up deal that had evolved into a massive environmental problem. Several hundred million cubic feet of salty mining wastewater from a potash mine and the decaying remains of thousands of tons of toxic sludge at a nearby dump site were seeping into groundwater and tributaries of the Dniester river, the water supply for the roughly ten million people living in western Ukraine and Moldova that runs into the Black Sea.

Environmental experts were warning me that the situation was potentially catastrophic. Wastewater at the site was just two meters from spilling over the crumbling walls of a 48-acre open mine known as the Dombrovsky Quarry.

None of the workers wanted to talk to me about it. The environmentalists and townspeople were worried about it. But everyone I spoke to wanted to talk about Yanukovych and the EU association agreement. They were all hoping he would sign it. Doing so would be the only way Ukraine would be able to realize the type of progress and modernization that neighbors like Poland had experienced years before, and thus the only way something like the potash mine and entrenched corruption could ever be cleaned up.

I was typing up my reporting on the evening of 21 November when news came across the wires that Yanukovych had backed out of the EU deal, citing pressure from the Kremlin. Instead, he said, he would turn to

Russia for financial assistance to help prop up a cash-strapped Ukraine and suggested joining Putin's Customs Union. There were rumblings ahead of the summit that this might happen, but that didn't make it any less shocking when Yanukovych actually performed the about-face. This decision would seal his fate and set in motion a series of events that over the next decade would reshape the world order, altering the course of history.

Anastasia told me to look at a post on Facebook from the journalist Mustafa Nayyem, calling for Ukrainians to come out to *Maidan Nezelezhnosti*, Independence Square, or simply the Maidan, to protest Yanukovych's move to back out of the EU deal. "RT!! Meet at 22:30 under the monument of Independence. Dress warmly; take umbrellas, tea, coffee, and friends," he wrote. "Spread the word." People gave the protest a name and a hashtag: Euromaidan. Maidan is the Ukrainian word – with Persian origins – for a public square.

Dozens of people waving EU and Ukrainian flags evolved into hundreds, and then about 2,000. The demonstration didn't seem like a big deal to outsiders, but many of us in Ukraine immediately sensed a shift was underway. There was something about this protest, in this moment, that felt different from so many other anti-government demonstrations before it.

Anastasia and I were watching this unfold from our hotel rooms in Kalush and wishing we were there. When Katya called me to say she thought it was a good idea for us to come back to Kyiv, we caught the next train.

On 24 November the protest swelled to more than 50,000 people. Ukrainians marched through central Kyiv to European Square in the biggest anti-government protest the country had seen since the 2004 Orange Revolution. The protesters waved Ukrainian and EU flags and chanted, "Out with the bandits!" and "Ukraine is Europe!" They carried posters demanding that Yanukovych resign. "Mr President, the Ukrainian nation will not forgive you for this treason," read one. The crowd sang the national anthem, "Ukraine Is Not Yet Dead," in a spontaneous display of patriotism.

The protests brought out the young and old, seasoned activists, and many who had until now been politically apathetic. They came from Kyiv and the regions, especially the western ones close to EU borders. My *Kyiv Post* colleagues and I interviewed several of them and published regular updates on a running online live blog.

"I'm here for a brighter future," said Serhiy Stoyanov, who brought his wife, six-year-old son, and two-year-old daughter to the demonstration. He had come alone to the first, smaller protests after Nayyem's call on

Facebook. He said he wanted his children to grow up in a "developed and civilized" place. "I want to live in a better country."

Many signaled their intent to protest long-term if the government didn't heed their calls. "If the right decision won't be made on November 28, there might be something even bigger than the 2004 Orange Revolution," said Tetyana Syrova, a resident of the western city of Lviv.

Some protesters tried to storm government buildings, but police in riot gear pushed them back with tear gas and batons in a heavy-handed and unnecessary response. In all, the protests remained peaceful and non-violent. But as anger deepened on both sides, it became apparent to me that most likely it wouldn't stay that way.

Yanukovych's stodgy prime minister, Mykola Azarov, delivered thinly veiled accusations of Western involvement and threats of violence to disperse the crowd.

"We know that these types of actions are financed. For example, if it's done within the framework of the law, this is normal. But if it's done in violation of the law, then the government will not act like it did in 2004, when before our eyes a technical dismantling of a lawful government was happening," he said in televised remarks on the ICTV channel. "We won't play around here."

The demonstrations continued and on 26 November, in a half-assed attempt to calm the protesters, Azarov announced that the Ukrainian government was still in talks with the EU about the association agreement and remained dedicated to "moving our country closer to European standards."

Nobody believed him. And when it was clear that there would be no turning back from Yanukovych's decision to cozy up to Russia instead of the EU, hundreds of the most hard-core, mostly student protesters set up a tent camp on the Maidan like the Orange Revolutionaries before them, and volunteers brought them food and hot drinks as they remained throughout the following chilly days and nights.

They called for Yanukovych and Azarov to resign, and the government to be dismantled. Prominent artists and activists delivered rousing speeches from a stage on the square. Among them was Svyatoslav Vakarchuk, frontman for the Ukrainian pop-rock band Okean Elzy. On 28 November the singer whose songs had inspired revolutionaries at the same spot nine years earlier encouraged the protesters: "Don't give up – everything is only beginning."

But the truth was, Euromaidan wasn't working to convince Yanukovych to change his mind. The next day I co-authored a story with my *Kyiv Post*

from the peaceful demonstration on the Maidan and marched up Institutska Street to Bankova Street, turning right toward the presidential building. Some carried crowbars, chains, clubs, and gas canisters. They pulled up cobblestones from the sidewalks. A man driving a front-loader accompanied them. They were ready for battle.

The rowdy mob was met by a steel barricade and a wall of heavily armored Berkut officers. The protesters shouted, "Death to enemies!" "Convict out!" "Bandits out!" Tensions escalated quickly when the group attempted to break through police barricades using the front-loader. The Berkut responded with a wave of stun grenades and tear gas.

I got stuck in the middle of the two sides while trying to film the melee and a gas canister that had been thrown back toward the Berkut lines struck me on the head and fell at my feet. The gas sprayed into my face and I choked on it as I struggled to find my way out of the crowd. Two men, including a photographer, threw their arms around me and dragged me to the side, where a medic dressed in a Red Cross vest doused my bloodshot eyes with milk and held me in her arms.

The Berkut managed to push back the protesters, but hundreds more arrived and they rushed the barricades again. Another wave of flash bangs and gas was lobbed from police lines. The scene repeated itself for hours.

With tensions reaching boiling point, the parliamentarian and oligarch Petro Poroshenko jumped in to try and calm the crowd. Speaking through a megaphone atop the front loader, he said that opposition leaders did not want to storm the building and that paid provocateurs had been sent here to fight with police. He urged the protesters and police to halt the violence.

"There are 1,500 titushki" – hired thugs – "who are armed and are here as provocateurs," he said. The crowd booed. Some responded to his words by throwing candy at him, a jab to his owning the country's largest confectionery, Roshen. He asked that protesters rejoin the peaceful demonstration on Independence Square.

At the same time the world boxing champion and leader of the opposition UDAR party, Vitali Klitschko, who was in a different part of the city but following developments on Bankova Street, condemned the attempt to storm the president's office and denounced it as an effort to provoke the government into declaring a state of emergency.

But their messages fell on the deaf ears of mostly young men who'd come with one purpose in mind: to break into President Yanukovych's office and drag him out to face justice.

Slava, a young man who carried a can of pepper spray, said that the group was determined to get inside. "We will take it. Yanukovych is a criminal and traitor," he told me, his voice cracking with anger.

Around 4 p.m. protesters and police forces exchanged blows. More stun grenades flashed all around and another cloud of tear gas filled the street. In the calm between clashes, a protester walked through the crowd holding up a helmet with a broken Berkut visor that he had seized, inciting loud cheers from the others.

The riot police were eventually able to disperse the demonstrators. Officers pursued the protesters as they fled, thumping them with batons and kicking them. I narrowly escaped a beating by climbing up and over a gate and hiding in a nearby courtyard. Many people weren't so lucky. Even those who had fallen on the ground or sat down with their hands in the air to signal they were peaceful got hammered and booted by police. Three policemen clubbed one photographer relentlessly as he crouched in the fetal position on the sidewalk. Blood ran from his head as he shouted in pain.

In all, dozens of people were carried to a nearby makeshift medical center with cuts, broken bones, and chemical burns, while those with more serious injuries were taken away by ambulance. Countless people suffered head wounds and many more gasped for air as they retreated to the Maidan.

The violence continued later that evening, after a few hundred of the young radical protesters made their way that evening to the Vladimir Lenin monument on Shevchenko Boulevard. The group wanted revenge and with large sticks, stones, and ladders they attacked a Berkut unit guarding the monument. The special forces responded with more stun grenades and gas, throwing them not only in the crowd attacking them but also into throngs of peaceful bystanders nearby. A group of officers fled the scene almost immediately.

The protesters pushed the riot police back from the monument, scattering them to a nearby bus. But two policemen were left behind and beaten by the group. One was seen being taken to the Prego Italian restaurant nearby. An ambulance arrived shortly afterwards.

With word that the riot police force had called for reinforcements, the angry mob swelled to over 1,000, shouting "Shame!"

The Lenin monument stood, for the time being. But the Euromaidan had entered a new phase. The Berkut attack had enraged the nation. People were fed up. Just months earlier, these same people were going about their ordinary lives, largely indifferent to politics. There was no way they could have imagined how things would change so quickly. As someone whose job it was to keep a finger on the pulse of the situation, I certainly couldn't see all this coming.

If the protests had begun as a demonstration of Western-minded progressives to pressure Yanukovych into signing the EU association agreement and moving Ukraine towards more Western integration, they had now transformed into an uprising of Ukrainians from all corners of society in support of bigger, more far-reaching goals. My friend Myroslava Petsa, a Ukrainian journalist working for Channel 5, described the change this way: "It's not about European integration anymore, and it hasn't been since the brutal crackdown by police on peaceful protesters on November 30 that resulted in dozens of injuries."

Now it's a fight against state-sanctioned intimidation, torture, and murder. It's about fighting for basic civil liberties and human rights. All those things that Yanukovych has worked to curtail so that he might become the dictator he's long aspired to be. And it's the most important fight in Ukraine's history thus far.

After filing my last story of the day, I spoke to Katya and Brian about procuring some sort of body armor and gas masks for myself and other reporters. "This is going to get a lot worse real fast," I told them. Then I tried to get some sleep.

The days and weeks ahead would push everyone on the ground to their limits, and beyond. It would be the most extraordinary thing many people had ever experienced, myself included. The personal walls that had defined the limits of Ukrainian society would collapse, and a diverse mix of people – including war veterans, retirees, entrepreneurs, artists, activists, students, politicians, nationalists, radical groups, and many others – would join together in a single, unified mission to overthrow the corrupt and violent government of President Yanukovych and his Party of Regions.

The Euromaidan protest was about to explode into a full-blown revolution.

"Slava Ukraini!"

In the early mornings, from the elevated streets of Old Kyiv, you could see Ukraine's revolutionaries, dressed in camouflage and military green, funnel down to the Maidan, their orange construction helmets and blue-and-yellow flags in tow. As Ukrainians from across the country streamed into central Kyiv, the statue-studded Maidan began to resemble a bizarre cross between a Renaissance fair and a twentieth-century war re-enactment. People were arriving by the thousands in the snow and bone-chilling cold to join thousands of others already on the square and central Khreshchatyk Street. Many had quit their jobs to be there or took a leave of absence or shifted their work schedules to ensure they could attend the big rallies, particularly the regular Sunday ones that always had turnouts in the hundreds of thousands, maybe even a million a time or two. People hopped charter buses, carpooled and hitchhiked to the capital, while taxi drivers offered free rides for protesters around Kyiv to the Maidan. Veterans of the Orange Revolution, experiencing a sense of déjà vu, couldn't get there fast enough. Grandparents came with their children and grandchildren. Couples arrived together to do their bit. It was a family affair. Illustrating this point, a meme began circulating that showed a mother wearing an apron and standing on her toes as she adjusts the black-and-red face mask of her revolutionary son dressed in black and carrying a Ukrainian flag over his shoulder. A lunchbox, apple, and thermos sat beside them, and text at the bottom of the image read, "Oh, mooom."

A student protester I met described the make-up of the revolutionaries to me this way: "Maidan was a convergence of ages, places, experience and ideas. It was a mishmash of ideologies. There was left-wing, there was right-wing, there was center, there were green activists, there were LGBT people . . . Yanukovych had pissed off everyone. People who hated each other before were actually holding hands, fighting against the police together."

Students made up a large and influential segment of the protesters and came from various Ukrainian universities in Kyiv and elsewhere. Born just before or right as the Soviet Union was breaking up, they were young, idealistic, and didn't harbor any nostalgia for the "old days." They viewed Moscow as out of date and uncool. The proliferation of the internet in the years leading up to the uprising meant they had seen what the West had to offer and how people in Europe and America lived. They filled cheap hostels, couch-surfed with friends, and crashed with perfect strangers. To lure more people to the protest, Kyiv residents began offering up spare rooms in Facebook posts. One young friend of mine and his girlfriend hosted a family of four from Ternopil, one of the major cities in western Ukraine. For nearly three months they would share a one-room flat with a mother, father, and two teenage boys. When I asked how they lived on top of each other in such a small space, my friend said it wasn't a problem. "We have a rotation," he said. "When we are home, they are on the Maidan. When they are home, we go to the Maidan."

Everyone dressed in thick winter gear, military garb, and patriotic clothing: many draped themselves in national flags or tied blue-and-yellow ribbons to their arms; some wore sunflower headbands or donned traditional *vyshyvanky*, colorful shirts, under their coats. Dozens of tents were erected, many adorned with flags indicating the regions from which their occupants hailed – Chernihiv, Vinnytsia, Kherson, Ivano-Frankivsk, Sumy, and so on – and field kitchens and cauldrons were brought in. Convivial babushkas and Cossack-looking older men with long handlebar mustaches and *oseledets* hairstyles (a long tress of hair flowing from the top of an otherwise shaved head) stirred pots of hot tea, chicken bouillon, hearty borsch, and *grechka* (buckwheat) amid clouds of white steam. Young volunteers walked around with trays of *buterbrodi* (open-faced sandwiches) covered with heavy smears of butter, slices of *salo* (salt-cured pork fat), rubbery yellow cheese, mayonnaise, stalks of green onion, and cloves of garlic.

Doctors and nurses set up medical facilities and a mental health center with psychologists on hand. Computer programmers and other IT specialists affectionately referred to as *IT-shniki* devised charging and wi-fi stations powered by generators. Grizzled Afghan war veterans, or *Afgantsy*, with their green army helmets, organized security patrols and held self-defense courses for people who'd never fought in their lives but were now preparing for the likely possibility of going into battle against highly trained police forces. There was a clothing distribution center, a library with political, cultural, and historical literature, and an open university offering free courses. Once I walked in on a screening of *The Square*, the 2013 documentary about the Egyptian protests and Arab Spring two years earlier. Afterward, Ukrainians discussed what they could adopt and use here.

Someone hauled in a yellow-and-blue-painted upright piano and a classically trained musician dubbed the "piano extremist" – because he wore all-black clothing with a balaclava covering his face and a bulletproof vest – played for crowds of onlookers who were mesmerized by how his fingerless-gloved hands danced across the keys in sub-zero temperatures. Protesters hovered over barrel fires singing folk songs and twirling about to keep up morale and stay warm.

Rising from the middle of the square like a Gothic spire was the metal frame of the New Year tree that authorities had begun erecting but failed to finish before the Euromaidan protests erupted. Instead of lights and ornaments, the crowd had decorated it with the flags of Ukraine, the European Union, and EU countries, as well as signs with various protest slogans and a large poster adorned with the face of the still-imprisoned opposition politician Yulia Tymoshenko. After the violence on 1 December, some started calling it the "Christmas tree decorated with blood."

Encircling the ever-growing encampment were makeshift barricades composed of tangled razor wire wrapped around cement flower planters, park benches, signboards, wooden pallets, tires, and myriad other objects. Anything that wasn't bolted to the ground – and even some things that were – had been dragged here and used to fortify the perimeter. When the snow fell, the protesters gathered it in sandbags and buckets and built walls of ice that were two stories high in some places. The fortifications connected with the buildings that outlined the square, which themselves became a part of the barrier around the camp, thus transforming the Maidan into something resembling a fortress. Many of those buildings, which housed government offices, were now occupied by the protesters.

Volunteer guards worked shifts at the handful of entrances around the Maidan's perimeter and imposed "face control" to ensure there were no undercover police, provocateurs, titushki, or drunks allowed inside. Alcohol was strictly prohibited. Generally, the Maidan camp did an impressive job of self-policing. Theft was uncommon. In a rare personal security lapse one day, I forgot my laptop bag on a chair inside a tent where I had interviewed an elderly man who had come with his son from Ternopil in the west. When I recalled this an hour later and halfway across the square, I panicked and darted back. But when I reached the tent, a man had my bag and a handwritten note that read, "Hold this for the American journalist." The older man had assigned another man to keep an eye on it for me.

On the Maidan, everyone trusted each other. People who were perfect strangers the day before were friends the next. Many treated each other with the care and respect of a long-time confidant, or close family member.

You could always tell who had been on the Maidan. The acrid smell of smoke from the fires clung to our hair and clothes. Black soot, ash, and dirt covered any exposed skin, filled forehead creases, and got wedged deep under our fingernails. Bathing and washing never wholly got rid of the odor and the grime – but nobody really wanted it to fade. In a way, these things were badges of honor. The spirit of the Maidan was intoxicating. For some, it was spiritual. Orthodox priests dressed in ornate robes prayed over the masses from the stage as protesters whispered prayers and crossed themselves.

As the uprising progressed, the Maidan became the sort of democratic state in miniature that most of the revolutionaries on the square wanted Ukraine to be. An alliance was formed by an eclectic mix of politicians, technocrats, businesspeople, civil-society organizations, activists and artists called the Maidan People's Union – *Narodne obiednannya Maidan* – to lay the groundwork for a post-revolution Ukraine, with a new government and updated constitution. Decisions were often made by consensus on the square. They outlined plans to overhaul the country's notoriously corrupt judicial system and impose new Western-oriented economic and foreign policies.

I was now working 20 hours a day and spending most of my time on the Maidan, returning to my apartment late in the night or early morning. When I slept, which was rare, I did so with my phone on my pillow beside my head in case I got a call from someone on the square and needed to rush down. Most mornings I dragged myself out of bed around 6 a.m., strapped on my newly acquired light body armor under my puffy coat, clipped my bicycle helmet to my backpack and stuffed my gas mask inside. Then I headed back out for another long day of reporting, passing neighbors in the stairwell who had just finished an overnight guard shift on the Maidan. On the way I popped into my regular coffee shop for a double espresso. One day I noticed the cashier had put out a tip jar. A handwritten note taped to its side read: "Free coffee for revolutionaries. But we accept contributions for a democratic Ukraine without Yanukovych." It was overflowing. All of Kyiv seemed to be on a revolutionary footing, including the baristas.

Meanwhile, the rest of the world was finally catching up to the events in Kyiv as Euromaidan protests morphed into a full-blown revolt. The administration of President Barack Obama, which had expressed "deep concern" following the brutal Berkut attack on peaceful student protesters, stepped up its rhetoric, warning Yanukovych that the United States was prepared to hit the Ukrainian government with sanctions if the violence continued. Leaders of European Union nations also threatened actions against the authorities and called for peace. In a phone call made to Yanukovych on 2 December, the European Commission President, José Manuel Barroso, said that "a peaceful and political solution is the only way for Ukraine out of the current situation." That day the crowd on the Maidan swelled to nearly 600,000 people, making it the largest in Kyiv since the Orange Revolution.

My inboxes were filling up with requests from Western editors wanting me to write for them. Major international media had sent their top hacks covering Eastern Europe to the southern Russian resort city of Sochi along the Black Sea to report on stories ahead of the Winter Olympics that would begin in February 2014. Very few were in Kyiv in early December. So, on top of my reporting for the *Kyiv Post*, I began working as a stringer for several newspapers, including *The Times, Daily Telegraph*, and *Independent*, and digital news startups like GlobalPost and Mashable. TV and radio news producers called constantly, asking for "live hits" from the Maidan. In days, my Twitter account, where I posted regular updates from the ground – including photos, video clips, and reporting that racked up thousands of likes, retweets, and comments – exploded. I went from a couple of thousand followers to tens of thousands in a few weeks.

Just about everyone I knew in Kyiv was playing some sort of role on the Maidan, including my Russian-speaking friends. We almost couldn't remember what life was like before the uprising, even though it was only a few weeks old. Days felt like weeks, and weeks like years. Soon it all just blurred together and time was dictated by events on the Maidan. All conversations and interactions now centered around what was happening on the square.

Meanwhile, in eastern Ukraine, only a little more than half of my friends were turning out to smaller satellite Euromaidan and anti-government rallies in Donetsk, Luhansk, and Kharkiv. Even fewer were making pilgrimages to Kyiv to join the big weekend rallies. Some were suspicious of what they saw in Kyiv. Meanwhile Yanukovych, being from Donetsk and still controlling most of the city through his vast "family" network of tycoons, local politicians, and goons, used his resources to quash the demonstrations there and keep them from taking hold like they had in Kyiv. Those in the east were predominantly Russian speakers and lived close to the border with Russia. Many of them regularly tuned into Russian television, which at best presented a distorted view of events and the people partaking in them, and at worst pushed blatant disinformation to discredit the uprising.

It was true that not all Ukrainians supported Euromaidan and the revolution emerging from it. Three prominent Ukrainian pollsters found that in December 2013 between 45 per cent and 50 per cent of Ukrainians supported Euromaidan, while 42 per cent to 50 per cent opposed it. Unsurprisingly, the most support for it was in Kyiv (about 75 per cent) and western Ukraine (more than 80 per cent). Those figures also aligned with where the protesters came from: about 55 per cent were from the west of the country while 24 per cent hailed from central Ukraine; just 21 per cent came from the east.

It was also true that ultranationalists and extremist groups on the far right of the political spectrum and from the margins of Ukrainian society came to the Maidan. The Kremlin pointed to their involvement as evidence of the uprising being a Western-backed "fascist coup" led by radicals who wanted to oppress the country's ethnic Russians and Russian speakers, which couldn't have been farther from the truth on the ground. Moscow cherry-picked events and groups to support its anti-Ukrainian and anti-Western propaganda. In particular, it pointed to the toppling of the Lenin statue in Kyiv, revered by diehard Communists but a symbol to many Ukrainians of tyranny and oppression.

It happened on 8 December, as hundreds of thousands of peaceful pro-European protesters were rallying on the Maidan. Meanwhile, just a few blocks south, at the intersection of Khreshchatyk and Chervonoarmiyska streets and Shevchenko Boulevard, a group of protesters gathered at the location where the red granite statue of the Bolshevik leader had stood atop a plinth overlooking the historic Bessarabska Square for nearly seven decades.

I was on my way back to the *Kyiv Post* office, situated about 200 meters around the corner on Pushkinska Street, when I saw the group of a few hundred athletic young men, some masked, using a winch and metal cable to tug down Lenin's statue. They shouted and cheered as he came crashing head-first to the ground, decapitating him. Then they began smashing him with a sledgehammer and breaking apart pieces to take as souvenirs.

"Yanukovych, you'll be next!" several shouted, mounting the fallen monument and burning red flares in triumph.

I made a short video of the event and then rushed to the office to publish it online with a short news story about what happened.

The Moscow-friendly Communist Party of Ukraine was quick to point the finger at the nationalist Svoboda Party and its members. "This act is testimony to what's happening in the country . . . that it is not a revolution or a democratic process, but a neo-Nazi revolt designed to seize power in the country," said Oleksandr Holub, a Communist Party lawmaker, echoing the Kremlin's messaging.

Yuriy Syrotiuk, a Svoboda spokesperson, said the blame didn't rest entirely with his nationalist party. "Participants of Euromaidan altogether toppled the monument, which was standing there illegally. There was a presidential decree about its abolition," he said, citing an edict from former President Yushchenko in 2009.

The Svoboda members did make up most of the group and were the ones operating the winch. But he was also right that there were other protesters there, many of whom didn't seem to represent Svoboda or any other party, but were angry and looking for a way to express their feelings. I saw them with my own eyes and interviewed many of them in Russian without any protest from them.

But the toppling of Lenin's statue – which would later spark a nationwide movement dubbed *Leninopad*, roughly translated as "Lenin-fall" – along with the occupation of the Kyiv City State Administration earlier on 1 December, would help cement Svoboda and its militant activists as key elements in the vanguard of the Maidan. Often wearing helmets and gas masks, armed with clubs and other hand-held weapons, they were ready to go into battle.

Svoboda claimed to be the torchbearer of the Second World War-era Ukrainian Insurgent Army, or UPA, a self-organized guerrilla force that fought against both Nazi and Soviet armies with an aim of establishing an independent and ethnically Ukrainian nation – and was accused of carrying out murderous campaigns against Poles and Jews. During that tumultuous period, some UPA members also briefly joined forces with the Nazis in a futile attempt to stop the re-occupation of western Ukraine by Soviet forces. It ceased activity in the mid-1950s. But by 1991, ideological descendants of these nationalists had founded the Social–National Party.

In 2004 the party became known as Svoboda. That year a controversial new member of parliament by the name of Oleh Tyahnybok was expelled following a speech in which he spoke of the UPA fighting against "scum," including Russians and Jews, and particularly the "Jewish–Russian mafia" controlling Ukraine. He found a home in Svoboda. Now that same stout, boisterous man, often dressed in a traditional Ukrainian *vyshyvanka*, was a lawmaker leading the party's faction in parliament and one of the leading political voices at the Euromaidan demonstrations.

Ironically, Ukrainian experts on the political situation told me, it might have been the rise of Yanukovych and his Party of Regions to power in 2010 that spurred the rise of Tyahnybok and Svoboda and led to the nationalist party winning 36 seats in parliament in 2012. It was also likely that their visible role on the Maidan had turned off some Ukrainians, particularly those in the south and east. It raised concerns for some protesters in the square who believed that collaborating with Svoboda and other political extremists could undermine the credibility of the uprising.

"Svoboda's presence at Euromaidan protests has cemented Yanukovych's electorate," said Taras Berezovets, a political consultant who worked for Yulia Tymoshenko. "People believed that Svoboda was the only party that can stop Yanukovych. But Svoboda's radicalism is something that scares the EU and keeps many would-be protesters away from Euromaidan."

To be sure, Western allies did look on nervously as Tyahnybok was offered space atop the Maidan stage and Svoboda was given a prominent role in the rallies. In conversations behind closed doors American and European diplomats regularly commented on or asked for my thoughts on his presence. But they were careful not to express their displeasure with the right-wing faction of the Maidan, so as not to help fuel Russian propaganda. Also, there were enough Ukrainians who accepted Tyahnybok and Svoboda – if not explicitly then implicitly – and thought their role and brand of nationalism was blown out of proportion or misrepresented by the Western media, and especially by Moscow.

"There is a lot of misunderstanding surrounding Svoboda," Olexiy Haran, a friend of mine and political science professor at the National University of Kyiv-Mohyla Academy, told me during one such discussion on the Maidan. "They are not fascist like people say. But they are radical."

Svoboda's people were also easy to spot on the Maidan, with their blue-and-yellow flags adorned with the party's three fingers' symbol – meant to mimic the *tryzub*, or trident, which is Ukraine's coat of arms, and as a nod to the Ukrainian independence demonstrations in the 1980s when anti-Soviet protesters would thrust their fingers in the air.

There was another reason why Tyahnybok appeared so prominently: he had something Vitali Klitschko and Arseniy Yatsenyuk, the two other main political opposition leaders, lacked – a certain charisma and magnetism. He was a skilled and fiery orator, beginning and ending his speeches from the Maidan stage with the same rousing calls that buoyed Ukrainian nationalist and independence movements of decades past.

"*Slava Ukraini!* [Glory to Ukraine!]" he shouted.

"*Heroyam slava!* [Glory to its heroes!]" the crowd answered back in rapturous unison.

"*Slava natsiyi!* [Glory to the nation!]" he continued.

"*Smert voroham!* [Death to enemies!]" the people responded.

And it wasn't just his Svoboda followers joining in the call-and-response – it was nearly the entire Maidan. Over time they felt less like the call of ethnic nationalism of decades past and more of the modern cry of a nation fighting for independence, as a majority of the diverse group of revolutionaries seemed to quickly adopt – or perhaps co-opt – the slogans and make them their own. *Slava Ukraini* was becoming synonymous with Ukraine's modern fight for freedom and democracy.

This sentiment was expressed to me by many on the Maidan from all corners of Ukrainian society. Among them was Natan Chazin, a Jewish Ukrainian with a crew-cut and a short, scruffy beard, who was originally from the southern port city of Odesa. He had emigrated years earlier to Israel and fought in the Israeli Defense Forces in the Gaza Strip before he saw the Euromaidan protests in Kyiv and the police violence against peaceful demonstrators. After witnessing that, he hopped on a plane and returned to Ukraine. I bumped into him after overhearing a conversation he was having with a foreigner in English.

"December 1st was tough. I remember walking to the Maidan for the big demonstration that day. And I heard them say '*Slava Ukraini! Heroyam slava!*' And, as a Jew, it sounded to me like these were nationalists and anti-Semites are there," he told me. "But I spoke to people and it wasn't like that. 'If you're here with us, you're our brother,' they said. After a few weeks, I was walking all over looking for these neo-Nazis that Russian propaganda was writing about. I didn't find them. Now when I hear 'Glory to the Nation!' and 'Death to enemies!' it doesn't sound anti-Semitic."

Chazin stuck around, excited to be "a part of modern Ukrainian history."

"I wanted to make sure that to anyone who will say that Jews didn't take part in the Ukrainian revolution we can say, 'No, here's the guy who was there. He did it,'" he told me.

He even began referring to himself as a sort of Ukrainian nationalist. "You could say I'm a *Zhidbanderovets*," he said, tongue-in-cheek, using a combination of derogatory and slang terms derived from the Russian and Ukrainian word for Jew and a word used to describe the followers of Stepan Bandera's far-right form of nationalism.

It didn't take long for people to see what Chazin could bring to the Maidan. "I could see the potential for danger there. I spoke to some of the protesters and asked them what they wanted," he told me. "They said they wanted to get to parliament. I told them, look, there are a small number of you. You need to be three, four times more, and with the same arms as those on the other side. And they looked at me and said, 'You know what you're talking about. So help us and tell us what to do.' I said, 'We don't have to be offensive. We need to be defensive and smart.' One thing I told them to do was to create a wall of fire, burn tires to create a smokescreen. I said this could be a real factor. In a few hours, people on the Maidan decided I was the guy who knew what to do."

Soon after, Chazin hopped on the Maidan bandwagon, forming and leading his own unit – the Jewish *sotnya*.

After the first clashes with the Berkut, the Maidan had decided it needed a more organized force to better defend itself and patrol the sprawling encampment, so it formed a volunteer security corps known as the *samooborona*, or self-defense forces. Coordinated by Andriy Parubiy, a member of parliament from the Batkivshchyna Party who had been involved in nationalist movements stretching back to Soviet times, the *samooborona* was composed of dozens of units called *sotni*. Literally meaning "hundreds," the term was derived from Cossack regiments dating back to the sixteenth century. Each Maidan *sotnya* – a platoon of dozens or even hundreds of fighters – represented a different region, political party, or segment of Ukrainian society for which they were often named. Fighters signed up at recruitment tables on the Maidan or responded to calls to enlist on social media. It was mostly men who were in the *sotni*. But soon, angered and frustrated by the sexism that many experienced on the Maidan and being told, for instance, that "men go to the barricades and women make sandwiches," a group of feminist activists organized a women's *sotnya*.

At a table on the Maidan where they were talking to recruits, I read over the oath that the women had to read and sign if they wanted to join. It read: "I ___ woman warrior of the First Independent Women's Sotni of Ukraine, swear with faith and truth to serve the people of Ukraine! I will do everything possible to preserve the territorial integrity of our State! I promise not to ask under any circumstances for political asylum in another country! I understand clearly that for fighting against the regime I face 15 years in prison! On behalf of Ukraine, I take this oath and promise never to violate it. God and Ukraine are with us! Freedom or death!"

Like Chazin, many other Ukrainians who had moved abroad or were from diaspora communities rushed back to their motherland to join the revolution. If they didn't join a *sotnya*, they found other ways to be useful.

One morning I bumped into Sviatoslav Yurash, a tall and slender multilingual 17-year-old international relations major enrolled at the University of Warsaw. He had decided to cut short his semester studying abroad in Kolkata, India, when the protests broke out and return to his home town of Lviv. "Younger people were talking about their dreams for the future and the loss of belief in this government and the need to change everything," he told me. "But older people were about the same opinion of '*You know, these kids, out there messing around, let them go to the square and have fun, and this will all be over in a few weeks.*' But then the beating of the students happened. And I called the same people who told me yesterday, these are just kids not knowing what to do. And they told me, 'We, the revolutionaries, the sons of Cossacks, we have to protect ourselves and show our strength.' And I felt a big change in their spirit."

After the police forces stepped up the violence in Kyiv, Yurash knew that he also needed to be there. "I felt that I needed to be here to be a part of my country's history," he said. "If I would not be here, I would not be a part of my country's story in the future, if I disregard this chance to put whatever skills I have – and I had none at that point except enthusiasm and ideas – to use, I would regret it."

With a giant bag of *salo* in tow, he rushed to the capital and found his way to the Trade Unions Building.

"I said, 'I speak English and I want to help. And then I showed them my bag of *salo*,'" he told me, recalling his first anxiety-filled moment on the Maidan. "It was the first bribe I'd given in my life." The salt-cured pork fat got him inside the doors.

"They welcomed me and immediately put me to work. I started as a translator. But I very much hated that job. I felt like I was an earpiece for someone when I had many questions and ideas of my own," he said. "Eventually, I managed to meet the civil leaders of Maidan. I had a conversation with them over tea and something I said I guess interested them. At the end of December, I proposed creating an international public relations office of the Maidan with specific goals. One was to work with the Ukrainian diaspora, communicating with them in a very structured way, helping them to get aid to the Maidan. Another was to assist the national organizations on the Maidan by facilitating conversations between them and the leadership of the Maidan. Third was PR, essentially working with foreign media, and it included publishing the information we wanted the world to know on our website. We had fixers for foreign correspondents, translators. We kept growing."

Volunteers started pouring in. A Belarusian man offered to translate news from Russian to English, as did a Russian opposition politician who arrived from Moscow. Western expatriates offered to edit translated texts before publishing them on the group's many online platforms. A group of Ukrainians pitched story ideas to foreign journalists and connected them with key figures on the Maidan. Soon Yurash was commanding a group of some 60 public relations volunteers who were translating, transcribing, and pumping out information in roughly a dozen languages, including English, French, German, Italian, and Polish, about events on the Maidan and around Ukraine. Calling itself EuromaidanPR, the operation was run out of the second floor of the Trade Unions Building, which had become the official Headquarters of National Resistance.

"Revolutionary Kyiv has an interesting allure to it," Yurash observed as we stood amid the hum of the EuromaidanPR office, where foreign journalists and Ukrainian fixers worked amid a tangle of wires and stacks of books and documents. "I love Kyiv, I see Kyiv as being full of possibilities, full of potential for any young person, even though now it's also full of chaos."

Naturally, everything EuromaidanPR did came with a pro-Maidan spin. And Yurash and his team were transparent about the fact that this was a propaganda effort – one for good. They believed it was essential to counteract the potent propaganda, smears, and outright falsehoods that were taking hold, as spread by the Yanukovych camp and Russian government. Still, Yurash and others were under no illusions that everyone on the Maidan was a saint, that the revolutionaries shared all the same goals and motivations, and that there were at times kernels of truth to some of the criticism leveled at the uprising, and even Russia's propaganda.

"If you get to the fifth floor and you speak to the guys from Right Sector, then you'll see that we have a problem that I think will be more apparent if we win on the Maidan," Yurash told me. "But right now we must focus on the moment and taking down the greater evil: Yanukovych."

Intrigued, I went upstairs to see for myself who was occupying the fifth floor. Stepping out of the elevator, I noticed a sign on a door that read "Nazis only." Standing beside it or seated on the hallway floor nearby were a bunch of masked men sporting black-and-red armbands. They wore balaclavas but many had them pulled down while they smoked their cigarettes. I asked one of them who they were. "*Pravy Sektor*. And who the fuck are you?" the man replied in Russian, blowing smoke in my face. "I'm an American journalist," I said, also in Russian. "I'm looking for your commander or a press officer." The man pointed to a room at the end of a dark hallway and then threw up a Nazi salute. "Heil Hitler," he said. "It's just a joke," the man next to him said, bursting into laughter. The first man then tried to explain something about it being an intimidation tactic when a young blonde woman passed and socked the men in the arms.

The place smelled like an army barracks, heavy with body odor and gasoline. Boxes, rucksacks, and cots were stacked along the walls. When I reached the room at the end, I knocked on a door and a voice shouted for me to come in. Sitting behind a large desk with his feet up was a squat man in army fatigues, a buzz cut and sharp scruff on his face. A guard patted me down before the man motioned for me to take a seat across the desk. He lit up a Lucky Strike and tossed the box down. "Who are you? What do you want?" he asked, with a slight lisp, in Russian. He wasn't expecting visitors.

"Christopher Miller. I'm an American journalist," I said.

"You have two minutes."

This was Right Sector's leader, Dmytro Yarosh, a 42-year-old former Soviet Army private and Ukrainian nationalist from Dniprodzerzhynsk in eastern Ukraine. Since 2005, Yarosh had served as the head of Tryzub, a strongly pro-Bandera, far-right paramilitary group whose goal was to create a Ukraine for Ukrainians. "Our enemies," Tryzub's declaration of principles stated, include "imperialism and chauvinism, fascism and communism, cosmopolitanism and pseudo-nationalism, totalitarianism and anarchy, any evil that seeks to parasitize on the sweat and blood of Ukrainians." On 20 November, Tryzub and similar groups, including Patriot of Ukraine and White Hammer, had created Right Sector and appointed Yarosh to lead it.

Yarosh told me that Right Sector was "the most revolutionary structure of Maidan." He said the group was prepared to use violence to achieve the goals of Maidan, which would "be justified," since Yanukovych's security forces had attacked protesters. Yarosh also said he encouraged Ukrainians who had legally registered firearms to join the protests.

"Why?" I asked him.

Because, he explained, he didn't believe that negotiations between Yanukovych and the major political opposition leaders could be successful – by that, he meant that they wouldn't lead to Yanukovych resigning. When I pressed him for details, he dismissed me and picked up his phone to make a call. But he said that his right-hand man, Andriy Tarasenko, could tell me more.

Tarasenko kept an office a few doors down the corridor, so I walked in to meet him. He was dressed similarly but was slightly taller than Yarosh, with dark hair and a dark five-o'clock shadow. Tarasenko, who was deputy head of Tryzub before Right Sector was formed, told me, "We believe in negotiations with Yanukovych only on the terms of his capitulation." He said the group was prepared to give the president a grace period for leaving the country and even provide him with personal security guarantees if he decided to stay in Ukraine after giving up power. I'm not sure I believed that, and it's safe to say Yanukovych wouldn't have either.

I mentioned that Yarosh had brought up the topic of firearms, and Tarasenko boasted to me about keeping a large cache of weapons down the hall. I asked him how many they had and if he could show them to me. He declined to provide any details. But as he walked me out, he showed me the inside of a janitor's closet with mops and buckets. Tucked behind them there were at least a few hunting rifles leaning against the wall and some stacks of boxes that appeared to hold ammunition. It wasn't a stockpile but it wasn't nothing either. Tarasenko said there was plenty more where that came from. "If they attack us again, you'll see more," he said.

Fire and Ice

The crowds on the Maidan swelled. Hundreds of thousands of Ukrainians came out on 8 December 2013, braving the snow and freezing temperatures, to demand the resignation of Yanukovych and his government. Opposition leaders called it the "march of a million." By any count, the crowd was the largest since the beginning of mass protests more than three weeks ago and resembled those during the Orange Revolution of 2004, the biggest peaceful demonstrations Ukraine has seen in its short history since independence.

The rally served as a platform for opposition politicians and civil-society leaders to clarify their demands. Besides resignations, they demanded the end of persecution of innocent protesters and a promise to sign the association and free-trade accords with the EU. Oleh Rybachuk, the leader of New Citizen, told me that they also wanted a round-table meeting with the government. Tymoshenko's daughter, Yevheniya, read aloud a letter penned by her mother in jail that rejected the idea of opposition parties negotiating with the government. "Yanukovych has lost legitimacy as president," the ex-premier wrote. "He is no longer the president of our state, he is a tyrant." Vitali Klitschko highlighted the need for justice for those protesters injured on 30 November and 1 December, and said, "We will fight and we are confident that we will win."

Farther up the street, the Party of Regions organized its own, smaller rally at Mariinsky Park, near the parliament building, in support of the president and government policies. It was a pathetic turnout of several hundred paid-for demonstrators, *titushki*, and state workers who had been forced to attend. I stopped by to speak to some of them. A small group of pensioners said they had been promised 200 *hryvnias*, roughly $20, to stand there and hold a sign in support of the president. They said they'd been brought there in a bus that was parked just around the corner. When I walked over to the bus, a few men with cigarettes dangling from their mouths were dolling out 100-*hryvnia* notes to some other old people. I asked the men near the bus what they were doing. "Nothing. You see? Nothing," one said, holding up his now-empty hands.

The Berkut began their next big attempt to clear the Maidan at 1:02 a.m. on 11 December. It was dark and freezing cold – just 10 degrees Fahrenheit – and people were exhausted, myself included. After more than two straight weeks on the Maidan, I went home to get some sleep. Everyone had their guard down. Katya Gorchinskaya, the *Kyiv Post*'s news editor, was on the square and said she'd call if anything happened. But nobody thought an assault would occur that night, not while the European Union foreign policy chief Catherine Ashton and US Assistant Secretary of State Victoria Nuland were in town. They were meeting with Yanukovych, who assured them that no force would be used against the protesters again. But he had broken his word and his police forces caught the Maidan by surprise. The first sign that the government was up to something came when an unusually timed power outage caused the lights to go out and the buildings surrounding the Maidan to go dark.

I was jolted out of bed when Katya called me in a panic and screamed into the phone at me: "They're fucking attacking again! Get up!" Hundreds of troops looking like black-clothed Stormtroopers in their helmets and body armor had been bussed into the government quarter. Stepping out into the snow and ice, we saw them form long, dark phalanxes. They marched in unison with their metal shields interlocked, towards the barricades on Institutska Street. When they got close, they shouted and stormed ahead, smashing and ripping down whatever was in their way.

The smaller group of revolutionaries on the square leaped into action. A group that included several opposition lawmakers was among the first to respond. Several of them were struck on the head with shields and truncheons. Calls for help went out across every available network. On the Maidan stage, the Ukrainian singer Ruslana Lyzhychko, who like Cher or Madonna goes by a single name – Ruslana – and was famous across the country for winning the 2004 Eurovision Song Contest, pleaded into the microphone: "We are a peaceful demonstration, remain calm and do not succumb to provocations!" she implored. "Stand strong in defense of your rights!" The clashes were so loud that it was hard to make out her words. Ukrainians posted urgent messages on Facebook and Twitter, called and texted friends and family, urging everyone to rush to the square. Taxi drivers picked up people on the street and rushed them to the encampment. Ukrainian streamers with their iPhone 4s strapped to their monopods and connected to mobile wi-fi routers with tape and wires filmed the attack live on Ustream, which was picked up and aired on opposition TV channels. Meanwhile, up the hill, 25-year-old Father Ivan Sydor sounded the ancient alarm, ringing the bells of St Michael's Cathedral to wake up the capital and call them to the Maidan. It was the first time its bells had rung out to warn of an attack since the Mongols invaded Kyiv in the thirteenth century. The bells could be heard across the capital, and they rang for hours as the assault unfolded. All of Kyiv was mobilizing. Within a few hours, the Maidan swelled from hundreds of protesters to tens of thousands. The national anthem blared on repeat from the stage speakers as protesters rushed to the camp's defense. Women were told to move toward the stage where a group of men encircled them for protection. It was an extraordinary display of patriotism, dignity, respect, and fury.

Hundreds of protesters and police were on the eastern side of the camp, crushed together in a gruesome shoving match. The front line was easily distinguishable because of the headwear worn by each side: the revolutionaries with their orange construction hard hats and the Berkut with their black helmets, bobbing and swaying together like a violent sea. The pressure in the middle of the throng was so great that it snapped some people's ribs. Many, unable to take a breath, nearly suffocated and fainted. Protesters dragged them to medical tents.

The Berkut then attacked from the north on Khreshchatyk Street from European Square. One of them rammed an armored personnel carrier into the barricades in an attempt to break through – and failed. Protesters climbed atop the barrier and hurled Molotov cocktails at the military vehicle, then it burst into flames. Just after dawn, the Berkut sent in another force to try to expel the protesters occupying the Kyiv City State

Administration and other government buildings. The protesters hosed them down. In the freezing temperatures, the water quickly transformed the street and sidewalk into an ice rink, and the police lost their footing. Several found themselves behind revolutionary lines, whereupon the protesters, instead of beating them, arranged a safe corridor for the policemen to retreat in a heartening display of mercy that the security forces certainly hadn't shown the protesters.

By 10:30 a.m., realizing they had failed to dislodge the camp, Yanukovych's shock troops pulled back. The protesters immediately set about re-erecting the barricades. The interior minister, Vitaliy Zakharchenko, issued a statement claiming the official reason for the raid was to clear roads so traffic could flow down Khreshchatyk Street and its surrounding arteries. "Main transportation arteries have been blocked by barricades, the necessity and appropriateness of which raise huge doubts," he said. That was absolute nonsense. Khreshchatyk Street stayed closed and traffic on the capital's main drag remained exactly as it had been.

For many Ukrainians, the ten-hour siege was another shocking and defining moment, another red line crossed. Each new, greater attack by the police forces had the opposite effect of what Yanukovych wanted; instead of terrifying the revolutionaries, it angered and galvanized them and brought more people to the Maidan. Katya marked the importance of the moment in a powerful column the next morning. "In a way, this is a war," she wrote. "It is a war for a new civilization in Ukraine. Based on values such as solidarity, dignity, respect for an individual and clear and equal rules of the game for all. This is no longer about Europe or integration – it's about who we are and where we want to go. This is about a nation being born, now and here, in Kyiv, and it's both painful and awesome. The only place to truly feel the pain and grandeur of this national awakening is to stand there right on Maidan."

Indeed, Euromaidan was gone. This was now a revolution of dignity.

Watching from behind the tall red walls of the Kremlin in Moscow, Putin must have been furious. He warned Yanukovych about letting the protesters walk all over him "like a doormat" and dangled a $15 billion bailout and reduced gas prices for the month if the embattled Ukrainian leader would stay his Russian course. "In no way is this connected with the Maidan or the European talks with Ukraine," Putin insisted. Always one to try to portray Russians and Ukrainians as one people, he said the offer was "an act of brotherly love."

Bloodlust

Tetyana Chornovol sat dazed in a wheelchair, her face bloodied, bruised, and swollen. She struggled to breathe. On Christmas Day the crusading, gonzo journalist and anti-corruption activist had been chased down the highway near Kyiv's Boryspil airport, run off the road, and dragged from her car by a group of men who then beat her to within an inch of her life. She filmed the chase on her dashcam. The journalist Mustafa Nayyem, who snapped a photo of Chornovol in the hospital and published it for the world to see, said her battered mug was "the face of Viktor Yanukovych and his entire regime."

Unable to stop the revolutionaries on the Maidan, the state stepped up its campaign of violence, cruelty, and intimidation against activists and journalists beyond the barricades. Later Yanukovych would be convicted by Ukrainian courts of treason for his efforts to crush the 2014 pro-western demonstrations that eventually toppled his government. A Maidan activist in western Ivano-Frankivsk was roughed up by *titushki*. Another in the eastern city of Kharkiv was stabbed multiple times. Yet another who was part of the group Road Control, which exposed corruption among traffic police, narrowly survived when he had his own gun turned on him while being assaulted by pro-government thugs. The rubber bullet penetrated the skin just two inches above his heart. Vyacheslav Veremiy, a reporter for the *Vesti* newspaper, was dragged out of his car by masked men and also shot in the chest. He died in the hospital. That attack happened late at night and it stuck with me because I had been on the same street, at the same time, just one block away, and heard the shot as I headed home from the office but wasn't sure exactly what it was. Dmytro Bulatov, a leader of the roving Automaidan group which used cars and trucks as a means of protest, went missing for more than a week. He turned up severely battered, bloodied, and missing part of his right ear. He said that his captors had also pounded nails through his hands, like they were crucifying him, and left him for dead in the freezing cold. These vicious attacks played out during all of January and February 2014 and grew more barbaric by the week.

I interviewed Ihor Lutsenko, a prominent figure on the Maidan, about the attack on him and another activist. Around 4 a.m. on 21 January he received a phone call from a colleague asking if he would drive another activist, Yuriy Verbytsky, to a hospital. Yuriy had suffered an eye injury during a clash with police and needed medical attention. Ihor picked him up but when they arrived at the hospital, a group of muscly *titushki* intercepted them. "Some men, maybe ten, came into the hospital . . . they didn't say anything and pushed past the doctors . . . just beat us and dragged us to a van," Yuriy told me from his hospital bed. They were driven to a rundown garage in a forested area outside of Kyiv, where their kidnappers tied their hands and legs and put plastic bags over their heads. The men said they were against the Maidan protests and wanted to see a "Slavic union" between Russia and Ukraine. They beat Ihor and Yuriy and tried to force them to confess that the protesters were being paid by Washington and the EU. It wasn't true, so Ihor and Yuriy had nothing to confess to. "I could hear Yuriy screaming from the beatings they were giving him," Ihor said. Hours later they were dumped separately on the side of the road in sub-zero temperatures. A passing driver found Ihor hours later and took him to a hospital.

When we met a couple of days later, his face was black and blue and swollen, his left eye flush with blood. He recounted the story despite now missing several teeth. But he was alive. He sat in his hospital bed picking at a plate of fluffy *grechka* and sipping hot coffee. Yuriy didn't fare as well. Having sustained more serious injuries than Ihor, he didn't have the strength to find his way to safety, and was discovered dead a day after being dumped in the forest near Boryspil, east of Kyiv. A plastic bag was still over his head and the remnants of duct tape were found around his mouth and hands. From then on, everyone associated with the Maidan took pains to be extremely careful. People were being hunted by what they were now calling Yanukovych's "death squads."

The kidnappings and beatings all happened around the time that Yanukovych's ruling Party of Regions was making a play in parliament to outlaw the protesters' actions and create legal justification for cracking down on the Maidan camp. On 16 January 2014, bypassing parliament rules and instead using a simple show of hands, the president's loyal deputies passed what the Maidan quickly dubbed the "dictatorship laws." The draconian legislation essentially made any form of anti-government protest, "extremist" and illegal action punishable by up to 15 years in prison. Among the actions now outlawed were: blocking access to or occupying government buildings; erecting tents and stages on public squares; driving in a column of more than five cars; blocking roads; slandering government officials; and wearing helmets.

Needless to say, the revolutionaries were furious with the new laws and defiant in their response. They didn't budge from the Maidan, and the next day people showed up with an assortment of headgear. Besides the orange hard hats, they came wearing bicycle and motorcycle helmets, vintage army tanker helmets, and pots and pans which they strapped to themselves with rope tied onto their handles and tucked under their chins. I saw a group of babushkas arriving with pasta strainers on their heads. They said it was their first day on the square but they were now there to stay.

The "dictatorship laws" brought even more people out and sparked the most violent clashes yet between the protesters and security forces. During a massive rally, some of the Right Sector and other radical demonstrators led people away from the main camp and attempted to march to parliament on the parallel Hrushevskoho Street. The riot police met them with a cordon of officers a dozen deep and a blockade of military cars, *marshrutkas*, and buses. "Dear citizens, your actions are illegal and are against the state," bellowed a voice from a megaphone on the police side of the line as the ground forces inched forward. The voice warned that any advance toward the cordon would be considered an act of aggression and prompt a violent response. More protesters gathered there. Priests holding crosses stood between the two sides, praying and pleading for calm. I don't remember exactly who cast the first stone or smoke grenade, but the street exploded into violence. Protesters attacked the police barricades with baseball bats, pipes, and crowbars. Officers whacked them back with their truncheons and hurled stun grenades and tear gas. Clouds from the gas burned our eyes and made it hard to breathe. I threw on my mask as I moved through the melee, snapping photographs, taking voice notes on my iPhone, and jotting down details in my reporter's notebook. For the first time on the Maidan, I felt frightened. I hadn't covered anything like this before and the situation was spiraling out of control fast.

Protesters began throwing cobblestones and Molotov cocktails by the dozens into the crowd of riot police. One of the Berkut caught fire near the barricade and the flames engulfed his helmet. I could see him smacking his head and waving his hands around as other officers tried to put it out. A human chain was formed to pass cobblestones, dug up from the road, from the rear to the front line. Nearby, groups of young and old women knelt behind the gates of the Dynamo soccer stadium and poured mixtures of oil and gas into empty glass bottles and stuffed bits of cloth into the tops. They filled boxes with the glass bottles. Some people took a more medieval approach. A man wearing plate armor and looking like he had just stepped off the set of *King Arthur* shot arrows from a home-made bow. Others, appearing more like they belonged in *Monty Python and the Holy Grail*, built a catapult and dragged it into the street. But the medieval weapon failed to work.

Protesters carried tires to the front line, doused them in gasoline, and set them ablaze. Just as Natan Chazin had said, the tires created a thick, black wall of smoke that extended beyond the height of the surrounding buildings. The fire moved to the police buses, which went up in flames. This all made it harder for the Berkut to attack on the ground, so they resorted to tougher means.

They used water cannons on the crowd, which covered everything in a thick sheet of ice. Then they fired into the crowd of protesters with shotguns and sniper rifles. I was interviewing a protester 100 feet back from the barricades on Hrushevskoho Street when he was hit in the leg and dropped to the ground, writhing in pain. I called for a medic and one ran over immediately. They carried him to a field hospital and I watched as they retrieved a brass, cufflink-shaped object from his thigh. After some research, I discovered that it was an armor-piercing projectile manufactured in Ukraine and fired from a 12-gauge shotgun. Security forces referred to it as a "car stopper" because it was often used to penetrate the metal of heavy vehicles and stop their engines. Over the course of several days, the Berkut fired dozens of these, as well as rubber bullets in a similar shape, and buckshot. It was only a matter of time before people were shot dead.

Sure enough, on 22 January, two protesters were killed. The first, struck with buckshot, was Serhiy Nihoyan, a 21-year-old Armenian–Ukrainian from Bereznovativka, a village outside the eastern city of Dnipropetrovsk. Nihoyan's Armenian parents had emigrated from the conflict-torn enclave of Nagorno-Karabakh to Ukraine in 1992, a year before he was born. "I was born in Ukraine and I live in Ukraine, that's why I came to support its people," Nihoyan told a reporter from the 1+1 channel on the Maidan four days prior to his killing. Nihoyan, a regular on the Maidan, cut a striking figure, with his youthful eyes, dark beard, and dark curly hair that flipped out from his red helmet. He often worked security on the western side of the protest camp and chopped wood to keep the barrel fires burning. You could see him from afar, with his red, blue, and orange Armenian flag draped around his shoulders. This morning, he had gone with thousands of other protesters to battle the Berkut on Hrushevskoho Street and was cut down by their bullets. He became an instant hero, or as many began referring to him, "Euromaidan's first martyr." A video circulated that showed him a month before his death standing at the barricades and reciting by heart a passage from Taras Shevchenko's famous poem "The Caucasus," about the Circassians' fight to free themselves from imperialist Russia:

And glory, freedom's knights, to you,
Whom God will not forsake.
Keep fighting – you are sure to win!
God helps you in your fight!
For fame and freedom march with you,
And right is on your side!

Mikhail Zhyzneuski, a Belarusian dissident, was the second to die that day. Despite the government's promise that live rounds wouldn't be used against the protesters, a sniper fired on him, killing him instantly. Three years later, he would become the first foreigner posthumously awarded the Hero of Ukraine medal, the country's top civilian honor.

Ironically, the bloodiest clashes yet broke out on Unity Day, the anniversary of the unification of eastern and western Ukraine in 1919. "Our goal is justice, welfare, free life in a free country," Yanukovych said in a flippant statement to mark the date, as his security forces continued to fire on protesters just blocks away from his administration. "We're so different, but we're united. Nobody can tear us apart."

Meanwhile, behind the police barricades, his Berkut troops were demonstrating what he really meant by unity. They nabbed the protester Mykhailo Havryliuk, a member of the fourth *sotnya*, on Hrushevskoho Street. They beat him, forced him to strip naked in the snow, and then stand there posing with a Cossack weapon for photos while they humiliated him. Bruises were visible all over his body. The riot police were so confident they'd face no punishment that their own captain released footage of the incident the next day.

The European Union's response to blood being spilled on Hrushevskoho Street was tepid at best. Afraid that stepping up support for the Maidan would anger Moscow, EU leaders and officials in Brussels took no tangible action to punish Yanukovych and his brutal regime, but released a series of statements expressing "deep concern." At the same time, the Obama administration in Washington was growing frustrated over the EU's lack of action and was determined to take a much more active role in Kyiv. It was also annoyed by the conflicting messaging among the political leadership on the Maidan, which failed to devise a coherent plan of action. All of this came out in a phone call that was leaked online in early February.

An audio recording of the intercepted call, between the US Assistant Secretary of State for Europe Victoria Nuland and the US Ambassador to Ukraine Geoffrey Pyatt was uploaded to an obscure YouTube channel on 4 February. But it went unnoticed until a source of mine connected to Yanukovych's security service and likely moonlighting for the Russian Federal Security Service, the FSB, tipped me off. When I opened the YouTube page to listen, I noticed that it had been viewed just three times. I pressed play and immediately recognized the voices of Nuland and Pyatt, whom I'd been in contact with previously. On the call, the two officials discussed how they believed the stand-off between Yanukovych's government and the protesters should end. And they made clear who their favorites were among the Maidan political leadership. "Yats," as Nuland referred to Arsenyi Yatsenyuk, was seen as the Washington choice to lead a new government, while "Klitsch" (Vitali Klitschko) just didn't have the political chops for the job and Oleh Tyahnybok was a "problem." Nuland also expressed Washington's frustration at the EU's handling of the crisis in three explosive words: "Fuck the EU."

I called the US Embassy for comment after I heard that and caught the press secretary completely off guard. "Um, Chris, I'm going to need to call you back." I briefed my editors at the *Kyiv Post* and we decided to give the embassy an hour to respond before we published a story on it. They didn't call back, so I hit publish. The story blew up.

By mid-February the mood on the Maidan had grown more serious and somber. People were exhausted and I could understand why. After two and a half months little progress had been made in getting the Yanukovych government to back down and accept any of the Maidan's demands. Attitudes were hardening – on both sides of the barricades. I noticed protesters growing increasingly militant as the government's troops took tougher and tougher measures against them. Maidan leaders at a mass rally called for a nationwide expansion of the *samooborona* to help protect the satellite Maidan demonstrations that had turned out in several cities, while Dmytro Yarosh of Right Sector said his group was preparing for "offensive" actions. "It's true that Maidan is radicalizing, but the reason is that the authorities aren't carrying out our demands," the parliamentarian Andriy Parubiy told me in an interview in his office inside the Trade Unions Building. "Every day of delay means a more and more dangerous atmosphere on Maidan."

As for the government, it was bringing in more troops and thugs to back its special riot forces. It formed an unofficial "defense" force of its own that it called Ukrainian Front. Heading it was a man named Evgeny Zhilin, who was staunchly anti-Maidan. He ran a group in Kharkiv called Oplot, which was named for a type of tank produced at the local factory where his parents worked. In an interview with Hromadske TV he said he was "preparing my people for a possible war."

It was a worrying thing to say and I had a bad feeling that things would soon turn much worse. But I was tired, too, from filing multiple news reports and dispatches daily and sleeping very little. So on 17 February, after filing a report on the clean-up of the Kyiv City State Administration building following the departure of the revolutionaries who had occupied it, I stepped away to mark my 30th birthday with a dinner among friends. I went to a speakeasy-style cocktail bar and had several Old Fashioneds. I drank late into the night and then went to bed without setting my alarm. My plan was to sleep long and hard into the next day.

But my phone rang just after 6 a.m. on 18 February. I ignored the first call but it rang again. And then again before I finally picked it up. A protester I'd interviewed earlier that week was on the other line. He said the Maidan was marching up Institutska Street toward the parliament building, where they would demand the passage of a series of laws promising constitutional change, early elections, and amnesty for the protesters so they couldn't be charged with serious offenses for taking part in the uprising.

It was Kyiv's first sunny day in a month and the blue sky was visible. I arrived on the Maidan just as hundreds of protesters were heading up the street. Many of them were armed with sticks, clubs, and stones. There were dozens from Right Sector, Tryzub, Svoboda, and other radical groups. They stopped at the corner of Shovkovychna Street, which police had blocked off with large trucks. The Verkhovna Rada was visible 200 feet away. I saw Pavel Podufalov, a *Kyiv Post* photographer, at the front of the group snapping photos. He climbed onto one of the trucks to get a view over the police lines when a protester smashed the cab window, reached inside, and removed the parking brake. Suddenly the truck lurched and protesters began pushing it back, creating an opening for many of them to sneak through. They clashed with police on the other side and then all hell broke loose.

Tear gas and smoke grenades came flying over the barriers toward the crowd. A group of people started crowbarring up cobblestones and passing them up a 100-foot human chain to the people at the front, who then hurled them at the police. The police sent troops to the rooftop of a nearby building. I watched them scurry over the slippery shingles in pairs, taking positions near the edge. Then they opened fire. At first they fired rubber bullets but then it became clear they had switched to some sort of metal pellet. A group of protesters found a way to the rooftop and chased them. But the police set themselves up elsewhere and continued shooting.

One of the projectiles struck the face of a 19-year-old man as I spoke to him. His head jolted backward as he reached for his eyes. He stumbled and then collapsed to his knees. Screaming in pain, he looked up and threw his hands in the air. They were covered in blood and I saw that his right eye had been dislodged and was hanging by a thin tendril from its socket. Blood gushed from the wound as I tried to help him to a bench. Others around me shouted for medics and two came running over and took him away in an ambulance.

Bullets were flying everywhere so I took cover in the entrance of the Glavcom news office, which was slightly below street level and provided a view of the scene with a little cover. I filmed the police as they advanced slowly down the street toward me and the protesters, firing more rubber bullets and tossing smoke canisters. One of them exploded and bounced into the doorway, temporarily blinding me and a group of medics. When the smoke cleared, I saw that the protesters had rushed forward to attack with Molotov cocktails and the police were moving backward. I filmed a short video of the moment and posted it to YouTube. The back-and-forth continued for more than an hour until the police got the upper hand. Phalanxes of Berkut in their riot gear and wielding clubs chased the protesters down Instytutska Street toward the Maidan. A few protesters tried to fight back with baseball bats but had to turn and run. There were dozens of bloodied faces and broken limbs. Medics bandaged people in the streets. Those with serious wounds were carried away by medics, who said the police had wrapped their grenades with nails and rocks to inflict greater damage on the protesters. The Berkut used large trucks to move some of the outer barricades, taking positions at the footbridge over Instytutska Street and at the October Palace performing arts center, which provided them with prime shooting positions. "You are fighting against your brothers and sisters!" someone shouted into a megaphone from the Maidan. The Berkut drowned out the crowd by banging their clubs on their metal shields. A group of women holding religious icons dropped to their knees and began praying aloud. The Berkut tossed Molotov cocktails on the tent camp, torching several tents. The protesters set tires on fire, creating a ring of fire and smoke that stretched hundreds of feet into the sky. The national anthem blared from the stage speakers as the Maidan burned. It was hellish, with gunshots and explosions every few minutes. There was a moment when people didn't speak but just stared in the fiery darkness. The police used green lasers and water cannons. And for the first time, I saw the lifeless bodies of people who had been gunned down.

It all happened so quickly that I got lost in the fracas and found myself trapped behind the police lines. With my hands in the air, I walked cautiously toward a group of Berkut troops, identifying myself as press. Surprisingly, they didn't attack me but said to follow them down the hill. We stopped at the Hotel Ukraine where they set up behind a concrete wall. Pointing toward the Maidan encampment, they claimed the violence had been started by the "fascists" and "extremists" there. I pushed back, saying that I didn't believe that. I said that most people I knew were peaceful and apolitical. One of the troops cursed at me. "Fuck off, American. Your Obama is financing them." He ripped my gas mask from my hands and said he was going to bash more skulls just for me. "I love it," he said. The first man, who identified himself as a captain, showed me three or four of his riot troops' shields, which appeared to have bullet holes in them. "Look," he said, "they're shooting at us, too." I wondered if Right Sector had brought their guns out but I hadn't actually seen guns used on the Maidan side yet. The Berkut, on the other hand, were carrying AK-47 assault rifles. They showed them to me and I snapped a photograph of them. As we spoke, a group of masked, elite-looking troops carrying sniper rifles approached. The Berkut sent me away and I heard the staccato crack of the assault rifles punctuated by what I believe was sniper fire. As dusk descended on the square and temperatures fell below freezing, the protesters there fed a ring of fire around the camp to fend off the police, who brought water cannons and hosed them.

At least 25 people were killed, including seven police officers. Most died by gunshot wounds but some were beaten to death. One was beaten and then doused with the water cannon. He died the next day after suffering hypothermia and a heart attack. The government's *titushki* also kidnapped some of the protesters. One man who was taken died from 20 knife stabs, medics would later determine. Another had his throat slit. His body was dumped in a building off the Maidan and found a week later. Another body turned up with signs of torture on Trukhanov Island across the river.

I went back to my apartment for just a couple of hours to change, eat, warm up, and take a power nap, then I returned to the Maidan to find the Trade Unions Building in flames. The Berkut had snuck into its upper floors from an adjacent building and attacked the Maidan headquarters, somehow setting it alight. Fire and smoke spewed from the windows of its upper floors as leaders of the protest called on demonstrators from the stage to help evacuate people inside and ready tarps and blankets for people who needed to leap to safety. The building burned through the night and into the next morning. Revolutionaries wandered the square in a daze, covered in black soot. The scene on the Maidan looked apocalyptic.

President Yanukovych agreed to meet with the leaders of the protest and a temporary truce was called, but everyone knew it was tenuous and wouldn't hold. Arseniy Yatsenyuk, one of the political opposition leaders, told the Channel 5 TV channel that the talks "ended with nothing."

Around 8 a.m. the next morning, 20 February, violence erupted again. I was there and I had no idea how it began or why, but one protester said the police started the fight when they threw an explosive at protesters, injuring several of them. And once it did, it couldn't be stopped. Gunshots rang out and their cracks reverberated across the Maidan. I could hear them and see the flash of the muzzles from the security forces' rifles. But there was also shooting from buildings around the Maidan that were controlled by the protesters. I walked across to the west side of the square to file a short news update using the McDonald's wi-fi and a bullet ricocheted off the bricks just a few feet above my head. I ducked and rounded the corner for cover.

Back at the front of the clashes, I followed hundreds of protesters up Instytutska Street as they slowly and methodically forced the Berkut and other police from their positions back up the hill beyond the October Palace, where a fire had broken out. A police bus also went up in flames. Protesters held up wooden shields in a futile attempt to protect themselves from snipers' bullets and rounds of assault rifle fire. I ducked behind trees for cover and tried to keep myself from being targeted. I stood for a moment beside an older man with a thick mustache and an orange hard hat. He was armed with the leg of a dining table. While we were being shot at, I asked what he was going to do with it. "I'm going to go up there and beat some sense into them," he answered, totally serious.

My gaze turned back toward the street, where a man was shouting in the direction of the square and waving his arms for people to follow him.

Then I heard a crack and saw a puff of red mist rise from his back. He was just a few feet from me. His legs gave out and he collapsed. The man beside me grabbed my arm and we ran to the street. He took the man's arms as I grabbed his legs and we shuffled down the hill. Other men ran over to help and we put the injured man on a stretcher. I followed as they rushed to a medical station behind the stage and noticed that the man was bleeding profusely and leaving a trail of blood. When I saw his arm fall lifelessly off the side of the stretcher, I knew he was gone. They tried to resuscitate him, but it was no use. When they peeled off his coat, I saw that he was wearing an armor-plated vest. It just wasn't thick enough. There were two bullet holes straight through it. I helped a group of men carry him to Khreshchatyk Street where they placed him on a blanket. A priest prayed over the body, offering what small comfort he could. A woman wept. A man, shaking his clenched fists in the air, shouted: "They are killing our heroes!" Someone laid a Ukrainian flag over the top of the dead man and I noticed how bright it seemed compared to his face, which was completely devoid of color. The person then placed a sign above his head with a warning for the president: "Yanukovych, you're next.". Within minutes, more bodies were brought over. And they continued to pile up as snipers picked off the protesters one by one. "It's like a safari for them," a man said.

Central Kyiv had become a war zone. Before 11 a.m. I had counted at least 35 corpses at four locations: Khreshchatyk Street, the Kozatskiy Hotel, the central Post Office, and Hotel Ukraine. The lobby of the latter had been transformed into a trauma center, with doctors in blood-stained white coats operating on severely wounded people right in the open. A makeshift morgue was arranged nearby and there were 12 bodies there. I asked Olha Bohomolets, the lead doctor on site, what she was seeing. Wiping the sweat from her forehead, she told me that the victims were shot with high-precision rifles and powerful ammunition. All had been shot in the head, neck, heart or lungs. Most were not wearing armored vests.

The bells of St Michael's Monastery rang out, echoing throughout the square, where thousands of protesters, their faces stained black, gave and obeyed orders to make Molotov cocktails and crush more paving stones for a human chain to pass them to the men fighting up front. Following each burst of gunfire, protesters could be seen toppling over. Some writhed and screeched in pain, grasping at the place on their bodies in which a bullet had entered. Smoke rose from the thigh of one man who was shot.

By nightfall, the death count had skyrocketed. Oleh Musiy, the head doctor on the Maidan, said that at least 67 people had been confirmed killed. In all, more than 100 protesters would die between 18 and 20 February. They would be remembered as the *Nebesna Sotnya*, the Heavenly Hundred.

Three visiting EU foreign ministers – Poland's Radosław Sikorski, France's Laurent Fabius, and Germany's Frank-Walter Steinmeier – said that they would stay in Kyiv for "a night of difficult negotiations" between Yanukovych and Klitschko, Yatsenyuk and Tyahnybok. In the meantime, at around 4 a.m., I went on Anderson Cooper 360° with CNN's correspondent in Kyiv, Nick Paton Walsh, to discuss the events of the past three days. I was exhausted and nervous. Nick cracked open a bottle of whiskey and we drank half of it before we went on air.

After six hours, the EU negotiators emerged to say that a deal had been struck. Its key components were: the restoration of Ukraine's constitution as it was between 2004 and 2010; constitutional reform before September 2014; early presidential elections no later than December 2014; new electoral laws; an investigation into the deadly violence; a veto on imposing a state of emergency; amnesty for arrested protesters; the surrender of occupied public buildings; and the forfeiture of illegal weapons.

The next evening, the three political opposition leaders walked out on the Maidan stage to address the crowd. Klitschko began to speak about the "small victory" they had secured, but the crowd shouted over him, "Convict out! Convict out!" There was sadness and fury in their eyes. They didn't want promises that could be broken and a delay in action. They wanted their main demand to be met now: Yanukovych had to go.

As the crowd grew louder, a group of men in camouflage rushed onto the stage. Volodymyr Parasiuk, an unassuming, floppy-haired young man from Lviv, snatched the microphone from Klitschko's thick hands. His voice cracked as he began to speak. "Here's what I want to say," he began. "Yanukovych will not be the president for another year! Tomorrow by 10 a.m., he must resign! My compatriot was shot down! He had a wife and baby! And our leaders shake hands with these murderers! Shame on them! I speak to you on behalf of my entire *sotnya* that my father also joined. If tomorrow by 10 a.m. you do not make a statement about Yanukovych's resignation, I swear we will go on an armed offensive!"

He then turned and handed the microphone back to Klitschko, who stood there, his brows furrowed, completely speechless. It was the greatest mic drop I had ever seen. The crowd roared. The Maidan rejected the terms.

Under the cover of darkness, early on 22 February 2014, Yanukovych hastily fled Mezhyhirya, his 343-acre palatial estate outside of Kyiv, allegedly taking billions of dollars in cash, artwork, and furniture, and other odds and ends. CCTV footage caught his security team loading what they could into trucks and then Yanukovych himself dragging two rolling suitcases across the helipad and onto a helicopter.

Word quickly spread on the Maidan that he was gone and the protesters rushed to the compound. There, they climbed the walls and opened the gates to see just what the president was doing with the money they say he had stolen from their country. The absurdly huge wood cabin-style mansion called "Honka," the faux ancient ruins constructed beside it, and the replica of a Spanish galleon docked in the bay drew much attention. But they also discovered a garage with dozens of collector cars, a zoo of exotic animals, greenhouses filled with banana trees, golden-headed monogrammed golf clubs, a boat hangar, and much, much more. Among the many other ridiculous extravagances was a nude portrait of Yanukovych that he had commissioned and a loaf of bread carved from gold. Nobody looted the place. Instead they immediately appointed someone to oversee the security of the property and a group of people who would preserve it as a Museum of Corruption for all to visit.

Perhaps the most important discovery came when a group of journalists found thousands of documents floating near a dock that jutted from the waterfront residence into the Kyiv Sea. They revealed evidence of unbelievable levels of corruption and an absurd spending habit: $2.3 million for dining-room decorations; $800 for fish food; nearly $1 million for a lawn watering system; $17,000 for tablecloths; $5.8 million to a group that monitored his critics. And there was a blacklist comprised of those who Yanukovych perceived to be his enemies, which included the name, photograph, and license plate number of Tetyana Chornovol, the journalist and activist who was chased down in her car and beaten by several men before being abandoned in a ditch in December, which was reported in the *Kyiv Post* on 25 December 2013. In all, nearly 200 folders filled with thousands of invoices, contracts, insurance policies, cash payment orders and other documents were recovered from the murky depths. The edges of some had been scorched, suggesting that before fleeing Yanukovych's people had tried to burn the documents before giving up and tossing them into the sea.

As protesters played golf on his private course and fed his ostriches, lawmakers in the Verkhovna Rada freed Tymoshenko, who came to the Maidan stage straight from jail in a wheelchair with her hair done up in her signature golden braids. "I am so proud of you!" she told the crowd. "I won't waste a minute making sure you are happy on your own land. Glory to Ukraine!" Few people applauded. Most booed her. Her message came off as patronizing and insincere. Oleh, an acquaintance who was standing beside me during her speech, rolled his eyes. "She's finished," he said. "The Maidan wants new blood."

Parliamentary deputies also declared Yanukovych unfit to rule and ousted him from office. A new government was formed and it issued a warrant for the former leader's arrest. He was now wanted for "mass murder." The government officially deemed him a wanted fugitive.

Ashes and Dust

Valentyn Nalyvaichenko stood amid the shattered glass, ash, and scattered papers, and cursed the traitors who had fled with a mountain of documents containing many of Ukraine's state secrets. It was 21 February 2014, and he and other Ukrainian spies woke to discover that the country's main domestic intelligence agency had been ransacked and torched by Yanukovych loyalists who had access to the building and its secured rooms and knew what they were looking for. The previous night, as the president prepared to flee to Russia with the help of Russian special forces, Yanukovych had apparently ordered his operatives to steal a trove of state secrets from the SBU, Ukraine's security service, according to Nalyvaichenko. During their raid, the thieves also stole data on more than 22,000 officers and informants, and files documenting decades of cooperation between the domestic intelligence agency and its Russian counterpart, the Federal Security Service, or FSB. What the burglars weren't able to carry in their haste to escape, they burned and destroyed. In the ruins the next morning, Ukrainian spies still loyal to the country found scorched paperwork and empty folders strewn about the floors.

"Every hard drive and flash drive was destroyed – smashed with hammers," a Ukrainian intelligence official told me. By the time he and his colleagues had arrived, "it was all ash and dust."

For a country in the shadow of Russia and preparing to embark on an uncertain path toward democracy, the break-in was devastating. As Nalyvaichenko put it, the thieves took "everything that forms a basis for a professional intelligence service."

Just days after the break-in, the Yanukovych-appointed head of the SBU, Oleksandr Yakymenko, also surfaced in Russia, announcing his defection along with four other top Ukrainian spies and dozens of subordinates loyal to Moscow.

In the following weeks and months, the security service would be thrown into turmoil as the agents' new allegiances played out. "We have no idea who we can trust right now," said a top SBU spy, still loyal to the government in Kyiv.

When Nalyvaichenko became the SBU's new chief on 24 February, he feared that he had inherited a spy agency filled with traitors. According to him, as many as one in five SBU agents had either worked for the Soviet KGB or studied at its training academy. How many of them saw their loyalty as being to Moscow rather than to Kyiv? And what were they capable of? And how would Russia use them?

6

"Little Green Men"

Simferopol, March 2014

The blood on the Maidan had barely dried and Ukraine's revolutionaries were still in a state of joyful shock over Yanukovych abandoning power, when Putin assembled his top security and military officials in Moscow for an all-night meeting on 22–23 February to plot out one of the most audacious power grabs of the twenty-first century. The Maidan's victory and the overthrow of Yanukovych had infuriated the Russian president, who saw a window of opportunity in the chaotic aftermath of Ukraine's revolution, as Kyiv scrambled to cobble together a new government. Now, inside the Kremlin, the Russian president and his top military brass would hammer out the details of a brazen operation that would upend the global order: Putin would use special forces to secretly extract Yanukovych from Crimea and deliver him to Russia while also stealthily invading Ukraine's Black Sea peninsula with the use of military forces already on the ground there and special forces that would sneak in and foment an anti-Kyiv uprising. He had always believed that Nikita Khrushchev's transfer of Crimea from Russian control to Ukrainian control in 1954 was an historical wrong that needed to be righted. And he recognized Crimea's strategic importance to Moscow. The port city of Sevastopol, after all, was the base of Russia's Black Sea Fleet, thanks to a controversial deal brokered by Yanukovych and then-president Dmitry Medvedev in 2010 known as the Kharkiv Pact. Besides allowing Russian warships to be moored in the port city, it permitted Moscow to station a maximum number of 25,000 troops at the base through 2042. Under a new, pro-Western government in Kyiv, who knew if the agreement would hold?

"When we parted, I told everybody: We have to start working on bringing Crimea back into Russia," Putin would admit a year later in a propaganda film about the covert operation, recalling the meeting that lasted until 7 a.m. on 23 February. But until then, he'd continued to lie about putting Russian boots on the ground in Crimea.

Later that same day, Maidan supporters, including a few thousand Crimean Tatars, rallied outside the parliament in Simferopol (as a de jure autonomous republic of Ukraine, Crimea had its own government structure) to demand that it recognize the new pro-democracy authorities in Kyiv. They chanted slogans from the Maidan and proclaimed that "Crimea is not Russia!" A counter-demonstration composed of several hundred pro-Russian locals suspicious of the revolution in the Ukrainian capital gathered nearby, waving Russian tricolors. The two sides were separated by police, but the security line was broken and scuffles broke out.

Tensions escalated over the next several days. Then just before sunrise at 5 a.m. on 27 February, dozens of masked men armed with Kalashnikovs stormed the Soviet-era building and encountered no resistance from the Ukrainian police officers on guard inside. In a matter of minutes, the building was occupied. By sunrise, the Russian tricolor had replaced the Ukrainian flag atop the building. Under orders from a shadowy and eccentric commander named Igor Girkin, the gunmen rounded up local lawmakers and forced them to call an extraordinary session in which they voted in a new local prime minister – Sergei Aksyonov, the leader of the unpopular pro-Moscow Russian Unity party. There were rumors of him being connected to local organized crime, allegations he denied. He had founded a political party that was deeply unpopular and failed to win any office in local elections, garnering just 4 per cent of the votes. But now, thanks to Moscow, he was the top official in Crimea. Girkin's guys also forced a vote for a hasty referendum on the separation of Crimea from Ukraine on 25 May. Later it would be bumped up to 30 March and then finally 16 March. The enigmatic Girkin, a former officer within the FSB and veteran of post-Soviet separatist conflicts, better known by his *nom de guerre* Igor Strelkov, meaning "shooter," would admit more than a year later on Russian television, and well after details of his life came to light, that most of the peninsula's government officials were against the move.

"I did not see any support from the [Crimean] authorities in Simferopol where I was," he confessed. "It was militants who collected deputies and forced them to vote. Yes, I was one of the commanders of those militants."

121

At the same time, another mysterious invasion force was calmly and methodically fanning out across Ukraine's Crimean peninsula. These were not scrappy-looking fighters like Girkin's forces; they were soldiers armed with modern, high-powered Russian rifles, driving state-of-the art armored vehicles, and donning neatly pressed and matching green military uniforms without insignia. They seemed to materialize out of nowhere. Russian media referred to them euphemistically as *vezhlivye lyudi*, meaning "polite people," due to the good behavior they demonstrated while calmly and methodically surrounding key military sites and government buildings on the peninsula over the course of a few days without firing a shot. The troops lifted their balaclavas and lowered their heads to receive kisses on their cheeks from babushkas, showed off their weapons and kit to fascinated young boys, and posed for photographs cradling cats in their arms. Many elderly locals nostalgic for Soviet times welcomed them with open arms. The bizarrely mute force refused to say anything about where they had come from, leading Kyiv to mockingly dub them "little green men." But everyone knew exactly who they were, even if they weren't talking about it openly: members of Russia's Black Sea Fleet. Fears by some in Kyiv who opposed the Kharkiv Pact had come true: the fleet was a Trojan horse that would move against Ukraine. But now the original 25,000 troops attached to it had swelled to a force of many thousand more, which included special forces units and unofficial military forces commanded by Girkin and other actors.

The "little green men" also closed road access from mainland Ukraine. For at least a day they managed to disrupt mobile communications and internet connections, and to shut down Simferopol International Airport.

The unmarked Russian troops were joined by thousands of much less disciplined pro-Moscow Crimean militiamen, Cossacks, and Berkut officers who abandoned their posts. They absurdly called themselves *samooborona* forces. On their coats, they wore black-and-orange St George ribbons – a symbol of the Soviets' victory over Nazi Germany that now signaled loyalty to Moscow – and carried various makeshift weapons. Some got their hands on Kalashnikov rifles. It was clear to most people that the Kremlin had assembled them to look something like the self-defense units that had organically materialized on the Maidan. They were caricatures but having them there provided the Kremlin plausible deniability (at least in Putin's mind) that its regular troops were up to something and gave the stealth invasion at least a small – if not completely absurd and unbelievable – semblance of a grassroots uprising. These toughs were used to crush any dissent. They attacked peaceful demonstrations. And they took over media offices, including main radio and television stations, dragging journalists out by their necks and sticking guns to their heads. TVs now aired Russian state-sponsored propaganda filled with falsehoods about the Maidan and the fledgling government in Kyiv, instead of Ukrainian television.

In Kyiv, Oleksandr Turchynov, a former director of Ukraine's security service, the SBU, and a prominent Maidan figure who had been elected as speaker of the Verkhovna Rada, as well as acting president and acting prime minister to fill the void after Yanukovych's departure, denounced Putin's moves in Crimea as military aggression and accused him of "provoking a conflict." "They're playing the Abkhazia scenario," Turchynov said of the Russians during a briefing inside the parliament building in Kyiv, referring to the 2008 invasion of Georgia that had led to the two breakaway regions of Abkhazia and South Ossetia.

In a live briefing from the White House pressroom, President Obama weighed in, warning Russia that there would be "costs" to military intervention. The Ukraine leadership wanted military help but they knew they'd get little more than reassuring words and some sanctions against Russia.

Meanwhile in Moscow, Putin shrugged off the threats and continued to deny that the soldiers on the ground were Russian. But he cited the deteriorating situation and the phantom threat of far-right "extremists" from Kyiv, who he claimed had seized power through a "coup d'état," as justification for asking Russia's State Duma to vote to allow him to send troops to Crimea. The pretext was that they would be "peacekeepers" working to protect ethnic Russians, who accounted for nearly 60 per cent of the peninsula's population. Russian lawmakers rubber-stamped a decree approving the option of sending military forces onto the territory of Ukraine. And within days, Putin's military was officially there.

This is the situation I found when my plane touched down in Simferopol, the Crimean capital, on 1 March 2014. The flight's only passengers were international journalists. Until we were on the tarmac many of us thought our plane might be forced to turn back to Kyiv. Some wondered aloud whether the Russians would be waiting to detain us when we disembarked. One veteran correspondent, who had worked in Iraq and Afghanistan as well as Russia's invasion of Georgia, suggested we write the mobile numbers of our emergency contacts on our forearms in case we were detained and our phones were taken away.

That's when I first thought about what I was getting into. I had only just covered my first revolution. Was I now dropping into my first armed conflict? *What the fuck am I doing?* I thought to myself. The *Kyiv Post* had no security resources. We operated on a shoestring budget. And my freelance contracts didn't include healthcare or risk insurance, let alone anything about aiding my release from captivity or extraction from dangerous situations.

"Ever covered a war?" the veteran correspondent inquired. He must have seen the look on my face at that moment as we began our descent and I watched the peninsula grow nearer in the window.

"Is this going to be a war?" I asked.

"Looks like it. The Russian army's on the ground."

"No, never covered a war," I said.

"You'll do fine," he told me. "Just act like you know what you're doing. Fake it till you make it."

To our surprise, the airport was still functioning almost as normal. Although it was now under the control of dozens of armed "little green men," who studied all of us as we took our things from the baggage claim and tramped outside.

I had no problem catching a cab. Drivers stalked us on the street, eager to overcharge Western foreigners with expense accounts. Driving through central Simferopol, I noticed there weren't many checkpoints yet. I'd seen photos and videos of the land border farther north where the militiamen and Berkut were stopping and interrogating people. Locals were out and about, sipping coffee, pushing kids in strollers. I checked in at a centrally located hotel with several other foreign correspondents. The staff greeted me in Russian with straight, stern faces and said I was eligible for an upgrade to a *lux* suite for the same price as the standard room I had reserved. I didn't know what I had done to deserve it but I was happy to take the bigger room. It all seemed weirdly normal. And it didn't look all that different to my previous visits, except for the chilled gunmen on the street.

I had been to Crimea twice before this. The first time was in the summer of 2010, when I visited Peace Corps friends in Armiansk, a drab city of trains and buses and heavy trucks that served as the northern gateway to the peninsula from mainland Ukraine. We then took a bus two hours southwest to the coastal city of Yevpatoria, where we spent the day on the beach, cooking *shashlik*, drinking cheap beer, and swimming in the Black Sea. The next time was the following summer, when I took Bri to Sevastopol. We were hosted in an AirBnB apartment in a high-rise building by a lovely young woman named Anna, who prepared lunch for us and hand-sketched a map of all the places we should visit, along with the bus routes we needed to take to get to them. We walked around the Port of Sevastopol and saw the Russian and Ukrainian navy ships moored there. We visited the ancient ruins of Khersones, where it is said that Vladimir the Great of Kyivan Rus had been baptized in 988 during his conversion to Christianity. Putin would later describe the area as Russia's spiritual ground and liken it to the Temple Mount in Israel, neither of which were entirely accurate but would help him to justify his seizure of the peninsula. We went to nearby Balaclava, a bayside city with ruins of a Genoese fortress situated high on a clifftop overlooking the Black Sea. Nearby was the site of a key battle during the Crimean War, and I imagined the British cavalry and its charge of the Light Brigade into what Tennyson would later dub "the valley of death" in a poem about the defeat. In Soviet times, when Balaclava was a closed city, its bay housed Russia's nuclear submarines in a cave carved deep into the hillside. We rented a boat and took it out into the sea, where we watched dolphins leap and play and swam with jellyfish. We went to Yalta to see Tsar Nicholas II's summer retreat, Livadia Palace, which would later serve as the location for the 1945 Yalta Conference between the Big Three – Roosevelt, Churchill, and Stalin – when they sliced up Europe into spheres of influence after the Second World War. We also met up with our friends Igor and Ira and watched the sun set over the water, which was the deepest and clearest blue that I had ever seen.

Crimea felt wild and gritty. I loved the mountains and seaside and the salty heat. It didn't look or feel like any part of Ukraine that I had been to. If you squinted, Alupka, Alushta, and Yalta, looked like cities on the Mediterranean, improbably built into rocky hillsides. The peninsula had long been a place of leisure for people from all over Eastern Europe. Russian and Ukrainian artists and authors had penned stories on its shores in imperial times. In the Soviet days, with its dozens of sanatoriums, Crimea was a favored summer retreat of the Moscow and Kyiv elite. It still was, with Yanukovych and other political leaders building elaborate mansions on pilfered land overlooking the coast.

Everyone spoke Russian here. I never heard Ukrainian. But nobody outwardly demonstrated a loathing for Ukrainian or a desire to part with Ukraine and join Russia. If they thought about splitting off or spoke about this, it was only a passing remark. Crimeans did, however, have their complaints, most of which came down to what was an inconvenient truth: Kyiv didn't think much about folks on the peninsula. The Ukrainian capital did its thing and Crimeans did theirs. Many Crimeans harbored resentment toward Kyiv because of this, and because many believed they paid a lot to the state without getting much in return. Many people on the peninsula certainly viewed Russia favorably and seemed to align more closely with it geopolitically. Polls showed a plurality of Crimeans were skeptical of the Maidan and of closer ties with the EU, and supported the prospect of joining Russia's alternative Customs Union, which included other former Soviet republics. Some people clearly had an emotional or nostalgic attachment to Russia. I didn't get the sense that a majority were itching to live under Moscow's rule, although some posited that they stood to get larger pensions, earn more money, and live more comfortably if that were to happen.

Standoff

Privolnoye infantry base and Belbek air base, Crimea, early March 2014
The morning after I arrived in Simferopol, I drove to a Ukrainian military base in the town of Privolnoye, about 20 miles away. I had heard the previous night that dozens of forest-green Ural military trucks, along with a handful of jeeps and armored personnel carriers, had brought hundreds of soldiers to the base. They'd set up tank traps on the roads and positioned themselves around the base in groups of three to five. At the entrance to the base, Ukrainian commanders trembled as they listened through an iron gate adorned with the country's coat of arms to Russian commanders issuing an ultimatum: surrender your weapons and pledge allegiance to Russia, or else we'll attack.

Oddly, the Russians didn't care at all that I was there, standing right at the gate, as they delivered the warning. Nearby, drunken, rag-tag local militiamen supporting the Russian troops bellowed like hype men as the threat was uttered. Volodymyr, one of the men in the group, walked up to me. He said he believed the new government in Kyiv had forced the hand of the Kremlin and Putin by ousting Yanukovych. With him gone,

Volodymyr claimed, and a new government that favored "Banderites" from the western part of the country, ethnic Russians in Crimea were going to be oppressed.

"The Maidan brought war here," he said. Nothing he said was true, but he did seem to believe it all. He also said he'd like Crimea to be a part of Russia. "This isn't occupation," he said, gesturing to the Russian troops, "this is a gift."

Tempers at the base flared as Volodymyr's group argued with journalists and blamed us for spreading lies and working for the CIA. Father Ivan, a Ukrainian Orthodox priest who had lived in Crimea for 17 years but was originally from Kyiv, tried to intervene. But Volodymyr and other men got in his face and shouted him down.

"Provocateur! Spy!" they yelled, angry that Father Ivan was speaking in Ukrainian.

"When people come and tell you how to live your own life, this is very bad. It is very hard now to keep peace," Father Ivan told me with a heavy sigh. "I pray that in a week this situation will de-escalate."

As he worked to keep the emboldened crowd calm and fresh, Russian troops replaced those who had stood guard throughout the night, and life went on as usual in the typically sleepy valley town. Children laughed and played in the yards of nearby apartment complexes, old men ate sunflower seeds and argued on benches, buses ran as usual, and stores stayed open for business. Many of their customers were the wives of Ukrainian troops stuck inside the military base. For weeks they were unable to leave and had gone without decent meals. The women would buy food in the day and then deliver the provisions to their husbands under the cover of night, hurling it over the concrete walls in tied-up plastic grocery bags.

But just because the Ukrainians refused to hand over control of their bases didn't mean they were opposed to Russia's takeover. One woman I met outside the base, Yulia, said that her husband was among the dozens stuck inside. She said they both aligned more closely politically and ideologically with Russia, but they had decided together that her husband would protect the base, as he had promised to do so upon joining the Ukrainian military. After all, she said, he was a man of honor.

"It's this new government in Kyiv making Russia and Ukraine fight," Yulia claimed. "These are brother nations. They shouldn't fight. But this is what it has come to."

Vera Kanayeva, a resident of Privolnoye since 1953, agreed. "Turchynov and Yatsenyuk are to blame for starting a war in the country," she told me, adding that Putin was "right" to send troops to Ukraine. "I am a Russian stuck in Ukrainian Crimea," she said. "But Putin will free me and the others."

Similar confusion played out at most military bases across the Crimea, and aboard Ukrainian naval vessels. Russian forces were using psychological pressure to wear the Ukrainians down and get them to surrender or defect. I watched as sailors aboard the Ukrainian warship *Slavutych* scurried frantically atop its deck with automatic weapons in hand, as a warship from Russia's Black Sea Fleet idled ominously some 200 meters in front of it, blaring the ultimatum from its on-board speakers. In preparation to defend themselves, Ukrainian sailors spread mattresses across the ship's rails and readied water hoses on the deck.

"Attention! You must surrender your weapons and pledge your allegiance to the Crimean people," I heard a deep Russian voice bellow from a loudspeaker. "Stand down and hand over the ship peacefully, or else prepare to be attacked!"

Nearby, the commander of the Black Sea Fleet, Vice-Admiral Aleksandr Vitko, was issuing the same warning to Captain Maksym Emelyanenko and his sailors aboard the Ukrainian Navy corvette *Ternopil*. Emelyanenko, an ethnic Russian with a Ukrainian surname, refused to surrender his vessel, telling Vitko, "*Russkiye ne sdayutsa!*" ("Russians don't surrender!"), a Red Army battle cry from the Second World War. Emelyanenko made it clear that he had sworn his allegiance to the Ukrainian state and he would not betray it. The clapback caught the Russian vice-admiral by surprise.

The sailors put on incredible displays of loyalty to Ukraine, holding out for days. But disoriented and without orders from Kyiv, they were finally forced to stand down.

There was one place where the stand-off between Russian and Ukrainian forces was especially intense: Belbek.

It was just before dawn on 4 March when Colonel Yuli Mamchur, base commander of Ukraine's 204th Tactical Aviation Brigade at Belbek, gathered his men. Enough was enough. For five days they had been under siege by unmarked Russian forces. The day before, the Russians had given Mamchur and his men an ultimatum similar to those delivered to troops in Privolnoye and elsewhere: surrender your weapons and pledge allegiance to Russia, or else face an assault by 5 a.m. Many of Mamchur's airborne troops – some of them boys, really – defected under the pressure. The rest of them stirred in the barracks throughout the night. Unable to sleep, they chain-smoked cigarettes and paced around bonfires until the sun began to peek over the horizon. When 5 a.m. came and went with no attack, Mamchur sensed a bluff. It was confirmed shortly after when a mysterious lieutenant colonel from the special forces who had them surrounded called in. He identified himself only as Dima and said the deadline had changed. The brigade had until 4 p.m. to surrender.

Mamchur wasn't going to let the Russians play mind games with his brigade. He assembled about 100 of them, ordered them to leave their weapons in the barracks, grabbed a Ukrainian flag and the red banner of the storied 62nd Fighter Aviation Regiment of the Soviet Air Force that had served in Belbek during the Second World War and battled the Nazi Luftwaffe over Crimea, and led the group onto the airfield about half a kilometer from the runway. They marched in unison toward four Russian military vehicles and several officers, some of whom fired warning shots in the air in an attempt to stop the Ukrainians from advancing. The Ukrainians halted only when the Russian soldiers aimed their automatic rifles directly at them.

"Stop! Do not come closer! We have orders to shoot! We will shoot to kill!" I heard a Russian soldier shout. I was among a small group of foreign journalists who had been embedded with Mamchur's unit. There, on a grassy bluff overlooking the Black Sea, the Ukrainians remained steadfast, even as camouflaged Russian troops encircled them, taking strategic positions atop small bluffs, behind concrete barricades, and in surrounding shrubs. The Russians trained their sniper rifles and machine guns on the group. Andriy Matchenko, deputy head of logistics, looked at me and raised his eyebrows. Spinning around to emphasize the fact that we were encircled, he appeared both frightened and entertained. I was more the former. The situation could easily have escalated should any of the Russians perceive any Ukrainian move as threatening and pull the trigger.

Mamchur spent the next couple of hours trying to negotiate with a man on the Russian side who would only identify himself as Roman. "We came this morning to demand that we be able to carry out our duties. This man, Roman, will not allow that," Mamchur told our small group of journalists in a huddle. "They say, 'We're not stopping you from working.' But how can we do our work when we are being occupied by invaders?" Roman, he said, also told him he did not have the power to make a decision on the matter. "We must wait now for someone on the Russian side who does, to come and negotiate."

And so the stand-off continued into the afternoon. Several Ukrainian soldiers used the downtime between negotiations to nap on the grass, while others called their wives to let them know they were fine. Several wives had spent the previous night next to the compound gates to "keep up morale," one of them, named Tanya, had told me. "Bunny, I love you. We are fine here," one of the men said into his phone, as his comrades whistled and hollered. Another group played soccer after someone tossed a ball over the fence. One man managed to tie a Ukrainian flag to a fence post, eliciting loud cheers from the soldiers. I began typing up a dispatch on my phone to file whenever this stand-off ended.

Meanwhile, a group of masked Crimean self-defense fighters came from behind Russian lines and positioned themselves in front of an armored vehicle. Two of them stepped forward to meet with Mamchur and tell him it was time to surrender. He did not comply, and so they stormed off.

Colonel Viktor Kukharchenko, the deputy commander of the Belbek base, motioned to Mamchur and our group of journalists that he had a phone call. He pressed the speakerphone button and held it up for everyone to hear. On the other end of the line was a Russian army colonel. He said that Putin was delivering a speech in Moscow. The Russian president, he explained, had reiterated that Russian troops were not occupying Crimea. But he had also ordered his troops to "stand down."

Mamchur grinned. His airmen shouted and slapped him on the back. It was just after 2 p.m. The brigade marched back to their barracks to fight another day. On the way, I asked Mamchur what he thought. "Today we achieved victory. But our Crimea is still a tinderbox."

Stand Down

Undisclosed location near the front line in southern Ukraine, north of Crimea, July 2022

Oleksandr Turchynov, dressed in a green Ukrainian military uniform, rested his rifle against the wall and took a seat at a table inside the bunker. It was a hot summer's day and the mosquitoes were out in full force. The Russians were nearby, too, lobbing mortars toward Ukrainian lines.

"Christopher, it's nice to see you," Turchynov said in a deadpan voice as he removed his cap and wiped the sweat from his brow. I told him it was good to see him, too, after several years of playing phone tag.

I first met Turchynov on the Maidan and had been trying to sit down with him again ever since but it just hadn't worked out. He became acting president and oversaw Ukraine's provisional government until elections in May 2014. And then he was tapped as secretary of the National Security and Defense Council. Our interactions were always short, professional, and focused on the events of the day. I'd get a question in during a press conference or security forum. What I wanted was more time to discuss the events surrounding Crimea and Russia's annexation. Then in April 2022, after Kyiv stunned the world by sinking the *Moskva* – Russia's flagship Black Sea Fleet missile cruiser – with a Ukrainian-made anti-ship cruise missile, I knew I had to try to get to him again. Somewhat surprisingly, I found him fighting as a soldier on the front line.

Here's why I wanted to speak to him. In March 2014 everyone wanted to know why Ukraine wasn't responding with its military and security forces to Russia's invasion of the peninsula. I was told two things by Ukrainian and US officials on the condition they could remain anonymous then: First, Kyiv was caught off guard, the Ukrainian military had been stripped down to almost nothing under Yanukovych, and it was in no shape to put up a fight; and second, the Obama administration didn't want to see Russia handed a reason to escalate in Ukraine any farther and it wanted to avoid a potential military confrontation between Moscow and the West. Finally, I could put these questions to the person who would know.

"Oleksandr Valentynovych," I began, addressing him formally by his first name and patronymic, "I want to talk about the situation around Crimea when you were acting president."

He painted me this picture: "So, the Revolution of Dignity wins, Yanukovych flees Ukraine, and then imagine this: there is no government in the country, no local authorities, no law-enforcement agencies. Nothing. I am elected speaker of the parliament, and because of the flight of the president, I am appointed the acting president of the country and the supreme commander-in-chief. And for a while I also led the government as prime minister. That is, one person was leading every government body. And in these circumstances, Russia begins its military aggression against Ukraine.

"So that you understand the state of the country's economy, at that moment, we had about 100,000 *hryvnias* in the treasury account. At the exchange rate at that time, this was about $10,000. For the whole country. And we almost completely lacked a combat-ready army. The army had been dismantled by Yanukovych, it was demoralized. The General Staff reported to me that they could only muster 5,000 troops in order to carry out combat missions. But there was no normal armament for them. Military equipment did not function. We had tanks without operators. Plus, in Crimea alone, more than 75 per cent of the Berkut, police, special forces, and soldiers immediately went over to the side of Russia. That was the situation. And yet, in this situation, it was necessary to somehow protect Ukraine.

"I turned to our partners, including the United States of America and the leaders of the European Union, for help, referring to the Budapest Memorandum, that Ukraine had given up nuclear weapons in exchange for security guarantees from them. But they told me explicitly that there would be no military help. Both the Obama administration and European leaders told me that they were categorically against the supply of any weapons to Ukraine. And they justified this to me by saying that they do not want to provoke Putin and increase the risk of Russian aggression. But there was already aggression, the occupation of Crimea was underway, and a war was brewing in the east. Throughout Ukraine, the special services of the Russian Federation, the FSB, military intelligence, was organizing separatist coups, which had to be suppressed. Our partners were not going to help us, so I realized that we must rely solely on ourselves.

"First, it was necessary to revive the army. I called a mobilization [in March 2014]. Then I realized that to restore the army it was necessary not only to train our soldiers and officers, it was necessary to provide them with modern weapons. I made it a priority to restore the country's military-industrial potential. I gathered all the leaders of the military-industrial complex and said that we have few resources, practically no time, but there are huge tasks that need to be implemented. We began to plan our missile defense, because in modern warfare, without missiles, in fact, a country cannot resist, it cannot be defended. We created the Stugna-P and Korsar anti-tank missile systems, and the Neptune anti-ship cruise missile system, all of which have now shown themselves to be very capable.

"And I want to repeat once again, we did not have any help. This is now being actively supported both at the level of the United States, and at the level of Great Britain, and at the level of the European Union. But in those days we were alone, opposing Russia on our own.

"We knew we had a big problem, which concerned the threat from the sea. Russia, having seized Crimea, actually dominated the Black Sea basin. And there was always a threat of landing on our Black Sea and Sea of Azov coasts. Moreover, we did not have such a fleet as the Russian

Federation, and this had to be defended against. It was decided to create an anti-ship cruise missile. It was named Neptune and was planned as a mobile launcher.

"You know, an hour after Russia's flagship Black Sea Fleet missile cruiser the *Moskva* was hit, I exchanged pleasantries with Oleg Korostylev, the general designer of the Ukrainian design bureau Luch, which helped with its production. We congratulated each other on the fact that this was an incredible result of our work.

"You know, there was one more ship, a large one, the *Admiral Essen*, which was actually, let's say, put out of action by us. Although it was able to get to a Russian port on its own and remained afloat. The problem was that it noticed the approach of our Neptune missile and was able to shoot it down. And only a fragment of a missile hit the ship and caused minimal damage to it.

"Therefore, when our air-defense forces planned to fire on the *Moskva*, our guys shot two missiles simultaneously and this allowed us to break through the air defense and they were able to strike and sink the target."

Homeland

Ana-Yurt, Crimea, early March, 2014

Aziz Ziyatdinov wobbled slightly in the road and rubbed his eyes. He hadn't slept much since Russian forces stormed the Crimean peninsula and empowered the rag-tag "self-defense" forces on the streets to start running around and rounding up their perceived enemies.

"We don't know who might come up this road," the 30-year-old told me, gesturing to a steep dirt pathway leading up to the Crimean Tatar village of Ana-Yurt. "We used to get a lot of sleep. It was very quiet until some weeks ago. Now it is very intense, and not safe for us."

He paced nervously, always keeping an eye on the horizon. He had come to prefer rain to clear skies, because the rain soaked the earth and made it almost impossible for even all-terrain vehicles to ascend the steep hillside atop which the village sat. Mud was its best defense.

Here, ten miles northwest of the Crimean capital of Simferopol, beyond a maze of serpentine dirt and gravel roads, sitting atop a dusty bluff that Ziyatdinov called "the mountain," he and 200 families of Crimean Tatars had built a new life for themselves after decades of living in exile in far-flung corners of the Soviet Union. They had homes of their own with gardens, various shops, and a mosque. It wasn't glamorous but it was theirs. And until recently they believed they might finally have not only that place but also some peace.

Moscow had persecuted Crimean Tatars, a Muslim people whose roots can be traced back to Turkic and Mongol tribes, for roughly a century. Thousands were deported or killed during the Soviets' collectivization in the late 1920s, and they suffered during the famine that followed. In 1944, under the pretext that they had aided the Nazis during the Second World War, Joseph Stalin deported more than 200,000 Crimean Tatars to Central Asia. They were kept there until they were free to return to their homeland on this peninsula decades later, just before the fall of the Soviet Union in 1991. About half of them had died of disease and starvation during their enforced exile in the Far East. Around 300,000 now called Crimea home. But once again, with Russia moving to forcibly annex the peninsula, their livelihood was in danger. Many feared a return to the darkest of times, and they had good reason to.

As gunmen forced Crimean lawmakers in Simferopol to vote for a referendum on secession, Ildar Ibraimov, who had returned to Crimea from Uzbekistan in 1991, fretted over what might become of him and his fellow Crimean Tatars should the peninsula be brought under Moscow's rule once more. "It has taken more than 20 years to rebuild our lives, and we are very worried it could all be taken away again," said Ibraimov, a local member of the Mejlis, the governing body of the Crimean Tatars.

Already the Tatars' lives had been made more complicated, with pro-Russia militia targeting and intimidating them. Several homes of Crimean Tatars in Simferopol and the city of Bakhchisaray, the one-time capital of the Crimean Tatar Khanate, had been marked by deep gouges or painted with a large "X" similar to that used by police under Stalin's order in 1944 to mark the homes of those to be deported. Many Crimean Tatars returned from shopping or visiting with friends to discover their homes burgled and vehicles smashed. "In such dark times appear hooliganism, robberies and general destabilization," Ibraimov lamented.

None of the homes in Ana-Yurt had been tagged with such marks yet, but the wall of a Crimean Tatar restaurant in the valley below had been marked in black paint with a large "X." I stopped in to speak with the owner and buy a *samsa*, a flaky and savory triangular pastry stuffed with minced lamb and onions. "It happened last week in the middle of the day," the owner told me. A group of men in a van sped into the gravel parking lot, jumped out, and tagged the restaurant. "Traitors!" one of the men shouted, before they sped away.

"They had no shame," said the owner.

But vandalism was the least of their concerns. Crimean Tatars were also disappearing. Reshat Ametov, a Crimean Tatar, was at a protest against Russia's troop presence in Simferopol on 3 March, when he was abducted by men wearing camouflage uniforms and frog-marched to a waiting car. His mutilated body would be found two weeks later. It sent a chill across Crimea, which is exactly what Russia wanted. Nobody would ever be arrested for his killing.

Eskander Japarov returned from exile in Russia to Crimea in 1992. He made his home in Ana-Yurt, a "beautiful" place. But now he was living in fear. With the vandalism, the marks, the abductions, he was afraid to stray too far from his home. "I don't go into Simferopol, because I believe these people will attack me," he said of the pro-Russian goons running around the peninsula's capital.

He and Ibraimov told me they were strongly against Crimea joining Russia, as it would mean "more repression," and that the referendum was illegal, a sentiment echoed by President Obama on 6 March, who said it "would violate the Ukrainian Constitution and international law."

The Crimean Tatar chairman Refat Chubarov had urged residents of the peninsula to boycott the referendum scheduled for 16 March and called the pro-Russia parliament members who voted for separating Crimea from Ukraine "lunatics" who had "lost their minds" and were "fulfilling someone else's will."

"The Mejlis of the Crimean Tatars does not recognize this referendum," he said.

Ibraimov wanted the referendum to fail, but he wasn't under any illusion that Russia would allow for a free and fair vote.

"We want peace, prosperity and development – and for Crimea to remain with Ukraine," he said. "But we are preparing for the worst: that we will wake up in Russia one day."

Ziyatdinov and others at Ana-Yurt weren't taking any chances. They assembled their own self-defense squad. They took turns patrolling the village streets day and night in rotating shifts, scrutinizing every new car and each strange face that emerged from the valley below. They knew they didn't have the manpower or the weapons to stop an organized attack by the pro-Russia militia groups should they come for them. But they had to try. And at least they might keep a few curious potential vandals away.

"You can see, we're not going to win a fight against 100 men," Ziyatdinov told me, gesturing to the small group that had gathered beside him. They chuckled, looking at each other, smacking each other on the backs. They carried flashlights and some farming tools.

"We don't have weapons, but we have men on the streets and in each yard, and we can protect from provocateurs."

7

Voting Under The Gun

Simferopol, Crimea, Ukraine, March–April 2014

Tensions flared between Ukraine and Russia in their respective capitals, and in Crimea between pro-Kyiv activists and the boisterous residents who supported Moscow's occupation as the referendum drew near. And for the first time since I'd arrived, I felt the mood on the streets change. There was a lot of fear and anger. People's fuses had gotten shorter. Heated arguments devolved into physical confrontations.

I heard from an activist that a group of pro-Ukrainian women were going to hold a rally outside a Ukrainian military base in Simferopol where troops had been trapped inside. It wasn't long before a pro-Russia group of around 50 men calling themselves Crimean self-defense forces arrived with shields painted the colors of the Crimean tricolor – a thin blue line, a wide white stripe, and a thin red stripe – and blocked the base. After several minutes of chanting "Ros-si-ya!" they charged at the group of women protesters. "Bitches!" "Fascists!" the men hollered while punching, shoving, and tearing apart handmade signs that read "Women for peace in Ukraine and Crimea."

The men, some of whom I recognized from other locations around the city, included several Cossacks who spewed Kremlin propaganda about "Kyiv fascists" from Right Sector coming to Crimea by train to attack Russian speakers and force the Ukrainian language on the peninsula. Except earlier when they went to the train station to wait for them, the "fascists" hadn't arrived. I had gone there, too, because I wanted to see what they would do when the train arrived empty of them. As the last of the ordinary passengers stepped onto the platform, the mob looked confounded and disappointed. But then one man suggested that the Right Sector guys had heard of their plan to confront them at the train station and chickened out.

"You are neo-Nazi scum sent here from Kyiv to destroy our Crimea!" shouted one of the Cossacks. He held a whip in his right hand and every so often would crack it in a display that was both sinister and silly.

A woman shouted back that she had been born and raised on the peninsula. "This is my home! I speak Russian just like you!" she told him. "But I'm not twisted and I don't fall for Putin's propaganda, like *you* do!"

He got in her face and raised his whip. I stepped in to separate them and that's when he and another Cossack threw me into the line of traffic. A sedan honked and slammed on its brakes. I flew onto the hood of the car and then rolled off as it came to a stop. A few foreign journalists and some of the women activists picked me up and checked to make sure I was in one piece. The Cossack cracked his whip to break up the crowd. "*Pedaras!*" ("faggot") he screamed at me, emphasizing the rolling *rrr* in the slur.

These were the people that Russian state news channels were depicting as grassroots activists, fascist fighters, and defenders of freedom. There was little coverage of the Russian soldiers. It was mostly b-roll shots without interviews. And the camera never lingered on them too long. Because, officially, they weren't there.

With armed Russian troops and gangs of militias roaming the streets, the referendum went ahead on 16 March, 60 years after Nikita Khrushchev gifted Crimea to Soviet Ukraine. The ballot showed two large, empty boxes alongside two questions: "Do you support reunifying Crimea with Russia as a subject of the Russian Federation?" and "Do you support the restoration of the 1992 Crimean constitution and Crimea's status as a part of Ukraine?" Despite the tricky language of the second choice, it was also a vote for separation. The 1992 constitution asserted that Crimea was an independent state and thus not a part of Ukraine. It was only later that language indicating the peninsula had autonomy within Ukraine was inserted into the constitution. There was no option to vote for the status quo and remain in Ukraine. Crimeans were confused by the options but that didn't matter. The outcome was a forgone conclusion. Putin was going to take Crimea no matter what.

On Simferopol's Lenin Square, pro-Russian voters gathered to celebrate as the results were announced: Crimea had broken away. Old Soviet ditties blared from stage speakers as people waved the Russian tricolor and the red flag of the USSR with its hammer and sickle. They danced under a sky of fireworks.

Russian officials claimed the final results of the vote showed that 97 per cent of people supported splitting from Ukraine. Mikhail Malyshev,

138

the Russian-approved head of the referendum election commission, said the next day that everything went so smoothly that the commission hadn't even registered a single complaint about the vote. Go figure. Of course, he was ignoring the countless protests from Ukraine and the international community. Kyiv called the referendum a "circus" masterminded by the Kremlin and conducted "at gunpoint." The United States, EU, NATO, and the United Nations, and pretty much everyone else save for adversaries of those nations, blocs, and organizations, condemned the referendum. They said it was "rigged" and called it a "sham" and declared it "illegal under international law." The White House Press Secretary Jay Carney said it was "dangerous and destabilizing." It was all of those things. "In this century, we are long past the days when the international community will stand quietly by while one country forcibly seizes the territory of another," Carney added. But in the end, the international community did little to prevent it from happening.

Putin wasted no time recognizing the outcome, signing a decree 24 hours after polling stations closed that officially – as far as Russia was concerned – acknowledged Crimea's independence. The move laid the groundwork for the illegal annexation of the Ukrainian territory the next day.

On 17 March the United States froze the assets of and banned travel for 11 Russian and Ukrainian political figures, including the Kremlin-backed Crimean leader Sergei Aksyonov, the Crimean parliament speaker Vladimir Konstantinov, the Russian Deputy Prime Minister Dmitry Rogozin, the Russian Presidential Adviser Sergey Glazyev, as well as Yanukovych and several others. The EU followed suit hours later with sanctions against 21 Russians and Ukrainians, but none as prominent as those on the US list.

"We're making it clear there are consequences for these actions," Barack Obama said in a televised statement from the White House briefing room. "The international community will continue to stand together to oppose any violations of Ukrainian sovereignty and territorial integrity."

The following day, Putin convened his top officials and both houses of parliament for an extraordinary session in the Kremlin's St George Hall. Horns announced his arrival. He strutted through oversized golden doors and onto the stage. "In the hearts and minds of people, Crimea has always been and remains an inseparable part of Russia," he said. When the Soviet Union collapsed, he added, ethnic Russians had found themselves cut off from the motherland, including those in Crimea. "Millions of Russians went to sleep in one country and woke up living abroad, as a national minority in former republics of the union. The Russian people became one of the biggest – if not the biggest – split-up nation in the world."

Lying through his teeth, he continued: "Don't believe those who try to frighten you with Russia and who scream that other regions will follow after Crimea. We do not want a partition of Ukraine."

Then he signed documents absorbing Crimea into Russia. And with that, Europe's first major land-grab in seven decades was complete.

The day after Putin's speech, Ukraine ordered its besieged troops and sailors to stand down and leave Crimea, and began moving them to the mainland. Besides taking Crimea, Russia also seized 51 vessels belonging to the Ukrainian navy. Among them were the submarine *Zaporizhia*, the management ship *Slavutych*, the landing ships *Konstantin Olshansky* and *Kirovohrad*, the minesweepers *Chernihiv* and *Cherkasy*. The *Cherkasy* was the last of the ships to have been taken following weeks of threats and ultimatums to surrender. It was finally chased down and overtaken by the Russian navy on 25 March after failing to slip past a blockade of two ships intentionally sunk by the Russians to trap it and other vessels in a narrow gulf, keeping them from escaping into the Black Sea. Ukraine had just ten vessels left in its navy's possession, including the frigate *Hetman Sahaydachniy*, the gunboat *Skadovsk*, the intelligence ship *Pereyaslav*, and the diving vessel *Netishin*.

Faced with the increasingly ugly mood many Ukrainians in Crimea, including Crimean Tatars whose allegiance was to Kyiv, saw the writing on the wall. The message from Moscow was clear: you're with us, or you're against us. Not taking a position was seen as taking the pro-Ukrainian side. A significant proportion of the population was against separating from Ukraine, but they would only say so in a whisper from the relative safety of their kitchens. There was no future here anymore. The peninsula was being dragged into the past. They began withdrawing their money from banks and heading north to the Ukrainian mainland. Many activists and journalists were among them. There wasn't enough time to sell their homes, so they were left behind. Who would buy in such circumstances? They packed what they could fit in their cars and left, uncertain that they'd ever be able to come back.

Moscow moved quickly after the illegal annexation to Russify Crimea. It replaced all Ukrainian flags with the Russian tricolor, which fluttered over official buildings. The Ukrainian *hryvnia* was replaced with the Russian *ruble*. Russian passports were issued to residents, as were stickers to transform Ukrainian license plates into Russian ones. Ukrainian language and history were removed from the school curriculum.

The Kremlin vowed to pour billions of dollars into Crimea and create a special economic zone to stimulate investment. It said tourism would see a huge boost and the peninsula would become something of a "Russian Las Vegas." Putin set about erecting a massive bridge over the Kerch Strait connecting Russia to the peninsula, an illegal project that would spark more Western sanctions.

But many of these promises and the dreams of the Crimeans who backed the referendum would not come true. Inflation would hit the peninsula hard. Visa and Mastercard would stop payments, forcing runs on banks. When I would make calls to my sources still there over the next few years, they would express remorse for voting in the referendum to join Russia. "We were duped," one would tell me. Crimean Tatars who stayed and didn't relocate to Kyiv would live in constant fear of Russia's security services and would be rounded up and imprisoned on bogus terrorism charges. Most of my Ukrainian friends would quit going to Crimea for summer holidays. They felt it was now tainted. And they didn't want to support Russia in any way. "Holidays in Yalta finance terrorism," a friend declared. Instead, they'd head to Odesa or to cities on the Sea of Azov – an inland sea connected to the Black Sea and shared by Russia and Ukraine – like Mariupol and Berdyansk. I, too, would not go back.

Over the next seven years, Russia would transform Crimea into a giant militarized zone, beefing up its air-, sea-, and land-based military infrastructure. And this infrastructure would play a key role in the full-scale invasion of Ukraine to come.

PART THREE

WAR

8

"Russian Spring"

The Donbas, March–mid-May 2014

No sooner had Russia stealthily invaded and forcibly annexed Crimea in February and March 2014 than the Kremlin turned its attention toward mainland Ukraine, launching a covert operation in the south and east of the country under the guise of a grassroots uprising. I had hoped to find time to visit Bri in the United States after three months apart. But the trip was put on hold and tensions quickly reached boiling point in my old stomping grounds.

While I was in Crimea in early March, pro-Russian demonstrations had erupted in cities across the Donbas, as well as in the regional capitals of Kharkiv, Mykolaiv, Odesa, Zaporozhzhia, and Dnipropetrovsk. Some, like in Kharkiv, turned violent and bloody when the pro-Russia crowd, wielding chains and clubs, tried to storm the regional government administration and clashed with police. Among the first and the largest demonstration was on Donetsk's central Lenin Square on 1 March. A few thousand people gathered around the statue of the Bolshevik revolutionary and Soviet founder to hold a "vote of no confidence" in the regional authorities. Andrei Purgin, the leader of the obscure pro-Russian group "Donetsk Republic," organized the event. But on stage, it was a little-known local by the name of Pavel Gubarev who led the rally. The 31-year-old had previously worked as an advertising agent and a part-time, for-hire Father Frost, the Slavic version of Santa Claus, at children's events. He was also a member of a handful of marginal pro-Russian political organizations with about as many combined members as a church book club; he was an odd choice as the face of the movement. Yet there he was, brazenly announcing that he was appointing himself the "people's governor of Donetsk" and leader of the "Donbas People's

Militia" from that day forward. And where were we now? According to him, inside the "Donetsk People's Republic."

The demonstrators repeated lines from Russia's powerful anti-Maidan propaganda widely consumed in the Donbas, which painted the new leadership in Kyiv as Western "fascists" and "Nazis" hell bent on wiping out every trace of Russian culture and oppressing Russian speakers. They wore the ribbon of St George, a military decoration harking back to the Russian Empire and Soviet Union. It was black and orange, apparently to symbolize gunpowder and fire. Anti-Russian Ukrainians would come to refer to those who wore the ribbon as "kolorady," as in the Colorado potato beetle with a similar striped pattern on its back side. They also waved the Russian tricolor and flags adorned with the image of Stalin and marched down central Artema Street chanting, "Ros-si-ya! Ros-si-ya!" Some carried banners so freshly made that the creases still showed. They read, "We are for a referendum" and "I'm Russian." Like Crimea, they wanted a vote on secession, which they believed would pave the way for Russian annexation. They planned to hold it on 11 May, two days after Russia celebrated Victory Day, a major holiday commemorating the Soviets' victory over Nazi Germany in 1945.

Looking on from Crimea, to me it all appeared strangely familiar and staged. In Washington, the Obama administration had the same sense.

"These do not appear to be a spontaneous set of events," the White House said.

A lot of people in the Donbas – maybe even most of them – had legitimate frustrations, anxieties, and complaints about how they had been treated by Kyiv in the past, and concerns over the path that the newly formed, post-Maidan government might take them on in the future. Many livelihoods were also tied to Russia. But beyond a minority contingent of Russian chauvinists, pensioners, and old communists who harbored nostalgic ideas of their Soviet days and feared integration with the West, and the oddballs like Ilya, my student's father who kept a separatist flag and Kalashnikov in the trunk of his Lada, I hadn't known people in the region to want to separate from Ukraine, let alone to join Russia. Polling data didn't show this either. That spring, surveys revealed less than 30 per cent support for living under Russian rule.

"I don't recognize any of these people. Where did they come from?" Oleksiy Matsuka, my journalist friend in Donetsk said when I called from Simferopol to ask about what was happening on the ground in the Donbas. "It all looks fake . . . There is no doubt of the Russian hand in this."

Acting President Oleksandr Turchynov and Prime Minister Arseniy Yatsenyuk warned that the demonstrations were being organized by Moscow as a pretext to launch an invasion of the Donbas and seize control over it. Turchynov canceled a trip to Lithuania and called an emergency session with the heads of the country's security and intelligence services. The newly appointed Ukrainian Interior Minister Arsen Avakov accused Putin and the deposed Yanukovych of "instigating and paying for the new wave of separatist riots." He ordered his police to squash the unrest. "A cruel approach will be used to everyone who directly conducts attacks on state buildings, on law enforcers and other civilians," he warned.

In our early reporting on the events, I and other foreign correspondents referred to what was happening as "pro-Russian protests" and the people involved as "pro-Russian separatists," or variations of those terms. Russian state-run media and Russian-friendly outlets in Ukraine began referring to the protests collectively as the "Russian Spring," a nod to the Arab Spring. But none of these descriptions adequately described what was going on. The true nature of the events was much more murky and complex. There were early signs of Russia's direct involvement in the unrest, although they were difficult to prove at the time and thus hard to get published. One clear piece of evidence was the influx of "tourists" arriving on charter buses from Russia. Once in Ukraine, Russian nationals were posing as locals to fill out the demonstrations. Eventually, it would become clear that Russian FSB agents were on the ground, whipping up tensions in the Donbas and paying people to protest, much like Yanukovych's rent-a-crowds before and during the revolution. And that Russian special forces and military intelligence operatives from the GRU were also present and fomenting violence. But early on, the Kremlin and its troops were absurdly insisting that the events on the ground had erupted spontaneously and that the armed fighters were merely local miners and factory workers.

Not all of Russia's efforts were successful, however. The anti-Kyiv protests in Kharkiv, Mykolaiv, Odesa, Zaporozhzhia, and Dnipropetrovsk fizzled out quickly. There just wasn't enough pro-Russian sentiment for the Kremlin and its agents on the ground to tap into and exploit. But in the Donbas, where skepticism toward Kyiv was greater and Russian television and state propaganda had been more widely consumed than Ukrainian programming, Putin found more fertile ground.

By mid-April, the pro-Russian rallies had turned much more violent and Ukraine was losing control over cities and towns in the Donbas.

Armed with makeshift weapons, the Russians and their local actors stormed and occupied the regional government buildings in Donetsk and Luhansk, declaring their own "people's republics" and demanding referendums on splitting from Ukraine. The first city to fall under their control was Slovyansk. It happened on 12 April, when Igor "Strelkov" Girkin, the former FSB officer and GRU colonel, led his group of Russian militants from Crimea into the eastern city and seized the government building, the police department, and the Security Service of Ukraine office. Other Russian fighters broke off and went to neighboring Kramatorsk. More fanned out across the region, seizing buildings in Druzhkivka, Horlivka, Mariupol and other cities. But it was Girkin who led the charge and boasted that he had "pulled the trigger" of war.

The occupiers included many of the same "little green men" who had helped capture Crimea, such as Arsen Pavlov, a Russian national from the northwestern Komi region who'd soon come to be known for his brutality and his call sign, Motorola, bestowed upon him by comrades because he enjoyed filming his battles on his cheap Motorola mobile phone. There were also regular Russian special forces troops and irregular Russian military veterans. Some came from Moscow and St Petersburg, but many came from the southwestern regions including the Caucasus. There were Chechens and Cossacks, Neo-Nazis, radical nationalists, and anarchists. They came to fight for Russia or money or power or blood, or because they hated Ukraine and Ukrainians. But the Russians had also recruited local military personnel, police officers, security service agents, and counter-intelligence officials from the area who were pro-Russian, disenchanted with the new central government in Kyiv, and saw opportunities for themselves in the unfolding chaos. In all cases, they drank heavily, looted homes and shops, and behaved recklessly. They held their fingers over the triggers of their Kalashnikovs and on more than one occasion I saw soldiers accidentally shoot either themselves or a comrade in the foot. The whole thing was a confusing and dangerous mess.

In Slovyansk, like in Donetsk, an unknown local actor stepped forward to declare himself the city's new political leader. His name was Vyacheslav Ponomarev. A Soviet Navy veteran who had most recently worked at a soap manufacturing plant, he had soft blue eyes, two gold lateral incisors that framed two false front teeth, two missing fingers on his left hand, and a penchant for black tracksuits. Ponomarev claimed he was the new "people's mayor" of Slovyansk, and ordered the elected mayor to be taken into custody.

From the moment he stepped into his self-appointed role, Ponomarev ruled like an angry little tyrant, detaining anyone who questioned him or looked at him wrong, including foreign journalists. He also ordered the week-long detention of seven foreigners and five Ukrainians working as conflict observers for the OSCE Special Monitoring Mission (See Associated Press, 29th May 2014.).

A shootout in Slovyansk on his watch greatly escalated things. It happened around 3 a.m. local time on Easter morning, 20 April, when a group of Ukrainian Right Sector fighters tried to storm the city. The DNR troops gunned them down, killing them.

Ponomarev used the assault to ask Russia to send peacekeepers to the Donbas to protect civilians from the Kyiv "fascists." He also placed a curfew on the city, barring residents from being outdoors from midnight to 6 a.m.

"They kill our people. They don't talk to us but just kill," Ponomarev told reporters at one of his press conferences. "The town has actually been besieged by the Right Sector."

I returned to the Donbas a few days later, just as it was beginning to look and feel like a war zone. Turchynov had announced an "anti-terrorist operation" – or the ATO for short – to try to oust the militants from the occupied buildings and quell the separatist unrest fomented by Moscow. Locals already angry with Kyiv or on the fence after the Russian forces rolled in didn't like the name and took it to mean that their own government considered them terrorists. Armored vehicles lined the highways and checkpoints were erected. The self-imposed authorities were now calling themselves officials of the "Donetsk People's Republic," or DNR. Their counterparts in Luhansk were doing the same, with their so-called LNR – the "Luhansk People's Republic."

Slovyansk was crawling with Russian forces and their local pro-Russian fighters. They liked to hang around on the central square, where a statue of Lenin stood in the middle of a flowerbed of red roses. The militants had barricaded the local government building with sandbags and stacked tires around it. Similar fortifications were erected around the SBU building on Marx Street where Girkin and his crew had set up shop, as well as the police station.

They were all armed with high-powered rifles and grenade launchers. Military trucks and armored personnel carriers rumbled through the streets with Russian and DNR flags jutting from their sides. Many of the fighters rode on top of them, waving to locals and shouting, "To Kyiv!" Nobody wanted to talk about where the weapons and vehicles had come from. I asked a group of soldiers who were lounging in the shade of a tree how they'd managed to obtain their kit.

"We just found them here one day," quipped a grizzled fighter. The group erupted in laughter.

"The Ukrainian army gave them to us," said another. "The army is with us. They opened their doors and said, 'Guys, take what you want.'"

That was partly true. On 14 and 15 April a demoralized Ukrainian army unit lost upwards of two dozen armored military vehicles to pro-Russian forces in Slovyansk and Kramatorsk when their local supporters blocked the road with cars and surrounded them. The group demanded that the soldiers surrender and switch sides. Unwilling or unable to respond with force, the Ukrainians simply gave up.

In those early days, Slovyansk was the center of power of Russia's military operation. And Girkin, the skinny, pencil-mustachioed war re-enactor, was in charge. He drove around town in a black Mercedes with a group of armed guards. He always kept an old pistol in a wooden holster on his hip. His office approved press accreditations as well. But many journalists were afraid to go in after some were briefly detained and threatened. I opted to stay in Bakhmut at Slava's apartment or my friend's hotel, the Atlantic. To keep a low profile, I sometimes rode into town in a *marshrutka* (minibus), which usually allowed me to avoid scrutiny at checkpoints, since the lazy fighters often just waved these vehicles through. But once I was caught, yanked off the marshrutka, and hauled into Strelkov's office. A hulk of a man with a snarling face sat me down and screamed at me for an hour. He called himself Balu, like the bear in *The Jungle Book*. And he told me he was going to kill me unless I confessed to being an American spy. I never confessed and eventually he was called into another room. A few moments later, a man walked in and told me to get the fuck out of the building. I moved so fast.

Girkin and his men in Slovyansk were especially brutal toward people who didn't fully agree to their takeover and revel in it, or were perceived as their enemies. To those who disobeyed orders or just fucked up, Girkin was also cruel.

Fighters rounded up dissenters, executed them, and tossed their bodies into mass graves. Among those killed were four members of the

Transfiguration of The Lord Pentecostal Church. They were dragged from the church one day and never returned. The Prosecutor General's Office of Ukraine officially charged Igor Girkin with war crimes in June 2020.

Soon, I would discover more information that brought to light the barbaric nature of Girkin's rule, which set the dark tone for the larger war to come.

As Ukraine's ATO got underway in earnest, the fighting in and around Slovyansk, Kramatorsk, and Donetsk exploded. There were skirmishes and ambushes, attacks with armored vehicles and heavy weapons. It was bloody chaos. Ukrainian forces dug trenches and erected countless checkpoints. Their enemies did the same. The front lines changed daily, sometimes even hourly. On some days, I'd pass through checkpoints on one road or highway and they'd be manned by Ukrainian troops and police. Then on my way back, I'd find the same checkpoints had been taken over by the DNR or LNR. Or vice versa. Everything changed hands in those early days more times than anyone could count. It was next to impossible to know who controlled what.

With the Ukrainians, I'd always flash my American passport and press card, including my new ATO accreditation that the SBU began giving out to journalists. But for the DNR or LNR, I showed only my press card and respective accreditation – and not my Ukrainian ATO card, lest I wanted to check into their basement dungeons for the night. The Ukrainians always ended with "*Slava Ukraini!*" And expected you to respond, "*Heroyam Slava!*" – Glory to heroes! The Russians and separatist proxy fighters would sometimes do the same, as a test to see whether you were a secret "fascist." But everyone always exhorted us to "*pishite pravdu*" – write the truth. (I'd often dream of these checkpoint encounters and the phrase would echo in my head for years. It got to be so distracting that I was forced to resort to drastic measures to try to remove it: I tattooed "*pishite pravdu*" on my body, symbolically removing it from the mental to the physical.)

One day, I was with the photographer Kostya Chernichkin, traveling on the highway between the two cities, when we were stopped by Ukrainian airborne forces. They had half a dozen armored vehicles parked on the road and we were forced to weave around them. At the last one, a Ukrainian soldier stopped us and asked where we were going. I told him we were headed to Kramatorsk and he warned us to be careful.

"We just smoked them," he said, apparently referring to the DNR fighters.

A mile up the road, we were stopped at gunpoint by jumpy fighters who were clearly dazed. The Ukrainians had just rolled in, blasted their checkpoints and roadblocks, and then stormed off. We were the first journalists to roll up since it had happened just minutes before. Everything was burning. A gas transport truck the DNR fighters had used to block the road had exploded and its tank was peeled back like a sardine can. One fighter, his face dirtied with smoke and grime from the blasts, tossed his gun over his shoulder and glared at me.

"You ask a question and I will fucking shoot you," he said.

I opted instead to approach a group of children who stood on the roadside. They said they had watched the attack unfold from one of the kids' yards. They held their hands out to show me several bullet casings they had picked up and were keeping as souvenirs.

Kostya and I rolled into the center of Kramatorsk, where we came upon another scene. Trolleybuses were in flames in front of the three-star Hotel Kramatorsk. A group of Chechen Cossacks lounging in the grass across the street said they had repelled a Ukrainian attempt to dislodge them from the city. Their rifles and spent anti-tank missile tubes were laid beside them. They were cheerful until they found out a foreign journalist was there. One demanded that I come with them and began moving toward me. By some miracle I squirmed out of the crowd that had gathered and got away, eventually making it back to our car. We got out of there.

9

Stamps

Donetsk, May 2014

The center of the DNR's power as it shifted away from Slovyansk was the 11-story regional administration building in Donetsk. As in Slovyansk, we needed a special press accreditation to move around the city and speak to people without being arrested, thrown in a basement or jail, or shot. The only way to obtain one was to bring a stack of hard-copy documents to the fifth-floor DNR press center, where there was a map hanging on the wall with "Rossiya" scrawled across it in red sharpie and a bullet jabbed into the heart of Donetsk.

But first, I had to get past the jumpy, sunburnt, and often drunken armed ruffians in faux Adidas tracksuits and fingerless biker gloves standing guard outside the front entrance.

To enter, I needed to show a press card, submit my backpack to a search, and then shuffle through a checkpoint piled high with sandbags, razor wire, wood pallets, and signs decrying fascism, Kyiv, Victoria Nuland, and President Obama.

Signs posted on the front doors and hallways inside warned against loitering and walking around the premises without a *propusk*, or a pass. A little old lady behind a small window gave them out upon you entering and showing your passport. Each pass was written by hand on a slip of paper, dated and stamped.

The press center was located on the fifth floor. While they demanded hard-copy documents with stamps and signatures of editors, they never seemed to be pleased with what they were presented.

"The stamp looks fake," an armed teenager with peach fuzz over his lip told me, rubbing his thumb over it.

"It's real," I said.

"The signature looks forged."

"It's not. It's my editor's signature."

"I'm going to have to take this upstairs."

He meant he'd need to run it by the warlords and grifters who had formed the DNR's security service, which, of course, they named the NKVD, in a nod to the Soviet secret police agency and predecessor of the KGB. It was located on the top floor and I hated going up there because I had to pass the sixth floor.

Heavily guarded by masked toughs and off limits to journalists, the sixth floor of the building was a mystery but obviously a terrible place. I always tried to catch a glimpse inside as the door was opened by a militant entering or exiting. Several times over months, I watched blindfolded men get frogmarched through its doors before they slammed shut. I heard screams and shouting from inside. I was never allowed in, but I was threatened with being dragged in for inquiring about what was going on there.

"We can show you. But we can't guarantee you'll be able to leave and write an article about it," quipped a grouchy fighter.

"I'm alright," I said. "Thanks."

Later, I'd interview several pro-Ukrainian activists and locals who'd run afoul of the Russia-backed authorities and who would provide some insight. They told me they had been accused of working for Kyiv. They'd been interrogated, beaten, tortured – even waterboarded. One man said someone speaking Russian with a Moscow accent had ripped off the man's pants, doused water on his testicles and then used jumper cables attached to a car battery to electrocute him through his genitals. Another told me he'd been injected with something that caused him to go "crazy." He described his eyes dilating and adrenaline coursing through his veins. His captors began questioning him and he couldn't stop talking, although he had no idea what he was saying.

"They were trying to get me to confess to spying," he told me. "I have no idea what I said."

Both were eventually let go – the first because a former friend who had joined the DNR government pulled strings to get him released; the second because nothing he said had checked out. His captors put a bag over his head, stole all his belongings, drove him to the edge of Donetsk and dropped him on the side of the road. They didn't even cut the ties they'd placed around his hands, leaving him to bite through them with his teeth, one of which was chipped in the process.

"Can I please show my documents to Claudia first?" I asked the gunmen. Claudia was the press secretary whose busy work made her prone to fiery outbursts. But she knew me because I'd been in there so many times.

She was short-tempered and skeptical of us from the West, especially from the United States. Every time I needed to renew my press card she would always do so reluctantly. But sometimes she was in a good mood, like the day she had come into a huge basket of strawberries. It was hot and her office windows on the upper floor were open. I peeked out to view the city from above and when I turned around she was standing right in front of me. I was startled at first and even wondered if she wanted to push me out. She had a fat, ruby-red strawberry in her hand.

"Open your mouth," she demanded, her face expressionless.

I did as she asked. Then she hand-fed me the strawberry and watched me chew and swallow it before backing away.

"Tasty, right?" she asked.

"Yes, very," I said.

"So, I will approve your accreditation," she told me. "But Christopher, I need you to do something for me."

"What's that?" I asked.

"Please, write the truth," she said. "I read some of your articles and I don't think you are writing the truth."

Of course, I knew what she meant. She meant she wanted me to write her truth. The DNR/Russia truth.

"I will always write the truth," I told her.

"Mhmm," she responded, mumbling something to herself as she looked me straight in the eye.

She signed my new press card, sealed it with a blue DNR stamp, and I was on my way. I never liked being inside the DNR headquarters longer than I needed to be. People had a way of disappearing inside.

―――――――――

Donetsk's new overlords also imposed a military curfew, and anyone on the streets after dark would be stuffed into a police or militant's car and hauled into an interrogation room, where they were deemed a spy and provocateur until proven otherwise. Some locals this happened to were never heard from again. The next day a soldier would go to their homes and confiscate their possessions.

155

The DNR fighters ran the street like their personal fiefdom. There were no rules. They would go to the rich neighborhoods and ask for "donations" for the military. If people didn't hand over cash, deeds, jewelry and the keys to their fancy cars – BMWs, Land Rovers, and Mercedes – their heads would be met with the butt of a rifle. Or they'd be tied up and questioned about where their allegiances lay. Some would be taken to jail, or worse – the sixth floor in the DNR headquarters.

Once, I was interviewing a man who'd been held for more than a week inside one of the DNR jails. We strolled through a park as he told me about being beaten and subjected to mock executions. He had owned and operated a stone company before the war but closed up shop a few weeks after it broke out, because business had dried up and he couldn't afford to pay his employees. At the end of the park was a pizzeria and a road, where several armed men were standing amid a group of black cars. The businessman pointed to a black Volkswagen SUV.

"That's my car," he told me, gesturing nonchalantly toward it with his head. He said the license plate out loud. It was a letter and number combo that he had memorized.

"They put a gun to my head and said to give them the keys," he explained. "They said it was a donation to the republic."

Indeed, Donetsk had become a much stranger and darker place than it was before the war. It was a place rife with delusions, denials, rumors, fear, violence, braggadocio and propaganda, where nothing and everything was real.

On city squares, children were exploited for propaganda purposes. One child poet, carrying a toy gun and wearing a camouflage bandana around her head, jumped on a stage at a separatist rally, giving a live mic performance in which she damned the Ukrainian "Nazi morons."

Another time, a group of school children performed a play in which they depicted Ukrainians as Nazis while black-and-white footage of World War II fascists played on a jumbo screen behind them.

Propaganda like this was ubiquitous. The city resembled the pages of a certain George Orwell novel, with gunmen roaming the streets reminding people to "speak the truth," and billboards portraying the current fight to that of the Second World War.

The message worked on many. They were being brainwashed to believe that they were fighting a continuation of their grandfathers' war against the fascists. Question firing squad executions, extrajudicial detentions or the parade of prisoners of war through Donetsk and you were likely to be called a fascist yourself and thrown into the makeshift prison called "Isolation" – a former modern art center with a chimney decorated as a lipstick container before Russia's gunmen seized it and turned it into a dungeon and torture chamber.

Against this bizarre backdrop, the Russian-imposed leadership wanted to project normalcy and give the impression that life could still go on as normal. To ensure schools would open on September 1, authorities visited classrooms and paid teachers one-time cash payments of about $231. They also began paying pensions to retirees who had not received any payments since May. They were bribing the population to quell any potential dissent and give the impression that everything was fine.

Credibility had been tough to come by for the Russian proxy government. Even supporters seemed skeptical about the future of "independent" Donetsk.

"We wanted to leave Ukraine – that's why we voted in the referendum," Maria Valeryevna, a 67-year-old pensioner told me one day on Lenin Square. But the thousands of lives that had been lost in the war, she said, "is too high a price to pay." She wanted her money back, so to speak. But there were no refunds in this undeclared war.

Between rocket salvos on a typical day in Donetsk, you'd see fighters swagger down the street, lugging big guns, as civilians scurried from shops to bomb shelters. Donetsk had a pre-war population of about one million. Hundreds of thousands of people, however, had fled as the fighting escalated, leaving the city full of soldiers.

The Russians sent by the Kremlin to take the political lead here, like so-called "prime minister" Alexander Borodai, a "political technologist" close to Putin's Ukraine point man at the time, Vladislav Surkov, strutted around with armed guards at his side, drinking top-shelf liquor and gaslighting everyone. He would come to the Ramada where I and many other foreign correspondents were and argue with us late into the night about the war and how Russia wasn't involved. The Russian soldiers would come in with him, wearing uniforms with Russian flags and badges of Russian brigades. But they weren't Russian soldiers – they were volunteers "on holiday." They'd come out of the goodness of their hearts to defend "the motherland," though most of them couldn't tell Donetsk from Makiivka, Volnovakha from Mariupol. They would sometimes ask my local driver for directions, and afraid of being thrown into a cellar or shot in the street, he would reluctantly abide.

The Ramada hotel was an oasis amid the chaos but also the heart of the weirdness. I drank and dined and worked there with correspondents from across the globe. Many grew so comfortable there that they'd walk around the place in a robe and white *tapachki*, little slippers that the staff left for us in our rooms. We would watch tanks trundle down the street from the terrace while we ate lunch. One time a car flipped completely over right in front of us. The driver had been fiddling with his gun and lost control of the wheel. There were artillery strikes around it that shook the walls and foundation. We taped our windows so they wouldn't shatter. When a strike knocked out the water supply for the week, the hotel staff pumped the chlorinated water from the pool so we'd all be able to shower. We smelled like a swimming team. The bar was crawling with sex workers looking to hook up with a Russian warlord or a Western journalist. They seemed to make good money because they kept coming back. On Valentine's Day the hotel would offer discounts on romantic dinners and rooms for couples. There was a whole dating scene, in fact. Here's one such date that I witnessed:

It was a warm September evening, and the camouflage-clad DNR gunman walked into the Ramada hotel lounge and asked for a terrace table with a view.

"Of course. We've already reserved a table for you," the uniformed hostess told him. "Your date is already here."

"Thank you," he said, shifting his Kalashnikov from his right shoulder to the left.

The gunman found his date touching up her glittery lip-gloss on a wicker bench seat overlooking the avenue. Seeing him approach, she stood to exchange a kiss on the cheek before they sat down side-by-side. He rested his rifle against the edge of their table.

A soft-rock cover version of Michael Jackson's *Beat It* sung by a woman with a hint of an Eastern European accent, played overhead as a server came over to take their order. The gunman wanted a beer and a hookah. His date was already sipping a colorful concoction from a florescent green bendy straw. They would also share a plate of sushi rolls, he said.

I watched from a table nearby, puffing on a cigarette and sipping a double whiskey neat while I banged out another dispatch on my MacBook.

As the food arrived, the gunman pretended to hand-feed her a salmon roll. Then, just before placing it in her glossy mouth, he pulled away and swallowed the roll himself, letting out a bellowing chuckle. Furrowing her brows while feigning anger, his date pointed to the rifle.

"Do it again and I'll shoot," she warned. "I know how to use it."

He laughed with his mouth open and continued the game throughout their meal.

There were a lot of influential Russian political figures who would come through, too. Some of them linked up with the militia forces and warlords like "Motorola," and they'd go out shooting at Ukrainian positions on what they liked to call "safaris."

One day, Alexander Prokhanov, a hardcore Russian nationalist and editor of the *Zavtra* newspaper, showed up in the Ramada. He wanted to see how Moscow's war was going and to get material for a column he planned to write that would explain why Ukraine and Ukrainians didn't deserve to exist. I knew because I'd overheard him speaking when he was drunk on the terrace. The next morning, I got the elevator to go down to breakfast and he was there with two armed guards. I asked him what he thought of Donetsk and the war and whether he thought what Russia was doing was wrong.

"It's a beautiful city," he said. "And this is a beautiful war."

10

"Look at Our Republic"

Donetsk, Mariupol and Bakhmut, Donetsk Oblast, 9 May 2014

On 9 May, two days before the referendum, the DNR held a Victory Day celebration on Donetsk's central Lenin Square. Among the many speakers was Denis Pushilin, a former security guard, casino croupier and candy salesman who then worked for MMM, selling shares in a notorious Russian Ponzi scheme that swindled thousands of people out of their savings. It was also his birthday. Addressing the crowd of mostly older people, including Soviet veterans the DNR had wheeled in with chests full of ribbons and medals, he cast the "republic's" struggle against Kyiv as a continuation of the Soviet's fight against European fascism. The crowd cheered and waved red hammer-and-sickle flags.

The only fascists I saw were right there on the stage. Among them was Aleksandr Zaldastanov, leader of the Russian biker group known as the Night Wolves. Beloved by Putin, he had been in Crimea, helping people self-determine their future, and was now in the Donbas to do the same by spreading the Kremlin's propaganda and scaring people into believing Nazis from Kyiv were coming for them.

At the end of the rally, I bumped into Pushilin and asked for an interview.

"There will be a referendum the day after tomorrow," he reminded me. "And there will be a good result. Let's talk after that."

"So you already know the result?" I asked.

"Of course. There is only one way forward," he said.

As the DNR celebrated, fighting flared in Mariupol to the south. Putin had wanted to see the seaside port city under Russian control. It was key to forming a land bridge from Russia to occupied Crimea. Plus, with nearly half a million people, it was the second-largest city in the region after Donetsk, and home to two large steel-manufacturing plants.

A shootout at the police station killed several people. Bodies lay in the street nearby and the building was in flames. I arrived the next morning to find the city crawling with DNR separatists. They had erected shoddy roadblocks and were burning tires to create smokescreens that would keep the Ukrainian army from storming the city and retaking control. There was more pro-Russian sentiment in Mariupol at the time than in many other places. But it was far from a bastion of separatism.

Hordes of rowdy pro-Russian separatists ruled the streets and they wanted blood. At least seven people, including civilians, had been killed and dozens more seriously wounded the day before. I stood where a man had been shot and killed. There was still a large bloodstain marking the spot and a discarded sheet that had been used to cover it. Angry locals swarmed the still-smoldering ruins of the police station and argued amongst each other about who was to blame.

Exactly what transpired at the police headquarters was still difficult to pin down. Police officers told me the fighting broke out when Ukrainian National Guardsmen and security forces rushed into Mariupol after receiving a phone call from a distressed police officer saying he and others had barricaded themselves on the third floor of the police headquarters when a mob of armed separatists stormed the building and demanded that they side "with the people." The officers said they were not sure what caused the separatists to break into the building and attack the officers, but that it was possible that word of police being ordered to forcefully remove separatists from the city hall building they occupied had spurred them into preemptive action.

Alexander Hadeyev, a local factory worker, said he was at the police station during the clashes and was among the group shouting at police with his hands in the air for them to cease firing.

"They just kept shooting . . . we had our hands up and they shot at us," he told me outside the police station. He and his friend Alexei corroborated the police officers' story of the police chief and other officers locking themselves in an office on the building's third floor.

"Yeah, they said they were calling for help. But for what? They needed only to speak with us and this would have been solved," he said, smacking his hands together in a wiping motion to indicate a deal could have been made.

With the police headquarters destroyed and the Ukrainian armed forces out of town, separatists ran amuck in Mariupol overnight and throughout the day following the clashes. Police branches and gun stores were raided, as were several mobile-phone shops. A Ukrainian armored personnel carrier captured by local separatists during the gun battle after it broke down was set alight in a central intersection. Explosions from ammunition still inside echoed throughout the city's streets. Nearby, separatists erected new barricades using discarded materials while others burned tires, creating a wall of acrid black smoke that rose high into the sky.

The whole scene disturbed Viktor, a middle-aged factory worker who had lived his whole life in Mariupol and never seen violence on this level.

"I am very afraid," he told me while standing next to the smoldering wreckage of the armored vehicle. "All through the night I heard explosions and bursts of gunfire. We are usually a quiet seaside city. I don't recognize this." If he had a choice, he said, he would move to Donetsk. But he doesn't have a choice. "I can't leave. Everything I have is here. This is my life." His only hope, he said, was that on 11 May residents of Donetsk and Luhansk oblasts would vote to secede from Ukraine and create the "Donetsk People's Republic."

"I am for the referendum," he told me. "Yesterday I was on the fence, but today I will vote for it."

His remarks elicited responses from bystanders nearby who said they also supported the idea of a quasi-independent state.

"You see, yesterday it was 50-50 here, and today, I think 90-10 in favor of the referendum," Viktor chimed in.

Amid the bedlam, I witnessed the incongruous scene of a young woman running down the main drag in a white wedding dress, a bouquet of flowers in her hand.

"We are getting married!" she squealed with delight, seemingly unaware of the violence unfolding just a couple of blocks away. Her husband-to-be picked her up, spun her around, and kissed her. A photographer standing nearby snapped a flurry of pictures.

I remember sinking into my bed that evening in the Hotel Poseidon and feeling down. For the first time that spring I really believed the Donbas was on the brink of a real war.

As the sun rose over the Donbas, Russia's puppet leaders were still hammering away on hastily erected voting booths and photocopying ballots on which residents of Donetsk would vote in the haphazard "referendum" whose outcome everyone knew was predetermined. It didn't matter what it would take, Russia's proxies were going to get the result they wanted – the Donetsk and Luhansk "people's republics" would be "independent" by day's end.

They framed the vote as a choice between fascism and freedom. Billboards advertising the referendum asked Donetsk residents to "make your choice!" and showed an image of a masked, bloody axe-wielding and Molotov-cocktail-carrying figure – meant to represent Maidan – beside a red X, and a smiling man in an orange miner's helmet carrying a bouquet of red roses beside a green check mark.

Some 800,000 ballots that had been printed were burned the day before, and so the DNR Xeroxed as many as they could overnight. No security markings adorned the ballots, making them vulnerable to manipulation and fraud. Also, no international observers were present to confirm the legitimacy of the referendum.

"Do you support the act of state sovereignty of the Donetsk People's Republic?" read the ballot in Donetsk. It came with an example of what to do with it, showing how to mark YES.

The DNR went ahead with the farcical vote in defiance of the fledgling government in Kyiv and acting President Turchynov, who had called the vote "illegal" and warned that they would be a "step into the abyss." (Putin had even asked that they hold off for a week, at least. He was taking a victory lap in Crimea on that day to extol the return of the Black Sea peninsula to Russia in front of a carefully curated crowd of thousands of people. It was his first trip there since his covert invasion and seizure. He wanted the spotlight.)

But that didn't mean the vote couldn't be fair, according to the separatists' head election official, Roman Lyagin, a 33-year-old former advisor to Yanukovych who was now the self-proclaimed chairman of the central election commission of the so-called DNR.

"Anyone who wants to observe the referendum can do so," he told me when I visited his office. "That's free and fair."

At the same time he was openly admitting that the whole thing was a sham. "Okay, it's not really in line with the law," he told the Reuters news agency.

At a polling station in central Donetsk, I saw several instances in which election workers simply stuffed ballots marked with YES into the ballot boxes. I looked inside and noticed a NO vote facing the plexiglass. Commenting on it, a middle-aged woman with bouffant hair grumbled, "Foo!" and scrunched her face. She told a worker to dig it out and toss it.

Several instances of people voting multiple times were reported by my friend Oleksiy Matsuka's *Novosti Donbassa* news site, which also said that one of its reporters had voted three times in the referendum and would continue to vote NO as many times as he would be allowed.

Many acts of intimidation were also reported. *Novosti Donbassa* said that its reporters witnessed referendum officials tearing apart those ballots marked with "no," while several foreign photojournalists told me that at the polling station inside Donetsk's School No. 1 two men with a pistol and shotgun had stormed in and ordered media to stop filming and photographing the voting process. They left after a few minutes and without farther incident.

That night, Lyagin called a press conference. There, he held up two sheets of paper displaying the results of the bogus referendum. He wore a gray suit and black bow tie and looked incredibly pleased with himself. Turnout was "off the charts" and more than 90 per cent of voters had cast ballots in favor of "independence," he told the room full of journalists and DNR officials. The former shot glances at one another that said, *Are you fucking serious right now?*, while the latter feigned surprise and elation.

"*Ura!*" the DNR representatives cheered.

I was driving from Slovyansk to Bakhmut one afternoon with my friend and trusty driver Volodymyr, who was called Vova or Cowboy, a nickname he'd earned because of the American-style cowboy hat that he wore to cover his balding head. With us was the photographer Kostya Chernichkin. We were fresh from reporting on armed battles in nearby Slovyansk and Kramatorsk. I hadn't yet been back to Bakhmut since the unrest and fighting erupted, and wanted to check in on the place and my friends there. It was days after the DNR and LNR "referendum."

We approached the northwestern entrance to the city and I could see a checkpoint ahead. There was a sign that read "STOP" in English and as we slowed to a halt, two scrappy, gun-toting fighters emerged from a little shack on the roadside. One of them told us to roll down our windows, as the other circled our car with his gun pointed at us. The first man leaned towards Vova, his right hand on his rifle and his left outstretched

"Documents!" he barked.

We handed them over and the soldier inspected them through dark, oversized sunglasses that kept slipping down the brim of his nose. Each time they fell, he took his hand off his weapon to push them back up. When he got to my blue American passport, he sounded out the English words in heavily accented Russian. Then he whipped off the sunglasses and thrust his head through the rear passenger window where I was sitting.

"Kreees!" he shouted. "*Ty vernulsya!*" – "You're back!"

"Ilya?" I asked, shocked.

"Da! Da!" he said. "Look at our republic!"

His long-shot dream of an independent "Donetsk Republic" had – sort of – come true. And he was pumped about it.

"Come to my block post later this evening for dinner," he said. "Not this one, but the one across from the salt mine in Paraskoviivka."

"OK," I said. "We'll come by."

Except for Ilya's band of armed misfits and the checkpoints around the city, Bakhmut looked mostly the same. Shops and hotels were open, New York Street Pizza was busy. The patrons were different, though. They were DNR fighters dressed in combat fatigues. My friends were there but keeping a low profile; they didn't support Russia or the DNR crowd. Only Slava had left; he was now living temporarily in my apartment in Kyiv. One change stood out: the DNR flag had been hoisted over city hall and the Ukrainian coat of arms that adorned the facade had been removed. (Later I found out that a student of mine from School No. 11 had found the coat of arms discarded besides a dumpster behind the building. He dragged it home and kept it hidden for weeks until the city was liberated, when he gave it to the local history museum, which displayed it alongside an exhibit of the war.) I heard that Mayor Reva had cut a deal with the DNR representatives who wanted to control the town: they could put their flag up wherever they'd like, but they wouldn't storm any buildings and take them over, and Reva would run the city. Like he'd done countless times before with the various political parties who'd come to power and then lost it over the decades, he was trying to keep Bakhmut from erupting into violence like Donetsk, Slovyansk, Kramatorsk, and Horlivka around it. He wasn't a collaborator, though some people whispered as much.

"He's a political chameleon," my friend Igor said of Reva.

I also discovered that the local DNR commandant overseeing Bakhmut was the son of a Russian teacher at School No. 11 who had tutored me for a while. He had taken up arms and was running the show in a stolen vehicle, guards in tow. Apparently the teacher was now boasting at the school about her powerful new son while proselytizing about the *Russkiy mir* – Russian world.

"She's brainwashing the children," another teacher quietly lamented to me.

Within a few weeks, though, the Russian teacher's commandant son would be killed in a shootout and she'd flee across the border to Belgorod.

That evening, I returned to Ilya's block post. It was more like a camp. He and several other men had set up tents in front of the mine's entrance and were keeping a watch around the clock on the comings and goings of its staff, while a group of Ukrainian soldiers and guards oversaw security on its premises. Their reason wasn't to stop or take over the production of salt. What they were after was something of local lore.

Stashed almost 1,000 feet below ground, inside the cavernous labyrinth of salt tunnels that were part of a system stretching 125 miles, was one of Europe's largest arsenals of Soviet-era weapons in the world. Compiled over decades, it held more than three million weapons, including Kalashnikov rifles and machine guns, and many millions more rounds of ammunition. I had tried to access it before – when I was a Peace Corps volunteer in Bakhmut and as a journalist, looking for a good feature story. But the military wouldn't grant permission to the public, let alone a foreigner.

If Russia's forces seized control of the depot, "it would change the game," a Ukrainian intelligence source of mine said. Ilya's guys had attacked it once before but failed to take control of it. Now he and his gang of motley fighters were waiting for an opportunity to give it another go. In the meantime, they wanted to be sure the Ukrainian army wasn't removing the weapons for its own use against them.

"We have explosives ready to block it if we must," the intelligence official told me. With the push of a button, the largest depot of Soviet-era guns and ammo could be crushed under the weight of tons of salt and earth.

I asked about whether a controlled explosion had recently been carried out to close an alternative entrance to the arsenal, something I had heard through my grapevine of army sources but hadn't confirmed. But the official kept that knowledge to himself.

"I cannot say yes or no to that question," he said.

11

"Some Fucking Militia"

Torez, Donetsk Oblast, 13 May 2014

The morning was met with an uncomfortable silence after a bloody day in which 14 people had been killed in gun battles in Donetsk and Luhansk. I slept in and did some writing. Then I got a call during lunch from a Donbas Battalion soldier who said there was a fight underway for control of a bridge in Karlivka, west of Donetsk. I told my friend Isaac Webb, a green reporter in Ukraine on a Fulbright Fellowship who had just started working at the *Kyiv Post*, that it might be good to check it out. This was his first trip to the east since the unrest began and he was eager to publish. We were on the road moments later.

But we didn't get far before I received another call. The person on the other line said there had just been an attack in Torez, the mining town east of Donetsk where I'd spent some time years earlier. This was intriguing, since it was deep inside Russia-controlled territory. I wondered, who was fighting there?

At the time, the Ukrainian army and its volunteer forces were actually regaining some of the ground that had been lost to the Russian and separatist proxy forces in April. In particular, some of the battalions were closing in on the H21 highway in an attempt to cut off the LNR from the DNR. There were skirmishes around that crucial road. And I thought this attack might be a part of that effort, and that we'd perhaps be the only ones there to cover it, as opposed to the fight in Karlivka, where every correspondent in town would likely be heading. I liked to zag when everybody else zigged. I told our driver and Isaac we were turning around.

We sped east on the H21 highway toward Torez, unsure of what we'd come across. I told Isaac to put on his Kevlar vest and helmet and handed him a pair of tourniquets, just in case.

When we arrived in Torez about a half hour later, I didn't see any signs of an attack. I asked a couple of older people standing at a bus stop if they'd heard of anything going on in town. One said that something had happened at the city-hall building.

We arrived there a few minutes later to find a group of men, including two guards, smoking outside. I walked up to ask what had happened and they told me there had been an attack.

"By whom?" I asked.

"Some fucking militia," one of the men barked.

"Were they in uniforms?"

"They were in black. With masks," the man said.

"Fucking ninjas," said a guard.

"Did they have guns?"

"Fuck – son of a bitch, did they have guns?" the man said, sucking on his cigarette. "Go inside and see for yourself."

The foyer was ripped apart and a guard station had been shot up. Shattered glass and bullet casings littered the ground. A police officer was writing something in a notebook. He looked up and pointed down the hallway without saying anything.

Inside an office at the end of the hall I found two more police officers. They were taking photographs of the room. They turned to ask who we were and after presenting our press cards we were let in.

They said that gunmen had burst through the front doors, ran towards the office where we now were, and opened fire on the two low-level DNR supporters who had been sitting, unarmed, at their desks.

A young man's body was lying face-down in a sprawling pool of blood that looked like thick liquid velvet. His mouth was open and more blood was slowly flowing out of it. He had a bullet hole in his head and another in his back that I could see. A part of his skull was sitting on the ground beside him. His arms were at his side and I noticed another gunshot wound to his left one.

There were at least five bullet holes in the wall around a "Donetsk People's Republic" flag that dangled by one of its corners. Several more bullet holes were scattered on the other walls. Desks and chairs were flipped over and documents were thrown across the floor. Two megaphones sat undisturbed atop the desk where the man had been sitting. A small religious icon of the Madonna and Child hung directly above where his head had come to rest.

Isaac recoiled at the sight and covered his nose. The room reeked of the metallic smell of the blood. I found myself transfixed by the scene. It instantly brought me back to the shootings on the Maidan on 20 February. But also, this man didn't appear to be much older than me, and he had dark hair and a similar build.

Police told me his name was Roman, and he had celebrated his 34th birthday 12 days earlier, on 11 May, the day the "Donetsk People's Republic" held its referendum, which he had helped to promote.

The police said that the attackers fired at least ten shots. Six slugs were pulled from the walls of the office and displayed on a desk. A second man was taken to the hospital nearby. I got the address and we drove over.

The second victim was a 25-year-old man named Oleksandr. He had been found badly wounded but alive when medics arrived. He had suffered three gunshots, including one in the neck and another in the abdomen, his family and a doctor told us. He would need to undergo surgery.

Myra, a relative, described Oleksandr to me as just an average man who "only wanted to live a normal life."

"Was he a big supporter of the DNR?" I asked.

"No, not really," she said. "He just went along with things."

"Did he carry any weapons? Was he part of the DNR army or something?"

"No, no."

I exchanged contacts with Myra before we left and told her to let me know how the surgery went.

In the car ride back to Donetsk, I found a video showing part of the attack that had been published on YouTube. It showed five gunmen clad all in black entering and exiting the Torez building. At the end of it, they jump from the top of the stairs and dash through the bush to escape.

In the video's description, I noticed a link to Facebook. I clicked it and it took me to a post by Oleh Lyashko, a member of Ukraine's parliament and head of the nationalist political party aptly named the Radical Party. He was taking credit for the killings.

With a baritone voice and a tidy John Edwards-style blowout, Lyashko was a provocateur infamous for his public theatrics, including picking fights and throwing punches in the Verkhovna Rada chamber. He was also a candidate in the upcoming presidential election on 25 May. Polling in single digits, the attack appeared to be a stunt to gain public attention and frame him as the leader who could cleanse the Donbas of Russian insurgents and their pro-Russian supporters.

"Soldiers from the Lyashko Battalion have cleared and liberated the city government building from the 'Kolorady' in Torez, Donetsk Oblast," Lyashko wrote. "Two terrorists were killed, while among our men were no injuries."

He added: "Glory to Ukraine!"

12

Volunteer Battalions

Dnipropetrovsk and Donetsk oblasts, 15 May 2014

The black-clad masked man with a Kalashnikov resting in his arms spoke confidently of the mission about to get underway. "We will act fast, like lightning, and we will be efficient," he said. But should things turn hairy, "We're ready for a war."

To prove his point, another man gestured to a rusty metal pipe with a hastily welded handle resting at his feet. "That's a Ukrainian bazooka. Light a match, and boom!" he said.

In the dusty courtyard of a rickety agricultural factory in this bucolic eastern Ukrainian town of fewer than 40,000 people, some 30 members of a pro-Kyiv militia unit created to fight Kremlin-backed insurgents was readying to storm police headquarters and city hall in Velyka Novosilka. And they had invited me along for the ride.

Days before, following the DNR referendum, local separatists had removed the town's Kyiv-appointed mayor from his office, seized control of the city-council building and raised the red, black, and blue flag of the DNR. Police officials stood idly by, letting it all happen.

Now, this ragtag militia group would storm in and reinstall Oleksandr Arikh, the 29-year-old mayor, take down the self-proclaimed republic's flag and hoist the blue-and-yellow Ukrainian one.

In final preparations before the mission, battalion members – donning full combat gear – went over logistics, as they filled their pockets with zip ties and grenades, and double- and triple-checked magazines before clicking them into their automatic rifles.

Squeezed into ramshackle Soviet-era vehicles, we drove fast in a column over bumpy roads toward the police station. When we arrived, the fighters told me to stay close, but not too close. Then they leapt from the vehicles and rushed the building, shattering its windows with the butts of their rifles and kicking in the doors. The raid was over within minutes, and a dozen trembling policemen were ordered at gunpoint to drop to the ground.

After disarming them and lecturing them about the importance of loyalty and duty to country, the group moved on to the city-council building, where they tore down the DNR flag and hoisted Ukraine's. In all, the mission lasted less than half an hour. Nobody fired a shot.

While the Velyka Novosilka operation was carried out without any hitches, those of other groups had ended in bloodshed. In an incident the following weekend, as separatists opened polls to vote in their farcical referendum on secession, members of the Dnipro Battalion had stormed a government building in another city to stop people from casting ballots. As rowdy separatists swarmed the entrance to the building that day, the militia – wearing assorted and unmarked uniforms, fired several warning shots into the air. Amid the gunfire, one man grabbed the barrel of a militiaman's automatic rifle. In response, the militiaman fired into the pavement, and the bullet ricocheted, hitting the civilian in the leg. That led to more gunfire and at least one man was shot in the back and killed.

With military counter-terrorism operations launched weeks earlier to wrest back control of areas in Donetsk and Luhansk from the grip of Russia's armed local militants proving largely unsuccessful, Ukrainians had started taking matters into their own hands, forming loosely organized militias, or battalions. There were dozens of them with names like Azov, Dnipro and Right Sector. One of the first was the Donbas Battalion, whose commander, Semen Semenchenko, a Donetsk resident with a nasty scar across his face often hidden beneath a black balaclava, invited me to meet him for what would be his first interview one morning.

We met on a road in the middle of nowhere, where he checked me out before leading me to a children's summer camp called *Druzhba*, meaning friendship. It would have been a serene setting for school kids on vacation from drab classrooms and teachers' instructions. Its gates were marked by signs adorned with colorful paintings of rainbows and flowers seemingly drawn by the untrained hands of children. Faded hopscotches decorated the pavement not far from a jungle gym.

Now it was home to Semenchenko, a former army reserve captain, and dozens of mostly men in masks and decked out in black combat gear. All had assault rifles. These were the fighters of the Donbas Battalion. The group was composed largely of ex-military men with experience operating in hot spots around the world as UN peacekeepers, and civilian volunteers, including many who were part of the *sotni* on Maidan. The group was first seen in action on 2 May, when a shaky video published to YouTube showed the black-clad battalion, wielding Kalashnikov rifles, destroying a separatist checkpoint near Krasnoarmiisk, west of Donetsk. During the raid, the militiamen captured 15 pro-Russian fighters and their weapons.

More than 100 militiamen had joined the group by the time I'd arrived, while a farther 600 were on a waiting list. All were unpaid volunteers who had signed up to "defend the motherland," Semenchenko insisted. Many had invested their savings in the battalion, but some money was raised through crowdfunding online. Semenchenko himself was active on Facebook, where he asked "patriots" to donate to the cause by wiring money to a bank account listed there.

Semenchenko told me they had recently caught three spies who attempted to infiltrate the group. They asked "too many questions" and "about mission logistics," he said. "We spotted them immediately." He did not say what became of the spies, other than they were "taken away."

Semenchenko told me the Donbas Battalion and other volunteer militias were crucial to Ukraine's defense, since the army was largely unable to respond.

On several occasions, Ukraine's army, faced with even mild resistance, had simply turned over their weapons and armored personnel carriers to pro-Russian fighters and even unarmed separatists.

"If we don't do it, who will?" Semenchenko said. Ukraine's military were "scared mice" who "give up without fighting."

"They have the authority, the guns. But they flee from armed and unarmed traitors," he said.

Another issue for Ukraine was its police forces in the east. Hundreds if not thousands of local officers had defected to the pro-Russian side, or had fled the region or simply stopped showing up for work, leaving a massive security vacuum.

The criteria for joining the ranks of the Donbas Battalion was straightforward: men and women had to be at least 18 years old, healthy, and show a great love for their Motherland. Then they underwent about 50 hours of training before they were "battle ready," Semenchenko said.

I asked to see how they were preparing for a war. He led me past the barracks to a gully at the edge of the camp, where a dozen fighters were holding target practice. Two of them looked unsteady and unfamiliar with their weapons. I asked them if they'd ever fired a gun before and they said this would be their first time. One was a middle-aged nurse who had tended to the protesters on Maidan during the revolution. She told me she was prepared to fight and die for Ukraine then, just as she was now.

13

"Live in a New Way"

Kyiv and Artemivsk, 25 May 2014

Two weeks later, Ukrainians went to the polls to vote in the first presidential election since the Revolution of Dignity and the overthrow of Yanukovych. I had never seen so many people turn out to vote.

In typical fashion, the ballot looked like a grocery list. There were 21 candidates in all, including several oligarchs and many familiar, old-guard types. Among them was Yulia Tymoshenko, the "Gas Princess" with her golden crown of braids, taking another shot at the presidency after several failed attempts. There were also some radical nationalist candidates, including Lyashko, whose bloodthirsty battalion was running around the east, hunting down pro-Russian separatists. Svoboda's Tyahnybok and Right Sector's Dmytro Yarosh had also thrown their hats in the ring. Then there was Petro "The Chocolate King" Poroshenko, the billionaire oligarch whose presence on the Maidan had been lackluster but not controversial. He'd had a somewhat embarrassing mishap when he climbed atop the tractor on 1 December, outside the presidential administration, and tried to quell the violent protesters, who responded by throwing candy at him. And there were some concerns about his past, including that he had been a founder of the Party of Regions back in 2001, and that he had been a part of the corrupt past that Ukrainians were trying to shake.

No matter who won, it was clear that the old guard would continue to be a feature in its post-revolution Ukraine. But Ukraine needed a manager. And most thought Poroshenko had the chops, even if they weren't excited about him.

Russia tried and failed to intervene in the elections. State-run propaganda channels ran a fake graphic they claimed had come from Ukraine's central election commission which showed Yarosh had won the election. It couldn't have been farther from the truth. In fact, Yarosh would

175

suffer an embarrassing defeat with less than one per cent of the vote. So would Tyahnybok.

In Kyiv, people laughed about what seemed like such a pathetic effort to paint Ukraine as a country of far-right extremists. But some in the occupied Donetsk and Luhansk areas, and in Russia, seemed to believe it, or at least wanted to believe that there was a chance the election had been rigged, if only to justify their support for Russia's military intervention.

In the DNR and LNR areas, authorities had done whatever they could to stop people from voting. In the days leading up to the election, they threatened, intimidated, and attacked local-election officials. They even went so far as to burn down election offices.

In Artemivsk, gunmen stormed into city hall, ordered everyone to throw up their hands, and started smashing everything in sight. They dashed up the stairs to the election office where Igor was working and ordered him and his colleagues to hand over local voter information and ballots for the upcoming presidential election. They told them to grab the ballot boxes adorned with the Ukrainian coat of arms and bring them outside. Igor and the others piled the boxes on the sidewalk out front and took a few steps back. Then the gunmen sprayed them with bullets.

"If we have elections tomorrow, they will kill us," Igor told me when we met at New York Street Pizza the day before the vote. He spoke under his breath in order not to draw the attention of the fighters stuffing their faces a few tables down, their Kalashnikovs resting on their laps.

I spent part of Ukraine's Election Day in Donetsk, where the DNR had organized an anti-election party with a huge rent-a-crowd on Lenin Square and dozens of Russian, Chechen, and pro-Russian Ukrainian soldiers from the Vostok Battalion who were brought in on military vehicles. They climbed out and lined up on Artema Street. Many wore masks. All were heavily armed. Upon command, they pointed their weapons into the air and opened fire with hundreds of live rounds.

The crowd, mostly composed of older women, cheered and planted big red kisses on their soldiers' cheeks. Two women waved a Novorossiya flag, which was identical to the Confederate flag, minus the stars.

Elsewhere, Ukrainians turned out in huge numbers to vote. In nearby Krasnoarmiisk, which later would be renamed Pokrovsk, they wore patriotic clothing and sang national songs, and cast their votes behind blue-and-yellow curtains.

Poroshenko won the election with an outright majority, receiving 54.7 per cent of the votes and avoiding a run-off. The Chocolate King was president, and Ukraine's first elected wartime leader.

"He was the least bad option," said my friend Anton, who voted for him. "Let's see if we can live in a new way," he added, riffing on Poroshenko's campaign slogan.

14

"This is a War Now"

Donetsk Airport, 26 May 2014

The next morning, I rushed from the Ramada to Donetsk's Sergei Prokofiev International Airport, but not to catch a flight. Overnight, all planes had been grounded and traffic to and from the airport had been suspended, after the DNR's troops had entered the terminals and seized a lot of the ground in and around the premises. The Ukrainians responded by moving to protect the runway and began advancing toward the terminals before dawn. Then all hell broke loose.

The airport had been a symbol of Donetsk's transformation from dull, post-Soviet malaise to vibrant modernity. Now it was a battleground for close-quarters combat.

Isaac was with me and looking terrified. I wasn't feeling great about what we were doing either, but I put on a brave face. Our driver refused to take us down the highway where the terminals were located, which was probably for the best. Two civilians in a black Toyota had come under fire there and one of them was shot dead as he tried to make a run for a patch of bush on the roadside. You could see his body just lying there, face down, with the blood slowly running out and onto the pavement. Above him was a sign that read "Arrivals" and "Departures."

The driver instead took us to a neighborhood wedged between the airport and the railway station. He parked beside a small home and told us we'd have to walk the rest of the way. We put on our helmets and vests and shut the door. Then the driver sped away, leaving us behind.

"What the fuck? Did he really leave us?" I said to Isaac.

"Dude. How the fuck are we getting out of here?"

I had no idea, but I'd worry about that later.

DNR fighters in military vehicles and ordinary civilian cars – Honda Civics, Toyota Corollas, Volkswagen Jettas – zoomed down the streets, their guns hanging out, masks over their faces. We made our way cautiously down a series of short roads, following the cracks of Kalashnikov fire and booms of RPGs, until we saw a group of DNR soldiers running past. Bullets whipped by and we found a place to take cover inside a brick bus stop. The fighting grew louder and dust was flying all around from the bullets striking the bricks and asphalt. I told Isaac to wait there while I ran 50 feet away to the outer wall of a cemetery to get a better view of the action.

Huge plumes of black smoke rose from the terminal. The Ukrainians had warplanes flying overhead and attack helicopters circling the area. Every few minutes, they came flying in fast and low, strafing the positions of the DNR soldiers, who opened fire on it with small arms. Drrr-drrr-drrr, drrr-drrr-drrr. The choppers' cannon fire was terrifying and insanely destructive. It ripped apart everything in its path. The DNR couldn't shoot it down and those who tried got blasted.

A group of fighters screaming in Russian came running up behind me and shoved me aside. One pulled out an RPG and crouched in a firing stance in the road. I had seen shoulder-fired grenades used in the movies and from a distance over the past weeks, but never up close like this. I wasn't a war correspondent and hadn't been trained to know how to operate on a battlefield. I definitely didn't know that being on the rear side of an RPG is also relatively dangerous. And so I didn't know that I should have had my mouth open to avoid having my eardrum ruptured from the air compression, or that the back blast was capable of throwing me to the ground. When the rocket exploded out of its launcher, I stumbled back and one of the fighters caught me. My ears were ringing. The fighter said something, but I couldn't make it out. I heard only *wah wah wah*.

The fighters ran forward and I followed. We ended up diving behind a cluster of trees, where there were other fighters and a bunch of journalists with cameras. Many were filming the fighting with the lenses pointed over the shoulders of the fighters. It looked incredibly stupid. Moments later, one cameraman was nearly struck when Ukrainian snipers opened fire on the position. A DNR fighter nearby was hit in the thigh and writhed on the ground in pain. I decided to get the hell out of there and ran back over to the bus stop where Isaac was. On my way I saw an old man walk into the middle of the street. He was carrying a white cross and a bible and mumbling some sort of prayer.

Without a car, we had to scramble on foot out of the fight. Eventually we made our way to the train station, where we found the body of a parking attendant lying on the ground. She'd been hit with a stray bullet. Minutes later, as we exited the other side of the station, another civilian was struck and killed by a stray bullet.

By nightfall, much of the airport was a mess of spattered blood, shattered glass, and mangled steel. The Ukrainians had managed to take back control of most of it, but the fighting wasn't over. Poroshenko, in his first day as president, vowed to stop it, and Russia's creeping invasion in the Donbas, in "hours." But the Kremlin's DNR forces would return with a vengeance. The airport battle would last months and see some of the heaviest and most grueling fighting of the war. Ukrainians defending it would come to be known as "cyborgs" for their superhuman efforts to defend the airport in hellish conditions for 242 days. But many of them would die doing so.

Back at the Ramada hotel, I frantically wrote stories about the events of the past 24 hours for several news outlets while chain-smoking and drinking heavily. I probably had six, seven, eight glasses of whiskey. On an empty stomach, too. I was too anxious to eat.

Kirill, the pro-Russian Ukrainian soldier, came over and sat down beside me.

"Chris, give me a cigarette, please," he said.

I held out the carton and he took two. My hand was shaking.

"You OK?"

"Seriously? No," I said. "This is a fucking nightmare."

"You'll get used to it," he told me. "You can get used to anything. Even war."

"This is a war now, huh?" I asked.

"Yes, this is a war now," he said.

The next morning I visited Donetsk's central morgue, where the new reality was on full ghastly display. Dozens of mangled corpses were carelessly piled as high as my waist. They spilled into the hallway. Some were headless. Most of the others were missing limbs. They had been ripped, shredded, crushed, twisted, broken, and filleted. The sight and smell were unbearable, even for the morgue workers, who gagged on the stench of death and fled outside to vomit. One worker offered some menthol rub to put under my nose and I obliged.

There were 33 bodies in all. And according to a stack of passports that I quickly rifled through before police officers came to remove me and several other journalists, almost all were Russian nationals. Some were from Moscow Oblast. Others from Chechnya and North Ossetia. I snapped several photographs of their bodies under examination before being scolded by one of the police officers, who was clearly on the side of the DNR.

"You're not going to tell the world the truth!" he shouted. "You're going to show lies!"

Outside, Sergei Khokholya, a police investigator, said the corpses were undergoing autopsies and then would be returned to their families.

"Where are their families?" I asked.

"Here," he said.

"But I saw they are almost all from Russia?" I asked.

"No, we haven't identified them yet because they have no documents," he said.

"But I saw their documents inside," I countered.

"No, no. It's impossible," he insisted.

I waited around for a couple of hours to see whether anyone would come by to claim the bodies. Just one family did. The dead man was a local Ukrainian. His head had been completely collapsed and then rebuilt by the mortician. They loaded him up in a black van and I watched his wife, mother, and another woman weep over the top of his open casket.

The rest of the bodies were later put into bright-red coffins that had been stacked near the morgue building and taken to an ice-cream factory, where they were refrigerated. That night, they were moved into a white truck marked Gruz 200 – a tag that came from the Soviet war in Afghanistan, signifying soldiers who had been killed in the line of duty – and driven under cover of darkness to the border with Russia, where they were repatriated.

15

Executioners

Slovyansk, 7 July 2014

In the early hours of 5 July, Igor Girkin went against the Kremlin's orders and retreated with his fighters from Slovyansk to Donetsk. Their departure followed more than two months of occupation and weeks of heavy fighting against the Ukrainian army and its volunteer forces. Girkin said it was necessary to avoid a devastating military defeat of DNR forces, which he claimed were on the verge of collapse. The move caught many by surprise, including the Kremlin and Girkin's own men, who were furious about the withdrawal.

Some 48 hours later, on 7 July, I arrived in Slovyansk by train from Kyiv with journalists Max Seddon, then of BuzzFeed News, and Noah Sneider, who was freelancing for *The New York Times* and *The Economist*. Slovyansk had been the first city to fall to the Russia-backed forces in April, and we were eager to see what it looked and felt like back under Ukrainian government control. We also wanted to know what the separatists had left behind, especially inside one building in particular: the local headquarters of Ukraine's state Security Service, the SBU, which was among the first buildings seized by Girkin and his "little green men."

We quickly made our way there, careful not to attract attention. The razor-wire-wrapped barricades that had been manned by menacing, gun-toting fighters days earlier were gone and the approach to the building was eerily devoid of activity. To our surprise, no Ukrainian soldiers were there, and the front door was ajar.

Inside, even in the light of the afternoon, the place was dark. It was also messy, reeked of gasoline, and a film of black soot covered everything. Mindful of booby traps, we tiptoed around overturned furniture and abandoned items, including Chinese-made coffee mugs adorned with the flag of Girkin's battalion. It was clear that the separatists had left in a hurry and had tried, unsuccessfully, to burn what they could not take with them.

In the basement where prisoners were kept, we found rancid food and a bar of soap used for washing on a windowsill. Stuck to a wall was a plastic bottle used to gather drinking water from a leak in the ceiling. On the floor were three damp mattresses covered in stains. Dozens of flies buzzed around the room, which was illuminated only slightly from a small window fitted with bars.

Back upstairs, we wandered into rooms where Girkin and his deputies had worked. Noah noticed a bunch of documents, some of them in plastic folders, scattered across the floor in a corner office. We picked some up and Noah began reading aloud from one of the sheets of paper. "*Zakaz*" – "Order," it began. And then, a few lines down, ". . . sentenced to death by firing squad."

We noticed a signature in blue ink on several of the documents. It read: "Igor Ivanovich Strelkov."

The three of us froze and looked at each other, at once realizing we had stumbled onto something big. Without much consideration, we quickly stuffed all the documents, many of them covered in soot or soaked with gasoline, into our backpacks and called our driver to come pick us up.

Our plan was to get back to the Ramada in Donetsk, a harrowing drive through military checkpoints and across the war's front line, where we had booked rooms for the week, and to start rifling through our discovery. On the highway, Ukrainian forces stopped us because a firefight was underway on the road ahead. After turning back, we got stuck in a convoy of Ukrainian armored vehicles. We sat there for several minutes until enemy mortar shells came raining down and exploded in the fields on either side of us. Bursts of machine-gun fire from Ukrainian troops then rang out. We were stuck, huddling with our combat gear and covered in grime, for another 30 minutes before we were able to break out of the jam.

With night falling and checkpoints on the roads closing, we knew we wouldn't make it to Donetsk, so we pulled over at a trucker motel called The Man in the town of Druzhkivka. There were no other guests; we booked three suites. In one of them, we began going through the documents that were dry enough to handle. Those that were not we carefully peeled apart and laid across the bed and floor, opening a window in an attempt to make them dry faster.

That was a mistake: a gust of wind blew several of them around and slammed the motel-room door shut, shattering its glass panel. The noise brought the manager running upstairs; she let us stay for an extra $50.

That night, we pored over the documents and slept little. What we found was the first hard evidence of war crimes committed by figures tied to the Russian state in the Donbas: the extrajudicial executions of three Ukrainian men by firing squad.

The discovery would cause a firestorm.

This is what the documents showed: Girkin's DNR forces came for Oleksiy Pichko on the afternoon of 17 June, three days after he broke into a neighbor's empty home and took two shirts and a pair of pants. They found the 30-year-old near his parents' cottage and hauled him into the SBU building's dungeon that had been occupied by Girkin and used as his occupation headquarters. "They came and took him . . . and we saw nothing else," one woman told us when we returned to the scene to report the information in the documents.

Pichko was beaten, interrogated, forced to write a confession, and then subjected to a sham "trial" before he was summarily shot to death by a firing squad under the orders of Igor Girkin.

His mother, Maria, and friends who sought out his whereabouts after he was taken told me that the executioners then discarded his body on a nearby battlefield, where it could be blown to smithereens by exploding artillery shells.

He wasn't the only person in Slovyansk to meet such a fate under Girkin's watch. The documents showed that three weeks earlier, on 25 May, two Ukrainian men who had joined the Russia-backed DNR army, Dmytro Slavov aged 32, and Mykola Lukyanov aged 25, had been arrested by their own comrades. Accused of marauding, armed robbery, kidnapping, abandonment of their military positions, and trying to cover up their activities, they were also interrogated before being lined up and executed by a firing squad, according to family members, acquaintances, former detainees, and two Slovyansk residents with knowledge of their so-called "trials" and deaths.

The documents showed that the fates of all three men had been decided by so-called "military tribunals" established by Girkin on the basis of a draconian law conceived by Stalin and imposed shortly after

Germany invaded the Soviet Union in the Second World War. The decree handed down by the Presidium of the Supreme Soviet of the USSR on 22 June 1941, and invoked by Girkin and his Russia-backed forces in 2014, allowed for capital punishment – a penalty abolished by Ukraine in 2000 and not imposed in Russia, where a moratorium has been in place since 1996 – for crimes that Girkin called "grave" but ranged from petty theft to murder.

There was also a third case. Another DNR fighter, Alexander Valeryevich Pyrozhenko, had narrowly escaped a firing squad when he was acquitted of treason following an incident in which he shone a flashlight at night during a firefight with Ukrainian forces, a move his comrades deemed to be "treason" for giving away their position. Pyrozhenko confirmed his case by phone when we called him. He said he was in Donetsk and that he didn't want to say anything more about it, especially with Girkin now in the city.

In the document ordering Pichko's execution, Girkin displayed the cruelty that he and his fellow Russians would impute to Ukrainians then and for years to come.

"I warn all fighters and commanders of the DNR militia, and also residents of Slovyansk and the Slovyansk area, that any grievous crime committed in the zone of military activity will continue to be punished ruthlessly and decisively," he wrote. "Punishments for crimes will be unavoidable, regardless of the status and service of the criminal."

The documents disturbed me more than anything I'd seen at that point. And I would become obsessed with them, spending the next five years piecing them together and tracking down the full identities and locations of all the Russian and Ukrainian members of Girkin's "court." I would even fly to Moscow to confront Girkin in person. He refused to talk.

I would also return every year to visit Maria Pichko, Oleksiy's mother. We would sit in her garden and talk about her son while she showed me old photographs of him as a child. He had been a troublemaker at times, she admitted. He had even done a short stint in jail before he was killed. But he loved his family and he was her son – which was what mattered most to her – and didn't deserve to be coldly shot dead.

In Oleksiy's handwritten confession, written shortly before he was killed, he attempted to appeal to whatever bit of humanity existed in his DNR captors. "I also have a pregnant wife, Rydkovskaya Inna Vladimirovna," he said. "I want to see her and raise children and be a useful member of society."

One summer afternoon, as the mosquitoes bit our arms, Maria confessed to me that she still lived in denial about her son's death and believed that he could walk through the front door.

"I believe he will come back to us," she said, wiping tears from her eyes. She gestured to the little girl playing in the sandbox beside us.

Warning

One hot July evening a few days after our stories about Girkin's firing squads had run, a United Nations representative who'd also been staying at the Ramada found me on the terrace eating a bowl of spaghetti carbonara. She had just left a meeting with the DNR authorities who had now sent their goons to search for us.

"They are looking for you," she told me.

"Me?" I said.

"Yes, you."

"Why? What do they want?"

"Why do you think? They were not pleased with your report."

"Right."

"They have people out looking for you now. There are only so many hotels in Donetsk."

"Shit."

"Yeah, there is some very ugly guy who is doing it."

I found Max and Noah and told them we needed to pack our things. Then I headed upstairs. When I got out of the elevator and rounded the corner, I saw a man I knew by reputation coming out of my room. I raced back to the elevator and caught it before the doors closed. Downstairs, I waited in a corner chair out of sight in the lobby until I saw him leave. There were two other men with him. They didn't see me. I asked a friend at the reception desk to go check on my room for me before I went back up. When she said it was clear, I went in to grab my things and then rushed to the car, where Max and Noah were waiting.

We were especially nervous about the checkpoints that day because we thought maybe our names had been on a list to stop and detain. The first checkpoint was a breeze. A group of four or five scraggly locals sauntered out of a ramshackle hut like they'd been on a bender the night before. They looked at us and told us, "Write the truth!" Then they waved us through.

At the second checkpoint we were waved to the side of the road. There were dozens of cars trying to pass in or out of Donetsk. We waited for 15 minutes before a *starshi* – the checkpoint chief – came over to look through our documents.

He left and took them into a small hut. Each minute that passed felt like an hour. I was growing concerned. I looked around to see what the gunmen were doing and if anyone appeared as though they were readying to drag us out. But they were gathered by a shot-up bus where they had recently ambushed and killed several Right Sector fighters. It stood there like some sick trophy and a dark warning to anyone trying to slip through their lines.

The commander finally came back out and asked us what we had seen in Donetsk and what we were reporting.

"The truth," we said.

"Very good," he said. "Safe travels." And he waved us away.

16

Fields of Death

I rolled into the *Kyiv Post* office after lunch. I was dragging myself after returning on the overnight train from the Donbas that morning and following another intense month on the ground in and around Donetsk. I'd hoped to rest up in Kyiv for a week before going back.

I was sitting at my desk when reports started trickling in that the DNR forces had shot down another plane near Donetsk. In the newsroom, we made calls and scanned social media to see what we might be able to find and confirm. At first, we all thought it had been a Ukrainian military transport plane. In the days and weeks prior, Russia's forces in the Donbas had managed to shoot down several of Kyiv's aircraft over the region, including one carrying dozens of Ukrainian soldiers. The celebrations rolling in on social media from Russian and pro-Russian fighters also hinted that the plane belonged to the Ukrainians.

Girkin wrote on VKontakte, Russia's version of Facebook: "We did warn you: do not fly in our sky."

He shared a video of the plane's debris falling from the sky and added that it had been "downed somewhere around Torez."

"The bird went down behind a slagheap, not in a residential district. So no peaceful people were injured," he continued.

I wrote up a story with what was known for the *Kyiv Post* and Mashable, and sent some lines of copy to international newspapers I was a stringer for. It was a few hours before anyone arrived on the site and photographs and reports showed that the plane was not, in fact, a military plane.

No sooner had Girkin's militants arrived at the crash site than they realized what they had done. Expecting to find debris from a military plane and evidence of a military victory, they instead discovered the bodies of hundreds of civilians – men, women, and children – scattered across the wide field.

Girkin deleted his VKontakte post and changed his tune. Now he was claiming the plane was downed by Kyiv with help from Western intelligence agencies as part of a bizarre plot to blame Russia and the DNR. "Corpses were entirely bloodless – as if their blood had clotted long before the accident," he wrote.

I grabbed my things and dashed to Kyiv's central railway station to catch the first train back to the Donbas.

—

Passengers began boarding the Boeing 777 at Amsterdam's bustling Schiphol International Airport a little before noon on 17 July. The manifest was a tapestry of the world: Europeans, Australians, Canadians, Indonesians, Malaysians, New Zealanders, and Filipinos were on the flight to Kuala Lumpur, along with 15 crew members from Malaysia Airlines. Some of the 283 passengers were going on holiday while others were headed home. There were several people traveling for business, including an international group of scientists bound for an HIV/AIDS conference in Melbourne, Australia.

A Dutch 15-year-old named Gary Slok snapped a toothy selfie with his mom, Petra, as they settled into their seats. They were on a trip designed for single parents with children.

Mohd Ali bin Md Salim, 30 years old, posted a short clip on Instagram showing passengers stuffing suitcases into the overhead bins. The captain could be heard on the intercom, announcing that boarding is complete and asking the passengers to switch off their mobile phones.

A Dutch musician named Cor Pan posted a photo of the Boeing plane at the gate to his Facebook timeline with a caption referencing Malaysia Airlines Flight 370, which had vanished without a trace, apparently over the Indian Ocean, a few months earlier. "In case we go missing, here's what it looks like," he wrote.

As the plane lifted off from Schiphol, Tom Warners, an amateur photographer, took a final picture from the ground.

Flight MH17 soon reached its cruising altitude around 33,000 feet, when passengers would have settled into their seats, scanned the in-flight movies or opened their iPads or books as the crew came down the aisles with drinks and snacks.

It would be a long flight to Kuala Lumpur – around 12 hours from Amsterdam – but outside the oval windows, above the clouds, the sky was a perfect blue.

Meanwhile, a group of soldiers from Russia's 53rd Air Defense Brigade dragged a Buk missile launcher from Kursk, Russia, across the battlefields of the Donbas. Around 11 a.m. a photographer from the French magazine *Paris Match* snapped a photo of the Buk moving east from Donetsk on Highway 21 on a flatbed trailer. The identification number 3X2 had been partly painted over but remained visible in the photograph.

It was just after 4 p.m. when MH17's pilot made contact with air-traffic control at Ukraine's Dnipropetrovsk International Airport: "Dnipro Radar, Malaysia one-seven, flight level 330."

"Good day, we have radar contact," came the response from the ground.

A little while later, the airport transmitted a navigation request: "Due to air traffic, proceed to waypoint Romeo November Delta."

The pilot acknowledged receipt of the new course at 4:19 p.m.

It was the last transmission from the doomed flight.

Two minutes later, air-traffic control watched as MH17 disappeared from the radar screen.

"Malaysia one seven, can you hear me, Malaysia one seven?" air-traffic control called to the plane.

It made two more attempts but received no response.

The black box would stop recording at 4:20 p.m., the moment the plane was shot down: 298 people perished.

Yelena Bratchenko, a 20-year-old bank teller, saw the Boing 777 passing over her village of Hrabove before it exploded.

She would tell me less than 48 hours later that what she saw on 17 July could never be forgotten.

The passengers, she said, "just fell very, very hard to the ground."

Other villagers described to me the explosion but hadn't seen the plane. Scared but curious, they emerged from their homes and approached the crash site. One of them was the mayor of Hrabove, 60-year-old Volodymyr Berezhnoi, who told me there was "mass panic." He was in his cottage when debris and bodies from the plane fell into the field nearby. When the larger pieces struck the earth, everything shook. It felt like an earthquake. It sent people running for cover wherever they could find it – basements, doorways, bathtubs. They clutched loved ones as they prayed for their safety.

They emerged to discover a hot, raging fire burning in the dry fields. Some grabbed hoses in a futile attempt to put out the flames. Once the flames finally dissipated, the villagers saw the evidence of death all around.

The DNR cordoned off the crash site, bringing in hundreds of people, including emergency workers and local coal miners, to comb through the fields. Wherever they found a corpse or human remains, the workers planted a stick with white tape attached. Passports and any other personal items that might help identify the victims were gathered in piles by the road.

Journalists, myself included, began to arrive early on 19 July. The scene was an absolute nightmare. Worse than anything I could have ever imagined. And it would keep me up for nights on end.

I could see the crash site from half a mile away as my car approached on the worst dirt road I'd ever driven on. I passed several *kopanki*, illegal coal mines, and gorgeous sunflower fields before arriving at the scene. A white cross stood on the roadside with the message "Heaven help us." But I saw only hell.

The field was black and smoldering. Plane debris was strewn across the torched ground. The stench of burnt flesh and jet fuel weighed heavily in the air. There were bodies everywhere. You could see it all from nearly half a mile away, as you approached

One man, face down in the field, was wearing jeans but his shirt and shoes were gone. There was a large hole in the middle of his back. The body of another man was fully clothed, but his legs had been torn off and his arms burnt. His face was nearly perfect, however, and frozen in fear.

Yet another body – this one of a young man or teenager – was completely stripped naked. His clothes had somehow ripped off during his rapid descent. But his body otherwise appeared pristine and, with his eyes and mouth closed, he looked as if he had simply lain down and fallen asleep right there. It was a sight I'd never be able to shake from my mind. So many impossibilities in one image.

Many more were still strapped into their seats. One man had an oxygen mask strapped to his face. I couldn't bear the thought of him and other passengers surviving the blast, to then be forced to contemplate their fate as they fell to earth.

The passengers' belongings were scattered all around, everyday objects made tragic by sudden, violent death. A photo album with pictures of a smiling family. Jewelry and handbags. Hand lotion and bottles of prescription medication. A Bali travel guide. An "I heart Amsterdam" T-shirt. A wedge of Dutch cheese and bottles of duty-free booze that had miraculously survived the 30,000-foot fall intact. A child's red Minnie Mouse lunchbox.

Across the road, the plane's tail fin was flat on its side. Farther down, the engines, landing gear, and central part of MH17's fuselage was sitting in a scorched area the size of half a football field.

A torn-apart cockpit came to rest in the middle of a golden field of sunflowers nearby. The red-and-blue letters on a crumpled panel darkly indicated its provenance: "Malaysia Airlines."

Horrified at the grisly scene, some of the Russian fighters, usually a hard-bitten lot, were sick in front of me. But others were disrespectful, kicking the possessions and rifling through them. They grumbled that their side couldn't have possibly been responsible. It had to be the "Nazis" and "fascists" in Kyiv who downed the plane.

A Ukrainian pro-Russian commander named Alexander Khodakovsky phoned one of his men at the crash site and ordered him to find the black boxes. Moscow, he said, was demanding possession of them. They fanned out to look for them.

Meanwhile, the miners bagged the bodies they found and piled them in dump trucks to be driven into Torez. There, they'd be deposited onto a train, which sat idle for three days before finally moving to Ukraine-controlled territory.

I sat beside a group of the miners as dusk descended on the field of death. One pulled a flask of samogon from his pocket and passed it around. When it got to me, I couldn't turn it down. I took a giant swig.

Meanwhile, the hunt was on for the crew who had opened fire on the plane and the weapon they had used. Later, an intercepted phone call between DNR commanders would indicate a Buk anti-aircraft missile system and its crew were responsible. But they had already fled to Russia with the weapon. It had been spotted on a flatbed trailer with one of its missiles missing.

There was little doubt among officials in Washington that the Russians were responsible for shooting down MH17, but more information was needed to prove it.

Within hours of the downing, the State Department had said it determined that a missile was launched near Snizhne, about 20 miles southeast of the crash site. Officials also released a grainy black-and-white photograph supposedly showing the missile's path. Another photo posted to Twitter by an anonymous account backed up the State Department's claim. It showed a vapor trail in the same area at the time of the downing of MH17.

17

The Launch Site

Pervomaiske, Donetsk Oblast, 21 July 2014

Visible over the wheat stalks, a small sedan was barreling down the bumpy road toward us. I was with Roland Oliphant of the *Daily Telegraph* and we were on the outskirts of Snizhne, ten miles from the Russian border.

"These look like real fucking soldiers," he said with a terrified look on his face.

"Let's get our story straight," I said.

We had only a moment. What was the story? We couldn't tell them that we were searching for a missile launcher, or traces of where one had been – not in the middle of nowhere and a war zone crawling with trigger-happy fighters who were no fans of nosy foreign journalists. So, we were idiot foreigners who had gotten lost.

When the beat-up vehicle came to a screeching halt beside us, three armed soldiers in camouflage fatigues stepped out. As if the maneuver had been practiced a thousand times before, they simultaneously lit cigarettes, thrust their Kalashnikov rifles over their shoulders, and shouted, "Documents!"

We gave them our passports and showed our DNR accreditations. "You think this will save you?" one scoffed. The fighters' eyes narrowed as they scanned our documents, noting aloud our nationalities. "Amerikanets. Britanets. Hmm."

"What are you doing here?" one asked.

"We're lost," I said, feigning ignorance. "We were on the highway and trying to find the plane crash site."

"Excuse us," Roland said. "Maybe you can point us in the right direction?"

We must have looked dumb or terrified enough to be believed, because they pointed north to Torez, returned our documents, and drove away.

Continuing our search, Roland and I trudged through the wheat field. We had planned our excursion the evening before on the Ramada hotel terrace. We had both spent days at the crash site, but the story was moving on from there. Everyone was now searching for clues that could help answer the many other still-open questions.

As the sounds of shelling rumbled through Donetsk, we pored over a post on a blog that caught our attention. In it, an amateur open-source analyst had claimed to have narrowed the possible launch site to three locations in a relatively small area southeast of Snizhne, based on a photograph of the missile's vapor trail that had been posted to Twitter. His findings seemed to align closely with the movement of the Buk missile system traced by Eliot Higgins, the open-source analyst who founded the investigative group Bellingcat, using dashboard-camera footage and satellite images. It would be a long shot, but with an early start and a smaller area to search than previously thought, Roland and I had a hunch that we might just get lucky.

We had set off early in the morning with a local taxi driver in a crappy old car, hoping to keep as low a profile as possible. Heading east from Donetsk, down roads cratered by artillery shells, we passed checkpoint after checkpoint. Beyond the city limits, the road and fields opened up and a feeling of uncertainty washed over us. We were deep in the heart of Russia-controlled territory, where a lot could go wrong and people who roused suspicions had a way of going missing.

A couple of hours later, we pulled into Snizhne, a depressed coal-mining city where anti-Western sentiment was prevalent. A Ukrainian air strike had also just hit an apartment building and killed several people. Fighters and locals here were fuming. I had been here before, during my Peace Corps days and found it to be dirty and rough. But it was in even worse shape now.

We drove through a neighborhood of cottages until we came to a dirt road that led to what had been a Soviet collective farm. This was one of the locations noted in the blog post that aligned with the MH17 crash site and the vapor-trail photo.

There, we found three very surprised men, covered in dirt and grime, working in a garage. They said they hadn't seen anything, though they were there when the plane was shot down. They declined to say anything more.

We left our taxi then and huffed it on foot through the wheat fields. That's where we ran into the soldiers in the car. But as they drove off, Roland noticed a large combine harvester cutting its way through the field a few hundred feet to the east.

We found Vasily, a local farmer, behind the wheel. Years of hard work under the sun had carved deep crevices into his tanned skin, while the noisy combine engine left him hard of hearing. He asked us to climb onto his machine to speak to him. He was working right in the middle of another possible location pointed out in the blog. Looking northwest from the spot, which rose slightly from the surrounding landscape, was a clear view of MH17's flight path. I remember feeling a rush of adrenaline that made my neck go cold in the summer heat.

But then Vasily said he had neither heard nor seen a missile launch nearby. "I can't even hear the shelling when I'm in the cab," he told us.

One thing struck him as odd, however.

"The field down the way was burning the other day. I don't know why," he said. "You might have a look there." He thought it happened on 17 or 18 July.

When we were back in the taxi, the driver headed down a tractor-worn path eastward across the field about a half mile, in the direction of the villages of Chervoniy Zhovten and Pervomayskiy, keeping a close eye on the northwestern horizon. Then we pulled around a thin tree line and stopped the car.

"This has to be it," I said.

The burned area was unmistakable and in any other circumstances perhaps unremarkable. There were no missile systems present. But in the context of MH17, it seemed as close to a smoking Buk as we were going to get.

The longer we were there the more it felt like we'd found what we were looking for. The area was crawling with soldiers and we could hear an intense battle raging at Savur-Mohyla, a strategic hilltop to the south. Roads to and from Russia were on either side of us, yet the tree line provided the perfect cover to hide behind.

"If you wanted to fire a missile at a plane flying from that direction" – Roland said, gesturing toward the MH17 crash site north of Torez – "then this would definitely be a good place to do it."

We scoured the blackened, oddly shaped area. As Vasily suggested, it didn't look like any ordinary crop fire. Numerous track marks ran near it and through it, along with detritus that suggested a group of people had idled there: discarded water bottles, beer bottles, and cigarette packs with Russian labels.

I photographed the area and filmed a short video of Roland walking around. We stayed for a couple of hours, scratching our heads over how exactly the shoot-down might have taken place and how we could prove that it started right here.

The fighting over at Savur-Mohyla grew louder and closer, and we knew we had a long drive back to Donetsk still ahead before dusk when the checkpoints closed. We got back in the car and told the driver to take us to Donetsk.

A few hundred feet away, where the field met a treeline along the road, a black, blue, and red flag of the Donetsk separatists emerged from the brush. Concealed from us the entire time was a checkpoint where a group of soldiers had been on watch. Three or four of them trained their eyes and weapons on us as we slowly approached with our windows down. "Journalists!" we shouted in Russian, offering our documents.

The interrogation was brief – Where had we come from? How had we gotten there? What were we looking for?

They shook their heads at our Western passports and then, curiosity apparently satisfied, we were released.

On the way back to Donetsk, Roland and I felt a heady mix of anxiety and excitement in the way journalists do when they've stumbled onto a big scoop. We were sure we'd found the missile launch site, but it would still be some time before it would be confirmed by the Dutch-led international investigation into the downing of MH17.

I made a solo trip to the launch site months later in the hope of finding an eyewitness. I followed a dirt road from beside the scorched field to the village of Chervonyi Zhovten just a kilometer away and on the opposite side of the field from Pervomaiskyi. I'd figured someone here must have heard or seen something. It was a one-dirt-road village surrounded by fields and composed of just a couple dozen dilapidated cottages. Dogs growled and barked from their kennels as I knocked on front gates and doors. At first it seemed like nobody was home, or at least they weren't answering their doors. But eventually I came across Pyotr Fedotav and his mother, who were working in their garden, just like they had been on the afternoon of 17 July.

Fedotav said he was harvesting some vegetables when he heard a blast so powerful that it shook the ground beneath his and his mother's feet, making them both tumble over.

"It was such a huge explosion," he told me, holding his hands out. "It was impossible to not see and hear it. It felt like the end of the world!"

He looked up and that's when he saw the cause of it.

"It was a big missile and it wobbled as it flew right over our house in the direction of Torez," he said, pointing in a northwesterly direction toward the town, which sits beside Hrabove. He kept his eye on it as it ascended and then . . . "Boom!" he said, smacking his hands together. The missile had struck a plane and fiery debris fell to the ground.

Fedotav's initial thought was the same as everyone else's – that Russian forces had shot down another Ukrainian military plane. Only later did he realize – along with the rest of the world – that the missile had struck MH17.

Fedotav told me he knew who did it.

"The militia were everywhere here, they controlled this area, and they were in that field," he said, referring to Russia's military forces.

"Which field?" I asked, for clarification.

"On the road between the village and the main road," he said. "If you turn from the main road, it's 150 meters."

It was the same field where Roland and I had discovered the scorch marks.

I was somewhat surprised that Fedotav told me he had witnessed the attack. He didn't hide the fact that he supported the pro-Russian side and was against the new government in Kyiv. Together with other evidence, his account was damning.

18

"The First Real Independence Day"

24 August 2014

Ukraine marked Independence Day with a military parade of soldiers and heavy weaponry down central Khreshchatyk Street and Maidan Nezalezhnosti. It was clearly a show of strength designed to show off a partly revitalized military force and boost morale among the nation's war-weary army.

Dressed in formal attire about 1,500 soldiers, 120 of whom had recently returned from the front lines, strutted in unison in a symbolic show of strength. On their heels were some 90 military vehicles, including armored personnel carriers and trucks hauling heavy artillery, as well as Grad multiple-launch missile systems and ballistic missile systems.

Tens of thousands of Ukrainians, many wearing *vyshyvanky*, colorful shirts, and waving blue and yellow flags, cried out, "Slava Ukraini!" and "Death to enemies!" before breaking into a spontaneous rendition of the national anthem.

Addressing a roaring crowd beneath sunny skies, President Poroshenko said Ukraine was fighting "a war against external aggression, a war for Ukraine, for her freedom, honor and glory, for her people and her independence." He said the parade marked the dawn of a new era for Ukraine's army. Military officials had said earlier in the week that the vehicles shown in the parade, as well as many of the servicemen, would be transported to the east immediately after the event.

Poroshenko used the moment also to announce his plan to pump 40 billion *hryvnia*, about $3 billion, into Ukraine's armed forces over the next three years. That would be "only a modest beginning" in resurrecting the army, but it would allow for the purchase of new warplanes, warships, and helicopters.

The military parade was the first of its kind since 2009. I watched it with Slava, who was still staying at my apartment in Kyiv to escape the fighting back in the east.

Seeing Ukraine's military on display like this filled him with pride. "I think this is the first real Independence Day for us," he told me.

But not everyone felt that way. Some parade-goers were more ambivalent. Retired university professor Iryna Kovalenko told me she supports Ukraine's military operation in eastern Donetsk and Luhansk regions, calling it "necessary," but thought the military parade at this time was in poor taste. "While we are showing off this new equipment in Kyiv, our boys are dying on the front lines," she said. "They need these guns there more than we do here."

I was conflicted about the whole thing. Seeing how it made Slava feel, I understood the importance for some, especially those who found themselves in Russia's crosshairs. But it was also surreal to watch crowds cheering as Grad rockets and Tochka ballistic missiles – weapons of death – rolled past.

Meanwhile in Donetsk, the DNR had organized an "anti-independence" celebration of their own. They dragged out destroyed Ukrainian artillery onto Lenin Square, where it was displayed in the shadow of the former Communist leader. And on Artema Street, soldiers with bayonets affixed to their rifles marched some 50 to 60 dejected Ukrainian prisoners of war, their hands tied behind their backs, past hundreds of sneering onlookers. Bruises and wounds were visible on the faces of some of the prisoners.

"Fascists!" the crowd lining the streets screamed. "Nazis!"

Some spat at them or hurled objects and rotten produce.

Following close behind the Ukrainian POWs was a street-cleaning machine, which washed the pavement where they had walked to "cleanse" it.

19

The Supply Runner

Dnipropetrovsk and Debaltseve, September and October 2014

Noah Sneider and I stopped in Dnipropetrovsk for a night on our way from Kyiv back to the front line in the Donbas. He had arranged for us to meet a woman we'd heard a lot about from soldiers at the front. Some said she was their "lifeline," others that she was their "good-luck charm." Ukrainian TV news called her "a legend."

Tetiana Rychkova was a 35-year-old former baker who for the past several months had been risking her life to run crucial supplies to Ukrainian troops fighting in some of the most intense battles and stuck in some of the most precarious positions in Donetsk Oblast.

Tanya, as she liked to be called, had decided to volunteer to help the military after visiting the 25th Separate Airborne Brigade camp where her husband, Vadym Rychkov, was serving as commander of the brigade's communications platoon. A neurophysicist by training, Vadym had joined the wave of Ukrainian men signing up for military service in March 2014, as Russia's forces were tightening their grip on Crimea and Kremlin-instigated disorder erupted in the Donbas.

"He saw how it was necessary for every man to stand up and fight against the Russian world," Tanya told us over coffee at a trendy Dnipropetrovsk cafe. "I saw the squalor that he and the boys were living in and decided something needed to be done."

She was dressed liked a soldier in military camouflage and tan combat boots but she was also strikingly beautiful, with dark, bluntly cut hair, dark eyes, and a bright smile.

And she had her own flair. She wore sparkly star-shaped rhinestone earrings and violet-colored lipstick. Her nail art was most impressive: on her right thumb, a parachute and the words "25th Airborne Brigade" had been painted in white, and on her left thumb was written the unit's motto,

"*Nikhto krim nas*" – "Nobody but us." She said it was to honor Vadym, who had been killed in action just a month earlier.

Through July and early August, Ukrainian forces had been routing Russian forces and their separatist armies, and recapturing serious ground. By mid-August the Ukrainians had come close to cutting off the Donetsk "people's republic" from its Luhansk counterpart. In fact, I had been in Torez at one point during that time when I stumbled upon a group of Ukrainian troops with infantry-fighting vehicles on the road. They were as surprised to see me as I was to see them.

After they waved my car to stop and saw that I was an American journalist, they asked me for directions to Shakhtarsk. They were a unit from western Ukraine and unfamiliar with the area.

"Back that way a few minutes," I told them.

"Dyakuyu," the soldier replied in Ukrainian.

So for a short time, at least, they had controlled a key segment of that main artery connecting the two Russian-controlled puppet republics.

Then, a Russian "humanitarian convoy" arrived from Rostov.

The convoys were well known to be cover for bringing in guns and ammo for the Kremlin's local fighters. But this time, regular Russian forces followed. Slowly the tide began to change in Russia's favor, and their forces clawed back the territory that Ukraine had just retaken. This culminated in the brutal battle of Ilovaisk, where hundreds of Ukrainian soldiers had become surrounded and were slaughtered by Russian forces as they retreated.

During a pitched battle for the towns of Nyzhnya Krynka and Zhdanivka on 17 August, a group from the 25th Airborne Brigade was caught under heavy shelling by a BM-21 Grad multiple-launch rocket system. Vadym and ten other soldiers and officers were killed.

Vadym would later be posthumously awarded the Order of Bohdan Khmelnytsky III degree for his personal courage and heroism, and given a Defense Ministry award "for military valor" as well as the rank of captain.

Even after Vadym was killed in action in August, Tanya didn't leave the front except to bury him. If anything, his death only invigorated her. She sold her bakery and the couple's summer cottage, withdrew all their savings, and headed back to the east.

By the time the three of us met, just a month later, she had completely dedicated herself to spending every minute of every day helping Ukraine's troops get what they needed to fight.

Noah and I wanted to see the people she was helping, so we asked to come along on her next supply run.

"You're welcome to come!" she said, while also cautioning us. "But it can be dangerous!"

A few days later, we were crammed into the back seat of a truck being driven by two friends of hers, Dmitry and Andriy, a paratrooper and a volunteer medic, who picked us up in Artemivsk. Having been liberated four months ago, the city had been transformed into a key staging ground for Kyiv's military operation in the east. Soldiers and supplies poured in. Meanwhile, internally displaced people fleeing from Russian-occupied areas settled there, too. It was a hive of activity.

Noah and I squeezed in the back of the truck between radios and bulletproof vests, ballistic helmets, camouflaged backpacks, night-vision goggles, and cartons of cigarettes, all stacked from floor to ceiling. Then we made our way to a checkpoint on the edge of town, where we linked up with Tanya.

Tanya was driving a white and silver Mercedes cargo truck that was riddled by bullet holes – reminders of past harrowing deliveries. Inside were medical supplies, including antibiotics, as well as power generators, tools, batteries, clothes, and more.

From the checkpoint, we headed south down the E-40 highway to a large Ukrainian army camp on the edge of Debaltseve. The city of some 25,000 people was a major railroad hub with tracks leading south to Donetsk and east toward the Russian border. Naturally, Ukraine wanted to hold it, Russian forces wanted to capture it. In the days before, they had began shelling and pressing on the city, surrounding it on three sides. There had never been a true ceasefire. The armistice agreed to by Kyiv and Moscow in early September under the observation of France and Germany in the Belarusian capital, Minsk, wasn't worth the paper it was printed on.

After a precarious 20-mile drive, past the charred remains of enemy armored vehicles and over a narrow bridge, we arrived at the army base, where hundreds of troops from the 25th Airborne were dug in deep.

They were hooting and hollering in celebration before Tanya even turned off the engine. She stepped out and jumped into the arms of one soldier who planted a fat kiss on her cheek before another wrapped her up in a bear hug. A crowd began to form and then the doors of the trucks swung open. The guys started rifling through everything and tossed packs of smokes around.

Inside the camp, the soldiers looked relaxed, even comfortable, despite their situation. They milled around, cooked meat over open flames, stacked crates of artillery shells in bunkers, and wandered through a maze of trenches as their artillery was working on the enemy.

Boom! Boom! Boom! their tanks and howitzers roared from just 100 meters away.

"We get 99 per cent of our supplies from volunteers," one soldier told me. He said that if it weren't for Tanya and others like her, they'd be "fucked."

After the war broke out, it became all too clear that Ukraine was short on supplies for the troops. So volunteers stepped in to fill the void. Many did it on their own. Some formed organizations such as Wings of Phoenix and Army SOS, and actively fundraised to equip the country's soldiers.

Mikhail, another soldier at the base, said that when he enlisted in June, he was only given one uniform, one pair of underwear, two pairs of socks, and a used pair of boots that were a size too big. He illustrated the absurdity by demonstrating how the boots' heels dragged when he walked.

"They told us these are supposed to last us two years," he said.

What's worse, the weather was changing and winter was coming. Soon the temperature would drop to below freezing at night, and the guys didn't have insulated coats to keep them warm.

"Look at this," said another soldier, pulling open his jacket to reveal its insides. "No fur, no insulation and no warmth."

The outgoing fire had slowed, which meant only one thing: return fire was on its way.

"We're still shooting – obviously," said one soldier as he gestured to a howitzer firing in the direction of enemy lines. "And so are they."

"It will never end," he added. "Russia will always want to fight us – at least until they take us all to our knees."

Sure enough, mortars started raining down on the camp, sending us all scurrying into shallow dugouts. We all crowded around a table and drank tea and smoked a pack of American Spirits I had brought with me while we waited it out.

Dispiriting news then came over the radio. Russian shelling had hit part of the bridge on the E-40, our only road in or out of Debaltseve.

"Are we stuck then?" I asked a soldier.

He said, unconvincingly, not to worry.

"They'll fix the bridge with something. But it will probably be several hours, so you should stay here until then," he said. "But there's another way out if we need it."

"Where's the other route to Artemivsk?" I asked. I knew this area well from my Peace Corps days. I used to get lost in the fields and villages on my bike on afternoons. There weren't many through roads around.

"Through the field," he said, pointing west. "You run. And then you cross the river. And there's a road."

Noah and I looked at each other and shrugged. Something felt very ominous here.

"They could really become trapped," I told him. "This could be another Ilovaisk."

"Exactly what I was thinking," Noah said.

There were thousands of troops and dozens of battle tanks and heavy weaponry, including self-propelled and towed howitzers at the camp. We had walked through earlier to check it out. It was a pop-up military town, with living quarters, large tents for sleeping, eating, and holding meetings, as well as lavatories and shower facilities. There was little cover from attacks other than the shallow bunkers that had been dug a few feet into the earth.

Three hours later, another call came over the radio.

"Bridge is repaired," a man's voice said.

"Copy," a soldier replied.

"Let's go?" asked Tanya.

"We're ready," I said.

We zipped back up the E-40. I watched out the windows as Russian artillery shells exploded in fields on both sides of us and plumes of smoke rose from their craters. We paused at the bridge to survey the damage. An entire chunk had been destroyed on one side. The Ukrainians had patched it up with some metal beams and wooden planks, then laid atop two steel tracks they had pulled off a military transport truck.

We lined up our tires in the grooves and drove slowly over them. Leaning out of the window, I peered down and could see the Luhan river directly below.

"Poyekhali!" Dmitry shouted.

We had made it.

Onward to Artemivsk.

20

City of Ghosts

Luhansk, October 2014

Lyubov Bolgarova came to look for her father in a desolate field surrounded by trees that the autumn cold had given a rust-colored kiss. Jutting from mounds of dirt were plain wooden crosses – more than a hundred of them by my count. Each was a grim testament to the toll of the war. Some were marked with names, others simply with numbers. The victims were all buried in a mass grave, in one of two long trenches dug with an excavator.

In August, when battles between Ukrainian forces and Russia's separatist fighters raged in and around the city of Luhansk, Lyubov's aging father, Oleksandr Bolgarov, awoke one night in a sweaty panic. He said he had heard a noise and believed an artillery shell had exploded in the family home. He moaned and twisted, flailing his frail arms in the air. The house was unscathed but a delirious Oleksandr, a survivor of the Second World War, was convinced that they were being besieged by the Nazis. He took to his bed and refused to leave.

"He lost his mind," his grandson Andriy, standing beside his mother, told me.

Tormented by fear and delusions, Oleksandr stopped eating and drinking. He suffered consecutive strokes, each farther incapacitating him. Three weeks later, one of them finally did him in.

When I met Lyubov at her father's shallow grave, she had with her a small porcelain mug. Andriy poured lager into it from a two-liter plastic bottle. Lyubov placed the mug at the base of the cross and whispered a prayer. Neither she nor Andriy shed a tear.

"We've already done our grieving," Lyubov said.

At that point in the war, few cities had suffered like Luhansk had. Once the epicenter of the country's metalworking industry with a pre-war population of almost half a million people, now it was bearing the brunt of the conflict. The provincial capital was of strategic importance because of the 464-mile border with Russia, across which Moscow funneled weapons and reinforcements to separatist fighters here. Although exact figures were hard to come by, the civilian death toll then was somewhere between 600 and 1,000 from the city of Luhansk alone.

For two months Ukrainian troops and Russia's proxy soldiers had fought grueling battles here, lobbing thousands of artillery shells at each other, turning entire neighborhoods and villages to dust. It gave the area a desolate – even post-apocalyptic – feel in some places. The roads into the city were lined with the destroyed military vehicles and tanks with their turrets blown off. One balanced impossibly on its side, and I thought what are the chances . . .

Electricity, running water, telephone and Internet services were knocked out for more than two months. Long bread lines and people standing for hours in front of the banks to take out money were common sights. Most businesses and cafes had closed, and the city was largely without basic services. The fighting had forced tens of thousands of people to flee, with some bolting east to Moscow and others going westward, headed for Kyiv. The exodus made Luhansk feel like a ghost town.

Yet the few people who remained were finding ways to survive. A restaurateur named Igor had stayed behind with his wife to watch over their business, The Brigantine. Located in the basement of an apartment building and decorated in a marine theme with porthole windows along the walls showing colorful fish swimming past other sea creatures in crystal-clear blue waters, the restaurant was as good a place as any still left to take shelter during heavy shelling. Igor and his family housed 49 other people inside The Brigantine for more than two months that summer.

"Together we listened to bombs explode outside for two months," Igor told me.

Their time trapped in the hull of this imitation ship in some ways did resemble life at sea. There was no electricity, no running water, and nowhere to go. They dined by candlelight and slept on tabletops, bench seats, and air mattresses on the floor. They played cards – specifically a popular game call *durak*, or fool – to pass the time. In the brief calm moments between rocket salvos they gathered sticks outside and burned small fires behind the building, over which they cooked thin soups seasoned with whatever smattering of ingredients they could find in the back of cupboards.

Four birthdays had been celebrated in The Brigantine during that time, including Igor's and his son's. "We celebrated as best we could," Igor told me. "We sang and danced. It wasn't all that bad. And we lived."

The pungent stench of the decaying corpses shocked my sense of smell even before they came into view. I shook my head stupidly as if that could expel the malodor and searched with my nose for a whiff of fresh air. No luck.

A habit of mine when in the war-wrecked towns of eastern Ukraine was always to visit their hospitals and morgues. They were always a good – albeit depressing – barometer of how bad things were. And I felt like they offered a true sense of the price of a war in which reality had become slippery. The living and the dead, the devastated, the stubborn, and the brave, all mingled together, and it was tough for any of them to tell a lie in those places.

Anatoliy Turevich, the 62-year-old director of Luhansk's main morgue, welcomed me inside his three-storied building one unseasonably warm afternoon in early October. The air was stuffy and stale and felt like it was clinging to my clothes. In one outstretched hand, he offered me a mask; in the other, menthol rub. I took the latter and smeared some beneath my nose. Anatoliy said his sense of smell had been so overwhelmed by the stink that he had finally lost that faculty.

It had been more than three months since he had been home – long enough, he said, for him to almost forget what it looked and felt like. Throughout the summer he lived in his office, sleeping on the sunken little sofa against the wall. With corpses coming in all hours of the day and night and nobody else to deal with their intake – five assistants had fled when the fighting broke out and one drove over a mine and was hospitalized across the street – he wasn't able to leave the morgue grounds.

"Not even once," he told me with a twinge of what was either pride or despair in his voice – I wasn't sure.

Inside his office stood a life-sized skeleton, and framed on one wall were medical diagrams and anatomical images of the human body. He had a small encased display of surgical tools on a shelf and stacks of paperwork he had neglected on his desk.

"So, you can see that I am very behind," he joked.

Another wall was covered with photographs of the Baltic and Black seas. Carefully erected model sailing ships sat perched atop a group of asymmetrically hung shelves. I asked about the nautical theme and he reminisced briefly of the days he had spent when he was a bright-eyed, 18-year-old member of the Soviet Coast Guard stationed in the Baltic. He pulled out a black-and-white photo of himself in uniform with neatly combed hair and a sharp mustache.

"It was boring but nice. Peaceful," he recalled.

It had been a long while since Anatoliy had seen, let alone been on, the sea.

"I've seen more of that lately," he said, gesturing to a real human skull resting on a table behind me. He walked over and holding it out in his hand began reciting from *Hamlet*.

"*To be, or not to be . . .*"

He had lost count of the number of bodies passing through his morgue since the war broke out, and since he could no longer access the digital records on his desktop computer.

"Almost 600," he said. "I don't remember exactly how many. And more will come."

Making his work particularly difficult was the lack of power, which had been cut for months, including in July and August – the hottest time of the year in Ukraine. A generator worked in fits and starts, allowing him to log data on his computer and keep some of the bodies refrigerated. But the maximum number of bodies able to fit inside the refrigeration unit was ten – and Anatoliy was sometimes receiving 15 or 20 at a time. So most weren't able to be kept cold, anyway.

He was forced to stack bodies in the halls and closets. He even used an office vacated by one of his former assistants. When those places filled up – and they often did – he placed the bodies in wooden coffins on the grass behind the building.

Among the coffins resting on the lawn when I was there were five unidentified Ukrainian National Guardsmen who had been left in the open for more than two weeks. They were wrapped in plastic inside the simple wooden coffins, but that hadn't saved them from the elements, of course. Bees and flies swarmed over them, and maggots squirmed out from the openings of the plastic wraps.

Some of the dead had been killed by gunfire, but shrapnel wounds caused most of the deaths of people who passed through Anatoliy's morgue. They were more gruesome than the injuries caused by the mining accidents that he was used to.

What fire-hot pieces of metal from an explosive are capable of doing to human flesh is unbelievable. They puncture, fillet, shatter, smash, and turn bodies inside-out.

Anatoliy lifted the lid of one of the coffins and pulled back the plastic.

"This one was ripped apart," he said, gesturing to a pile of severed limbs.

Anatoliy said the bodies had been recovered after the battle for the Luhansk airport, which now looked like little more than a heap of twisted metal, ash, and rubble. The fight there was fierce, and in the end Ukrainian forces had lost.

Anatoliy was waiting to get word from either the Russian-backed leaders in Luhansk or the authorities in Kyiv about what to do with the National Guardsmen.

"The Ukrainians haven't told me what to do. The Luhansk people's republic hasn't told me what to do. I don't know what to do," he shrugged. "I am waiting for a body exchange, or something."

"We can't bury them here," he added. "We have no more room in the cemeteries."

Anatoliy hadn't brought it up and I couldn't glean it from our conversation, so I asked him which side he supported in the war.

"I'm agnostic," he said, looking me straight in the eye. "But the ghosts in these halls talk to me. So I know what is happening."

Across the road from the morgue, inside the trauma unit of Luhansk's main hospital, I found Svitlana stirring anxiously and rubbing a cross that dangled from her necklace as she waited for doctors to update her on her son's condition.

Oleksiy, 29, was a volunteer fighter for the Russian-led separatist army. The day before, he had been struck by shrapnel when a volley of rockets believed to have been fired from a nearby Ukrainian position exploded around him while he was manning a block post in the nearby town of Stanytsia Luhanska. The metal shards had torn open his right thigh and penetrated several other parts of his body.

With the town's sole hospital destroyed by a rocket attack weeks ago, Oleksiy had to be transported more than three hours over rough and dangerous back roads to Luhansk, to the operating room of Dr Volodymyr Anatolyevich.

With tears streaming down her cheeks and her voice trembling, Svitlana prayed that her son would survive, "even if he must have his leg removed."

Good news came as we spoke, however: Oleksiy would live and likely even keep his leg.

"He's very lucky," Dr Anatolyevich said.

"*Slava bogu! Slava bogu!*" – Thank God – Svitlana cried. "I want him to come home. I just want everything to go back to normal."

———

I thought there was something poignant about the Luhansk central maternity ward sitting right across from the morgue – the beginnings and ends of lives separated by a bumpy little road.

Dr Valentina didn't find that thought to be as interesting. But then she didn't have much time to think or listen to me wax philosophical.

When I waltzed into the ward to see about an interview, the place was a buzz of activity. I was surprised, I guess because for some reason I didn't think that babies could continue to be born while so many people were dying, that new life could be made amid so much death.

Little Oleksandra screamed and kicked and threw her arms around.

"She's our miracle," said Tanya, the young aunt of the newborn, sobbing. "She is named for her father."

Two weeks earlier, the baby's father, Oleksandr, had been killed when the tank that he and his pro-Russian comrades were driving struck a mine and were ripped to pieces.

They collected what remains they could and took them to the morgue days later. Then they buried him in a row of graves with a little wooden cross.

21

POWs

Ilovaisk, Donetsk Oblast, October 2014

Ruslan Tinkalyuk cut a forlorn figure as he took a long drag on a Chesterfield cigarette. Dirty and unkempt, he was curled up by a small barrel fire amid the rubble of an apartment destroyed by a rocket in this war-torn eastern Ukrainian town, Ilovaisk. He should have been with his family in Ivano-Frankivsk, a charming provincial city nestled at the edge of the Carpathian Mountains, watching autumn turn the sprawling forests their vibrant seasonal hues.

Instead Tinkalyuk was here, a prisoner of war, being closely guarded by gun-toting, pro-Russian militants.

I found him doing forced labor in the town of Ilovaisk one day. I'd come with the Russian photographer Evgeny Feldman to see what the town looked like in the aftermath of the deadliest battle yet.

Ukrainian troops had entered Ilovaisk on 14 August. Their goal was to split the occupied territories in half, isolating Donetsk from neighboring Luhansk to cut off an all-important supply line. But the tide of the battle changed and the troops were encircled and forced to take shelter inside a local school.

Hunkering down, they waited for days for the reinforcements promised by Kyiv. But the cavalry never came. Instead, a "green corridor" was negotiated through which the Ukrainian troops could retreat. But it turned out to be a trap. They were ambushed by Russian forces who bombarded them with artillery and rocket fire. Hundreds of Ukrainian troops were killed and dozens more were taken prisoner. Kyiv called it a "massacre."

The Ukrainian losses led to the first controversial ceasefire deal known as the Minsk Protocol (Minsk-I), which was hammered out and agreed on by Kyiv and DNR and LNR representatives, as well as OSCE officials, in the Belarusian capital on 5 September.

Inside Ilovaisk, we ran into a DNR commander, who offered to show us some of the repair work being done. That's how we ended up at an apartment building being fixed up by a group of Ukrainian POWs, including Tinkalyuk.

Tinkalyuk considered himself "one of the lucky ones," having escaped from the ambush in which scores of his comrades were killed.

He and others were held in cold, dark basements and weren't allowed to communicate with the outside world. They slept on grimy cots and soiled mattresses thrown onto floors that crawled with insects drawn to the squalor. Each prisoner had just one set of clothes, no changes of underwear or socks. And while coats had recently been handed out to the prisoners, many lacked insulation and were ripped at the seams. Some of the Ukrainians were seriously wounded and ill and not being treated.

Their captors woke them at dawn every day, and they did forced manual labor until sundown.

Andrei was a brawny DNR commander who watched over the POWs as they repaired an apartment rooftop destroyed by shelling. He was eager to tell me about the prisoners' comfort, noting that they had access to showers and bathrooms and were given a television to watch "romances and comedies, but nothing patriotic that would excite them."

Holding a matchstick between his lips, Andrei kept flicking the safety on his rifle up and down with his right thumb and index finger. He then offered a cigarette to one of his prisoners.

"We're not monsters," he said.

Oleksiy, the prisoner who had taken the cigarette offered by Andrei, said that POWs were fed three meals a day, but that they consisted solely of bread, cold oats, and watery soup. On good days, they got a piece of cheese and sausage.

"It's not enough really," he said. "But it's better than nothing."

It was his only criticism in an otherwise positive review of his captors. He said his idea about the DNR fighters had "changed 100 per cent."

I had a hard time believing that. Then I glanced over my shoulder and saw Andrei standing nearby, clearly listening in on the conversation.

"I think we understand each other," Oleksiy continued, looking at Andrei. It was unclear how heartfelt the sentiment was, given the presence of Andrei's rifle. Another Ukrainian soldier later pulled me aside and said that he thought Oleksiy might be suffering from Stockholm syndrome.

"He's not the same anymore," he told me, making a twisting gesture with his finger to the side of his head.

The soldiers were waiting to be set free in a prisoner exchange, but many of them were concerned that Kyiv didn't even know they were here and alive. They feared that perhaps their names had ended up on a list of troops killed in action in Ilovaisk. Prisoner swaps had also slowed because Ukraine didn't have many DNR and LNR captives left to hand over. In more than one case, in fact, the Ukrainian government was found to be releasing common criminals rather than bona fide fighters.

Staying sane in such gruesome conditions was difficult. Maxim, a thin, pale-faced POW, told me he daydreamed about the future, and that had kept him going. Focusing too much on reality got him down.

"The thought did cross my mind of killing myself," he said. He fumed over the fact that he had been made "a prisoner in my own country, by my own people."

"We simply survive," he said, choking up. "We eat, sleep and work. And we hope that someday we will be released. What else can we do?"

He and Tinkalyuk and several others told me they wanted me to publish their names or photographs or both in hopes that they might be seen by their government and families.

"They don't know that we're still alive," Tinkalyuk said.

When the guards were called away momentarily, he was quick to pass on the contact information of a relative.

"Give me your pen and notebook," he said. I handed them to him and he scribbled down a name and number. "If you can, let them know I'm alive and healthy."

The relative, his sister-in-law, lived with his brother in western Ukraine. When I returned to Kyiv, I called her up and gave her the news. Then I sent her a photo of Tinkalyuk. She wept loudly into the phone.

"We last saw him on 31 May," she said. "When he finally returns home safely, we will hold him tight and never let him go."

Just before Christmas, Ukraine and the DNR would agree to another prisoner exchange. It was meant to be a gesture of goodwill around the holidays. When I saw the names of the Ukrainians who'd be released, I noticed Tinkalyuk's, as well as those of some of the other men I'd met in Ilovaisk.

The Ukrainian government had added their names to the list of people it wanted set free after my story was published.

22

The Body Collectors

Marinovka, Donetsk Oblast, November 2014

The dead Ukrainian soldier clutched a cell phone in the hand of his outstretched right arm, which was already in deep rigor mortis. Yaroslav Zhilkin snapped on a pair of latex gloves and pried the Nokia device loose by carefully peeling back the charred fingers encasing it.

"We'll access the SIM card and try to locate his family," he said.

Similarly, the blackened corpse of a second Ukrainian soldier offered few clues as to who he had been in life. He didn't have a cellphone on him or any identifying papers, and there were no distinguishing features or tattoos visible on his crispy skin. The only obvious thing seemed to be that the soldier's death had been horrific. His head tilted back with his mouth agape like Munch's *The Scream*, and his arms were outstretched like he had been reaching for a lifeline as he was burned alive. I wondered if he had had enough time to let out a yell and what it would have sounded like as he was engulfed in flames.

Zhilkin had been collecting bodies for months by the time I met him in Marinovka, a pastoral, poverty-stricken village near the Russian border, which had been home to a couple hundred mostly elderly residents before being caught in the middle of an artillery duel over the summer. Zhilkin's macabre but essential job, and one he was doing voluntarily, had earned him a nickname: The Body Collector. He had a mystique about him that fascinated people, including myself. And the singular and precarious nature of the work won Zhilkin the admiration of his compatriots and made him something of a celebrity in Kyiv. More importantly, it had earned him a respect that allowed him the rare ability to operate on both sides of the front line.

Every few days, after negotiating with commanders on the ground for access, the 43-year-old Zhilkin would drive out to the battlefields with a motley crew of Ukrainian men to collect the corpses of the fallen as they piled up. Zhilkin's team called itself Black Tulip after the cargo plane that had transported the bodies of soldiers killed during the Soviet war in Afghanistan. They drove large white vans daubed with red crosses on the hood and sides. Signs taped to the windshields read "Cargo 200," a military code used across the former Soviet Union to identify vehicles transporting slain soldiers.

It was on a breezy October afternoon that I followed the Black Tulips from Ukrainian government-controlled territory to the Russian proxy-held area of Donetsk. We took winding back roads, passing checkpoints manned by hulking men with machine guns who scrutinized our documents and our purpose for being there. And we weaved around rocket craters, burned-out carcasses of tanks and military trucks. It was several hours before we reached Marinovka.

Zhilkin was tall and bald with brawny shoulders and strong, thick hands. The other Black Tulip members were equally burly, sporting coarse beards and thick, callused hands. If not for their bright orange workers' vests, it would be easy to mistake them for soldiers. The crew wore the vests to give them an air of authority and identify them as emergency workers to inquisitive passers-by.

"We don't want people to mistake us for fighters," Zhilkin said. "We're a peaceful mission."

For Zhilkin, interring fallen soldiers had been a preoccupation even before the war broke out. An enthusiast of the Second World War, he had founded a group called National Memory Union. Its members spent their weekends tracking down and identifying the remains of Soviet soldiers buried in mass graves across Ukraine. They kept meticulous logs of the work in an office in Kyiv lined wall-to-wall with history books and maps with shapes drawn on them in bright marker pen.

Zhilkin was motivated by what he said was a great injustice of this war: the Ukrainian government's lack of action when it comes to returning the country's "heroes" to their homes for a proper burial. He contrasted Kyiv's lackluster casualty–recovery efforts with those undertaken by the United States when two American soldiers went missing in Afghanistan in 2006 and more than 8,000 troops and a team of forensic scientists were dispatched to find them.

In Ukraine, there was only Zhilkin's team of 37 volunteers.

His team had recovered more than 150 fallen Ukrainian soldiers just in the month before we linked up – dozens more than the official government KIA count for the same period of time. One of every seven soldiers killed then remained unidentified, Zhilkin told me. Those without names were buried in mass graves marked by wooden crosses adorned with colorful plastic funeral wreaths and tiny makeshift headstones that read: "Temporarily missing-in-action defender of Ukraine."

Many corpses that Black Tulip came across were mangled by violence or wild animals, and had often been left to the elements for days.

"Feral dogs and the foxes complicate our work," Zhilkin said, grimly.

He and his men sometimes found the bodies to be rigged with booby-trapped explosives set to detonate when they're moved.

Before putting the unknown troops in the ground, Zhilkin's team took DNA samples so that someday they could be entered into a database to help with identification. At the time, Ukraine had no such database. Complicating matters farther was the fact that neither Ukraine's regular or irregular fighters were issued dog tags with personal information when they enlisted.

Zhilkin led me down a dirt road, past homes with their walls blasted through by artillery shells. There were only a few older local people left there. The only other people in the village were Russian soldiers and pro-Russian Ukrainian fighters.

Half a mile down the road, we found two local fighters standing beside a destroyed military truck. It was punctured with shrapnel and charred black and orange from an intense fire. The bodies of the Ukrainians were inside the cabin. Zhilkin got to work.

He said the soldiers would likely be buried in a makeshift grave with many others like them, and without their families knowing of their fate.

"But all of Ukraine will know that this man died a hero," he said as he folded the body of the man with the Nokia into a bag and zipped it closed.

The local fighters thanked him for coming and asked whether Zhilkin would return to help recover and possibly identify some of their comrades. Zhilkin said he would discuss it with commanders on both sides. If they would approve the request, he would return to help.

"Nobody is fighting with the dead," Zhilkin said.

23

City of a Million Roses

Donetsk, 22 January 2015

One moment they were seated in a bus at the bus stop in Donetsk's southern Leninsky district, ready to catch a ride to work. The next moment they were dead – 13 of them. All civilians. Any promise of a ceasefire or prospect for a lasting peace also seemed dead.

I was at the Ramada when it happened and heard the explosions. I hurried to the scene and when I arrived minutes later I saw the victims' bloodied and ripped-apart bodies splayed across blue bus seats. Some appeared to have survived for a few minutes and tried dragging themselves into the street. A lengthy trail of blood followed the body of one person who'd come to rest a foot short of the sidewalk. Among them was a woman who had been carrying bouquet of roses. Donetsk was called the "city of a million roses." The grim scene struck me as darkly symbolic.

The attack happened on Unity Day, celebrated every year in Ukraine on 22 January. Many, including President Poroshenko, would say the war here had united the country in a way it had never been united before. But the harsh reality was that Ukraine had been carved up by Russian forces and their pro-Russian proxies, and farther divided between Ukrainian patriots who stand for peace and others who want to fight an insurgency that threatens the sovereignty of their state. The entire peninsula of Crimea had been seized, and Ukraine's Donbas was being torn apart by a bloody war.

There was a hatred that had grown and festered that wasn't present before.

At the scene of the bus attack, a handful of people stood on the shrapnel-scarred pavement, near a swept mound of bloody glass, weeping as Russia's proxy fighters paraded in a dozen or so Ukrainian prisoners of war who'd been captured in battle at the Donetsk Airport.

Earlier, a Ukrainian colonel had been brought alone to face a similarly angry mob at the site of the bus attack. People punched and kicked him before he was tossed into the back of an SUV and hauled away.

"Kyiv calls us terrorists. But look at this!" shouted Ludmila, a Donetsk resident in her seventies, gesturing to the spot where a shell had exploded that morning. She turned to the POWs who were now being forced to their knees by gunmen.

At that moment, several other people gathered around us. One woman, fighting back tears, her face puffy, told me she had watched a neighbor friend of hers die a slow death on the synthetic blue seats of the yellow passenger bus that was hit. One minute, she was greeting her "Good morning," and the next, "she was screaming for help with blood on her face."

"We will never forgive you, and we will never forget what you've done!" the woman cried at the Ukrainian POWs. She then spat on one sunken-faced soldier while a man dealt a punch to the back of the head of another, causing him to fall to his face on the rain-soaked pavement. Several of the other battered and bruised Ukrainian prisoners, including one who appeared to be missing part of his right hand, were similarly abused.

Egging the crowd on were a group of jittery, gun-toting fighters in mismatched uniforms. One was checking press cards, and warning foreign media to "tell the truth" about the "Kyiv junta" who they said perpetrated the attack.

"You, American, and your Obama are also guilty," he said as he scanned my DNR-issued press accreditation.

Just then seven truck-driven multiple-launch Grad rocket systems trundled passed. Their tubes, which can hold up to 40 rockets, had been emptied.

Throughout the morning, sounds of outgoing Grad rockets and mortars reverberated through the city. Near one road to the airport, Russian forces fired shells in the direction of Ukrainian positions northwest of the complex, where they retreated overnight after enduring days of intense fighting that ended with the Russian side detonating explosives that collapsed two floors of a building, killing dozens of Ukrainian soldiers.

Despite Russian and Ukrainian officials in Berlin the day before agreeing to adhere to the Minsk ceasefire deal that had been hashed out in September but routinely violated since, rhetoric from the two sides suggested that fighting – and the death and destruction that had come with it – would continue.

Ukraine and Russia and Donetsk exchanged accusations of terrorism. Speaking to reporters at the scene, Alexander Zakharchenko, the DNR's figurehead, accused Ukrainian forces of carrying out the attack and vowed to go on the offensive.

"There is no ceasefire. We will fight. I promise," he said.

In Kyiv, Yatsenyuk said the blame rested with Russia, suggesting their forces carried out the shelling in a false-flag attack.

"Today Russian terrorists once again committed a terrible act against humanity, and the Russian Federation bears responsibility for that," he said.

Back at the Ramada, I asked a pro-Russian local fighter what was next. He answered with the bravado I had come to expect of everyone who carried a gun here.

"We have won Donetsk Airport. Now, onward to Kyiv!"

"Welcome To Hell"

Horlivka, Donetsk Oblast, 6 February, 2015

The two scruffy young fighters raised their hands and automatic rifles as my car approached their shabby checkpoint of sandbags and tree trunks stacked like Lincoln Logs and dusted with fresh snow.

"Pull over," one ordered, waving my driver to the side of the road.

It wasn't the first nor would it be the last to pass through, as my driver and I approached Donetsk. But visible through the windshield was a spray-painted sign that seemed to set this block post apart.

"Welcome to hell," it read in Russian.

Six months earlier, under a searing summer sun, it was here that half a dozen masked rebel fighters dragged me at gunpoint out of my car and into their bunker.

"We take CIA spies to the basement of the police station," one said, berating me about the United States' backing of Kyiv, as he rested his finger on the trigger of a Kalashnikov.

They phoned their commander, the mustachioed and notoriously brutal Igor "The Demon" Bezler, one of the most feared warlords in eastern Ukraine. They wanted to know what they should do with me. This was just after a video surfaced of Bezler mock-executing two Ukrainian policemen taken prisoner.

"Check his documents and his index finger," I heard him shout to his men through the phone. The finger check assessed whether there was a buildup of calluses, something a seasoned sniper might have on their trigger finger. "And what does his face look like?"

219

My finger was smooth and my face unremarkable, so they sent me on my way after four hours, several cigarettes and cups of tea. "Good luck on the road," the fighters said.

These types of brief detentions and encounters had become routine here. You learned to deal with them, or you didn't, and wouldn't be able to work here.

Days later, I was with one of my regular drivers headed back across the front line. We were relaxed, singing along to a remixed version of Depeche Mode's *Personal Jesus* and then Jason Derulo's *Wiggle*, featuring Snoop Dogg, which played on a Russian radio station. Then we saw a checkpoint come into view.

Two armed DNR fighters stepped into the road and motioned for us to pull over and exit the car. They handled their weapons like Hollywood gangsters would – low and away from their bodies, as if they were about to blow someone away. It was a dead giveaway that they were amateurs.

They carried themselves like tough guys, smoking and lowering their voice to sound intimidating, but they looked like teenagers. These weren't Bezler's guys. Their demeanor changed the moment they saw my passport.

"Can we take a photo with you?" one asked. "I've never met an American before."

This was the cost of passage. After my other checkpoint run-ins, I didn't think it was too much to pay.

"Tyler"

Artemivsk, early February 2015

As a new wave of fighting exploded in the Donbas, I returned to Artemivsk. Peace talks had fallen apart, and Russian forces, eager to snatch up more territory, were on the warpath. After launching a fresh offensive two weeks earlier, they had captured some 200 square miles of new territory, including the fiercely contested and symbolically important Donetsk Airport. Even if it had been reduced to ruins and was of little strategic use, it was a highly symbolic prize.

The focus of fighting was now shifting to the crucial transport hub of Debaltseve, 45 miles northeast of Donetsk. There, some 8,000 government troops were now facing off against Moscow's DNR forces and new units of Russian regulars. The Russians were closing in on the Ukrainians fast, creating a ring of fire that rained down hell in the besieged town.

As a result, Debaltseve was being decimated, and deaths in the town were piling up. Kyiv said about three to five soldiers were being killed and around a dozen wounded there every day. But medics and troops in Artemivsk, where they were being medically evacuated, said it was more like "three times that."

Natalia Nazar, a petite 41-year-old mother of two who'd previously worked as a teacher of medicine at a medical university in Lviv before volunteering to be a front-line medic, told me she was transporting upwards of 80 wounded soldiers from Debaltseve every day — and in rickety, decades-old ambulances and donated Soviet-era sedans, including one with a vanity license plates that read, "Putin, fuck off."

We met at the Artemivsk central hospital one afternoon. The city was swarming with ambulances and military helicopters, which landed on the field of the old soccer stadium to evacuate soldiers with the most severe wounds. Nazar was dressed in camouflage fatigues and combat boots. Her dark hair had been perfectly straightened and her eyeliner applied with the utmost care.

"I wake up at 5 a.m. every day so I have enough time to paint it on," she told me. "I'm Ukrainian nationalist and a soldier. But I'm also a woman."

She told me she'd treated the gunshot wounds of several of the Maidan revolutionaries who'd been shot down by sniper fire the year before. But she had never in her worst nightmares imagined that she'd be in the middle of a war, as many people in an hour as she had in the worst day of Ukraine's Revolution of Dignity.

She wiped tears from her eyes and hugged me before jumping into her ambulance and setting off on another run to the front.

I knew where else I could go in Artemivsk to get a sense of how bad things were: the morgue. Ruslan Fedonyuk, the director of Artemivsk's mortuary, looked exhausted. He said he had seen the corpses of 160 soldiers come through his facility in the past month alone. He'd taken in 40 bodies just in the day before I arrived. I could smell them from down the hall. Ironically, death has a sweet, almost fruity scent to it. It's hard to pin down but it's unmistakeable.

The corpses, many with grisly battle wounds that made them impossible to identify, were coming in at such a fast rate that Fedonyuk and his staff of nine people couldn't keep up. They were used to seeing about 120 bodies a *year*.

"It's like a conveyor belt," he said. "They just keep coming."

I paid one more visit to the central hospital before nightfall. The operating rooms were full and ambulances streamed in with more badly wounded Ukrainian troops. The toll was visible on the faces of the sleepless doctors and nurses.

A Ukrainian military medic with innocent eyes and a scruffy goatee lit up a Marlboro Red and took a long drag. He had just carried a soldier with a severed leg into an operating room and watched another with more serious injuries die right in front of him. Nothing could've been done to save the man, who was about the same age as the medic.

I was making notes about what I had just seen, when the medic approached me. He noticed I was scribbling in English.

"Do I know you?" I looked up and squinted. "Oh my god, Bohdan! Hey!"

It had been more than four years since I last saw him sitting in the front row of my English class. He was 16 then, a curious and searching kid, who'd talked to me about struggling to decide what he wanted to be when he grew up. "Call me Tyler," he said.

He was in the military now and had given himself a *nom de guerre*. He borrowed it from Tyler Durden, the imaginary character in the American film *Fight Club*. In the movie, Brad Pitt plays the uninhibited manifestation of Edward Norton's repressed id with manic zeal. His service had changed him, Tyler explained, and he sometimes felt like two people.

Tyler had fled university in Luhansk in 2014, after gun-toting locals backed by Russian special forces threatened to coerce him and other students into joining them. He had been on the front lines in the Donbas ever since.

"I couldn't just sit on my hands, you know?" he said.

Tyler's bloodstained fingers put the cigarette to his lips. Despite the obvious danger, he wanted to go back to the front line, but he had promised his mother he wouldn't. She had lost her husband, Tyler's father, a year earlier.

"She told me if I die that she will have no man in her life."

As we spoke, an ambulance pulled up. There were punctures from shrapnel all up the side of it. The driver jumped out and shouted, "Fucking bitches!"

He had just been in Debaltseve and was rushing out with a wounded soldier when they came under rocket fire. It was a narrow escape.

"I just had my second birthday," he said, giving Tyler a bear hug.

24

Left Behind

Debaltseve and Verkhnya Krynka, Donetsk Oblast, February 2015

Petro Kohikov didn't want to leave his home of some 60 years. But the war had come to their doorstep, and his wife, Olena Koshikova, had had enough. She pleaded with Petro to pack up their things and leave. She was going with or without him. After five months of debating, and only when the bombs came crashing down on their neighborhood, did he give in and agree to go with her. Where, exactly, they didn't know. Away from Debaltseve would be enough, for now.

But their hesitation would cost them. The next day, they missed their bus out of town. Hobbling toward the central square. Olena cried out and Petro raised his arm in the air as they watched it pull away. They were too old and fragile to chase it down.

When I found them, they had taken shelter in the musty basement of Debaltseve's railway station, along with scores of other local people. Petro had developed a wheezing cough and looked to be in a bad shape.

"I'm very worried," Olena said, caressing his face with her hand. "He is all that I have now." I was with three other journalists in a car without extra space. But I said that I would pass along their name and details to volunteers in Artemivsk. And I did. But I would never find out if they managed to escape. And their faces would be among so many I'd see when I closed my eyes at night and wondered if there was more I could have done to help.

Poroshenko and his government had promised to evacuate civilians from the hardest-hit areas, but they claimed Ukraine's resources were limited to taking out only a few hundred people each week. And they used the increase in fighting as an excuse not to try any harder. They also imposed punitive measures, including a blockade, that slowed or stopped passage through checkpoints across the front line. As a result, many thousands of desperate Ukrainians who supported Kyiv were left behind.

It was an open secret that the Ukrainian president, despite his patriotic chest-thumping, and his government were suspicious of those who had stayed until then in the Russia-controlled territories. Many in Kyiv, in fact, believed residents in the east had remained there for so long because they supported Moscow or pledged allegiance to the self-proclaimed DNR and LNR "republics."

"All the people that are left on the occupied territories have made their choice and refused to leave," said Semen Semenchenko, the commander of the Donbas Battalion who I'd met the previous spring and summer. He had shed his mask and was now a member of parliament, elected in the autumn.

"All this nonsense that old people and children are starving, it is not true and it is a manipulation of the facts," he claimed.

Of course, it was true. I saw it every day – on both sides of the front line. The human suffering was evident, and nowhere more so than in the rural areas of the Donbas.

In Komunar, a town of some 2,000 residents about ten miles from the front line, people were living on a meager diet of grains, pasta, and tea, without gas and electricity in subzero temperatures. There were no doctors left, residents told me when I visited. And the town's only pharmacy had been closed. It was a terribly dire situation in a place where most of those who had been left behind were elderly and incapable of caring for themselves.

Dressed head to toe in layered wool clothing and wrapped in blankets as she huddled next to the warmth of her wood stove – her only means of heat – 96-year-old Vera Martinovskaya recalled to me her struggle living through the Second World War. Her family had had very little food. Many of her male relatives had gone off to fight – and would die. It was a nightmare that she never wanted to experience again. But war had returned. Trembling as explosions from artillery boomed in the distance, she told me that she was having flashbacks to the hell she endured seven decades earlier.

"How can it be?" she asked, grabbing my wrist and looking me in the eyes. "How?"

I had heard that residents in the neighboring town of Verkhnya Krynka, where the only way in and out is a makeshift road over a field marked with deep craters and covered in a thick sheet of ice, were in a particularly grim situation. The few hundred residents whose homes were bombarded by artillery shells last summer when Verkhnya Krynka temporarily became the front line of this war, relied solely on shipments of humanitarian aid, which were now few and far between because of the heavy fighting surrounding the village, and the snow and rain that had transformed the dirt road into an impassable quagmire.

My driver and I were barely able to make it into the village. We were stuck momentarily, until I got out to push the car from the back.

There was a pervading and palpable sense of desperation in Verkhnya Krynka. Old women sat on benches outside the gates of their homes, their toothless mouths agape like ghosts and their hands outstretched like they were begging for food. We stopped and I gave two women what I had – some bananas and bottles of water.

In the town center, the only sign of life was a woman dragging a cart with a box marked with the Red Cross emblem.

"Is there an aid point nearby?" I asked her.

"There," she said, pointing to a tiny schoolhouse.

Inside, a woman was organizing bags of flour and pasta and other goods into boxes. She was going to distribute them around the village and invited me to come along. She asked if we could use our car to take some of the supplies, and I said that we could. We loaded up several boxes and set off down the road.

Around the corner, we found two homes with elderly women inside. Their husbands had died long ago and their children were somewhere in the west of the country. One of the women, Valentina Panchenko, aged 66, said their only sustenance had been tea and plain pasta noodles. They cried as they recounted to me the horrors that had descended upon their village.

Panchenko pointed to a house two doors down. She said it had been the home of a 55-year-old widow named Valentina Mazur. They had been friends for decades and watched each other's children grow up. But a few months ago, Mazur had retreated into her home and fallen into a deep depression. Her husband and brother had died earlier in 2014, just before the outbreak of the war. And her daughter had enlisted in the pro-Russian militia in the summer.

Making matters worse, Mazur "had no money, no food, nothing," Panchenko said.

Two days before Christmas, Panchenko and another woman went over to check on Mazur and found her front door unlocked, which was unusual. The women stepped inside and called for their friend. "Valentina! Valentina!" There was no response.

One of the women then noticed something hanging from a roof beam.

"I saw it was a rope and I thought, that's strange," she recalled, describing how her eyes moved down the rope. "I didn't even see that it was wrapped around Valentina's neck until several moments later."

25

The Woman in the Grass

Kramatorsk, 10 February 2015

I was enjoying a bowl of warm borsch when the missiles struck. The explosions were so close they shook the cafe walls. My server shrieked and dropped a tray of sodas that crashed to the floor. I dove under the table and covered my head with my hands. The attack lasted a couple of minutes, but it felt like it was dragging on for hours. My heart thumped and my breathing quickened. I wondered if I was going to die.

I walked out of the cafe a few minutes later to find Vova smoking beside his white Mercedes van. He'd stayed in the passenger seat the whole time.

"Son of a bitch!" I exclaimed. "You OK?"

"Da! Chris, I heard screaming. There must be injured people," he said. "Look there – smoke."

I threw on my helmet and vest in case there would be a follow-up attack. About 100 feet away, I saw a spent canister from a rocket wedged deep inside the earth and recognized it as one that stored cluster munitions – little bomblets that are released as the rocket approaches its target and explode over an area the size of a football field. Nearby, I saw a body lying supine in the middle of the grass. It was a woman. She was dressed in a winter hat and puffy jacket with black knee-high boots. I rushed over and saw blood coming from her head. When I knelt down I noticed the color had fled from her face and she was white. Her eyes were open and her mouth was slightly agape. I spoke to her but there was no response. I put my fingers on her neck to check for a pulse but there was nothing. A group of people came over and I told them the woman was dead.

"When will it stop?" a woman cried as her friends comforted her. She did not know the woman, she said, but "it could have been any of us. We are safe nowhere!"

I stood up and walked around the block. There were six more large rocket craters and several more bodies, too. The target was probably the military airfield nearby, I thought. The rockets had overshot their target. Then again, Russia's forces had no problem firing on and killing civilians. It could simply have been an act of terror.

26

The Cossack Bomb Squad

Debaltseve, March 2015

Early on 18 February, Ukrainian forces began to retreat from Debaltseve. Russian forces had nearly encircled them, the highway was under their fire control, and the bridge was blown out, making the Ukrainians' position in the town untenable. The withdrawal wasn't easy. Thousands of soldiers desperately fought their way out, walking or crawling through frozen fields under heavy fire until they reached safety on the outskirts of Artemivsk. It would be one of the biggest and most consequential defeats of the war.

Ukraine shouldn't have had to pull out of the town, because a deal known as the Minsk II agreement signed days earlier and meant to stop the fighting and lay out a path to peace had designated it a part of the territory that was to remain under Kyiv's control. But that wasn't how Putin saw it. The Minsk deal was hammered out in an all-night meeting between the Russian leader, Poroshenko, German Chancellor Angela Merkel, and French President François Hollande. It was a bad deal for Ukraine, but Kyiv didn't have the momentum in its favor at that moment. Russia's forces on the ground had the upper hand, and without the deal it was possible that more territory could be lost. After signing it, however, the Kremlin went ahead and took a few more towns, Debaltseve included, without any consequences.

Shortly after, I wanted to see what was left of the town and what the Russians were doing there. So I set off one day with Evgeny Feldman, my Russian photographer, from the Donetsk Ramada. Then I made what was one of the dumbest decisions of my life: I embedded us with a Russian Cossack bomb-disposal squad.

They called themselves the First Strike Company. One wrong move could have meant the difference between living and dying, and the sappers' leader, 31-year-old Denis "Raven" Zaitsev, liked to remind me of that for no other reason, it seemed, than to terrify me.

"It's like dancing with death," he said, doing a little jig. His comrades were rolling with laughter.

By this point, after a year of war, the battlefields of eastern Ukraine were covered with mines and various unexploded rockets and mortars and shells. The UN was calling the Donbas one of the most mined places on earth. Now I was going to roll around collecting them with a bunch of guys with death wishes.

A grizzled Cossack who went by the *nom de guerre* Gazeta ordered me into a Soviet-era military van that looked like a sad, green version of the Scooby Doo Mystery Machine. He was wearing a traditional black hat and camouflage fatigues. In his hands he cradled a 82mm mortar round that had failed to explode when it struck a residential neighborhood.

Up front in the van, Raven and another member of the team chain-smoked Lucky Strikes, their Kalashnikovs resting in their laps. An Orthodox priest, wearing a long robe and gold chain, poked his head inside to say a prayer and shower us with holy water before we set off.

Also in the van – more worryingly – were boxes of explosives, land mines, and anti-tank mines, as well as the anti-personnel bounding fragmentation mines that jump when tripped, exploding into a bazillion lethal shards. There were grenades and blocks of C-4 (plastic explosive). Beneath our seat were two 155mm howitzer shells. All of it collected from Debaltseve.

"We disarm about 30 mines, explosives or booby traps every day," Raven said.

Now these dud munitions were rattling around the floor beneath me and slamming into the back of my boots each time the driver would come to a stop. I truly feared these might be my last moments as we bounced over cratered roads and fields, en route to the former Ukrainian army camp I'd visited earlier with Noah, in order to blow up all the ordnance.

I shot a look at Evgeny that was meant to say without actually saying it, this was a damn stupid fucking idea. But he looked back at me with wild eyes. He was getting a kick out of it, snapping photos of it all.

Raven, sensing my concern, tried to put me at ease. "Christopher, you can't die twice, and you can't avoid dying once," he quipped, borrowing a quote from Tolstoy.

Soon we stopped at a home on Pioneer Street where Raven pulled a spent Uragan cluster munitions rocket from a rooftop and Gazeta examined an unexploded missile rammed into the garden. Many residents who fled Debaltseve during the fighting had returned to find mines and missiles in their yards. The owner of this house had called a hotline for ordnance removal and the Cossacks had put him on their daily rounds list.

Two teenagers peering over the fence told each other the rocket shell looked "cool" and they asked Raven if they could have it. He took one more look at it as if to check that nothing could explode, and threw it over to them.

Amid the conflict, a new hobby had emerged: children here collected shell casings – the bigger the better. I'd seen several kids with collections that included bullet casings and rocket fins and spent anti-tank canisters. But because they often didn't recognize unexploded ordnance, sometimes their fun turned deadly. Weeks earlier, two boys in Artemivsk had stumbled upon unexploded mines in a field near my former Krasne village school. Danil Zverkovsky, a former student of mine who was 16 at the time, was killed when the shell exploded in his hands. A ten-year-old boy with him was badly wounded. Around the same time in Debaltseve, two more young boys found an IED (Improvised Explosive Device) and picked it up to have a closer look.

"They dropped the IED, and then . . . corpses," Raven told me, shaking his head.

This wasn't Raven's first time defusing ordnance, nor was this his first war. But he was tight-lipped about the details of his past. He admitted that he was not Ukrainian, but from Pyatigorsk, a city in Russia's North Caucasus region. And he was here to fight for what he believed was "my land . . . Novorossiya," using the Tsarist term employed by Putin and the DNR and LNR crowd to describe southeastern Ukraine.

As for his crew, some had worked as engineers and had a general understanding of weapons systems from their time in the Russian and Soviet armies. Others learned the ropes as they went along. Gazeta was from Khartsyzk, an impoverished industrial town 20 miles east of Donetsk. I'd been through there several times before. It wasn't much to look at. A devilish grin on his face, he said quizzically that he couldn't remember where he had learned to disarm bombs.

During their daily sweeps the First Strike Company sometimes found unexploded ordnance dating back to the Second World War, the last time a bloody war had been fought here.

Raven kicked one across the pavement toward me and it came to rest at my feet. "We found this one the other day," he said of the corroded howitzer shell.

Whatever the First Strike Company found, the team blew it up in controlled explosions. As our battered van trundled to the former Ukrainian camp, the dugout that would be used to destroy a ton of explosive munitions came into view.

We stopped beside the tarnished hulk of a destroyed Ukrainian tank, and Gazeta walked over. He noticed a middle-aged couple, who'd been made homeless by the war, curled up in an adjacent bunker that they'd been living in. The Cossacks waved their rifles at them and told them to fuck off.

Gazeta went to work neatly stacking the day's collection underground. When it was all there, he slapped some C-4 to it and lit the fuse. Evgeny, myself, and the others ducked behind the van and waited for the blast.

Gazeta wasn't even 40 feet away when it detonated, and a ball of flames exploded from the bunker, the shockwave throwing concrete slabs, logs, and dirt into the air. The earth shook beneath my feet.

Pleased with the job, Gazeta lit a cigarette and surveyed the smoky blast zone.

Turning to me and nodding in approval, he said, "That's how it's done."

27

PTSD

Kyiv, April 2015

Officer Sergei Yatchenko closed the curtains in his cluttered bedroom, sat down on his bed, and poured himself a drink. Then he took a deep breath and squeezed his eyes shut. It was quiet here, far away from the war in the east and weeks after the Minsk II ceasefire deal. But there was still no peace. Not for Ukraine and certainly not for Yatchenko.

"I feel terrible," he told me, slowly opening his eyes. I was sitting at his desk. He reached over me and grabbed a large dagger. Pulling it from its sheath, he held it in front of his chest, sizing it up.

Somewhat nervously, I asked what he was thinking.

"I'm not living. I'm existing," he said. "I can't call what I'm living life."

Returning home from the war had been as hellish as being in the shit at the front line.

"Have you seen *First Blood*?" he asked, referring to the 1982 film starring Sylvester Stallone as John Rambo, a Vietnam veteran who winds up in rural Washington state looking for an old friend, but is met with intolerance by the community and abuse by a local sheriff. "It's like that."

Yatchenko wasn't a trained soldier. He was a 35-year-old licensed child and family psychologist who had joined the 25th Kyivan Rus Territorial Defense Battalion after the war began. He signed up because he wanted to do his part. And he thought, given his professional experience, he'd be able to at least handle the mental and psychological – if not the physical – elements of war.

"I had to face horrible things there at the front. But I have to deal with even harder things here at home," he said. "Ukrainian society is not ready to accept war veterans."

After months of grueling battles around Donetsk, Yatchenko had returned to Kyiv to find that he had developed dependent personality disorder and an acute reaction to stress, as well as post-traumatic stress disorder, or PTSD.

There were thousands of soldiers here like him, men and women coming home only to face a new, internal enemy, or "invisible injuries," as Yatchenko called them. But nobody was talking about them. Not journalists and certainly not the Ukrainian government or military.

Ukraine was woefully unprepared for the war itself. It certainly wasn't ready to have to deal with its fallout.

"We train soldiers to kill, not to take care of their mental health," Serhiy Hryluk, a Ukrainian colonel in charge of the military's social–psychological center had told me.

Before I met Yatchenko in Kyiv, I'd been in Artemivsk. There, inside a military hospital, I visited with Ukrainian troops still recovering from physical injuries suffered during the battle of Debaltseve. Many told me their mental wounds were worse. A soldier named Slavik was among them. He'd been shot in the leg. Over tea, he recalled a night two weeks earlier when he awoke delirious and thought his roommate was an enemy soldier.

"I was ready to kill him," he told me.

A nurse found Slavik talking to himself as he stood over the sleeping soldier with a six-inch knife in his hand.

"Thank God she was there," he said.

Another soldier I met, named Serhiy, was a middle-aged, bulky volunteer fighter with a graying walrus mustache who had fought with the 43rd Battalion. He asked me to call him by his *nom de guerre*, "Wolf." Wolf wound up in the hospital after a grenade he tried to throw toward enemy lines exploded prematurely in his hands, blowing off several fingers.

"Give me a bottle of vodka and I'll be fine," he told me. He had turned to drinking to block out memories of the horrors he'd experienced on the battlefields.

"Dogs were growling and chewing the arms and legs of corpses," Wolf said. "How the fuck can I ever forget seeing that?"

Next to him was 18-year-old Seryozha. His call sign was "Jester" and it suited him. He had jokes for days. Not even being stuck in this grimy hospital kept him from smiling and laughing. His chuckle was infectious and sounded like a child's. But his face and scars were those of a war-battered man.

Like Wolf, Jester had lost several fingers in a grenade blast. It happened when he threw himself atop an enemy grenade that had landed inside his bunker, in order to save his fellow soldiers. When it failed to detonate and he realized he was still alive, he grabbed the grenade and moved to toss it back. That's when it exploded.

His mental health had never been a concern. Jester believed he was sent to war to fight and die.

"Our commanders told us, 'We are going to war and we won't return,'" he told me. "I really thought we'd all die, so why would I think about returning home?"

Interlude

Ukraine, 2015–2021
After the Minsk II agreements and a last gasp of fighting in and around Debaltseve in winter and early spring 2015, the 250-mile front line that cut through the Donbas suddenly froze, and the war moved from a boil to a simmer. The Minsk II agreements had outlined a path to peace, but there would be no lasting truce. Putin didn't want his war against Ukraine to end – not without bringing the country completely under his control. The Donbas was just a slice; he wanted the whole pie.

Over the next six years, Putin would tighten his grip on Crimea and the Donetsk and Luhansk oblasts, using them as leverage to try to control Kyiv and influence Western decision-making in the context of Ukraine. He would dial up the war when he saw a need to do so, threatening to expand it, or to try to dissuade Washington and other Western governments from supporting Kyiv with weapons or from hitting Russia with new sanctions. Then Putin would turn down the fighting to make it appear as though he would be willing to negotiate an end to the conflict.

He would also begin attacking Ukraine in multiple other, unconventional ways, notably with cyberattacks and a covert campaign of assassinations targeting Russian dissidents and Ukrainian military personnel inside the country. These were attempts to soften and undermine the country from within.

Meanwhile, Ukraine's pro-Western government would work – and struggle at times – to carry out crucial reforms and combat corruption, as it laid a path toward its revolutionary dreams of becoming a member of the European Union. Politically, socially and culturally, Ukraine also would move farther from Russia and its Soviet and post-Soviet past, as it launched a sweeping decommunization program and began promoting Ukrainian language and culture. It would grow stronger and more united.

And a new generation of Ukrainians would come of age who were proud and determined to fight against Moscow's persistent attacks.

As for me, I would be banned by Russia and its DNR and LNR proxies from ever returning to the areas of Donetsk and Luhansk that it controlled, meaning much of the Donbas would be off limits to me. The reason? The Kremlin considered me a Western "spy," and it punished me for writing critically of its brutal and unprovoked invasion of Ukraine and not telling "the truth." My name would be added to the top of a blacklist of hundreds of journalists who had once been granted accreditation and access. But I still had my sources inside and I'd speak to them regularly.

As much of the world turned its attention away, Moscow would move to "Russify" the DNR and LNR areas. It stripped them of all freedoms and privileges afforded to Ukrainians living in Kyiv-controlled areas and treated them as extensions of Russia. The Kremlin also handed out Russian passports to hundreds of thousands of people and played them against their own government.

What many feared but didn't want to believe during that whole time was that Putin was regrouping, building up his army and waiting for the right moment to again invade Ukraine and try to bring it to its knees.

PART FOUR

FULL-SCALE INVASION

28

Warning Signs

Kyiv, early 2022

Volodymyr Zelensky paced across the ornate parquet floors of his office, the clack of his black, size $8^{1/2}$ oxfords echoing through the cavernous building, as he studied the contents of a red folder. A stamp at the top read "top secret." It was for the Ukrainian president's eyes only. Inside was an intelligence briefing compiled by his National Security and Defense Council. The information contained within was so urgent and alarming that the secretary of the NSDC, Oleksiy Danilov, had rushed across town in his aging Audi to deliver it himself.

"Sir, information from our Western partners indicates your life is in grave danger," Danilov told Zelensky. The document outlined a Russian capture-or-kill operation targeting the president.

Zelensky furrowed his brows and scrunched up his face.

"Hmm," he grumbled. "Thank you."

He left the folder on his desk, dismissed Danilov, and headed down the hall to another meeting.

It wasn't the first time Zelensky had been warned of such a thing and he was, frankly, tired of hearing about it – even if he was finally beginning to believe it.

For weeks, the United States and other Western nations had been alerting him to the threat of a Russian invasion, the goal of which, they said, was to capture Kyiv and install a pro-Russian puppet government. On a secret visit to the Ukrainian capital in mid-January, CIA Director Bill Burns had also told Zelensky that there was a threat to life, my sources in the president's office would later tell me. Burns warned that the Kremlin had compiled a "kill list" of Ukrainians who were to be assassinated or sent to prison camps. The list included government officials, journalists, activists, ethnic and religious minorities, and LGBTQ Ukrainians. But

Zelensky himself was at the top. And shortly before the intelligence report landed in Zelensky's hands, Ukraine's foreign minister, Dmytro Kuleba, had been briefed in Washington. "I was received by President Biden. And then we had a meeting with Secretary Blinken. We delivered our comment to the press and then I was asked to go to a separate room," he told me later. "And in that room I received an update, a pretty detailed update on the Russian preparations. And the guys who were speaking with me said the invasion was likely to begin within like 48 hours."

The Biden Administration was especially and unusually vocal about the looming Russian threat. It had first sounded an alarm in March and April 2021, when Russia began massing thousands of personnel and military equipment near its border with Ukraine and in occupied Crimea. Russia withdrew some troops that summer but left the equipment in place. Then, in October 2021, Washington sounded a second alarm when it noticed Russia was moving its forces back toward the border and deploying more units on new fronts. By December, US intelligence was saying that roughly 120,000 Russian troops, along with fighter aircraft and ballistic missiles, were in place, and that the troop numbers were likely to increase to 175,000, maybe more. American General Mark Milley, head of the Joint Chiefs of Staff, called Russia's troop buildup "larger in scale and scope . . . than anything we've seen in recent memory." President Joe Biden showed solidarity with Ukraine, warning the Kremlin of severe consequences should Vladimir Putin give the order to invade.

Zelensky's annoyance was evident to the public three weeks before Danilov walked into his office, when the president held a press conference on 28 January. Foreign media, myself included, gathered at the baroque-styled Mariinsky Palace, the official residence of the President of Ukraine, designed and built in the eighteenth century. Crystal chandeliers hung from the ceiling of the gilded room. There were samovars filled with coffee and tea. Servers dressed in uniform and white gloves opened doors for us and offered pastries and fruit. The mood among us journalists was tense. We had, of course, been the ones writing about the Western intelligence warnings. Some of us had received off-the-record briefings ourselves from our respective government sources, who said that it might be a good idea to leave Kyiv and head west, where Russia was unlikely to invade. "I know you probably want to be in the thick of it when it happens, but I'm telling you this isn't going to be like 2014," a senior U.S. official who I'd known for many years told me. But the Ukrainians appeared less anxious. I chatted on the sidelines with Zelensky's press secretary, Sergii Nykyforov, before the event. He was calm and reassuring. "I think it's possible Russia might do something, but I'm not sure it will be like they are saying," he told me.

I was seated in the front row when Zelensky strutted in, clean-shaven and wearing a black suit and tie. He flashed a little smile, greeted us with hello in English and Ukrainian. "Can I be without mask?" he asked in English as he walked past me and gave a little bow before plopping down on his chair in front of a row of Ukrainian flags. It was a reminder that we hadn't seen the end of one crisis while another one was looming. COVID was still ravaging Ukraine. Hospitals were full of coronavirus patients; ventilators were in short supply. Just about every foreign correspondent flying into the country caught it within 72 hours. An entire crew of some 20 CNN journalists were infected at the same time at the Intercontinental Hotel. I had had it in December and spent more than a week cooped up in my room at the Radisson Blu, dining on room service.

It was immediately clear at the presser that Zelensky was irritated by the West's repeated warnings. In particular, he was concerned about the impact they would have on Ukraine's already struggling economy and cause panic among the population. But that didn't mean he wasn't taking the threats seriously, he said. Shrugging off questions about whether he was in denial about Russia's military build-up, Zelensky referred to the Netflix movie *Don't Look Up*, a satire about astronomers trying to warn the world of a comet threatening mankind's extinction but are ignored by the US president, who is more concerned about her popularity. The film was wildly popular in Ukraine, where quick-witted social media users following geopolitical events created memes of Zelensky as the president in the movie.

"It's like your film, *Don't Look up*. We're looking up. We do understand what's happening and we're talking about this. We're talking about this with our people," Zelensky said. "But we are also looking on the ground.

"Do we have tanks on the streets?" he continued. "No. When you read reports in the media, you get the image that we have troops in the city, people fleeing. That's not the case."

He wasn't saying Russia couldn't or wouldn't invade. He was saying that it already had back in 2014. "Escalation already happened," he explained. "The [Russian] threat is imminent. The threat is constant."

While he respected Biden and appreciated his support, just like the American president knows better about what's happening in Washington, he said, "I'm the president of Ukraine and I'm based here, and I think I know the details better here."

And he had one more thing to say. He was unhappy about the US, the United Kingdom, and Canada evacuating its embassy staffers. "Diplomats are like captains," Zelensky said. "They should be the last to leave a sinking ship. And Ukraine is not the *Titanic*."

Several months after the invasion, Zelensky would defend his words to me in an interview, saying that despite the public warnings by US officials, Kyiv was never given intelligence it could act on about the impending Russian attack. "Nobody showed us specific material saying it would come from this or that direction," he said. A US official would tell me otherwise. "We told them exactly where the Russians would come from and how they would do it," the official said.

But by the time Zelensky had received the intelligence briefing from Danilov, he had finally started to come around to the US assessments and believed, at the very least, that Russia would invade Ukraine again – he just thought it would be an incursion aimed at seizing more of the Donbas.

Hours before Danilov placed the folder in the president's hands, Putin had gone on Russian state television and recognized the "independence" of the Donetsk and Luhansk oblasts in eastern Ukraine, all but confirming attacks there. Citing false and unproven reports as a justification, the Russia strongman said he would heed the appeals of his puppet leaders on the occupied parts of those regions, who had asked for military support, and deploy his troops there under the guise of a bogus "peacekeeping mission."

Zelensky was looking for more details on that when he walked into his next meeting late that evening. He had called to his fourth-floor office the leaders of all the political parties serving in parliament, so that they, too, could be brought up to speed. Knowing they were on the verge of renewed all-out war, he asked them to set aside their differences now and unite for a common cause: the defense of the country. Also present were Denys Shmyhal, Ukraine's prime minister; Valery Zaluzhny, the commander-in-chief of the Armed Forces of Ukraine; Ivan Bakanov, Zelensky's childhood friend who'd been tapped without any relevant experience to head the Security Service of Ukraine; defense minister Oleksiy Reznikov; and General Kyrylo Budanov, a former special-forces operator who was still new in the role of head of the Defense Ministry's Military Intelligence Directorate. There was a conversation about whether to announce mobilization in response to the latest US intelligence. But Bakanov and Reznikov said that wouldn't be necessary, because there'd be no full-scale invasion and another incursion in the Donbas could be met this time around with Ukraine's reformed military that it already had entrenched there.

Then Budanov, the youngest among the officials at 36 years old, stood up and quieted down the room. He spread a map across the large table in the middle of everyone before calmly and clearly delivering a message that one person present would later tell me "drained the blood from their faces." The Russians would invade in the Donbas from the east, yes, Budanov told the group. But Putin's army would also attack military targets across the country with missiles and rockets. Attack aircraft would follow. And ground forces would invade with tanks and other armor from Belarus in the north, Russia in the east, and occupied Crimea in the south. Drawing his fingers across the map to show which routes the Russians would advance on, he detailed an invasion plan more ambitious than anything seen since the Nazis invaded Poland in 1939. What Russia had in store would reorder the post-World War II security architecture and reshape the global order.

That night and through the next day, Zelensky repeatedly tried to call the Kremlin. He wanted to tell Putin himself that it would be a "great mistake, a great tragedy" to invade Ukraine, he would later tell me. However, the Russian leader refused to take his calls.

Unable to reach Moscow by phone, Zelensky turned to the airwaves. He called into his office his chief of staff, Andriy Yermak, speechwriter Yuriy Kostiuk, and Daria Zarivna, Yermak's press secretary. He said he wanted to deliver an address – not to Ukrainians, but to Russians. It was 11 p.m. on 23 February when they finished and the president's video team began recording him. Five minutes before midnight, his office posted the address online.

Zelensky looked into the camera and spoke in Russian: "Today I initiated a phone call with the president of the Russian federation. The result was silence . . . That's why I want to address today the people of Russia. I am addressing you not as a president, I am addressing you as a citizen of Ukraine. More than 2,000 kilometers of shared border is dividing us. Along this border your troops are stationed – almost 200,000 soldiers, thousands of military vehicles. Your leaders have ordered them to make a step forward, onto the territory of another country. And this step can be the beginning of a big war on European continent.

"They told you that Ukraine is posing a threat to Russia. It was not the case in the past, not in the present, it's not going to be in the future . . . I know that [the Russian state] won't show my address on Russian TV, but Russian people have to see it. They need to know the truth, and the truth is that it is time to stop now, before it is too late."

29

Servant of the People

Kyiv, early 2019

The first time I ever saw Zelensky deliver an address on television was three years earlier. It was just before midnight on New Year's Eve, traditionally the biggest holiday of the year in Ukraine. Families and friends were gathered wearing fur coats around tables overflowing with giant bowls of mayonnaise-laden olivier salad and herring, *kholodets* (a meat jello dish), boiled potatoes with dill, various pickled vegetables and cured meats, *holubtsi*, buttered bread covered in caviar and more. They were buzzed on *horilka* (moonshine) and Artwinery sparkling wine when they switched on their televisions to watch the traditional presidential address at midnight.

For those tuning into the 1-Plus-1 channel, owned by the controversial and famously vulgar Ukrainian oligarch Igor Kolomoisky, they were in for a surprise. In the run-up to midnight, the channel had been airing *Evening Kvartal*, a regular comedy program put on by a troupe called Kvartal 95. Zelensky was a writer, director, actor, and leader of the troupe, which was composed of friends who all grew up on the same block (*kvartal*) in the south-central industrial city of Kryvyi Rih and went to university together. His wife, Olena Zelenska, was a scriptwriter for the program. *Evening Kvartal* was made up of various sketches poking fun at Ukrainian culture, society, and politics. It was more *Benny Hill* than *Monty Python*. Like a cross between *Saturday Night Live* and *Mad TV*, though more slapstick and racy. The first time I ever watched it was exactly ten years earlier. Igor and I were working through a two-liter bottle of Lvivske 1715 beer. It was a frigid February evening in Bakhmut and the city was shut down. We tried to entertain ourselves by boiling pots of water on the stove and then tossing them out the window to watch them transform instantly into white powder in the -20 degree cold. But that didn't pass enough time. So we went into the living room to watch some comedy. Igor pulled up a skit on YouTube by Kvartal

95, which at that point I was unaware of. It was the 31 December special from a little more than a month earlier. In it, Zelensky played a traffic cop who stops a driver on New Year's Eve. Both are wasted and spend almost ten minutes staggering around. Another skit involves another actor impersonating Yanukovych. It was funny but not *that* funny.

A few years later, Kvartal 95 produced a hit political comedy series called 'Servant of the People', in which Zelensky played Vasyl Petrovych Holoborodko, a humble high-school teacher who, in the first episode, is secretly filmed by a student while unleashing a profanity-laced tirade about the rampant corruption plaguing Ukraine. Holoborodko becomes an internet sensation overnight after the student posts the episode online. Then the unthinkable and absurd happens: he's miraculously elected president and thrust into a role as the only moral leader in a crooked system. This show, I enjoyed.

The clock was about to strike midnight when *Evening Kvartal* switched to a scene with a New Year's tree decorated in lights and ornaments on a stage shrouded in red curtains. But instead of President Petro Poroshenko, out walked Zelensky, then 41, wearing a white buttoned-up shirt with no tie and his sleeves rolled up. He was grinning. His hair was floppy. He looked nerdy and nervous, a lot like Holoborodko.

"Good evening, friends," he began. "Soon we will celebrate the New Year and continue *Evening Kvartal*. In the meantime, I have a short break, so I decided to talk to you frankly, as Volodymyr Zelensky."

He continued: "You know, unlike our great politicians, I don't want to make you empty promises. So now, a few minutes before the New Year, I will promise you something and immediately fulfill it. Dear Ukrainians, I promise you to become president of Ukraine, and I will fulfill it right away . . . Happy New Year! To the new servant of the people!"

Ukrainians were stunned. I was stunned. I texted my Ukrainian friends from New York, where I was spending time with family. "WTF?" "Zelensky??" I wrote. Shrug and laughing emojis flooded in. "Welcome to Ukraine!" one responded.

Zelenska, his wife, was equally surprised. He hadn't told her of his plans before the announcement. "I learned about it like everyone else, watching the program," she would tell me later with an eye roll. "I was angry. He could have told me. But I do remember those days. That was a very tense period of time for him. There were lots of events happening. So I pretended that he had just forgotten to tell me about it. I didn't want to fight or aggravate the situation."

To call Zelensky's speech a coup would be an understatement. Poroshenko was "boiling mad," one of his advisors would tell me during the ensuing presidential race, adding that the president had even called Zelensky to try to convince him to back out. "Poroshenko told him he was making a terrible mistake, and that he would crush him," the advisor said. "Zelensky told him, 'Petro Oleksiyovych, don't let the door hit you on the way out.'"

The next four months were a whirlwind. Ukraine's presidential campaigns, with their dozens of contenders, oligarch candidates and clones (people with the same name as a leading candidate or someone who legally changed their name to that of a leading candidate for money and planted maliciously on the ballot by opponents to trick people into voting for the wrong contender, thus costing crucial votes) were always a colorful yet exhausting circus. But Zelensky's candidacy injected a new level of absurdity into the 2019 race. His staff was formed from Kvartal 95 actors. He registered a political party called Servant of the People and the production style and music in his political ads were the same as the sitcom. Season 3 of the show was airing as he began campaigning, leading people to wonder, where did Holoborodko end and Zelensky begin? But some of my Ukrainian friends who were disillusioned with the same old established political faces quipped, does it matter?

"I think he's a lot like his character in real life," my friend Ihor Bidenko, a 21-year-old bartender, told me as he stirred my boulevardier cocktail at the hip Podil East India Company one evening. "But for me, it matters more that he is someone new." The rest of the bar nodded in agreement.

Zelensky's slick campaign together with him being a political novice and his instant recognition – he'd already been a household name from winning Ukraine's spinoff of *Dancing With The Stars* in 2006, voicing Paddington Bear in the Ukrainian versions of *Paddington* and *Paddington 2*, and playing Holoborodko – instantly shot him to the top of the polls. He breezed through the first-round vote in March, topping all candidates and setting him up for a head-to-head run-off with Poroshenko in April.

The weeks leading up to the second round were wild. Zelensky and Poroshenko pulled no punches in their attacks against each other. Poroshenko claimed that Zelensky, who'd performed in Moscow and was popular in Russia, was "pro-Russian," claiming that a vote for the comedian was "a vote for Putin." Poroshenko plastered billboards across the country with his nationalistic campaign slogan, "Army. Language. Faith," in an attempt to portray himself as a savior of Ukraine from Russia. The candidates challenged one another to live-streamed drug tests and held a raucous debate inside Kyiv's Olympic Stadium that was a cross between a tailgate party and a prize fight. As a member of the press, I had a front-row seat to the action.

"A war against the Russian aggressor cannot be led by an actor," Poroshenko told the crowd. "The price that tens of millions of Ukrainians will pay could be very, very high."

Zelensky snapped back. "I'm not a politician. I'm just a person. A simple man who came to break the system," he said. "Petro Oleksiyovych, I'm the result of your mistakes and missteps."

The difference between them was stark. Poroshenko may have participated in the Revolution of Dignity and been elected in the wake of it, but for many he didn't represent Ukraine's future. Many were frustrated by his handling of the war and they saw the Minsk Accords as a bad deal with Russia that froze the front line and led to long-term occupation of the Donbas. Zelensky, who didn't partake in the revolution but did call for Yanukovych to resign, was a wild card, sure. But he was also a chance to shake things up and start afresh. He vowed to keep Ukraine on a westward path while also making two major promises: he'd stand up to the oligarchs and root out corruption; and he would bring an end to the war in the Donbas. He said he could sit down with Putin and hash out a deal that would finally bring peace. There were signals from the Kremlin that they might even be willing to negotiate with him. To a country that had already lost more than 14,000 lives, seen more than a million people displaced, and cities destroyed in an unnecessary war, that sounded like a chance worth taking.

Inside the Poroshenko campaign office, officials were clearly befuddled. His staff carried themselves as if defeat was inevitable. Nothing they tried worked; everything Poroshenko did came off as scripted and rigid. He lacked Zelensky's charisma, quick wit, and authenticity. And Ukrainians didn't want more war, which is what they believed they would get with Poroshenko at the helm.

On election night, I visited Zelensky's campaign headquarters, located in the swanky, high-tech Parkovy Center on the bank of the Dnipro river. There were photo booths and table-tennis tables. There was an endless buffet of pizzas and a bar with cold beer on tap. The crowd skewed young, with Ukrainians in their late teens through early thirties making up a majority of Zelensky's staff. Svyatoslav Yurash, who I'd met during the revolution when he was running the EuromaidanPR center, was there. Now 23, he was working as an advisor to Zelensky.

"Zelensky's wide support shows how much everyone is tired of the political elite," he told me. "He's popular not just with the young people but with all age categories."

Zelensky's office was upstairs and every once in a while he would come down, roll up his sleeves, and crack some jokes for the room. It was packed when the results came in: Zelensky had trounced Poroshenko with 73 per cent of all votes. The room exploded in applause. Confetti fell from the ceiling. Champagne flowed. Zelensky entered the room to the Servant of the People theme song. In his first speech as president-elect, he reiterated that ending the war was his top priority.

Meanwhile in Moscow, the Kremlin was watching with great interest. It had long viewed Poroshenko as someone they couldn't do business with. Russian Prime Minister Dmitry Medvedev wrote on Facebook that the election showed "a clear demand for new approaches in solving Ukraine's problems." He said he saw "chances for improving cooperation" between the two countries.

Two months later, I found myself sitting on a fluorescent green beanbag chair across from a newly elected President Zelensky, who had sunk into a giant pink bag. I'd been invited along with several Ukrainian journalists to one of the president's official residences, deep in a forest outside of Kyiv. The residence was a multi-story log cabin-style estate. Zelensky gave us a tour and sneered at the decor. He said it was too ostentatious for his taste and said he would consider opening it up to the public. He had caterers bring in wine and food, including *shawarma* (a roasted meat wrap). "It was my favorite as a kid," he told me as he chomped on his wrap, careful not to drip onto his white shirt and black tie. Poroshenko never had a good relationship with the media. He saw us as adversaries. Zelensky was skeptical of journalists but he knew how to work a crowd and seemed to want to restore relations with the press. These were some of Ukraine's top reporters and editors. But in Zelensky's presence, many of them instantly transformed into fans, posing for selfies with the newly elected leader. Most of the conversation was light and jovial. But there were moments when I and others put questions to him about serious issues, one of which was the war and his promise to end it. As we indulged in our shawarma, I asked if he was intent on speaking with Putin and how he planned to deliver on his promise to end the war.

"We must talk," he said. "I will not give up any territory of Ukraine but we must save people's lives."

I pushed for more, but he was pulled aside by the editor of a top Ukrainian news site for a photo.

Zelensky took great pains during his first year as president to be the antidote to Poroshenko, including in his dealings with Russia. He made it a point not to insult Putin personally. For instance, while Poroshenko referred to him as a terrorist, Zelensky simply referred to him as the Russian president. He knew he'd have to face him down at some point and he wanted a fresh slate to work with.

There was some progress in those first months. Zelensky and Putin managed to agree on a prisoner exchange in September that allowed prominent Ukrainian prisoners of war to come home. Among them was Oleg Sentsov, a prominent filmmaker from Crimea who'd been in Russian captivity for five years. The swap had helped Zelensky's approval rating soar to new heights.

Then in December 2019 the Ukrainian and Russian presidents met in person at the Élysée Palace in Paris, alongside German Chancellor Angela Merkel and French President Emmanuel Macron. There was very much a "now or never" vibe to the high-stakes event conducted by the four great powers. Zelensky came with some ideas for how to appease Putin. He floated the idea of unblocking a dam that had stopped water flowing from mainland Ukraine to Crimea, which had dried up the peninsula. And he said he would consider a level of autonomy for Donetsk and Luhansk oblasts that would be roughly similar to what Crimea had enjoyed prior to its illegal annexation and occupation. But Russian troops would need first to withdraw from Ukrainian territory. Putin fiddled with his pen and moved his eyes around the room, simply going through the motions and looking disinterested. Russian troops weren't in Ukraine, he insisted, adding that he wanted Zelensky to deal directly with the puppet leaders in occupied Donetsk and Luhansk, which would be a way to legitimize them. In the end, the two agreed to hold more POW swaps and meet again in four months. But there were no major breakthroughs.

"I would like to have seen more," Zelensky told a press conference afterwards. Putin said relations between the two countries, which he described as having been "frozen" since Yanukovych's ouster, were now "thawing." But he said the two sides were still nowhere close to a peace deal, which he saw only working on his one-sided and unjust terms.

Over the next two years, the war in the Donbas continued to simmer. I made several trips back to the front lines, which remained frozen. The troops had very much settled into the rhythm of a grinding war of attrition. Neither side was attempting any offensive. They were all holding out for a political solution that felt like it would never come. Zelensky began making moves against pro-Russian political operatives in Kyiv, in particular, Viktor Medvedchuk, Putin's close pal and the leader of the Opposition Bloc – For Life party in parliament. (Medvedchuk had told me in one of our three in-person interviews that he vacationed with Putin in Crimea and had bestowed upon the Russian president the title of godfather to his daughter, Daria. "We are good friends," he admitted to me once. "But I don't want to speak about our personal relationship.") Zelensky shut down TV stations connected to him over what Ukraine's National Security and Defense Council said was pro-Russian and anti-Ukrainian propaganda. Indeed, the channels were blatantly anti-Ukrainian and anti-Zelensky. Anytime I tuned in to hear what the stations were saying, it was clear they echoed popular Kremlin lines about Kyiv and the president. I called Medvedchuk to ask for his comment and he told me it was "political repression." Zelensky's government later charged him with treason, placed him under house arrest, and seized his assets, including a pipeline that transported Russian gas to Europe. Medvedchuk was furious at Zelensky over the moves, and so was the Kremlin, who now took a hostile position toward Zelensky, with whom it believed it could no longer negotiate. On 21 February 2021, Russia's Defense Ministry announced that 3,000 paratroopers would be deployed to the border with Ukraine for "large-scale exercises" that included practicing how to "seize enemy structures and hold them until the arrival of the main force." They would be the first troops sent to the border of Ukraine as part of Russia's pre-invasion military buildup.

30

Keep Calm and Party On

January–mid-February 2022

A light snow fell over the Ukrainian capital one evening in late January 2022, as bells from the golden-domed St Michael's Monastery rang out. Nearby, I watched two men stop to pay their respects at a memorial honoring the thousands of Ukrainian soldiers killed in the Donbas. It stretched almost 200 feet along one of the monastery's walls, with small portraits of each fallen hero. Besides the memorial, there were few outward signs in Kyiv of the armed conflict that continued to chew up lives in the east.

Nearly three years into Zelensky's presidency, his shine had worn off and his approval rating had plummeted from more than 70 per cent to just 25 per cent. And with the looming threat of the war escalating once again, some Ukrainians feared they might have put a man into office who wasn't up to the task of being a wartime leader. Zelensky's trips to the east to visit the troops over the years when the fighting had cooled to a simmer and was localized was one thing. Leading the defense of a country under an all-out invasion would be another.

But as Zelensky continued to play down the Russian threat, the Ukrainian capital and its more than three million residents kept humming along, not totally ignoring the Russian forces massing around them but choosing, it seemed, to believe they weren't about to do the seemingly unthinkable.

"In the morning people go to work. In the afternoon they are preparing for war. And at night people are going clubbing," Liubov Tsybulska told me. She is the owner of two of the city's hippest cafes who leads a double life as a Russian disinformation specialist and advisor to the government. As we sipped coffee inside Kometa, young Ukrainians in Carhartt beanies and platform shoes chomped on New York-style pizza and elaborate sushi rolls, as Unknown Mortal Orchestra blared from the sound system. We could have been in Portland, Brooklyn, London, or Berlin.

TsUM, the high-end mall on Khreshchatyk Street, buzzed with fashionable shoppers. People lined up for films, like one titled *Everything Will Be Alright* playing at the Zhovten Theater in the historic Podil neighborhood. They packed the city's incredible bars, like Parovoz and the Who & Why speakeasies, enjoying swanky cocktails one carefully considered sip at a time. And they put on their dancing shoes to gyrate with friends at quirky bars like Gnezdo.

Vitaliy Andronov, a 3D designer originally from Donetsk, was there celebrating his 36th birthday one night. "I was in Donetsk in 2014, when jets were flying up to the city and where there was bombing, and I was looking at a guy who was aiming an AK-47 at me," he said. "Now in Kyiv it's not so scary as it was in 2014." He wasn't going to change his daily life in light of the recent tensions, except that he would think about getting a license to keep a shotgun at his home.

On a walk back to our hotel one night, Pete, my photographer, and I stumbled upon a group of women singing and laughing. They were sharing a bottle of Ukrainian brandy beside the Golden Gate, the ancient entrance to Kyiv. Their howls could be heard a block away. Offering us a healthy pour, one woman, a university teacher, said war was the furthest thing from their minds. In fact, they had just left a performance at the opera. But if an invasion were to happen, she conceded, they would have their party first.

"Cheers!" they roared as we clinked our plastic cups and poured the booze down our gullets.

The calm resolve of Ukrainians came from living for the past eight years with Russian guns aimed at them and an even longer history of facing threats from their former imperial ruler. And Kyiv had felt like it was a far cry from the battlefields of the Donbas. There were no checkpoints or roadblocks. Nobody was piling sandbags in front of windows or taping large Xs across them, a preventative measure meant to keep glass shards from spraying everywhere in the event of an explosion.

"It is not the first Russia crisis we are living through. We've been under attack since 2014," Aliona Osmolovska, director of the reform support team at Ukraine's Ministry of Energy, told me. "The initial shock with Russia's latest military build-up this winter turned into annoyance. Then we burst into what we are good at in crisis modes – humor. People are posting memes. There are jokes about how our daily routines now fluctuate between normal office work, family chores, and training at the range or passing a first-aid course."

Whether Ukrainians were taking their cues from their president can be argued. But many seemed to agree with him that the threat of a new Russian invasion wasn't something to panic about.

Yet beneath that steely exterior there was some worry and uncertainty among people. And Liubov Tsybulska admitted that there is growing anxiety here, even if it's hard to see. A recent wave of bomb scares in schools had put people on edge. The government said the number of them had risen sixfold in the past several weeks compared to last year. Danilov, the secretary of the National Security and Defense Council, told me that the threats were coming from individuals associated with people in Russian-controlled Crimea and the Donbas. Danilov said he suspected Russian special services were behind them. The goal, he added, was to destabilize Ukraine's internal security, creating chaotic conditions that would be favorable for Russia should Putin decide to invade.

There was no chaos, but some people did begin to make preparations as January turned to February, as the Western warnings grew more frequent and worrying. Kyiv began renovating and stocking its 4,500 bomb shelters, including dozens of metro stations deep underground, built after the Second World War, and shared their locations on a publicly available Google map. Ukraine's military veterans began teaching self-defense and first-aid courses, and training local Territorial Defense Forces composed of civilian volunteers to fight a guerrilla war against Russian forces. Families started packing "emergency suitcases" filled with essential items that they could grab and flee with at a moment's notice. And some people temporarily relocated to western Ukraine, where they could be closer to NATO countries and troops, and where roads led to EU countries.

Still, a vast majority of Ukrainians stayed put in Kyiv and other cities. And as they hunkered down and waited to see what Putin would do, many began using the time to locate and spruce up their local bomb shelters.

I managed to visit my friends in Bakhmut one wintry January day, while Pete and I were reporting out in the east. The streets and squares were busy as usual and the mood was calm despite the front line being just 15 miles southeast. Igor invited us to go with him and his son Sasha and a group of other young boys and their fathers for what had become a weekend ritual. We gathered at a snowy soccer field to watch a model-plane hobbyist fly three home-made aircraft. The planes zipped through falling snow, performing loops and barrel rolls. One with a Ukrainian blue-and-yellow ribbon attached to its tail conducted a low fly-by near the boys, who roared with excitement.

"You know, they haven't seen real airplanes in the sky," Igor said. I had almost forgotten about the empty skies over the Donbas at that point. Planes no longer flew over eastern Ukraine, not since MH17 was shot down in July 2014. Igor, noting that the boys had been born after the tragedy, turned to me and shook his head.

"It's a strange life for them," he said.

I asked whether he and Ira were planning to take Sasha and their new baby girl Nastya and leave Bakhmut.

"No, not right now," he said. "We will see what happens first."

Meanwhile, in the apartment building where I had lived together with Igor and Ira a decade earlier, some of the neighbors were prepping the bomb shelter. Constructed with the building in the 1940s, after Nazi occupation, the bomb shelter had a thick steel door that led to a hallway and several rooms. It was musty and filled with junk that people had discarded there over the decades. The two toilets in the back didn't work and the plumbing needed to be fixed.

"I hope we won't need it," Igor said.

Back in Kyiv, a few nights before Russia would invade, a group of my friends – both foreign and Ukrainian journalists – arranged a dinner at the trendy Publicist restaurant. There were a dozen of us. We drank copious amounts of wine and cocktails and stuffed our faces with beef carpaccio, various types of tartar, racks of lamb and assorted cheeses. We darkly joked that if we were on the verge of a big war, we should eat well one last time. Katya Sergatskova, the editor of the online news site Zaborona, asked the waiter to snap a photograph of us to mark the moment. The photograph captured us all smiling somewhat awkwardly. "The last supper!" someone quipped.

31

The Battle of Kyiv

Kyiv, 24 February–29 March 2022

Early in the morning on the day that would change everything as we knew it, Ukraine's leadership was fast asleep. The president's staff and government leaders had been in late-night meetings and Zelensky had been writing and recording his speech to the Russian people. "He came home and everything was so tense because of this possible attack. We spoke for a while but we didn't discuss any of the details, like what I should do with the children, what he should do," Olena Zelenska, the First Lady, would tell me later, recalling that night. "We weren't sure anything would happen. So we went to bed."

Zelensky was startled awake by his phone ringing around 4:20 a.m. On the other end of the line was Interior Minister Denis Monastyrsky.

"It's begun," he told the president.

"What exactly?" Zelensky replied, still groggy.

Monastyrsky explained that dozens of Russian cruise missiles were in the air over Ukraine and that several had already struck their air defenses, airfields, radar batteries, ammunition depots, and other strategic military structures. The attack was coming by air, land, and sea. There were reports of Russian ground forces breaching the border in the north, east, and south.

"This is it," Monastyrsky said.

Zelensky didn't need to hear more. "It took a moment because I was asleep. But I knew he meant this was the invasion," he would tell me later.

Olena woke up moments later to the roar of explosions in the distance and rolled over to find her husband wasn't in bed. She got up and walked into the other room, where he was throwing on a dark-gray suit and white shirt, eschewing a tie.

"What's happening?" she asked, rubbing the sleep from her eyes.

Zelensky repeated Monastyrsky's line: "It's begun."

"His face was serious and he showed no emotion at all," she told me.

She peered out of a window into the cold darkness and saw a fighter jet zoom past. She didn't know if it was one of theirs or Russian. Air-raid sirens screamed across Kyiv as more explosions rocked the capital.

The couple peeked into the rooms of their children, 17-year-old Oleksandra and 9-year-old Kyrylo, and just looked at them for a moment. Then Zelensky kissed his wife goodbye.

"I did think, maybe this is the last time," Zelenska told me.

Meanwhile in Moscow, just before 6 a.m. local time, Vladimir Putin was declaring war on Ukraine in a pre-recorded televised address. Seated at a wooden desk covered in old-school telephones and wearing a black suit and maroon tie, he announced the beginning of what he called a "special military operation" to "protect people who, for eight years now, have been facing humiliation and genocide perpetrated by the Kyiv regime."

"To this end, we will seek to demilitarize and denazify Ukraine," he continued. "It is not our plan to occupy the Ukrainian territory. We do not intend to impose anything on anyone by force."

His eyes narrowed and his lips curled with anger. Moscow had been left with "no other opportunity to protect Russia other than the one we will be forced to use today," he said.

Spewing more lies, he addressed the Ukrainian military directly: "Your fathers, grandfathers and great-grandfathers did not fight the Nazi occupiers and did not defend our common Motherland to allow today's neo-Nazis to seize power in Ukraine. You swore the oath of allegiance to the Ukrainian people and not to the junta, the people's adversary which is plundering Ukraine and humiliating the Ukrainian people. I urge you to refuse to carry out their criminal orders. I urge you to immediately lay down arms and go home. I will explain what this means: the military personnel of the Ukrainian army who do this will be able to freely leave the zone of hostilities and return to their families." Standing in the way of his invasion force, he added, would "lead to consequences that you have never faced in your history."

Within minutes of Putin wrapping up his announcement, explosions rocked Kyiv, Kharkiv, Odesa, Dnipro, the Donbas, and several other locations across Ukraine, as more than 150 cruise and ballistic missiles fired from bombers, warships, and submarines struck military targets and infrastructure. Russian troops with hundreds of tanks and armored vehicles broke through border crossings in the north from Belarus and Russia, the east from Moscow-controlled areas of the Donbas, and the south from occupied Crimea. Security video showed them streaming into Ukraine and meeting little resistance, at first. I watched the videos with a couple of dozen journalists from the bomb shelter below Hotel Kramatorsk, stunned by what I saw. Putin was attempting to shock and awe the country, then launch a blitzkrieg in which his forces would swoop into Kyiv in three days, be greeted as liberators, raise the Russian tricolor, and declare victory.

Zelensky arrived at the presidential office on Bankova Street shortly after 5 a.m. Several of his cabinet members and staff were close behind. Like the Ukrainian president, they had all been asleep when Putin launched his invasion. One of the first to arrive was Ruslan Stefanchuk, Speaker of the Verkhovna Rada. He awoke like many Ukrainians that morning, "to the sound of explosions," he would later tell me. He was on the eastern side of the city, across the Dnipro river, and was close to several of the missile strikes. He rushed to Zelensky's side in the presidential office, flouting protocol. According to Ukraine's constitution, as head of parliament he was next in line to the presidency, and thus should have remained apart from Zelensky in case the Russians managed to reach one of them. When he arrived, security guards, soldiers and police officers were scrambling to erect barricades around the building and at the northeast and southwest ends of Bankova Street. They grabbed whatever they could to reinforce the gates and guard stations and moved vehicles in front to use as roadblocks.

Once inside, Zelensky convened an urgent national security meeting, which he began with a memorable pep talk. "He was in a very, very, I would say, combative mood," Stefanchuk said. "He said, look, history has chosen us. Fate has chosen us. And now we have to live up to that."

"It was like his *Independence Day* moment. You know, like the Hollywood film, when the president comes out and gives this big speech and inspires everybody. It was that type of a moment," Stefanchuk would recall, referring to Bill Pullman's famous scene as President Thomas Whitmore when he says that humankind is "fighting for our right to live, to exist!"

"We have to stand and fight or there will be nothing left!" Zelensky told the group, slamming his fist on the table.

Several important decisions were made in a matter of minutes. Zelensky wanted Stefanchuk to round up lawmakers and get them to approve presidential decrees on imposing martial law across the country and announcing a national mobilization. The president also ordered the government to split up to ensure continuity of government in the event of a worst-case scenario: those from his cabinet and parliament responsible for security and defense would remain by his side in Kyiv whereas the others would get on a train bound for western Ukraine. Those who were ordered onto the train didn't know where they were going at the time, one of the ministers aboard would tell me later. The train took a roundabout path out of the capital, eventually arriving the next morning in the city of Ivano-Frankivsk.

Around 6:30 a.m., Zelensky's iPhone began ringing again. Recognizing the caller ID, he answered and put it on speaker phone for several people in the room to hear. It was British Prime Minister Boris Johnson, the first Western leader to call that morning. He wanted to express his support and ask Zelensky what he planned to do.

The Ukrainian president shouted into the phone in English: "We will fight, Boris! We will not give up!"

A series of other high-level calls followed, including one on a secure line with President Joe Biden. Zelensky pleaded with Western leaders to make public statements and send weapons needed for Ukraine to repulse Russian forces. In a call with EU leaders, he would bluntly illustrate just how high the stakes were, telling them: "This may be the last time you see me alive."

Meanwhile, his chief of staff Andriy Yermak received a call of his own. It was Dmitry Kozak, Putin's deputy chief of staff and point person for Ukraine. For days, Zelensky had tried to reach the Russian president and his office was finally returning his call. Yermak answered. Ukraine should surrender or else be prepared to face the full might of the Russian Army, Kozak told him. "Fuck you!" Yermak replied and hung up.

At 8:48 a.m. Zelensky released a video address on his social media. "Today, Putin started a war against Ukraine, and against the entire democratic world. He wants to destroy our country, and everything we have been building," he said. "But we know the strength of the Ukrainian people. You are indomitable. You are Ukrainians."

He continued: "Today I ask you, each one of you, to remain calm. If it is possible, please stay home. We are working. The army is working. The entire security and defense sector of Ukraine is working."

Zelensky assured Ukrainians that he'd stay in regular contact, a promise that would lead to him sharing a nightly address similar to Winston Churchill's radio broadcasts and Franklin Roosevelt's fireside chats. "We are ready for anything. We will defeat anyone," he said. "Glory to Ukraine!"

At the same time, Danilov and other national security officials were inside the president's Situation Room on a conference call with the heads of Ukraine's regional administrations and security forces. But one of them wasn't calling in. "Where's Kherson? Can someone get in touch with Kherson? Fuck! Can someone from Kherson join us?" a livid

Danilov shouted. Little did he know, General Serhiy Kryvoruchko, head of Kherson's SBU directorate, had ordered his officers to evacuate the city before Russian troops stormed it, against Zelensky's orders, a source in the Ukrainian president's inner circle told me, and according to the Ukrainian security service. And Colonel Ihor Sadokhin, his assistant and head of the local office's Anti-Terrorist Center, was tipping off Russian forces heading north from Crimea about the locations of Ukrainian mines and helping coordinate a flight path for the enemy's aircraft while he fled in a convoy of SBU agents going west, the source in Zelensky's inner circle told me, and alleged by the security services. As a result, Kherson would quickly be captured by Russian forces.

As Danilov raged, secret-service agents burst into the Situation Room. Russian saboteurs were fighting Ukrainian troops in the streets around the government quarter and were only a few blocks away from Bankova, they said. The agents wrapped up Zelensky and quickly ushered him down to the building's bunker. Later, everyone underground would be given bulletproof vests and assault rifles in case the office was breached.

Yermak and highly placed intelligence sources would later tell me that saboteurs from Russia's FSB had infiltrated the ranks of the Ukrainian security service to steal critical information, while local collaborators were paid off by Medvedchuk to work with them. They had been living as sleeper cells for weeks and months and quietly moved into safe houses close to the government quarter until they were activated. When Putin launched the invasion, they emerged with high-powered assault rifles and attempted to storm Zelensky's office with the goal of capturing or killing the president. Instead, most of them would themselves be killed while a few managed to escape.

"Honestly, we were lucky," a top official in Zelensky's camp told me, recalling how unprepared the presidential office was for the targeted assault. "It was a very close call."

32

Control the Skies

Vasylkiv, south of Kyiv, February and early March 2022

Lieutenant General Anatoliy Kryvonozhko, head of Ukraine's Central Air Command, was laid up in a Kyiv hospital recovering from a tough bout of COVID, when his phone rang before dawn on 24 February.

"Sir, the attack has begun," his chief of staff said on the other end of the line.

Kryvonozhko was in isolation, wheezing and aching. At one point several days earlier he had been close to being put on a ventilator. He still had an IV drip stuck in his arm. Now, with Russian fighter jets and cruise missiles in his skies, he didn't care about any of that. "I was cured of coronavirus in that moment," he would tell me later in early June, when we met for what would be his first interview since the invasion.

He ripped the IV out of his arm as soon as he hung up the phone, threw on his clothes, and jumped into action, brushing off the concerns of his doctors.

Ukraine's air force wasn't unprepared. While in isolation, Kryvonozhko had held calls with his staff to make sure preparations for a possible Russian attack were carried out. "Each commander was instructed and knew his combat mission in advance," he said. He ordered Ukrainian fighter jets and air-defense units to be relocated days before the invasion. They did so under the cover of night and set up decoys in their places. He also instructed his pilots to fly rotations after Putin's 21 February announcement, so that if there would be an attack, they would already have someone in the air ready to respond. As a result, Kryvonozhko said, "most of Russia's strikes that were planned on our territory, they, so to speak, did not achieve their goal." He conceded, however, that there were some strikes that did hit their targets. For instance, several smashed into buildings and military infrastructure in the garrison city of Vasylkiv, home to the central air-command center overseen by Kryvonozhko that protects the capital and central Ukrainian oblasts. A little more than 20 miles southwest of Kyiv, it's also home to a top-flight school that has trained generations of Ukrainian top guns. One missile struck a fuel depot, sending a ball of flame and black cloud of smoke into the air. Another missile hit the barracks of the 138th Radio-Technical Brigade. But the 50 airmen inside survived. "How? I don't know," Kryvonozhko said, adding that an alarm signaling an air attack that should have sounded had failed to go off. "It was a miracle."

Kryvonozhko gave a pep talk to his units when he arrived in Vasylkiv. He didn't mince words. "I told them it would be the biggest fight of their lives and many of them wouldn't make it out alive." Some of the pilots had experience from 2014, when Ukraine's air force was briefly used in the Donbas. But for most, this would be their first crack at actual combat. The older pilots volunteered to fly first and told the young guys to stay on the ground. "They said this was their duty and we couldn't argue with them because they were senior pilots," a 29-year-old Ukrainian fighter pilot who goes by the call sign Juice told me. Kryvonozhko ordered the younger pilots to grab shoulder-fired surface-to-air missiles known as man-portable air-defense systems, or MANPADS, to defend the Vasylkiv airstrip. The strip was important not only in that it housed the central air command's pilots and planes, but if the Russians captured it and were able to land paratroopers there, it could serve as a bridgehead from which they'd be able to launch an attack on Kyiv.

"A little more than an hour after the first Russian missile strikes, our aircraft were taking off and starting to work," Kryvonozhko said.

The Russians believed the initial missile strikes had taken out Ukraine's air defenses. So when they entered Ukrainian airspace, they flew as if they would be able to conduct their missions without much, if any, resistance. "They were surprised to find us here," Kryvonozhko said. "They entered the airspace and we immediately engaged them."

Even so, the enemy had numbers on its side. Looking at a radar screen on his digital tablet, Kryvonozhko could see the Russian aircraft crossing into Ukrainian airspace and closing in on targets around Kyiv. "There were 15, 20, sometimes up to 30 aircraft all grouped in one raid," he said. He saw so many Russian aircraft that at one point he couldn't tell them apart. "They appeared as one large red blip over a huge area of Kyiv region." It was never a fair fight. "It was often two against six. Sometimes even worse, like two of us against 12 of them at once."

Aiding the Russian air force in its aerial assault was a Beriev A-50, a Cold War relic used by the Soviet Union, Kryvonozhko said. NATO uses the code name "Mainstay" when referring to the plane. The airborne early-warning and control-system aircraft, based on the Ilyushin II-76 transport plane but with a large rotating radar antenna on its back, detects and identifies airborne objects, determines their coordinates and flight path data, and transfers the information back to command posts on the ground.

The Russians had so many flight crews that they could afford to only fly their pilots just twice a day, allowing them time to rest. By contrast, Kryvonozhko and Juice said many Ukrainian pilots flew three, four, even five sorties a day and slept for 30 minutes to an hour in between flights. They often eschewed pre-flight checks, took off from partially destroyed runways, and landed on civilian roads to refuel.

"We have a large airfield infrastructure in Ukraine, both a military airfield and civilian airfields, as well as these sections of the road where you could put the aircraft down, refuel, rearm with missiles, and then fly away," Kryvonozhko said, to my astonishment. "Yes, there are certain sections of the highways that allow you to land a plane. There are highways that are even wide enough to allow several planes to land and take off."

Some of the Ukrainian pilots were in the air so long that they nearly ran out of fuel. "There was such a case when after a battle with an Su-30 group, one of our jets was severely low on fuel and just as it was landing the engine turned off," Kryvonozhko said.

Not a single pilot asked for a break in the first days until he was commanded to do so. Even then, Kryvonozhko said, they needed to be forced to rest. "I decided to give some teams a little rest and told them to stay grounded. In the evening, the brigade commander called me and said, 'Why don't you give us a task? Have you forgotten about us?'" he said. "They had lost so many comrades, I thought it was good to give them a break. But they only wanted to get back in the sky and fight." No pilot showed fear that day, he added. "The adrenaline simply drowns out the feeling of fear, the feeling of self-preservation. They are focused on only one thing: destroying the enemy."

Ukrainian pilots did destroy several Russian aircraft in the first hours and days of the invasion. Many were shot down in dogfights but most were downed by surface-to-air rockets operated on the ground. Several Russian jets shot down their own aircraft by mistake in friendly-fire accidents. "They shot down many of their own planes and helicopters," General Vadym Skibitsky of Ukrainian military intelligence told me. "They lost skilled pilots."

After the first few days, the Russians wised up. They changed tactics, began flying sorties at different times with different approaches. They flew at different heights. "They finally realized that our air-defense systems were still viable and effective," Kryvonozhko said. "So their main efforts now were to continue working on the farther destruction of the air-defense system."

To preserve those units, the Ukrainians kept moving them around. It was a game of cat and mouse. But Kryvonozhko said the Russians were getting good intelligence and were able to track several of them thanks to sabotage and reconnaissance groups on the ground.

Natalia Balasynovych, the mayor of Vasylkiv, told me when I visited the city on 28 February, that like in Kyiv a group of Russian spies had purchased apartments in a new apartment complex near the aviation university and moved in with their families for cover. As we spoke, a call came in to her guard sitting with us: a group of Russian saboteurs had been captured near a checkpoint on the edge of town. Some had been shot dead but at least one was alive and talking. Balasynovych threw on a bulletproof vest and ordered her security team to drive us to the site. "I want to look him in the eye and talk to him," she said as we weaved through checkpoints. But while en route she received a call from the National Guard forbidding us from seeing the saboteur, leading me to wonder whether it was all a show.

A few days later, a missile struck another fuel depot at the airfield, causing a massive explosion. Pete, my photographer, and I were driving nearby when it happened, heard the blast, and saw black smoke rising from the strike. We peeled off the highway and snaked through a neighborhood until we reached a road parallel to the base. As we approached the airfield, I noticed an SUV on our tail. Moments later it sped up and cut us off on the road. Two Ukrainian Special Forces-type guys burst out of the car with guns drawn and rushed toward us. "Who are you!? Hands up!" they screamed. "Journalists! American journalists!" I yelled back in English and then Ukrainian, as we threw up our hands. After showing them our press badges and passports, they asked if we had seen another white SUV like ours driving in the area. "Saboteurs?" I asked. One of the guys looked me in the eye but didn't respond. "Get out of here," he said.

Ukraine's pilots became heroes overnight, symbols of hope and resistance. But their bravery came at a great cost and sacrifice.

"Of our pilots who flew on 24 February, several died," Kryvonozhko admitted. He wouldn't give an exact casualty figure, citing security reasons. "After our victory, I'll tell you everything." But we know some of the pilots who fought bravely for their country and gave their lives. One of the first to be killed in combat was Yarko Vyacheslav, who along with his wingman shot down five Russian jets on the first day of the invasion. But Vyacheslav would also be shot down. While he managed to eject from his aircraft, Russian forces fired on him while he parachuted toward the ground, killing him. He would be posthumously awarded the title of Hero of Ukraine and awarded the Order of the Golden Star.

"Basically, they had pistols and we fought them with knives," Kryvonozhko said, describing the fight in the sky in David-versus-Goliath terms. "They had more aircraft, more pilots, more missiles. But we had the fighting spirit in us."

He added: "You could make a film about each one of my pilots that would be better than Tom Cruise's *Top Gun*."

33

"Who would like some tea?"

Hostomel, northwest of Kyiv, late February 2022

The Russian helicopters took off from Belarus and headed south, flying fast and low through the vast Dnipro river valley to avoid Ukrainian radars. North of the capital, they banked west where the river widens to become the Kyiv Sea and approached their target: Antonov Airport. Located in the heart of the suburb of Hostomel, about 20 miles northwest of Kyiv, the cargo airport and testing facility was home to Ukraine's and the world's largest cargo plane. The An-225 Mriya, whose name means The Dream, boasted a 290-foot wingspan and six engines. It had carried massive wind turbines, generators and, at the height of the COVID pandemic, crucial medical supplies to countries across the world, including the United States. Mriya was an object of Ukrainian national pride and a marvel of technology. But what the Russians really wanted was something else.

The airport was also home to an especially lengthy runway to accommodate such large aircraft. During a secret visit to Kyiv in mid-January, CIA Director Bill Burns had warned Ukraine that Antonov Airport would likely be targeted by Putin's forces because of this, as well as its proximity to Ukraine's center of power. Under Russian control, the Antonov base could be used as an air bridge through which it could ferry troops and military equipment on massive transport planes to Hostomel. And, from there, it would be a quick hour-long journey by armored vehicle to Kyiv.

Ukrainian National Guard Lieutenant Andriy Kulish, a 36-year-old former communications professional who had joined the military in 2014, following Russia's first invasion, was preparing tea for himself and two other guys when he heard the distinctive hum of helicopter rotors growing louder. The men had come to the airport shortly after dawn, following news that it had been targeted by a Russian cruise missile around 7 a.m. The missile exploded near an apartment building that housed the families of civilians working at the airport and left a massive crater in the ground.

After that, Andriy told me, "We were expecting something. We had our armor and helmets and rifles." When he heard the helicopters he swung open the door and looked out to see them approaching, their dark silhouettes ominously set against the overcast sky. "The first thing I asked was whether the guys had any cigarettes," Andriy said. "Second, who would like some tea?" The men burst out laughing as the attack began.

There were more than 30 Russian helicopters in all. Ka-52 Alligator attack helicopters led the air assault, strafing the airfield with a barrage of rockets and machine-gun fire and sending Andriy and his comrades diving for cover. Civilian employees at the airbase ran for safety in the bomb shelter beneath the airport canteen. Some were too far away and ducked behind buildings or crawled into sewers to get out of sight. Larger Mi-8 helicopters carrying hundreds of elite Russian airborne troops followed. After the initial barrage, the helicopters split into teams of two or three, attacking Ukrainian positions around the base and then circling back for more. Some of Ukraine's air defenses located around the airport were hit and destroyed.

"The helicopters would arrive, fire their rockets, find some targets, shoot their automatic cannons and go away. And then another wave would arrive," Andriy said.

His National Guard unit was an elite Rapid Reaction Brigade with experience fighting in eastern Ukraine. But on this day, it was short of troops, notably many of its most battle-hardened ones. Those fighters and much of the unit's equipment had been deployed weeks earlier to the Donbas, where it was expected that Russia would focus its attack.

"We had two company tactical groups, which is less than 200 people. And those 200 people included women, civilian workers, people who were on a sick leave, guys that had finished their contracts and they were about to quit and stuff," Andriy said. "They were basically there doing basic services needed to keep the base running."

Now they were thrown in the fray. Everyone grabbed whatever weapons they could find. Machine guns, Kalashnikovs and Igla shoulder-fired air-defense weapons. "We didn't have any anti-air cannons. Zero," Andriy said.

They made do with what they had. Andriy grabbed the keys to a pickup truck and jumped behind the wheel while another soldier loaded a machine gun in the bed. "We drove around finding good positions to shoot at the Russians," Andriy said.

The guardsmen managed to down the lead Ka-52, as well as several other helicopters. "Six of them were destroyed completely. And a bunch more of them were damaged by our fire," Andriy said. Among those shot down were three Mi-8s. "That's the funniest thing to me. The Russians advertised those things as flying tanks and yada, yada. But we shot them down using our assault rifles and a machine gun."

An hour after the fight began, fires raged and huge plumes of black smoke rose from the airfield. The Mi-8s then touched down in fields and dropped off the Russian airborne troops before lifting back off and rejoining the air attack. The airborne troops fanned out in fields, using patches of evergreen trees for cover before moving on foot toward the airfield as they opened fire.

"They approached our base and they tried to capture our gate and we had a major shootout," Andriy said.

By that point, the Ukrainians were running dangerously low on ammunition and were out of missiles. The brigade commander made the call to withdraw from the airport and regroup.

Meanwhile in Kyiv, military intelligence officials had gotten word that 18 Ilyushin Il-76 transport planes were preparing to take off from Belarus and bring in hundreds more Russian troops. Valery Zaluzhny, commander-in-chief of the Armed Forces of Ukraine told his subordinates that that couldn't happen.

"He told the 72nd Mechanized Brigade to come and help us fight," Andriy said. Air-assault brigades and foreign volunteer fighters also responded. "It was only because of these reinforcements that we were successful."

Ukrainian forces fired heavy artillery at the Russians and the airstrip, blasting holes in the runway to prevent any invading planes from landing on it. And Lieutenant General Kryvonozhko ordered Ukrainian bombers from his Central Air Command to finish it off.

Fighting raged. As the Russians tried to dig in, the Ukrainians counterattacked, and as the evening wore on, they managed to stop the Russians' momentum. It was around this time that a call came in from military intelligence. The Russian transport planes had aborted their mission and were turning back.

After an exhausting day of fierce back-and-forth fighting, the Ukrainians had managed to deal a significant blow to the Russians, disrupt Putin's plan for an air bridge, and kill some 300 paratroopers. They also regained control of the airport, but only briefly. The next morning Russian mechanized troops, storming south in massive convoys through the Chornobyl exclusion zone and the town of Ivankiv, would push the Ukrainians out of the destroyed airfield. And the invaders would soon capture the rest of Hostomel, as well as several other nearby towns and villages, fully believing that their plan was more or less still on track.

34

"Ya tut"

Just after midnight on 25 February, Zelensky appeared again in front of the camera, looking haggard but defiant. He had swapped his suit and collared shirt for military-type khaki garb that would become his famous wartime wardrobe. He announced the first casualties of Russia's war: at least 137 Ukrainians, including military personnel and civilians, had been killed. Another 316 had been wounded. The true figures were likely higher, and would soon climb into the many thousands.

"We are not afraid to defend our country, we are not afraid of Russia . . . I remain in the capital. My family is also in Ukraine. My children are in Ukraine," he said, looking straight into the camera. "The enemy has marked me as target No. 1, my family as target No. 2. They want to damage Ukraine politically by destroying the head of state."

Ukrainians were glued to their TVs and phones watching Zelensky's speech from basements and bomb shelters. I was also watching from the discomfort of my car two stories underground in the Radisson Blu parking lot. A few dozen people were scattered around me. They had made makeshift beds on the concrete ground and wrapped themselves in blankets. The hotel staff served coffee, tea, and sandwiches. The room was in low spirits. Zelensky's words and the fact that he was appearing at all and was still in Kyiv were somewhat reassuring. But rumors of Russian troops closing in were growing and many wondered if we'd wake up to fighting in the streets around us. Would we find ourselves besieged? If we did, would we be able to leave? Would Kyiv fall? At that point, much of the world thought it was possible. Western governments and military analysts were looking at Russia's army, supposedly the second most powerful in the world, and comparing the amount of manpower and equipment it had with what Ukraine had, which was significantly less. Putin and his troops, with their pressed military parade uniforms in tow, certainly believed they would be raising the Russian tricolor over Bankova Street and the Maidan by the end of the weekend.

American and British officials offered to send in special-forces teams to evacuate the president and his team to someplace in the west of Ukraine or eastern Poland, where he could set up a government in exile. But Zelensky wanted no part of it. It was in response to Washington's offer that he supposedly delivered his now famous line: "The fight is here; I need ammunition, not a ride." (Four members of Zelensky's team, including his press secretary, told me that they never heard him utter this phrase and weren't confident that he'd said it, but they liked the sound of it and were happy to let it stand.)

Just before dawn on the second day of the invasion, Russian cruise and ballistic missiles struck Kyiv again, rocking the capital for the second straight morning. Checking social media and statements from the Ukrainian military, I saw that government troops had blown up several bridges across the country where Russian forces were threatening to advance, in a desperate attempt to halt them. Several of the bridges were around Kyiv, northwest of the capital. Ukraine's Defense Ministry said that some Russian forces had even managed to enter the Obolon district, a bedroom community a few miles north of central Kyiv, where a fierce gun battle broke out. The ministry urged residents to stay indoors and to "prepare Molotov cocktails" to fight the invaders.

"Last time our capital experienced anything like this was in 1941 when it was attacked by Nazi Germany," tweeted Foreign Minister Dmytro Kuleba. "Ukraine defeated that evil and will defeat this one."

Around 8 a.m. Pete and I decided to go outside for some fresh air and threw on our helmets and vests, something I never could have imagined needing to do in Kyiv. We found a ghost town. There was no traffic. Cafes and shops were closed. The streets in Kyiv's old town were almost completely empty. The air-raid sirens howled periodically, reverberating between the city's historic brick buildings. Other than that, there was little sound. The haunting silence made the caws of crows seem especially loud. We walked past the Golden Gate, where I'd typically find people hustling to work and sipping espresso, and there was nobody. Turning north, we wandered towards St Sophia's Cathedral to find the square in front of it also empty, save for the monument of Bohdan Khmelnytsky, the Ukrainian Cossack Hetman, atop his steed with his *bulava* (ceremonial mace) in hand and his back toward Moscow. It felt like a scene from an apocalypse movie where the main characters wake up to find themselves the last people left on earth.

Soon, though, other people emerged. Journalists spilled out from hotels and residents from their apartments. Chaos and confusion ensued, as everyone tried to figure out what to do. Of Kyiv's more than three million residents, around two million decided to flee. Those with cars stuffed whatever they could fit inside, while others huffed it with backpacks to the central railway station. Many foreign correspondents did the same after consulting with their security teams. My security team at BuzzFeed News left the choice to me and Pete and Isobel, my BuzzFeed News team. But if we wanted to stay in Ukraine, they asked that we at least move someplace outside of the city center, in case the Russians managed to get in or surround the city. Being someplace on the southern edge provided several possible escape routes that would take us west. So we packed into the rented white Ford SUV and set off, unsure exactly where to go but in touch with a group of other journalists who decided to do the same.

By mid-morning, in Kyiv and everywhere else across Ukraine, people were mobilizing. The army rushed to all corners of the country where Russian troops were advancing. Territorial Defense Forces composed of ordinary civilians who just days earlier were reporting to work at tech companies, schools, supermarkets, legal practices, and everything in between, gathered in predetermined meeting places to get armed and hear their orders. Ammunition depots swung open their doors at the request of Zelensky and handed a rifle to anyone with a passport willing to fight the Russians. Faction leaders in parliament sent a mass text to lawmakers to let them know that "weapons are being given out at the National Police headquarters on Volodymyrska Street."

On the road, we found a massive traffic jam of people fleeing. There were mile-long queues at gas stations and lines of people outside pharmacies and supermarkets, as those planning to stick out the attack looked to stock up on food and essential supplies. Defensive lines were being built everywhere in between the major military ones set up around the inner and outer rings of Kyiv. Checkpoints were erected with cranes moving massive concrete blocks onto highways and major arteries leading to the capital's center. Police and Territorial Defense volunteers dug trenches with excavators and shovels in yards and flowerbeds. Government buildings were barricaded with dump trucks and police vehicles while the windows were reinforced with sandbags. The bridges over the Dnipro river were closed. In the streets, people were making Molotov cocktails by the hundreds with empty booze and beer bottles. I saw several empty bottles of sparkling wine from the Artwinery factory in Bakhmut used to make the home-made firebombs. Among the materials were blocks of polystyrene foam that people broke into tiny bits and added to the explosive mixture so it would stick better to their targets and burn for longer.

We also came upon people tearing down and covering road signs with black paint. Taking a page from Britain in World War II, Ukravtodor, Ukraine's government agency responsible for the national highway and road system, had put out a call on social media for "all road organizations, territorial communities [and] local governments to immediately begin dismantling nearby road signs." It wanted Ukrainians to rip them down or else paint over them to confuse the invaders. Ukravtodor's post included a mock-up of a highway sign that underscored the public's attitude toward Russian troops. "Fuck off," it read beside an arrow pointing ahead. "Fuck off again," read the words beside an arrow pointing left. And next to a third arrow veering to the right was a demand to "Fuck off to Russia."

"The occupier must understand that he is not welcome here and [we] will resist on every street, every road!" Ukravtodor added. "Let's help them go straight to hell."

That day and in the following days, we passed several colorful messages now scrawled across the traffic signs. One appealed to the enemy's humanity: "Russian soldier, stop! How will you look into your children's eyes? Leave!" Another, spray-painted over in red, served as a warning: "Welcome to hell, you Russian motherfuckers!" Billboards were also plastered over at record speeds with messages such as "Those who come at us with a sword will die by a sword." That one was paired with the image of Kyiv's Towering Motherland statue wielding her sword in one hand and Putin's head in the other. Similar messages were also shown on electronic road signs above highways typically used to transmit information about water conditions and traffic accidents. Several of them broadcast the first battle cry of the new war: "Russian warship, go fuck yourself," they said. It was an homage to the final communication made by Ukrainian border guards stationed on Snake Island, a small rock off the coast of Odesa, just before the Russian missile cruiser *Moskva* opened fire on them in the first hours of the invasion.

Our convoy collectively looked for AirBnB spots we could rent together or any hotel with available rooms. The only place we could find was a motel on the side of a main highway. It was on the southern part of the outer ring of the city and could give us a jumpstart if Russian troops stormed into the capital from the north. But we realized after we had already paid and checked in that it was only ten miles east of Vasylkiv, a main Russian target. The first clue was the mobile 9K35 Strela-10 air-defense system parked 100 yards north on the side of the highway. The second was the constant roar of fighter jets overhead. We were beneath their flight path. Luckily, they were Ukrainian and Pete snapped several shots of them with his telephoto lens, which allowed us to see that the country's air force was still alive and working, and armed with various missiles on their wings. They zoomed fast and low in pairs about every 30 minutes for most of the evening, heading north to engage Russian aircraft, then turning back south to refuel and reload.

The hotel's kitchen was closed but the hotel operator, a nervous man who was careful to write by hand all of our passport details before turning over the room keys, let us dine in the restaurant area and use plates and silverware from the kitchen. The only condition was that we keep the lights off. So our group of foreign correspondents dined on a meal of Lays potato chips, bread, cheese, smoked sausage, tomatoes, olives and Snickers bars, washing it all down with Staropramen tall boys, by candlelight.

Afterward, I tucked myself into a bed that was covered with a hand-stitched blue-and-white quilt that had little hearts on it. Inside the hearts were the words "Home sweet home," in English. I called Bri, who was sick with worry back at our home in Brooklyn, to let her know I was safe.

Before I dozed off, I saw a new post on Zelensky's social media accounts. It was a video. He had emerged from his bunker and with his top aides at his side walked out to Bankova Street to film what might be the shortest yet most important address he would ever make.

"Good evening, everyone," he began. "*Ya tut*" – I'm here. "We are all here. Our soldiers are here. Civil society is here. We are defending our independence. We are defending our state. And this is how it will be from now on." The president's video was proof of life with a crystal-clear message: he was still at the helm, steering the ship. "Slava Ukraini," he said as he signed off. The rest of the group responded: "Glory to heroes!"

35

Heroes

On the Outskirts of Kyiv

On day three of the invasion, we found a temporary base where we would spend the next two weeks living and working. Johnny O'Reilly, an Irish filmmaker and freelance journalist, had befriended an architect with a home in a gated community on the southern edge of Kyiv. The man had left town with his wife and child and said we were welcome to stay in his house while they were away. The place was incredible and it felt a bit strange to be living there while the country was under attack. In a village of mostly classic dachas, or summer homes, this was a modern two-story abode of polished concrete and black metal, with a large yard, a security gate, an alarm system, filtered water (a big deal because Ukraine's tap water isn't drinkable), and various other gadgets and gizmos. It had four rooms and a large sofa in the living room, plenty of space for me, Pete, Isobel, and Johnny, as well as Shaun Walker of the *Guardian* and his driver Dima.

But our presence there piqued the interest of the neighbors and concerned some who were understandably wary of strangers at that moment, especially ones who show up unexpectedly with multiple vehicles and lugging helmets and bags of equipment around. About an hour after we arrived, there was a knock on the gate. A group of about six or seven men, including the village head, had come by to question us. They weren't hostile and after a quick call to the homeowner they were at ease. Later, the village head told us that we were nearly raided by SBU agents after one of the neighbors called the local contact responsible for fielding tips about Russian saboteurs and told them a group of suspicious people had just arrived. "I told them I'd go over and speak to you first," the village head told us, recalling his chat with the SBU agent who was readying a team to burst into the house and detain us. "Lucky for you all, we believed you and said you were fine."

The house was a great place to work and live and only a 30-minute drive from central Kyiv. But we were doing a lot of driving to and from the city, and especially when the situation to the northwest of the capital escalated and we'd drive there nearly every day. Gas quickly became hard to find. Stations were running dry and were slow to be refilled because the whole supply chain in the country and across Europe had been disrupted with the closure of Ukraine's airports and ports, and the logjams at the land border crossings. I wondered what to do about our dwindling gas supply and the Ford SUV that didn't get great gas mileage. Then we came up with a plan. Johnny knew a guy with a private car-rental company and he happened to live just ten minutes away. We called him up and he said he had two Volkswagen Passats that he could rent. Both had full tanks of gas. I told him I'd rent both. We picked them up that day for $500 each and a handshake deal that we wouldn't get them shot-up, and suddenly we had a fleet of vehicles that would last us the next two weeks.

The owners had some food in the cupboards and refrigerator and they said we could help ourselves to anything perishable. We made a family trip to the supermarket down the highway to stock up on other items. But when we got there we found the place picked over. The first to go had been perishable items including meat and vegetables and fruit. But so were a lot of the frozen foods, including meats, pizzas, *varenyky* (stuffed dumplings), fish sticks, as well as canned goods. We split up and rushed through the aisles blindly grabbing whatever was left. At the register, we realized that we'd gathered about $1,500 worth of sardines, prosciutto, pasta, bread, butter, sunflower oil, dried fruit, coffee and instant coffee, tea, soda, Snickers bars, and an assortment of other things. We weren't able to find any fresh meat or eggs, but I noticed a freezer shelf fully stocked with Beyond Burger patties. Even in such dire circumstances, Ukrainians, apparently, had no interest in vegan burgers.

We also picked up several bottles of whiskey, scotch, vodka, and wine. Booze, besides helping to calm the nerves and settle us down after long, stressful days, also had other uses. For instance, we could use the vodka as a disinfectant. We barely made the cut-off before the Kyiv mayor, Vitali Klitschko, banned the sale of alcohol across the capital and the store clerks began wrapping the shelves in plastic and taping off the liquor, beer, and wine aisles.

Our routine during these days was as follows: wake up before dawn, take turns showering, have breakfast, grab our gear, and get out the door just after sunrise. We would head into central Kyiv to see what was going on and maybe stop for interviews on the street. We'd also set up interviews with politicians, diplomats, military contacts, humanitarian workers, and other types. There were press conferences from time to time at one of the Ukrainian news offices or the presidential administration or government offices that we'd attend. Just before dusk, which in late February and early March was around 5 p.m., we'd head back to our compound to go through notes, call our editors in London and New York, write our story of the day, and then cook a family dinner. Each night we dined together under dimmed lights on meals of pasta, rice, the occasional vegetable, and of course cured meats and assortments of pickled things. Like everyone else in Kyiv and most of Ukraine, we closed the curtains at sundown and kept the lights dimmed or off to avoid being targeted by Russian planes or saboteurs and spies on the ground. We drank the wine and booze until we ran out, and then we nicked a few bottles from the owner's stash. All of us were exhausted but also in a constant state of awareness. Having a couple of drinks before turning in to bed helped to calm our minds and bodies so we could get at least a few hours of sleep each night.

It was impossible to talk or think about anything other than the situation we were all in. We weren't paranoid but we were certainly hyper-alert. Every time a door closed or a window was shut with a bit of force, we'd lift our heads and glance at each other. We'd briefly pause our breathing and our ears perked up like a dog's. "Was that . . . an explosion?" we'd ask each other.

———

The first days and weeks of the invasion tested Ukraine and its fortitude in ways nobody could have imagined or fully prepared for. But without hesitation, millions of Ukrainians leapt into the fray as the country mobilized for its defense.

So many checkpoints were erected in the first days that it seemed like there was one every 1,000 feet. Sometimes we'd find two on the same suburban road. On a drive from the south of Kyiv to the northwest of the city, I counted about 30 checkpoints we passed through. By the second week of the invasion, Zelensky would have to ask authorities to order that some be removed because they were slowing down traffic, including military transportation.

The checkpoints were mostly manned by police, Territorial Defense Force volunteers and the National Guard. At checkpoints on the main highways and streets, there would often be one SBU officer or senior military person.

276

In the suburbs and more rural areas around the capital, there would be a colorful hodgepodge of local men and women standing guard at their hastily built roadblocks. As we made our way to a new location on the third day of the war, we passed through one area where villagers had set up three checkpoints in a one-mile span of road. We were stopped and questioned at all three. Despite no law-enforcement credentials, the locals, armed with hunting rifles and shotguns, demanded to see our passports and press cards, and to look inside our vehicle. We obliged and at the last one I asked if we could pull over and interview some of the people in the group. We made it a habit to try to get to know the *starshiy*, or senior person, at the checkpoints that we most frequently passed through, so we knew who to ask for if we got into a bind or got caught on the road just after curfew.

Among this group was Aleksandr, a 50-year-old who gladly showed off his American-made Remington shotgun. He was one of a couple of dozen men guarding a checkpoint built of sandbags and concrete blocks on the outskirts of Kyiv. Born in Russia, his family had moved to Donetsk, eastern Ukraine, when he was eight years old and he had lived there until 2014.

"I always felt like a Russian, but in 2014 I said that I'm a Ukrainian, because I saw [Russia's] aggression, because I saw what Russia was trying to do with Ukraine, and I said to myself, 'No, that's it, I'm not Russian,'" he told me. "I became Ukrainian that day."

Formerly, he had been the owner of a women's fashion shop. Now, Aleksandr said, he had a new profession: "I'm a hunter of Russian occupiers."

Aleksandr had never fought in a war or fired a gun before that week, but like millions of his compatriots he was ready to defend Ukraine – even if it meant turning against his country of birth.

"Of course, if it's a tank, in this terrain there's nothing we can do and we need to run. But if it's anything less than a tank, we will fight."

———

There were, of course, many others with prior military experience who volunteered to join the many arms of Ukraine's defense forces. I had heard that a Ukrainian veteran of the 2014 invasion who went on to found a successful veteran-owned-and-operated pizzeria had been accepted into Kyiv's police-patrol unit and was organizing a group of friends to join the squad. They gathered inside the Veterano pizzeria in downtown Kyiv. Peter, Isobel and I stopped in one morning at the invitation of the owner, Leonid Ostaltsev.

Muscly and tattooed with dark hair and a thick beard, and a seemingly endless catalogue of old war stories, Leonid was a bad-ass figure. Inside the pizzeria, about two dozen guys in their thirties and forties, dressed in camouflage and dark street wear, milled around, cleaning their high-powered assault rifles and filling their magazines with bullets. They cracked jokes and teased one another. Considering the seriousness of the situation, the mood here was light, even fun at times. It turned out, many of the guys had gone to school together and were old friends. Some of them had gone off to live in other parts of the world. There was one Ukrainian who went to Los Angeles to work as an actor and had returned to fight the Russians. In a way, this was a reunion for them.

Among the group was Andriy Khlyvnyuk, who I recognized from across the room. He was one of Ukraine's biggest rock stars and the front man for the popular group BoomBox. On 27 February, the third day of the war and his first day as a police officer, Khlyvnyuk posted to Instagram a video of himself singing "Oh, the Red Viburnum in the Meadow," a battle hymn about Ukrainian freedom, in the same spot that another Ukrainian freedom fighter had sung the same song a century earlier. The haunting, bare-bones rendition shows him in his new combat uniform, rifle slung over his shoulder, and wearing a New York Yankees cap. Standing beside the ancient St Sofia Cathedral, he belts out lines calling for Ukraine to rise up that were written about the Sich Riflemen, Ukrainian soldiers of the Austro-Hungarian army who fought in the Ukrainian War of Independence from 1917 to 1921. Ukraine's Armed Forces shared the video on Twitter the next day, where it went viral, racking up millions of views. Months later, Pink Floyd's David Gilmour would create an original song around Khlyvnyuk's vocals and release it to the world.

I walked up and introduced myself and Khlyvnyuk offered me a coffee. Then we walked into a side room to sit for an interview. He wasn't supposed to be here, he told me. He had a hectic March lined up, with ten concerts planned in four countries over 25 days.

"I have a weekend in Miami. The day before I was in LA, and some days before in San Francisco. I'm on tour in the US and Canada right now," the 42-year-old Khlyvnyuk said, rattling off the places where he should have been. But that was before the Russian bombs started falling on his country.

Instead, Khlyvnyuk swapped his microphone for a gun and his leather jacket for an armored vest, and was now fighting side by side with his Ukrainian compatriots against invading Russian forces.

"This is my duty. Ukraine is my home," he said. "And it's not that easy to push me out of my home."

Khlyvnyuk, who is tall and bald and wears a single-hoop earring that dangles from his left ear, said he was in shock when Putin launched his invasion. "After a day or two, you accept reality," he said. For him, that meant joining the fight. Khlyvnyuk sent his wife and daughter someplace safe in the west of Ukraine and stayed behind to defend the capital. He bought a high-powered assault rifle and immediately linked up with his old pal Leonid.

Their unit helped with humanitarian missions but also patrolled the streets, hunting for Russian saboteurs, and backed up front-line soldiers with anti-tank weaponry.

Many other Ukrainian celebrities, including pop icons, tennis stars, ballet dancers, playwrights, and top chefs, pushed pause on their old lives and joined their country's fight for freedom. Some took up arms like Khlyvnyuk, while others helped with humanitarian and fundraising efforts. But in one way or another, they were all now playing major roles on the front line of the biggest land war in Europe in 80 years.

"Used to be rackets and strings, now this," tweeted the retired Ukrainian tennis player Alexandr Dolgopolov alongside a photograph showing a Soviet-designed AK-74 assault rifle, a magazine, a large knife, an armored vest, and a helmet.

"We are no longer businessmen, bar owners, rock stars for the next I don't know how many days," Khlyvnyuk explained. "We are soldiers. Some of us are police officers."

Khlyvnyuk found it hilarious and ironic that he was now an official badge-carrying police officer, considering some past run-ins with the cops. After he and a friend were caught urinating on a monument of the Soviet Union leader Vladimir Lenin many years ago, police officers detained them and he released a remake of "I Shot the Sheriff."

"It was called 'I Shit in a Police Car,'" he said. "And now I'm a sheriff driving a police car."

Later in the morning, Leonid called the guys over to the bar to talk about the day's tasks. They were to split up into pairs or teams of three and patrol areas of Kyiv, keeping an eye out for saboteurs. They had special permission to be out after dark, when most Russian saboteurs and collaborators moved around and marked roads and buildings with mysterious symbols. Some of the symbols were simple red-painted crosses or Xs. Others looked more like targets with a cross inside a circle. The Ukrainians said the marks were used by Russian aircraft and advancing ground forces to designate important locations to capture or destroy.

Before I left, I mentioned to Leonid that I was a fan of his pizzas and had spent several summer evenings with friends eating and drinking on Veterano's back patio. The pizzas were gone, for now, he said, but they'd be back.

"We have NLAWs [next-generation light anti-tank weapons] here," Leonid boasted, puffing on a cigarette in his storage-room-turned-office and bunk. As he walked me out, he pointed toward the kitchen, where several light anti-tank weapons recently delivered to Ukraine by the British government were leaning against the wall.

—

As much as NLAWs and their American cousins, Javelins, were helping Ukrainian troops keep the Russians at bay, an army needs food to fight. So while many pizzerias and other dining establishments closed because of the invasion, several others remained open, albeit serving in a different capacity.

The restaurant of Ievgen Klopotenko, Ukraine's most famous chef, the country's Jamie Oliver if you will, was one of them. Charming and witty with piercing eyes and wild curls that spring from his head, Klopotenko told me one busy March morning that his high-end restaurant *100 Rokiv Tomu Vpered* – 100 Years Back to the Future – where he playfully reimagined Ukrainian cuisine, was also on a war footing.

"To feed and cook for the army is like the same importance to stand with the gun and fight," he told me. "If the guys with the guns don't have food they will die."

He had four cooks working with him, including a 23-year-old cold chef who had been preparing salads and appetizers before the invasion. Her name was Nadia and she had grown up in Crimea. When I walked into *100 Rokiv* and met her, she was preparing rice and chicken hearts.

"We just got like 100 kilograms chicken hearts. So this is like the second day we are serving them," she said.

They used the food they had left in their refrigerators first. And then volunteers began bringing in food, and restaurants that had closed up gave them what they had left over. Everything they made went to Ukraine's army and National Guard soldiers, Territorial Defense Forces and police officers. Once the food was ready and put into travel containers, a pair of volunteers with a van would come by, load it up, and drive it to the front lines around Kyiv.

"I feel grateful that I'm able to do this and help people. If I was just sitting at home this war would eat at me inside," Nadia said. As much as anyone, she knew what was at stake. "I lived in Russian conditions," she told me, recalling the threats, intimidation, and abductions of Ukrainians in Crimea after Russia's illegal annexation. She was just 15 years old then. "I was studying in school and didn't realize what was going on. My mom called me and said something was going on and I just went to my next lesson." But as she grew older, Russia's terror campaign on the peninsula came sharply into focus. She moved to Kyiv in 2019 and had made the capital her new home. She didn't want Russia to again storm in and upturn her life and the lives of her friends and family.

Similar scenes were playing out in some of my favorite haunts across the capital. The Crimean Tatar owners and chefs at the popular Musafir restaurant chain, which had been displaced back in 2014 and reopened in Kyiv, were cooking up *plov* and lagman soup. At the Kyiv Food Market, a collection of food stalls where Ukraine's hipsters sipped craft beers and cocktails and dined on fancy hot dogs and sweet pastries, volunteers were preparing salads and stewing chickens.

Every location was producing 300 to 600 meals a day. Klopotenko called it "fuel for our defense."

"When we peel potatoes, we are powering the army," he said. "We are all soldiers."

He wanted to make one more thing clear: "You know, the Russians will lose. They can't defeat us. We are very courageous people."

As quickly as Russian forces advanced toward Kyiv, stories of acts of unthinkable bravery by Ukrainians ascended into legend, boosting morale and galvanizing a nationwide resistance that had already proved formidable in the face of Moscow's attack.

Several videos of Ukrainians stopping tanks emerged and were shared around the world as the spirit of defense gathered momentum. One video showed a man standing in front of an approaching Russian tank, reminiscent of China's Tiananmen Square resistance movement. The man can be seen standing in front of a Russian armored personnel carrier and gesturing, forcing the vehicle to swerve to avoid him. Another video showed a man physically trying to push back a tank and a middle-aged woman throwing herself at the tank. Dozens of unarmed Ukrainian self-defense volunteers in puffer coats marched toward a Russian tank in another video. And in yet more incredible footage, a man can be seen carrying with his bare hands an anti-tank mine placed by Russian forces near a bridge in southern Ukraine, and with a lit cigarette dangling from his lips.

It was clear that the Ukrainians were going to resist, no matter what.

But not everyone wanted to or could stay and fight.

36

Escape

Kyiv and Irpin, west of the capital, early March 2022

The scene at Kyiv's central railway station when we arrived on 1 March was shocking and distressing. People threw themselves and whatever possessions they were able to carry onto the departing trains. There were thousands and thousands of them, all desperate to flee as Russian troops inched closer to the capital. Some even tried to climb through the windows.

In the chaos, a young mother got separated from her daughter when a police officer hoisted the girl onto the train that began rolling away before the woman could jump on. As she let out a blood-curdling howl, the mother ran alongside the moving car until she was able to grab the outstretched arm of an older man who yanked her on board. A pink unicorn backpack that the mother had slung over her shoulder didn't make it and tumbled onto the platform before falling onto the tracks.

People frantically asked those around them which train on which track would go to Lviv, Rakhiv, Kamyanets-Podilskiy, and other western Ukrainian cities that might provide safe haven or an onward passage to European Union countries. Some had their questions answered and dashed to where they needed to be. Others were left stumped. Even more didn't care and just tried to get on any train that was heading west out of Kyiv. Tickets were obsolete. Nobody working at the station checked to see if anyone actually had them, they just ushered people on board.

The situation was too much for some people. Many gave up and left or sat down and dropped their head in their hands, accepting defeat. An older woman fainted from exhaustion and had to be carried away to an ambulance.

There weren't enough trains or space on them for everyone who wanted to leave. Police and railway workers prioritized women and children and the elderly on the trains. Because President Zelensky had ordered a general mobilization of the population to fight against Russian troops and declared martial law, men between the ages of 18 and 60 were barred from leaving the country. When a man tried to muscle his way on board a train that was about to depart, two police officers shoved him back and shouted at him and other men on the platform. I saw a police officer console a man standing with a stroller that couldn't fit inside the carriage, as he waved to his family on board who were pressed against the window in the aisle. Amid the havoc, on another track, I watched a man in plain clothes hold a pistol in the air in an attempt to control the crowd.

Pets were another issue. Small ones that could be easily carried or fit into shoulder bags were allowed on the trains. But larger ones weren't let on board due to the limited space and were handed over by their crying owners to friends staying behind.

Outside the station entrance, huddled against the building's stone wall, Serhiy pondered what to do as his wife, Veronika, rocked their infant daughter, Sofia, to sleep. The couple had come with their neighbors to find a train that would take them south to Odesa, where they had family and friends.

They said they were aware of attacks also in and around the Black Sea port city, but they believed it would be safer there than in their Kyiv apartment. They had spent four nights there sleeping in the hallway of their home behind solid walls and one night in a bomb shelter because the artillery fire was so close and loud.

"It's an absolute nightmare," Veronika said.

It was especially so for the foreigners trying to leave, many of whom didn't speak Ukrainian or Russian and had less experience with the train system. Muhammed Ali, a student from Turkmenistan who had been studying programming at Kyiv's Drahomanov National Pedagogical University until it closed its doors earlier that month, had come to the station with five friends. When I bumped into them, they were staring at the jump electronic screen that showed train arrival and departure times. But the times for both weren't accurate because of so many delays. Muhammed and his friends were attempting to get to Romania, where they hoped to find flights home. He said the group didn't expect to get seats, but were praying for standing-room-only spots in the corridor between carriages.

Emmanuel and Sylvester, IT professionals from Nigeria, said they were heartbroken to leave Kyiv, a city they'd come to love during the last four years. After not leaving their apartments for five days and sleeping the night before in a bomb shelter, they'd come to the station hoping to find a train that would take them west, where they could cross into the EU and catch a flight home.

"My mother told me she would kill me before [Putin] if I didn't leave," Emmanuel said.

They chose to try and reach Hungary after reading reports that Ukrainian police and border guards had harassed Nigerian citizens trying to flee, and that Polish authorities were denying entry to people of color.

Nearby, Molvina, a mother of two daughters aged ten and five, wept on the floor of the international hall of the train station. Along with their small terrier Kompot, named after the home-made fruit juice that's popular in this part of the world, she hoped they would be able to make it to Poland.

"We don't know what to do after that," she said. "Everything we have is here now." All she could manage to take were three small bags of possessions and the dog. "We hope we will be back soon. We *will* be back soon," she said.

There was a dark irony to her situation. This wasn't her first time fleeing from invading Russian troops. She had left Georgia for Ukraine after Russia attacked her home country in 2008. She had spent the last 14 years building a new life, only to have Putin destroy it yet again.

Behind her, people queued at the international hall's France cafe, which typically serves buttery croissants and steamy cappuccinos. Now it gave out simple Lipton tea in plastic cups and plain slices of white bread. When the tea ran out, the cafe handed out hot water so that people could keep warm while they waited.

Natalia, a retired teacher, was among those waiting for something hot to drink. She wanted to travel to her daughter's home in Ivano-Frankivsk. I approached her as she nibbled on her last home-made bun filled with mashed potatoes. She had given the rest of the buns to the Ukrainian soldiers and Territorial Defense Force fighters who were fortifying positions and manning checkpoints around her home in Kyiv in anticipation of an attack.

"It's important that they are strong. They're defending our country," Natalia said. "I'm an old woman. I'll be dead soon. But Ukraine will live on."

The situation in Irpin was growing worse by the hour. Pete and Isobel and I drove up there to cover the intensifying fight and the evacuations that were underway. Russian troops, their advance stalled in Bucha a few miles northwest of Irpin, had begun pounding the town with all sorts of artillery. The Ukrainians inadvertently were doing the same as they returned fire. Residents who hadn't fled were caught in the crossfire and were now faced with the impossible decision of whether to hunker down and pray that they'd survive or try to escape on foot through streets that had become a deadly no man's land.

Katerina Oleksiivna chose the latter after brave volunteers arrived to evacuate her. When she emerged from the basement of her home where she'd taken cover from Russian missiles, mortars, and tank fire after ten days underground, she found everything within view completely destroyed and dead bodies littering the street. The 74-year-old told me when I met her at a staging point for the volunteers that most of the past week and a half she had had no heat, no electricity and no water. She survived mostly on canned vegetables and stale bread. She hadn't seen or read any news but could hear the explosions above ground and feel the force of them reverberate deep beneath the earth. Terrified and confused, she trembled and stammered as she tried to make sense of the dire situation. To see Russia's war and the death it had wrought up close, she explained as she made the sign of the cross with her hands, was devastating.

"Is the war everywhere?" she asked me through tears.

As she tried to say something else, a series of explosions rocked the evacuation point where she stood with dozens of other Irpin residents. Each blast threw Katerina slightly off balance as she hobbled with a cane behind a brick wall, where she took a breath and sobbed. I rubbed her back and told her everything would be okay, knowing that I didn't really believe my own words.

The fighting was relentless in and around the once-quiet bedroom community, which had the unfortunate luck of sitting on a crucial road heading toward the center of Kyiv. A mortar round exploded in the middle of a street where a family were attempting to make their escape. A father, mother, and child were killed. The Ukrainian journalist Andriy Dubchak caught the moment of the deadly strike on video and the American photojournalist Lynsey Addario documented its aftermath in a photo published in the *New York Times* that would define Russia's war at that moment.

Irpin's mayor, Oleksandr Markushyn, said about eight people died from Russian shelling on that single day. "Two children died in front of my eyes," he said.

It was all proof that Putin was lying about his army not targeting civilians in his so-called "special military operation," and about establishing safe corridors for people to flee the deadly violence. In his evening address that night, Volodymyr Zelensky said he had information obtained by his intelligence officials from captured Russian troops which proved that bombing civilian areas had been part of Putin's plan from the beginning. It was "pure evil," Zelensky said.

While the evacuation in Irpin went ahead despite the difficulties under heavy Russian shelling, plans to evacuate residents of the cities of Volnovakha and Mariupol in eastern Ukraine collapsed because the artillery fire was too intense and targeted the supposedly safe "green corridors" that civilians were meant to use. It was clear that Russia didn't give a damn about people or sticking to its promises.

We returned to Irpin three days in a row, as it became the biggest unfolding story and the place where Russian troops saw their best chance to break through Ukrainian lines and capture Kyiv. But it was growing more dangerous by the day. Now journalists were being wounded and killed, some accidentally as they were caught in the shelling crossfire, others deliberately in their cars as they tried to get closer to the action. And a few were purposely targeted and murdered. Among the latter was my friend Maks Levin, a prominent Ukrainian photojournalist who had dedicated much of his life and work to covering Russia's war against Ukraine and the Ukrainians impacted by it. He was among the first journalists to head to the Donbas when the war broke out in 2014, and he narrowly escaped the encirclement of Ilovaisk in August of that year.

"Every photographer dreams of taking a picture that will stop the war," Maks had said. Maks was flying his drone in the north of Irpin when it went down. He went to look for it and ran into Russian troops. Evidence uncovered later by Ukrainian authorities and investigative journalists suggested that the Russians detained him, interrogated him, tortured him, and then executed him. It is thought that a friend who was with him, Oleksiy Chernyshov, had been burned alive. Maks was 40 and the father of four boys.

In Irpin, most people had no idea where they would go. They just wanted to be anywhere they would be safe. They only had with them what they could carry on their backs and in their hands. They were visibly exhausted and stressed from surviving heavy bombardment for the past week and a half. At a staging point where more than 20 yellow buses arrived to move people to Kyiv's central railway station, families and friends separated in the chaos frantically searched for one another, worrying that someone might have been left behind. And people from other cities showed up to look for relatives in Irpin with whom they had lost contact.

"Is there anyone from the Capital Apartment Complex?" asked one man, who was searching for a cousin that he'd lost contact with after the invasion began.

When a man I met named Vadym and his family reached the other side of the blown-up Irpin bridge and arrived at the evacuation staging area, they were shell-shocked.

"We can't even talk; can't you see?" Vadym's father said.

Vadym and his family said they had nowhere else to go but were trying to come up with a plan as they stood in the street with their rucksacks and a couple of plastic bags. At that moment, a car pulled up and offered them two free seats and transport to the train station. But Vadym's family had to turn down the offer because there were six of them and they didn't want to be split up.

Nearby, Tetiana, an Irpin resident, cut up bits of white sheets to tie around the neck of her six-year-old son and her nieces and nephews to identify them as civilians so they wouldn't be shot while trying to evacuate. "We couldn't leave until we found someone to look after our bedridden relative. All those who can't walk are stuck there," she said. "We left all the food we could find with them." Tetiana described seeing Russian tanks going down the central streets of Irpin and witnessing "the kind of battles that have flattened houses." It was a "nightmare," she said, covering her face with her hands to hide the tears streaming down. "When they said there would be a war, I laughed and said, 'Oh, please!'"

Now she was fleeing her home with her children, including the two older children, aged 23 and 27, for whom she was waiting to cross over the bridge and reach the evacuation area.

"We don't know where we're going. We're just going anywhere," she told me. "It was just so scary." Tetiana shook her head in shock. "We just don't understand why this is happening. Maybe you know the answer?" she asked me. I did not have the answer. I also wanted to know why, as much as anyone.

"We don't understand. We have half our family in Russia. And everyone is calling saying, 'Don't worry; tomorrow you'll be part of Russia,'" Tetiana said. "But we're in shock. Why do we want Russia when we can live in Ukraine peacefully?"

Another Irpin resident, 60-year-old Sveta, said life for the people still stuck in the war-stricken town was hell and she didn't know what they were staying behind for. "The food supplies will end pretty soon. There's no gas, there's no electricity, there's no internet. There are tanks shelling residential buildings," she said.

Sveta said the Russians pushed into the western side of Irpin on 5 March, and now controlled part of the city. "Russian tanks came down Mechnykova Street," she said, referring to a main road through town. "There are no Ukrainian tanks there; there are Russian snipers shooting."

Roman, a Ukrainian Territorial Defense fighter, told me that he expected Russia to launch a major offensive from Irpin to try to capture Kyiv in the coming days. He said Ukrainian Special Forces, army soldiers, and armed volunteers like himself were preparing for a bloody battle and that he hoped to kill as many Russian "invaders" as possible.

"In a few weeks, you're going to see fat homeless dogs and you will know why," he told me.

We returned to Irpin the next day and found the fighting even worse. I parked the car on the side of the road facing the way out, then Pete and I made our way on foot to the bridge. People scrambled over wooden planks as water rushed over their feet, desperate to escape before Russian bombs flattened their homes with them inside. In the endless column of civilians, there were old women in headscarves being helped along by soldiers, young mothers dragging children who wore tiny backpacks and clutched stuffed bears, and wounded people being carried on stretchers. Their cries were punctuated by the booms of artillery shells exploding all around. And their faces wore the shock and pain of a war none of them had ever thought would blow into their town with such devastating fury.

They had survived – though some of their neighbors had not – with no power, no heating, no water, and no communication with the outside world while huddling in basements while Russian air strikes and artillery fire pulverized their town. But even as they fled, they weren't safe.

"Rockets! Get down!" a Ukrainian soldier barked at the endless queue of fleeing people. Some of them dropped to the ground, but many were just too exhausted to move in any direction other than another step forward.

An old man whose legs crumpled upon hearing the soldier's order looked like he might die of fear. A police officer knelt down and told him, "Breathe, grandpa, breathe."

A brief reprieve came in the early afternoon, when the Ukrainians went on the offensive. We fell back a few hundred feet to watch from a distance, worried that the Russians would respond with mortars.

"We're hitting them because they've run out of artillery shells," said Anatoli, a 19-year-old Ukrainian soldier whose helmet had the words "Time of the strong" scrawled on his helmet. We were standing at a checkpoint back from the bridge, watching smoke from the Ukrainian counterattacks rise over the horizon. "We can say that Irpin is theirs. But we will cut them off now that the people are out," he told me confidently.

He and other Ukrainian soldiers told me that thousands of residents were being urged to leave immediately because Russian forces were not only shelling Irpin but were also moving in, squatting in their homes, stealing food, gas and other supplies, and destroying everything else.

Anna, a woman in her sixties, had just fled her home. She told me that if it weren't for enemy soldiers breaking in, "we wouldn't have left."

In the face of the worst fighting that Europe had seen in decades, Ukrainians were defiant. Oleksandr Markushyn, Irpin's mayor, said Russian forces had sent him a death threat and a demand to surrender the city to them. "I am surprised that these monsters still don't understand that Irpin doesn't surrender, Irpin is not for sale, Irpin is fighting!" he said. When I saw him in his office several months later, he would remind me of these lines while swinging a large sword above his head like he was slicing through the Russians. "I warned them," he'd tell me later.

Oleksandr Irvanets, a prominent Ukrainian writer and poet who was among the crowd leaving Irpin, said his fellow citizens would fight for every inch of Ukrainian land. The former Fulbright scholar, who lived in Philadelphia in 2005 and 2006, was joined by his partner Oksana Tsyupa, a textile artist, and their cat Matsuo Bashō, named after the famous Japanese haiku poet. Oksana said they didn't know where they would go because they'd never thought they would need to run away.

They left behind their sixth-floor apartment where they lived with Oksana's 92-year-old mother, who had dementia. She had been brought out by a rescue team two hours before them and taken to a Kyiv hospital.

"Did I think about war? No. For many years, Russians tell us, 'We're brothers! We're one people!' But look – they're killing us!" Irvanets said. "They're mad. This is terrible. They want to take us into Russia. But we won't go! We want to be independent. We don't want to be with this fucking Putin!"

Confined to his apartment while a battle raged outside, Irvanets had spent his time contributing his part to Ukraine's defense – composing a poem that might inspire his compatriots. He said he hoped it wouldn't be the last poem written in the couple's home. I asked him to share it with me. This is what it said:

From a city shattered by missiles,
I will shout to the whole world:
This year on Forgiveness Sunday
I won't forgive anyone!
World-world, well, you left us!
But in the hell of these sufferings, patience
Still stands the golden-domed Kyiv,
Bucha, and Hostomel, and Irpin.
We will overcome everything and endure!

Oleksandr and Oksana's ride never showed up, so I offered to take them to the hospital myself to visit her mother.

37

"It feels like I'm doing something wrong"

Kyiv, eastern bank of the Dnipro river, mid-March 2022

There was something different about the three soldiers who were brought in to Vitaliy's operating room. They were wearing Ukrainian-type uniforms and claimed they were from Kyiv, but they couldn't speak a word of Ukrainian, name a single neighborhood in the capital city, or offer up any documentation to prove their residency. They spoke only Russian – and with an accent more common in Moscow than in Kyiv. And they behaved in a somewhat cold manner toward the medical staff treating them, refusing to answer many questions. Hospital staff and Ukrainian police were eventually able to confirm the men were Russian soldiers, said Vitaliy, a young doctor from western Ukraine who was doing a surgery apprenticeship in Kyiv when the invasion started.

"They were very scared," he told me about the Russians.

Deputy Defense Minister Hanna Malyar had posted on Facebook on 25 February that Russian forces had "seized two Ukrainian army vehicles and changed into Ukrainian uniforms" during a failed assault on the northern Obolon district of Kyiv. The soldiers who Vitaliy operated on were among those who participated in that assault on the capital.

Vitaliy said the soldiers were conscious when they arrived, but they had been shot several times and one of the men's legs was broken. "One of them was very seriously wounded and he died," he said. The other two survived and were being kept in a small jail inside the hospital while they recovered.

I wasn't able to meet Vitaliy in person because the bridges were closed and I couldn't cross the Dnipro river. So we spoke by phone. He was a friend of a Peace Corps volunteer who had served in his western Ukrainian town. He'd just finished a long day of surgeries when we spoke.

When I asked about the Russians, Vitaliy told me he felt deeply conflicted about helping to save enemy lives.

"I think we should help them but of course sometimes the feeling I have about it is horrible. It feels like I'm doing something wrong," he said. "Like, I can be helping my people, but I have to spend time helping that piece of shit."

It was especially hard to show compassion given the brutality that Putin and his military were unleashing on Vitaliy's people. Bombs and shells had razed entire towns and more were being demolished every day.

"But we do our job because it's our job and our duty," he said, referring to the Hippocratic oath by which medical professionals abide. "And, of course, after they recover we can exchange them. So I tell myself that this can help to get Ukrainian soldiers back."

Both Russia and Ukraine had taken prisoners of war. The more Kyiv had and could keep alive, the better, since they could be traded for their own soldiers.

Vitaliy had treated dozens of civilians and soldiers. There were so many that his hospital had run out of space and was sending them to other medical centers. What he and his fellow doctors saw were "mostly gunshot wounds" among the wounded soldiers. "Some of them had a combination of explosions and gunshots," he said. He described horrific wounds caused by shrapnel.

"When [shrapnel] hits your body, it can make a hole in your leg and come out of the stomach," Vitaliy said.

In the first two days of Russia's invasion, the surgeons didn't have a lot of work. But as the attacks intensified, an influx of patients were wheeled through their doors and they were quickly overwhelmed. For a week in late February and early March, Vitaliy worked at the hospital without a day off. He caught only a few brief hours of sleep inside the hospital's on-call area for staff during that time.

Most of the wounded were Ukrainian soldiers and volunteer fighters from the Territorial Defense Forces. Vitaliy said Ukrainian civilians began arriving in large groups to donate blood. "In one or two days our blood bank was full," Vitaliy said.

He confessed that the work was stressful and taking a toll on him and his colleagues. But he said they wouldn't stop.

"We cannot think. We try to focus on our work. When we aren't doing operations we are always scrolling the internet and watching the TV to be informed," he said. "We are working under fire."

38

The Brothers Vyshyvaniy

Duliby, western Ukraine, March 2022

The bodies were piling up – not only in Kyiv, but also along the front lines in Ukraine's east and south. Funerals weren't an everyday occurrence – they were being performed practically every hour. Death was everywhere. Mortuaries were overflowing and the country was running out of body bags.

Pete and I headed to the west of the country for a breather when we stumbled upon a memorial service for four fallen soldiers – Kyrylo Vyshyvaniy, Oleh Yashchyshyn, Rostyslav Romanchuk, and Serhiy Melnyk – at Lviv's baroque Saints Peter and Paul Garrison Church. Hundreds of mourners had gathered to pay their respects. They lined the street and watched silently as the four were carried in polished wooden caskets inside. During the service, people took turns to approach the men in their caskets, touching them, and placing large bouquets of flowers atop them. Many made the sign of the cross, glanced upwards, and mumbled prayers under their breath. Tears streamed down their faces. A man sang haunting funeral hymns as mothers hugged the boxes holding their boys and wept while priests doused the bodies in holy water.

When air-raid sirens and warnings to take shelter blared from Lviv's city hall mid-funeral, the mourners defiantly stood their ground.

Yashchyshyn, Romanchuk, and Melnyk were laid to rest at Lviv's historic Lychakiv Cemetery. But Vyshyvaniy was loaded into the back of a hearse and driven 35 miles southwest to Duliby, where he would be buried beside his younger brother, Vasyl.

When I found out that two sons from one family had been killed, I felt I needed to go and see how his family and village mourned and honored him.

Ahafiya Vyshyvana raised her sons Kyrylo and Vasyl Vyshyvaniy to love their country. In the pastoral village of Duliby in western Ukraine, far from the bustling capital of Kyiv, they grew up to become patriots and soldiers

– defenders of the Motherland – fighting against invading Russian forces. But in a window of six days in March, Vyshyvana had buried them both, side by side, in plots that had been reserved for her and the boys' father. The roses piled atop Vasyl's grave had barely wilted before she would put Kyrylo in the ground beside him.

When we arrived, the entire village of Duliby, a population of 3,000, was waiting. They had gathered to pay their respects to the older brother. Hands clasped in prayer, they lined the streets as pallbearers carried Kyrylo's body into a small wooden church. It was an incredibly moving sight and I stood there in awe of them.

Priests delivered the eulogy "Memory Eternal," spoke of Kyrylo's bravery, and said he had made the ultimate sacrifice for his country and people. A church choir sang haunting funeral hymns. The lips of battle-hardened troops in uniform quivered. And a sweet scent of incense hung in the air.

The mourners then moved in a solemn procession from the church to the village cemetery, passing people who stood and kneeled outside their homes. When they stopped at the gravesite, boyish soldiers in neatly pressed uniforms played their horns and performed a customary gun salute, firing four shots into the air. The cracks of the rifles startled some of the war-weary people in the crowd. Many placed their hands over their hearts and sang the national anthem, which begins with the line, "The glory and freedom of Ukraine has not yet perished."

After nearly two hours, the blue-and-yellow Ukrainian flag that had covered Kyrylo's casket throughout the day was folded and given to Vyshyvana by a Ukrainian army officer.

"Accept this flag as a symbol of the state that your son served faithfully to the end," the officer told Vyshyvana, who was too distraught to accept it and deferred to a family member.

It took a ten-man rotation 20 excruciating minutes to fill Kyrylo's grave with dirt. Vyshyvana wept uncontrollably the entire time and at one point collapsed to her knees and tumbled onto the grave of Vasyl. "Why, God? Trade me for them! Please take me!" she cried out.

"We are so proud of you boys. The country is so proud of you," she repeated until she was out of breath and the words faded into a chilling whisper.

Beside her, wearing a black head wrap, was Mariana Lopushanska, the girlfriend of Vasyl. Overwhelmed with emotion, she fainted and fell at the foot of his grave.

"God takes the very best ones," Halina, a neighbor, said of the Vyshyvaniy boys.

Vasyl was a 28-year-old senior lieutenant and paratrooper when he died. He had first joined Ukraine's armed forces as a fresh-faced 20-year-old in 2014. He was killed by Russian forces on the southern front in Mykolayiv on 3 March. I was told by Josef, a long-time family friend with a Cossack-style haircut, that the fighting had been so intense there that it took days for the army to recover Vasyl's body and evacuate it to Duliby. His casket arrived sealed shut. He had been buried in a similar ceremony on 9 March.

Vasyl loved playing soccer and was on the village team when he was younger. He had fought in eastern Ukraine. Kyrylo, 35, supported that decision and in 2017 he himself had joined the armed forces.

Natalia Bodnar, their older sister, told me that she had helped raise her brothers and said the boys used to joke and laugh together. We spoke beside the graves of her brothers after everyone else had departed. Bodnar had spoken with Kyrylo for the last time just a few days earlier. She said he was worried about their mother's health and specifically her heart. After Vasyl's death, she had been briefly hospitalized with what they believed was a small heart attack. "I think it was broken," Bodnar said, wiping tears from her eyes and gesturing toward her mother, who was being helped to a car nearby.

Kyrylo was killed the morning after they spoke by a barrage of Russian missiles that struck the International Center for Peacekeeping and Security in Yavoriv, a town that sits ten miles from the border with Poland and had hosted US National Guard troops until a few weeks before the invasion. I had been there just weeks earlier, watching the Americans train their Ukrainian colleagues to use Western anti-tank weapons. Kyrylo was one of 35 people killed in the attack; 134 more were injured.

Captain Roman Bilyakovskiy, a close friend of the family, told me that he had last seen Kyrylo inside a building at the training center as the attack unfolded. Kyrylo had told him to run and seek safety while he stayed behind to help others. Moments later, the building took a direct missile hit and Kyrylo was buried under the rubble. It would take a full day to dig out his body.

Bodnar said Kyrylo, who left behind a wife and infant daughter, was solemn the last time they spoke, and he told her matter-of-factly that he believed he would soon join Vasyl in the afterlife.

"He told me, 'You can bury me beside Vasyl.'"

39

Savagery

Kyiv region, Spring 2022

By mid-March, the tables had turned and it became clear that Russia's invasion was for the Kremlin, in fact, a fuck-up of historic proportions. Ahead of the invasion, its troops positioned to Ukraine's north in Belarus and northeast in Russia were led to believe they had been deployed to training grounds to conduct exercises. They were unaware until hours before they received their orders from commanders that they would be crossing the border on a very real mission. Even then, as the troops rolled into Ukraine relaxed, sitting atop their armored vehicles, they had been told that they'd meet little or no resistance and would be welcomed as liberators by the Ukrainians. The Russians had no maps to help guide them to Kyiv or they used old maps of the city from 1989, which showed them roads that were no longer there, terrain that had long been altered with new towns and infrastructure. They carried little food and no spare clothing items except parade uniforms they believed they'd be wearing as they marched victoriously down Khreshchatyk Street in a few days' time. And they over-extended their supply lines. Many didn't even believe they would see combat.

Upon entering Ukraine, they quickly found things to be very different. The Ukrainians met them with fierce resistance – and the Russians didn't handle it well. Putin's troops never adapted to the situation, and instead repeated the same failing tactics over and over, with the same devastating results. They took wrong turns; they tried to punch-throw Ukrainian defenses with huge armored columns, including one more than 40 miles long; and they ran themselves into traps, where Ukrainian troops and volunteer fighters armed with Javelins and NLAWs easily picked them off.

Ukraine turned the fight into a war of ambushes and skirmishes, deploying a hodgepodge of regular army soldiers, National Guard troops, Territorial Defense Force volunteer fighters, and civilians. They were armed with rifles and hundreds of Western anti-tank weapons, and had limited heavy weaponry and armored vehicles. Yet they managed to stop what was thought of by many as the second-most powerful military in the world. What the Ukrainians lacked in firepower they made up for with creativity, flexibility, and determination. Not to mention they were fighting on their land and knew every square inch of it better than any of the Russians.

"We funneled them into long, narrow streets where they had no protection and then we would sneak up and hit them from both sides," explained Lutiy, commander of the Wild Ducks, a volunteer unit formed from a group of friends in Makariv and surrounding towns and villages west of Kyiv. "We always aimed for the first and the last vehicles, so they would be trapped. Then it was like shooting orcs in a barrel," he told me in April, using a term taken by Ukrainians from J.R.R. Tolkien's *Lord of the Rings* novels to describe the Russian invaders. Why orcs? "Because they are inhuman," Lutiy said, listing on his fingers a number of heinous crimes that Russian troops would be found to have committed during their occupation of Kyiv Oblast.

Volunteers were essential to Ukraine's victory in Kyiv, especially those who didn't have guns. They fought with weapons like smartphones, messaging apps, and hobby drones. In an interview with *Ukrainska Pravda*, Brigadier General of the 43rd Brigade Oleg Shevchuk underscored the crucial role they played. Using what he described as "wedding drones" – small quadcopters available over the counter – locals in towns where the Russians were passing through would record videos and send them over WhatsApp to his troops, who would open fire on the invaders with their massive, Soviet-era 2S7 "peony" self-propelled heavy artillery systems. The 203mm shells were used to destroy Russian airborne forces in Hostomel as well as a snaking column of Russian troops in Brovary, east of Kyiv.

By 19 March the Russian forces in Kyiv Oblast had suffered such great losses and were so demoralized that they were no longer capable of conducting offensive operations. It was clear that their blitzkrieg campaign around Kyiv had failed, now they were desperately trying to consolidate control over the areas they occupied around the capital. They dug trenches and revetments and continued to try and resupply and reinforce their units, but it wouldn't be enough. The Russians had been significantly weakened and were in complete disarray.

They retaliated with missile strikes on civilian areas, including a shopping center in Podil that killed eight people. And in the towns they got stuck in and occupied, they terrorized the local population.

In late March, Russia's military leadership began trying to save face by reframing the objectives to focus on eastern Ukraine. We all saw that as a sign that Russian troops might soon pull out from Kyiv Oblast. Sure enough, a few days later, they began to withdraw.

By 2 April, the Russians were gone. With its surroundings free of the invaders and back under government control, Ukraine declared victory in the battle for Kyiv. But Russian forces had left a trail of carnage behind them.

The scope of the atrocities conducted in occupied areas outside the Ukrainian capital was tremendous. Bearing the brunt of Russia's campaign of terror was Bucha, where hundreds of bodies of civilians were discovered. Days after Russian troops had arrived in the city, the Ukrainian army began their attack on the invaders. They lit up the Russian tanks and armored vehicles with anti-tank rockets and artillery, destroyed a Russian column on Vokzalna Street, a main thoroughfare. Around 20 vehicles burned after a massive attack. The torched husks of them remained until the Ukrainian authorities entered Bucha in April. But the Russians would return, and in occupying the city they would show no mercy to its residents.

A mass grave filled to the brim with the bodies of 67 people was discovered behind a Ukrainian Orthodox church. Two more mass graves were discovered nearby. Many of the bodies had their hands tied behind their backs, some of them showing signs of torture and rape. Others were found mutilated. They were old and young, men and women and children. About 40 bodies were found just on a 4,000-foot stretch of Yablunska Street, which divides Bucha from Irpin.

The Russians had set up in factory buildings and schools. Snipers sat perched in a high-rise building, picking off civilians who ventured outside. The invaders beat, raped, robbed, tortured, and mutilated civilians in their homes and yards. Some were executed with gunshots to their heads or had their throats slit.

The horrors uncovered would make Bucha, once a quiet, leafy suburb, now synonymous with Russian barbarity. But they would also galvanize the international community into providing greater political and military support for Ukraine as it fought for survival.

On 4 April, President Zelensky entered Bucha with his top aides and bodyguards. He was wearing his khaki military clothes with an armored vest over his top. Dozens of journalists followed. Appalled by what he saw, Zelensky compared Russian fighters to ISIS militants and Nazi war criminals. "There is not a single crime they would not commit there," he said. He called the torture and cold-blooded murder of so many Ukrainians "unforgivable," adding that the Russians "treat people worse than animals."

A year later, marking the first anniversary of the invasion on 24 February in Kyiv, Zelensky would tell journalists that of all the horrors of the past year, Bucha was the most gut-wrenching thing he'd seen. "I saw that the devil was there," he said.

The savagery in Bucha would also kill any prospect of negotiations.

"It is very difficult to talk," Zelensky said, choking up. "It is very difficult to negotiate when you see what they did here."

It wasn't relief or calm that washed over the constellation of towns and villages west of Kyiv when the Russians withdrew after their month-long occupation. It was horror and unnerving silence. Those who survived the carnage cautiously inspected what was left of their badly damaged neighborhoods and began searching for those who were lost.

In March I interviewed the families and friends of five men killed in three instances, just a few miles apart from each other in Kolonshchyna and Kalynivka, a few miles south of Bucha, the district center that encompasses the villages. In each case, the men had been unarmed. Two of the men were found together, hastily buried in a shallow grave; two others were found shot to death in a burned-out car; the third man was discovered inside the trunk of his own sedan – his body booby-trapped with an anti-personnel mine. The information provided by the families about their loved ones was corroborated by local police and Territorial Defense Forces I spoke to.

The cases accounted for a fraction of the number of alleged war crimes that were being logged by Ukrainian and international prosecutors. They said that the total was likely to have constituted the largest number of atrocities in Europe since the Second World War.

Andriy Nebytov, a top National Police official for the Kyiv region, told me in late April that investigators had examined more than 1,200 bodies of civilians killed by Russian troops in the area. And the cases would continue to pile up. While a majority of the alleged war crimes had been recorded in the suburban towns of Bucha, Hostomel, Irpin, and Borodyanka, where large mass graves were discovered, similar acts of barbarity were carried out in smaller towns and villages.

Vira Tyshchenko spent hours every day for weeks poring over thousands of images of mutilated corpses, bloody clothing, and personal items. She thought that among the remains and detritus she might recognize her younger brother Serhiy, or something that belonged to him. But she also hoped not to see any signs of him, because she wanted him to still be alive. The images were compiled by authorities and shared in a group on the Telegram messenger app created for residents of the western district of Kyiv searching for loved ones who had gone missing while Russian troops occupied the area between late February and late March. A Ukrainian friend had tipped me off about the group. I counted more than 2,400 haunting photographs of roughly 500 corpses and personal effects found with them that had been uploaded.

Finally, on 3 May a series of images posted there would catch Vira's attention. She couldn't identify the man by his face, which was bruised, swollen, decomposed, and caked with mud. But she immediately recognized the tattoos on his body, including one on his right forearm that read in Latin, "dum spiro spero," or "while I breathe, I hope." It belonged to her brother Serhiy.

When we met on the street in central Makariv, it had been more than a month since Russian troops withdrew from their positions around Kyiv. And yet bodies and mass graves were still turning up on a weekly if not daily basis, underscoring the scale of atrocities committed by Putin's forces during their month-long occupation near Ukraine's capital.

Russian troops arrived in the area on 27 February, three days into Putin's full-scale attack on Ukraine, where they hoped to make a push for Kyiv. But strong Ukrainian resistance forced them to hunker down and occupy several towns and villages, set up bases, and bring in heavy artillery. They rounded up locals – men in particular – whom they suspected of spying or having ties to the Ukrainian military and local Territorial Defense Forces, and they shot civilians walking down the street in unprovoked attacks.

"When the orcs came here they just started killing us," said Svitlana Tyshchenko, Serhiy's other older sister. She described to me a wave of terror and violence unleashed by the Russians on the civilians in the area and recounted one instance in which she witnessed a group of eight Russian soldiers riding atop an armored personnel carrier who casually opened fire on a man walking down the street. "He wasn't doing anything," she said.

Their father, Volodymyr Barchuk, his voice cracking and tears streaming from his eyes, said their family had laid 25-year-old Serhiy to rest in the Kolonshchyna village cemetery the day before.

"Barbarians!" he cried. "He was my boy. He did nothing to them. He wasn't a threat."

Serhiy wasn't ignorant of the seemingly callous violence when he was riding his bicycle with a friend, 33-year-old Dmytro Luchynya, through Makariv on 19 March. During the ride, he told a friend over the phone that a Russian tank was coming toward them and that he would call back soon. The return call never came. What exactly happened to Serhiy and Dmytro isn't clear. But Volodymyr and his daughters Vira and Svitlana believe Russian troops detained the men and interrogated them for hours or even days, possibly in an attempt to get information about Ukrainian military activity.

Their bodies were discovered later, on 29 April, 41 days after they had disappeared and long after Russian forces retreated from the area. A tip led authorities to a shallow mass grave where Serhiy and Dmytro were found with their hands tied together by a single rope.

Vira said investigators told her Serhiy had likely been tortured before his death. Medical examiners found that his spine had been broken in several places and his neck had been snapped in a manner that suggested murder. "They broke his neck," Vira told me, demonstrating with a quick twist of her hands how she believes it was done. She said his abdomen was also cut open and his organs were exposed.

Dmytro's cause of death appears to have been four gunshots to the head. But investigators said he had also been shot in each of his limbs and he had other wounds on his body suggesting he was tortured before being killed.

Serhiy's family didn't know where he was going with Dmytro the day they disappeared. One theory was that Serhiy was trying to get to a recruitment center to rejoin the Ukrainian military or to join the Territorial Defense Forces. In the days after Russian troops invaded their area, he had expressed an interest in fighting.

Serhiy had enlisted in the Ukrainian Armed Forces shortly after his 18th birthday in 2014. He was based at a military facility in Desna, a city north of Kyiv, but was never deployed to the front line in the eastern Donbas region, where Ukraine has battled Russian and pro-Russian separatist forces over the past eight years. Afterward, he struggled to find his place in life, bouncing from job to job, Vira recalled. "He was trying to find himself," she said.

She spoke to me beside her brother's grave at the Kolonshchyna cemetery, as a funeral for Dmytro was taking place. A pine-tree branch was placed atop Serhiy's fresh grave, a symbol that he was unmarried. His family had hoped that he would someday find a partner and settle down.

"He loved women. A lot of women," Volodymyr said with a wry laugh. "He had a girlfriend. No, he had two girlfriends."

Dmytro, a road-construction worker, was eulogized by several of his colleagues. "We all die but Dima was taken from us too soon," said one man, noting that Dmytro's daughter would now go through life without a father. "They were so cruel to him."

Down the highway in nearby Kalynivka, a sleepy village of gas stations, truck stops, and car-repair shops that straddle the E-40 highway, Lyudmyla Kyrpach was still struggling to figure out what her life would look like after Russian soldiers murdered her husband Oleksandr in early March.

"We did everything together. He always thought of me," she told me in the yard of her cottage. She wept as we spoke, threw her hands in the air and looked up, as if to ask why.

Oleksandr, a 47-year-old mechanic, had organized a local Territorial Defense unit in their village the day that Russia's invasion began, calling on friends Oleksandr Radchenko, who was 52, and Serhiy Zaborovets, 51, to join him and round up the rest of the men. None of them owned firearms and they knew they didn't stand a chance against Russian troops with just crowbars, hammers, and various other tools. Their plan was to blend in and watch the enemy, taking note of their movements to provide intelligence to the Ukrainian army. The Russians entered Kalynivka on 28 February, whereupon the shooting and shelling began.

On 1 March, according to Valeriy Spasichenko, an acquaintance of Radchenko and Zaborovets, the men set out by car to see if they could locate the Russian troops' positions, which they hoped to then share with the Ukrainian military. They never returned. When Oleksandr didn't hear from his friends late in the afternoon, he went looking for them. "He said he would be right back," Lyudmyla said. But he also didn't return.

Lyudmyla was awake all night, worried sick. Early on 2 March she set out to find him. In a wooded area just off the road less than a mile from their home, she spotted his sedan. The car was riddled with bullet holes and the rear window had been shattered. She peered inside but there was no sign of her husband. The keys were still in the ignition, though, which she thought was weird and concerning. "Maybe he needed to run into the trees for safety," she wondered. She shouted for him in the forest and listened carefully for any response, but there was nothing.

She returned the next day with one of her husband's friends to continue searching. The friend, Yuriy, noticed a peculiar pattern of bullet holes along the trunk of the car. When he turned the key, the trunk flung open to reveal Oleksandr folded inside. Lyudmyla shrieked and lunged at his body, but Yuriy grabbed her by the shirt and pulled her away. He had heard that the Russians were booby-trapping the bodies of people they killed and was worried that Oleksandr's could be wired to explode.

On 4 March they returned with a rope and tied it around Oleksandr's limbs. Then they moved a safe distance away, and slowly started tugging. The car exploded in a ball of flames, sending body parts and pieces of the car flying into the air. The Russians had placed Oleksandr atop a weight-sensitive mine that was set to detonate when his body was moved.

Lyudmyla spent the rest of the day picking up the pieces of her husband. She placed them gently into a box. Back at the home they made together, she dug a shallow grave and buried what was left of him in the garden where they planted vegetables each spring. He lay there under a thin layer of black soil until the Russians retreated later that month, and then she transferred his remains to a plot in the local cemetery.

Days later, Lyudmyla's neighbors discovered the bodies of Radchenko and Zaborovets in the car they drove on the day they vanished. It was just a few hundred meters away from where Lyudmyla had found Oleksandr. The men's corpses were riddled with bullet holes.

As Kyiv was coming to grips with the Russian occupation of the capital's region, the retreating Russian troops were regrouping. Soon they would be ordered to another front in the war, in Ukraine's east. The eastern battlegrounds where the war had simmered for eight long years was about to heat up.

40

A Storm on the Horizon

Avdiivka, Mariinka and New York, eastern Ukraine,
January–February 2022

I had been at my home in Brooklyn in November and December 2021 when American sources first began sounding the alarm about a potential Russian invasion. The reports were worrying, and looking at the numbers of troops and types of weapons Putin was deploying around Ukraine, I knew that Moscow was building up to something. But I'd be lying if I told you that I believed a full-scale invasion was destined to happen at that point. Like many people, I believed it would be centered on the Donbas. After all, Russia and Ukraine had unfinished business there. The Minsk II deal in February 2015 had dialed down the intensity of the war, halted the Russian advance, and reduced the bloodshed. But it hadn't solved anything. In reality, it solidified Russia's hold over the occupied areas of Donetsk and Luhansk and, as we know now, allowed Moscow to regroup and prepare its forces for another shot at attacking Ukraine. For seven years the war there simmered and soldiers continued to die. But much of the world stopped paying attention and moved on.

I even moved on briefly. After 11 years in Ukraine, I decided in February 2021 to try my hand on another beat. It was just after the insurrection on the US Capitol on 6 January and BuzzFeed News asked if I'd come back to New York to cover domestic extremism. So I moved home. But then the Russian military build-up happened. I returned to Ukraine in mid-December, and soon I was back out in the Donbas.

Moving around the front line while reporting with Pete and our friend Inna Varenytsia, a Ukrainian journalist with the Associated Press, it became clear that a larger war was looming on the horizon.

It was Private Ihor Tychyna's turn to keep watch.

It was just after 2 a.m. on 27 December 2021 and light snow was falling over New York. Not the shimmering American metropolis of skyscrapers, Times Square, and Central Park. But New York, the eastern Ukrainian town of some 12,000 people that sat smack on the front line of the grinding war in the Donbas. Only recently the town's name had officially been changed from Novhorodske back to its historic title, which dated to the nineteenth century. The origin of its name was a matter of great debate in the town. Some believed it was named New York by German Mennonites who moved there from Jork in northern Germany. Others claimed that a founder of the town who had married an American from the Big Apple and brought her back to eastern Ukraine had named it for her so she wouldn't feel homesick. Others said it had always been called New York and they had no idea how it got its name.

In any case, the lanky 20-year-old Tychyna of the 95th Air Assault Brigade was stomping through the neck-deep maze of trenches that divided New York from Russian-controlled territory in Donetsk Oblast when he reached a shallower segment of the channel that hadn't been fully dug out yet. With the mud squishing beneath his feet on this unusually warm winter night, he almost certainly didn't hear the quiet chirp of the sniper's bullet fired from a bluff 2,000 feet away before it penetrated the left side of his head, just an inch below the bottom of his helmet.

"It was a *Mission Impossible* kind of shot," Denis Ivashchenko, a 21-year-old officer to whom Tychyna reported, told me. "It was dark and snowing, and he was moving. The sniper had to be a professional."

Ivashchenko found Tychyna moments later, slumped over. There was a hole in his skull and blood was pooling beneath him in the fresh snow. Tychyna was rushed to a nearby hospital but died on New Year's Day, making him the first Ukrainian soldier to be killed in 2022.

It was three weeks later when I found Ivashchenko and Andriy, a 21-year-old soldier with a carefully trimmed beard, digging with a pickax and shovel at the very spot in the trench where Tychyna had been shot.

"It should be deep," Ivashchenko said, monitoring Andriy's work. Andriy shoveled dirt and tossed it over his shoulder. Now, the top of his helmet was nearly a foot below ground level.

"The fighting in the Donbas has been more frequent and intense than has been reported by both sides," Ivashchenko said. He wasn't sure if the military or government was suppressing the information they were reporting to them about the situation on the ground. But he was certain that it was worse than people knew. As we spoke, there were bursts of small-arms fire nearby. He told us to keep our heads down.

Nobody here had been on the offensive for years. But danger still lurked around every trench corner, mostly from sniper fire and landmines. Soldiers here knew never to let their guard down. But after eight years of this, sometimes they did.

I wrote a dispatch for BuzzFeed News in which I described this as Ukraine's own forever war, where generations had fought and come of age. Fathers who first took up arms in 2014 now had sons like Andriy, Denis, and Ihor who were teenagers when Russia annexed Crimea and invaded the Donbas. Andriy, who came from a military family, said his father had fought in the Debaltseve battle and was lucky to be among those who escaped encirclement and death. Now, these young men were the first line of Ukraine's defense at the front.

I spent a week embedded with them and other units in three strategic positions along what was then a 250-mile front line – in New York, Avdiivka, and Opytne – to find out what they were seeing and how they were preparing for a new Russian invasion. I found that the fighting in the Donbas had intensified to a degree much greater than was being reported. There were once again daily skirmishes and the Russians had brought back heavy artillery to their positions. The Ukrainians told me they were seeing more tanks, too, and showed me them through binoculars.

"My guess is he will move in, he has to do something," President Joe Biden said about Putin around that time. A full-scale invasion of Ukraine would be "the most consequential thing that's happened in the world in terms of war and peace since World War II," Biden added.

"Ukraine does not want a war, but Ukraine must always be ready for it," President Zelensky said in a televised address, urging Ukrainians to remain calm. "We are not afraid because we protect our land. We will not give up because there is nowhere to run."

The Kremlin kept denying that it had any plan to invade Ukraine again, saying that what it does with its military forces on its own territory is its business. But it had also delivered a list of demands to Washington and NATO that it said must be met or else it would respond militarily against Ukraine. Diplomacy had so far failed to de-escalate the situation. Almost nobody believed that Moscow wanted to find a peaceful solution. And so Ukraine and its partners in the West braced for what was shaping up to be a devastating new war.

The soldiers I met on the Ukrainian front line said that Russia's latest military moves made them nervous, and there was palpable anxiety mounting on the front. But the troops had also been preparing for this moment for several years.

"We're not scared. We've had time to grow stronger. We're real soldiers now," 24-year-old Platoon Commander Valentin Trusov told me down the road from New York, in the village of Opytne, where just about 28 residents remained, living without electricity and heating.

We reached him from a desolate road that was so close to the Russian front line that we had to race at high speed in order to avoid Russian gunfire. In peacetime, the drive would have been an idyllic one, with golden fields of sunflowers and tall grass lining the highway. In fact, I had ridden my bicycle down a similar road through the area years earlier while in the Peace Corps. I remembered it because I had punctured two tires in less than a mile.

Now soldiers here referred to it as a "road of life," as it offered an escape from danger. But sometimes it's also a road of death. Two soldiers had been killed by an anti-tank missile while on a supply run here a few months earlier.

Shortly after we arrived in Opytne, a small volley of grenades fired from an automatic grenade launcher came in. Trusov told me to keep my head down as we toured his unit's forward-most positions. The destroyed Donetsk Airport, the once glimmering symbol of progress in the rough-and-tumble coal-mining region, was just 600 meters away. Through a scope, I could make out craters on the runway left from fighting more than seven years ago. This was the closest I had come since I had been here with forces fighting over it in 2014. It felt strange to be so near and at the same time know that it was impossible to step foot on the former airport's grounds.

"They fire on us all the time. Every day," Trusov said. Lately, his troops had increasingly been targeted by Russian artillery. Pointing southeast toward the former airport, he showed me the enemy battle tanks positioned behind a tree line.

Amid the ruins of the former tire factory on the outskirts of Avdiivka, we linked up with the 25th Airborne Brigade, where I met First Lieutenant Ivan Skuratovsky, a 30-year-old married father of two from Dnipropetrovsk Oblast. After an unsuccessful search for a well-paying engineering job in early 2014, he had joined the army. It was just months before Russia invaded Crimea and war broke out in the Donbas. His father was displeased. He had hoped his son would leave Ukraine after getting his engineering degree, thinking he would have a brighter future abroad. Skuratovsky's father was also fond of Russia and not exactly a Ukrainian patriot. He watched Russian state propaganda and repeated the lies they told about the Revolution of Dignity, for example.

When the war broke out in the Donbas, he pleaded with his son to quit the army and leave the country. But Skuratovsky, just 22 at the time, was vehemently against Russia's invasion and saw it as his duty to fight back. And he would – in some of the fiercest battles of 2014 – as a gunner on a Ukrainian version of the US Bradley Fighting Vehicle. He survived, but his unit lost seven soldiers and the battalion another 25 between August and November of that year.

Over the years, Skuratovsky and his father struggled with their relationship. "He watches a lot of Russian propaganda. He thinks everything they say is true," Skuratovsky told me. That included what Russian propagandists were saying about Washington's warnings of a looming invasion. "He is worried, but he thinks that it will be better when Russia will win."

Now, in 2022, the young Skuratovsky was in a leadership role and one of the most senior people in his brigade. The 25th had been positioned in Avdiivka's industrial district since August 2021. Known as the *Promzona*, the area was the site of some of the most intense fighting over the years. Almost everything was pockmarked and bent out of shape from rocket barrages, artillery strikes, and machine-gun fire. It was a *Mad Max*-like scene with the burned-out husks of cars and machinery littering the grounds. Feral dogs roamed the wreckage, and other than their growls and the whipping winds, the only sound you could hear between the sporadic cracks of gunfire and thuds of mortars was the eerie creak of flapping sheet metal.

We followed Skuratovsky through a maze of trenches and found Oleh, a 43-year-old commander, fiddling with his machine gun. A sign beside him read, "Hell is empty and all the devils are here." Oleh, it turned out, was a Shakespeare fan, and he'd borrowed the quote from *The Tempest*. Dressed in snow-white camouflage, he pointed through a small wooden cut-out to where his enemy stood just 150 yards away. Through a scope, he could sometimes see their breath rise above their open trenches. The two sides were so close that he could also hear the clanking of weapons and conversations being had by the very people who were trying to kill him.

"We can hear them prepare their provocations," he told me. Russia-backed fighters often took potshots at the Ukrainian soldiers in hopes of getting them to return fire and, as Oleh put it, "pick a fight."

He could also hear them "curse and complain" when they'd be given orders to dig new trenches or carry out other laborious tasks, giving the impression that morale among the local Russia-backed forces was low.

I'd seen evidence of that in photos provided by a source and on social-media accounts of those still living in the occupied city of Donetsk: advertisements offered monthly payments of around $300 for new recruits to join the "Armed Forces of the Donetsk People's Republic" – which was little else but a more poorly armed and poorly trained branch of Russia's military. Composed mainly of local Ukrainians who chose Moscow's side, they had been used as cannon fodder in battle, sustaining most of the casualties, while Russia's regular forces were used sparingly, often when their proxies were losing a fight in order to turn it around.

Lately, however, there had been an increasing amount of sniper fire, as well as an increase in reconnaissance and sabotage.

"Snipers fire and machine guns cover his position," Skuratovsky told me, "masking" the sound of the shot.

On 31 December 2021, three hours before midnight, Junior Sergeant Stanislav Bohuslavskiy, aged 23, was on patrol when he was hit in the head by a sniper's bullet. "He made a mistake" by letting his guard down for just a moment, Skuratovsky explained. "It was a really good sniper. And we think he had thermal vision on his rifle."

Skuratovsky remembered Bohuslavskiy as a funny guy built like a club bouncer. He would be the last soldier killed in 2021.

To Skuratovsky, the manner of his death suggested professional Russian soldiers had returned to the front, likely in preparation for a new offensive. But until that happened, Skuratovsky's men were unable freely to return fire. For the past several months, they had been under orders not to fire back except in serious circumstances and under direct threat. If it was merely a potshot, they were supposed to let it slide. The order, which trickled down from President Zelensky to the military's top brass, was intended to de-escalate the fighting along the front line so that Russia wouldn't be given a pretext to launch a large-scale attack.

The soldiers hated this. When I asked about it, they rolled their eyes, clenched their teeth, and complained.

"It's hard for our guys to understand," Skuratovsky said, recognizing the frustration of his soldiers.

In September and October, Skuratovsky said, they did meaningfully return fire after being bombarded by "really heavy artillery," including 122mm shells. Most days, though, they took much more than they gave. Lately, it had been a lot of grenade fire from automatic systems and under-barrel launchers. "They're like little mortars," Skuratovsky said. "But they can do a lot of harm."

Inside a bunker made of logs and adorned with colorful children's drawings sent from across Ukraine to keep up the troops' morale, Skuratovsky stood among several computers and printers. He complained that he and his soldiers were pushing more paper than they were pulling triggers at the moment.

"We have a joke," he told me. "A soldier calls on the phone and says, 'Commander, they are attacking us. Can we return fire?' And the commander says, 'Wait, we must file a report first.'"

But the situation on the battlefield was about to change dramatically. Skuratovsky and I would keep in regular contact by phone when he had downtime in the trenches and voice messages over WhatsApp. He would become simply Ivan, a friend. And months later, when he would come under attack and take shrapnel in his back and have to undergo surgery, we would speak over video calls while he recovered. He would tell me war stories but mostly we'd talk about his children and how little he had seen of them since the war reignited. More than anything, he wanted victory for them.

He spent a few weeks with them while he recovered, and then he was sent back to the front line in the east. The battle of the Donbas was in full swing, and Ukraine needed every soldier it could get to hold off Russia's assault.

One place where the increase in fighting was especially evident ahead of the invasion was Mariinka, a town just a few miles west of Donetsk where I had spent a lot of time in previous years. I had been on the phone with Alina Kosse, my friend who was the administrator at the Mariinka city youth center, and she was growing increasingly worried that Russian forces would soon launch a large-scale attack there. With the front line running through the eastern edge of Mariinka, it had always seen some fighting and once or twice a year there would be a spike in shelling. But Alina was now seeing heavy weaponry being used and shelling on a daily basis.

"Chris, it's so much worse. We're scared," she told me on the phone. I could hear the rumble of incoming artillery on the line. Videos posted to social media from residents also showed the artillery attacks on the town.

We arrived the day after our call, I saw fresh damage from the shelling in the town's center. Inside the local government office, I found Oleksandra Sisenko, a city employee who filmed a video of an attack. She had grown so concerned that she was now considering moving with her third-grade daughter out of town.

"We want peace," Oleksandra said. "We want to build a future."

But like everywhere along the front line, I also found people in a state of denial and numb to the hostilities after eight years of war. They didn't believe a peaceful solution could be found and that this would be their reality for the rest of their lives. Their stoicism was on display as they mingled around a depressing little market with just a few older women selling jars of pickles.

Past the market was Alina's office. I walked up to the second floor and found her laughing with some colleagues. It was typical Alina, finding humor somewhere in the middle of hell. She wrapped me in her arms and kissed my cheek. We chatted like we usually do over cups of instant coffee, and then she walked me around to see what the children were up to.

Masha, an especially petite 16-year-old, was singing love songs in the auditorium, totally alone with the sound system blaring – loud enough to drown out the sound of shelling in the distance. She said singing helped her forget about the war outside. "Everyone needs love," she told me.

Down the hall, 12-year-old identical twins Veronika and Yeva were hard at work piecing together extravagant beaded necklaces. I noticed tape on the window and asked Alina what had happened.

"Sniper," she said, peeling back the tape to reveal a bullet hole. "This happened just yesterday."

The shelling was growing louder and closer. I motioned to Pete that we should maybe get going. Veronika and Yeva didn't bat an eye as the explosions thundered and shook the building. They remained focused on threading string through their tiny beads. I asked if they were scared. They told me that they had heard it all before.

"We have learned to live with war," Alina interjected.

Valentina Gordeyeva had been waiting for a bus in central Mariinka the day before when the Russian rocket exploded beside her. Fire-hot shrapnel struck her in the left hand and lower abdomen. She was waiting to go to a medical center for a checkup – instead, she landed in the trauma ward of the district hospital.

"I ran when I heard the artillery start," Valentina told me from her hospital bed in the neighboring town of Kurakhove. She was dressed in black tights and a red cable-knit turtleneck sweater. A white bandage was wrapped around her hand. It was unclear what the Russians were targeting. The only buildings around her were a school, a small grocery, and civilian homes. She had tried to make it inside a grocery when the attack began but she wasn't quick enough. The shrapnel struck her down in the street.

"My blood was everywhere," she said as she fought back tears.

The 65-year-old retired schoolteacher told me her home sat smack on the front line. It had been damaged by a rocket eight years ago, when the war first broke out, but was patched up. The last years had been hard on her. She suffered from high levels of stress and anxiety. Now there was the shooting pain from her physical wounds. And she worried that the attack was the precursor to the return to full-scale war.

"It felt like 2014 and 2015 all over again," Valentina told me.

She had a daughter who lived in Florida but didn't know how she could get there. The American Embassy was closed and the diplomats had left. It was now impossible to get a visa. She asked me if I knew how to get her to the States. I didn't. I gave her some phone numbers of people I thought might be able to help. I'm not sure if she got through to them. And I never found out what happened to her.

Taken together with the spike attacks in Avdiivka, Opytne and elsewhere, this seemed to be part of a broad, coordinated assault by Russia's forces, a softening of the battlefield before the launch of a major offensive. If I wasn't convinced before that a new, major war was on the horizon, I was now.

41

Trouble at Sea

Mariupol, southeastern Ukraine, January 2022

Second Captain Roman Varianitsyn, dressed in blue and gray camouflage that blended in with the sea, was on high alert. He surveyed the horizon through a steamy window as waves slapped the side of our small armed cutter. Beside him, a helmsman navigated the growing swells as another man stayed glued to a green radar screen. A fourth man in the rear of the vessel stood at a machine gun, his finger resting beside the trigger. They were all on the lookout for Russian warships that Putin had dispatched to the Sea of Azov to probe and provoke the Ukrainians.

It was one month before Russia's full-scale invasion, and tensions were not only rising on land, they were also escalating on water. I wanted to return to Mariupol because I knew it was of great strategic importance, and because I was fond of the city. Conveniently, Varianitsyn had invited me, Pete, and the AP journalist Inna Varenytsia to join his crew of Maritime Guards of the Border Guard Service of Ukraine on a patrol. In recent days, there had been several dangerous approaches made by the Russians. Sometimes their navy boats steered directly toward Ukrainian vessels like they were playing a game of chicken, before breaking away moments before collision.

"They come directly near our ports. They record and control and monitor all of our activities," Varianitsyn said. "They are constantly monitoring the situation near the Ukrainian coast and everything that happens here."

It was no secret that Mariupol had always been a main target of Putin's, who was still sore about his forces losing it in 2014. Moscow was moving several large landing ships from its Baltic Fleet towards the Black Sea. That movement, along with the Russian presence on land nearby and the build-up of ground forces around Ukraine's border, had the Ukrainian Maritime Guards very worried. They believed that if Russia launched a new invasion of Ukraine, which seemed more and more likely by the day, it would almost certainly be a multi-pronged attack that included a push east from occupied territory toward Mariupol with another attack from Crimea in the southwest and some type of naval operation in the Azov itself. After all, Mariupol and neighboring Berdyansk were home to Kyiv's only ports in the Sea of Azov. For Moscow, controlling them would mean controlling all of the sea and its ports, and it would create Putin's long-desired land bridge connecting Russia to annexed Crimea.

The scenario had been talked about for years and it stuck in the back of the minds of the half a million residents of Mariupol, who knew the Kremlin was itching to try its luck once more at capturing the strategic city. But Ukraine had built up its defenses around the city in the years since 2015. To try taking it now seemed silly to some. But others were growing more concerned that Putin might attempt it.

We were five nautical miles out at sea when a Ukrainian vessel appeared. The *Donbas*, a patrol boat named after the eastern region. It boasted two double-barreled 30mm anti-aircraft guns, a heavy machine gun, and several smaller machine guns. We shadowed it for several minutes, keeping our eyes peeled for enemy vessels on the horizon and green blips indicating them on the radar screen. The faces of the Maritime Guards were serious. They radioed to other Ukrainian vessels nearby to ask whether they'd spotted anything. We bobbed around for an hour or so but the Russians never appeared. But everyone knew they were lurking somewhere in the same waters, monitoring and awaiting orders.

There had been several incidents and close calls between the two country's navies on the Sea of Azov over the years that had raised tensions to a dangerous level and threatened to spark a new outbreak of fighting. Most notable was the incident on 25 November 2018, when Russian FSB coastguards opened fire on and captured three Ukrainian navy vessels and 24 sailors as they attempted to transit from the Black Sea into the Sea of Azov through the Kerch Strait. The sailors were released only after months of tense negotiations and international pressure on Moscow.

Ukraine narrowly escaped another attack in December just as new tensions between Moscow and the West were on the rise, when Russian navy boats claimed that the Ukrainian command ship also named the *Donbas*, a 400-foot Soviet-era vessel, was acting provocatively in the sea; Kyiv said it was carrying out a routine training exercise. In the end, a crisis that could have sparked renewed large-scale fighting in Ukraine was averted.

In the years since Russia invaded Ukraine, it had significantly increased its presence in the Sea of Azov and the larger Black Sea, tightening its grip on the strategic bodies of water that wash both Russian and Ukrainian shores. The Russian fleet here was composed of dozens of vessels including warships much more powerful than anything Ukraine had in this shallow body of water slightly larger than Lake Erie.

"They have the advantage [on the sea] – the advantage in the number of ships and in firepower," Roman Varianitsyn lamented.

Ukraine never boasted a powerful navy, and it lost 70 per cent of the fleet it had back in 2014, when Russia annexed Crimea and seized Sevastopol, the Black Sea port.

Since then, Ukraine had worked to rebuild its fledgling naval force and had received some help from the US in the form of used Coast Guard patrol boats. But it was still a far cry from what it used to be, let alone anything that could rival Russia's navy.

On several trips made to Mariupol between 2015 and 2020, I had visited the Ukrainian Navy and Maritime Guards, who showed me their modest fleet of 14 vessels, including the armed cutter-class ship *Lyubomir*, two patrol ships – the *Donbas* and the *Onyx*, which were smuggled out of Crimean ports during Russia's annexation – and 12 small cutter patrol boats, four of which were fresh camouflage paint jobs to cover rusting hulls on a 2018 visit. The Ukrainians called it a "mosquito fleet" that would be able to pester the Russians and maybe deter them, but nothing powerful enough to stop them.

Back on land, the mood was tenser than I'd felt it in Mariupol in years. The port city had long been one of my favorite places in the east of the country. As a Peace Corps volunteer, I traveled there several times to see friends and wade into the sea. We spent hot afternoons on the sandy beaches there and would sometimes catch a bus to the nearby resort town of Sedove, just two kilometers from the Russian border. It was kitschy, with its many beach stalls, but fun. One time, I bought a speedo to blend in with the locals, much to the amusement of my American friends in their board shorts. The wind was so strong that while floating in the sea it flipped me off my air mattress, which then blew into Russian waters to be lost forever.

Every time I rolled into Mariupol I'd snap a photo of the towering steel worker at its entrance – a monument celebrating the industry that powered the city – and pull off the highway at one particular observation point where there was this incredible view of the hulking Ilyich Iron and Steel Works, one of Ukraine's and Europe's largest metallurgical plants.

Since the front line of the war had frozen eight years prior, Ukraine and its Western partners had invested millions in Mariupol, transforming it into a vibrant modern city. A series of decentralization reforms implemented by the government after the 2014 revolution largely contributed to Mariupol's revitalization by shifting power and spending decisions from Kyiv to the local government. There were tech hubs and co-working centers, hipster barbershops and cafes that rivaled those in Kharkiv, Kyiv, and Odesa. I went to cocktail bars and art galleries when I'd come to town and then dine at a seaside restaurant. Afterward, a little buzzed, I'd walk the beachside train tracks, following them to the new piers that jutted into the sea, where couples smooched against the backdrop of the sunset. There was a burgeoning theater scene, new bike paths, and sports clubs with turf fields.

The last time I had visited Mariupol was in November 2020. I had followed Zelensky there for the Mariupol economic forum, which the president hoped would show representatives from major companies, international financial organizations and diplomatic missions that, despite the still-simmering war, the city of roughly half a million residents – as well as the rest of Ukraine – was full of potential and open for business.

I flew from Kyiv to Zaporizhzhia airport, then hired a car to take me to Mariupol. At the entrance where the steel worker stood, we passed gigantic concrete tetrapods adorned with colorful paintings of flowers, fruits, and vegetables, and traditional Ukrainian folk art. There were dozens of other journalists, too. But they were less interested in Mariupol and Zelensky's ambitious domestic agenda. They wanted to corner the president to get him to comment on the deepening political scandal that he had been sucked into involving then President Donald Trump half a world away.

In a phone call that July, Trump had seemed to pressure Zelensky into opening investigations into the Ukraine dealings of Hunter Biden, the son of his political rival Joe Biden. Trump had ordered $391 million worth of crucial military aid to Ukraine just three days before the call. The story broke in September, causing a transatlantic firestorm.

Zelensky managed mostly to dodge questions about Trump in Mariupol, thanks to a large security presence that followed him everywhere and kept journalists at a distance.

Addressing the forum's audience in his keynote speech, Zelensky boasted of Ukraine's capacity for transformation. "We're the Apple starting out in the garage. We're Lance Armstrong defying the odds," he said. The problematic comparison to an admitted cheater seemed to be lost on him. Nevertheless, the crowd applauded, and during a coffee break many of the high-profile guests expressed their satisfaction with Zelensky.

But the war wasn't far away. It had simmered for years just 15 miles to the east, at the edge of the one-time resort town of Shyrokyne. I had visited the town several times over the years with Ukrainian troops. On a reporting trip in 2018, I rode up and down the front line with Julia "Taira" Paevska, a tough-as-nails volunteer medic who was based there. We had met previously during a heavy battle in Avdiivka to the north, when she was treating wounded soldiers. "Be careful where you show your head here. A sniper can shoot it off," she told me as we walked through a desolate area where Ukrainian and Russian troops regularly exchanged gunfire and engaged in mortar duels.

Now that simmer was turning to a boil. For the first time in years, the Russians were using rockets and other heavy artillery in the area. And Ukrainian forces saw them bring back tanks and other armored vehicles to the front line.

"This is such an important and dangerous moment for us. We need serious defensive help from the United States," Halyna Odnorih, a Mariupol-based activist told me over coffee at our regular meet-up spot, Time Out cafe on central Metalurhiv Avenue, just around the corner from the Mariupol Drama Theater. She was convinced a new Russian invasion was imminent and that Mariupol, with its large factories, warm water ports, and a mostly Russian-speaking population that has long enjoyed close ties to its larger neighbor to the east, would be a key target.

Albert Khomyak, a military chaplain and widowed father of 16 adopted children, agreed. Stroking his silver goatee, he told us that he had already begun making preparations to evacuate his kids to cities in central Ukraine, where he believed they'd be safer when – not if, he said – Russia attacks. However, he conceded, "if Russia wants all of Ukraine, nowhere is completely safe."

"In this situation," he told me, as he rubbed the cross around his neck between his fingers, "I'm afraid there is nobody who can help us. It may be up to God only."

42

Siege

Mariupol, 24 February–April 2022

The Ukrainians expected the Russians to try to break through the eastern front line when Putin ordered his invasion to begin. Soldiers fortified their positions and dug new trench systems. The military brought in extra weaponry but not a whole lot of it. They didn't bring in many reinforcements. They weren't anticipating that Russian forces would storm through the land crossing in northern Crimea to mainland Ukraine and then sweep so quickly and without much resistance to the east, through Kherson and Zaporizhzhia Oblasts, reaching the western outskirts of Mariupol in just over a week. But that's what would happen.

By 2 March, the Russians had Mariupol surrounded and were laying siege to the city. They pummeled it with heavy artillery from all directions. Nowhere was safe. Within days, local authorities declared a humanitarian catastrophe was unfolding. Power, gas, and water lines were cut almost immediately across the entire city. Cell-phone, radio, and television towers were downed. There were food shortages. The cold winter weather exacerbated the situation. Residents were forced to cram together into cold, dark bomb shelters and basements. They came up only for a breath of fresh air or to search for food, which they prepared over open fires on the street. When it snowed, they scooped up the snow and melted it to drink.

By mid-March, Russian tanks were rolling through the center of Mariupol. They fired upon buildings indiscriminately, turning nine-story apartment buildings to rubble in an instant. Civilian deaths piled up as the invaders tightened their noose around the city. On 9 March an air strike destroyed a maternity and children's hospital, killing at least three people and wounding 17 more. Photographs taken by Ukrainian journalists Mstyslav Chernov and Evgeniy Maloletka showing bodies being thrown into mass graves, buildings engulfed in flames, and a pregnant woman being carried on a stretcher amid the death and destruction, shocked the world. Both the woman and her baby would die.

Escape was risky if not impossible. People who tried their luck on the roads sometimes came under fire or faced harsh interrogations from Russian troops. Ukrainian marine and National Guard forces in Mariupol had nowhere to go. They tried to hold back the Russians but were eventually forced to take shelter in the city's massive factories.

It was impossible to believe what I was seeing and hearing about Mariupol, knowing it as I did, and having just been there a few weeks before. My brain couldn't process the images coming out of the city. I stayed awake at night thinking about the nightmare that those stuck inside Mariupol were living through.

Senior Lieutenant Valentina Strutynska of the 36th Ukrainian Marine Brigade, along with Captain Oleksandr Demchenko, an anesthesiologist in Ukraine's medical service, and Oleksandr Voronenko, a major in the 56th Motorized Brigade, were among them. Strutynska and Voronenko said Russian forces had been shelling Mariupol for days before the invasion began. But on 24 February the ferocity with which Putin's army attacked the city really picked up. As the fighting escalated, Strutynska and Voronenko retreated with their units into the fortress-like grounds of the Ilyich Iron and Steel Plant. There, they found protection and supplies inside the factories' bomb shelters – concrete bunkers several meters below ground that had been partly renovated to include ventilation systems and food pantries.

As Russia stepped up its rocket and artillery attacks on Mariupol, Ukraine's remaining forces in the city, along with hundreds of civilians, hunkered down in Ilyich and its neighbouring plant, Azovstal. But supplies began running low. That's when Ukraine's military devised a risky plan to help those trapped there.

Demchenko was part of a secret mission in late March to fly in reinforcements and supplies, and to evacuate several of the most badly wounded troops and civilians. He likened the mission to "a jump from a plane without a parachute."

"Mariupol was already surrounded by that time," he told me. "I understood that this was probably a one-way ticket and there would be no turning back."

He and another doctor were put onto separate military helicopters with several Special Forces troops.

"They split us up so that if one helicopter was shot down, at least the other would have a chance to make it through," Demchenko said.

The helicopters took fire from Russian troops as they swept low along the Sea of Azov coast, their rotors slicing through the chilly sea air, before banking toward the Port of Mariupol. Amazingly, they weren't hit, and managed to land. From there, the medics jumped into a small boat and zipped over the choppy water to the Azovstal plant.

Inside, Demchenko immediately set up a makeshift hospital and operating room to treat the wounded, many of whom he found in terrible condition. Over weeks, he performed blood transfusions in almost complete darkness; treated gaping head wounds; tied up abdominal injuries that saw internal organs spill out; set shattered bones; and amputated limbs – sometimes with little or no anesthesia.

One badly injured man had a tourniquet applied to his leg for 15 days. "Something completely unthinkable," Demchenko said. Gangrene had set in when the medic found him and he had to amputate the leg above the knee. "Miraculously, he survived."

"The most terrible thing was the massive air strikes by the enemy aircraft," Demchenko recalled.

He said Russian planes dropped massive bombs on top of Azovstal. One of the blasts sent flames whirling through the ventilation shafts and threw him five meters across the room into a concrete pillar. Another caused three floors of concrete to collapse on top of the medical ward, killing several patients.

"Death was instantaneous for them," Demchenko said, adding that in a way they were fortunate.

But the concrete piled on top of them was too heavy to move, and because the temperatures had begun to rise as spring set in, the bodies began to fester and stink.

Small quadcopter drones were constantly hovering above them, dropping explosives.

A failed breakout attempt on 14 and 15 April led to dozens of deaths and injuries, Demchenko said.

"We had only three operating tables for all these people. We didn't leave the operating room for more than 30 hours."

One soldier's heart stopped four times while they worked on his badly wounded head. But he survived and opened his eyes hours later.

As the Russians bore down and pounded them with heavier and heavier weapons, the Ukrainians were finally forced to surrender – first the marines in the Ilych power plant in mid-April, and then another group of marines and National Guardsmen from the Azov Regiment in May.

But they had managed to hold out for long enough to force Putin to divert resources away from invading troops in Kyiv and Kharkiv, leading to the Russians' retreat of those areas and ultimately changing the course of the war.

The Ukrainians would be transferred to several prisons over the course of six months, including the notorious Olenivka prison. It had been under the control of Russian forces since Putin's first invasion of Ukraine in 2014. In July 2022 an explosion would destroy a wing of the prison where Ukrainian troops captured in Mariupol were being kept, killing 53 POWs and injuring 75 more. Kyiv and its intelligence agencies said Russian forces had blown up the building to conceal its torture of Ukrainian captives and it published audio recordings to support the claim. Moscow said without evidence that Ukrainian forces had used US-provided missiles to destroy the barracks. Fortunately, Strutynska, Demchenko and Voronenko, who all spoke with me after they had been released six months later, had been transferred before the explosion.

The troops had suffered abuse and torture for months. In the first days of captivity, the soldiers were piled on top of each other in their tiny cells and not given blankets or pillows. Food was scarce and what they were given, they said, was rotten and disgusting and mostly composed of various porridges. They were given buckets of muddy river water to drink, which made some of them sick. Only occasionally were they given tea.

"Everyone was dehydrated and exhausted," Demchenko said. At one point, he was down 45 kilograms from the 117 kilograms he had weighed in February.

Strutynska said more than 40 women soldiers were put into a cell meant for four people.

"We slept on top of each other," she said.

But she said they were treated better in Olenivka, in a prison run by pro-Russian Ukrainians, than they were later when they were transferred to a prison in Taganrog, Russia.

There, Ukrainians said they were physically and verbally abused, while also subjected to Russian propaganda.

"It was absolutely continuous propaganda and streams of hatred [toward Ukrainians]," Voronenko said of the programs they were forced to watch on Russian television.

Strutynska said she and other women sang folk songs and pop hits by the Ukrainian band Okean Elzy. On 24 August, Ukraine's Independence Day, they sang the national anthem, "Ukraine Has Not Yet Perished."

As autumn came, the nights began to get colder and there was no heating in their cells. They huddled together for warmth while holding out hope for a prisoner swap.

On 21 September the Ukrainians awoke to Russian guards in the cells. They were all blindfolded and had their hands tied painfully behind them. They were unsure what was happening – some thought that perhaps they were being transferred to another prison, or were being moved back to Mariupol for a sham "trial" of defenders captured in the city that was rumored to be in the making. In fact, to their surprise, they were being exchanged for a group of Russian POWs and Viktor Medvedchuk, the pro-Russian MP and close friend of Putin's who had been charged with treason. At the time, it would be the largest prisoner exchange since Putin had launched his full-blown invasion.

Two bus rides, two flights, and many hours later, Strutynska heard someone shout, "Glory to Ukraine!" As her blindfold was removed, she was home, after five hellish months in Russian captivity.

Strutynska, Demchenko, and Voronenko recounted their stories to me a little more than a month after they had returned home to Ukraine.

Demchenko and Voronenko spoke to me by phone from a base in Poltava, where they were recovering. Demchenko was trying to get his weight back up. He hoped that sharing his experience would help other doctors save more soldiers' lives. Voronenko had plans to undergo surgery to remove two bullets that had been lodged in his leg since he was in Mariupol. "I never even cried from my wounds," he said. But returning home had been "emotional."

Strutynska met me in a cafe in Kyiv. It was a day after her sixth wedding anniversary, which she had celebrated alone. She showed up not in her military uniform but in a pink puffer coat, fashionable jeans, and sparkly sneakers. She wore shimmery lip gloss and smart glasses. Much to her dismay, her husband, Yevhen Strutynskyi, also a Ukrainian soldier, had not been included in the prisoner swap. She had not seen or been in contact with Yevhen since they were captured in mid-April and had no idea of his current whereabouts. "Home," she said, choking up, "is not the same without him."

A few weeks after our meeting, I got a message from her. "He's home!" she wrote. I didn't have to ask what she meant. When I looked at her Facebook page, I saw that she'd posted a photo showing her and Yevhen wrapped in each other's arms. A message beside it read: "My hero. My beloved husband is home."

43

Filtration

Mariupol, February–April 2022

Oksana had just woken up her children to get them ready for school and was taking the last sip of her coffee on the morning of 24 February, when Russian bombs began raining down on Mariupol. She had heard the rumors about a new invasion of Ukraine but like many people in the southeastern seaside city, she had brushed them off.

"Everyone thought it was just some kind of panic. We didn't understand how dangerous it was," she told me. "For the past eight years we have listened to the distant sounds of shooting and we understood that we were at war already."

In the years since the battle for Mariupol in 2014, the city had been largely out of firing range, as the hot phase of the war gave way to a grinding battle of attrition. Oksana and other residents had grown relatively comfortable living adjacent to a static front line and the occasional rumble of artillery fire sounding in the distance.

"We shrugged our shoulders, so to speak," Oksana said. "We thought Putin was just trying to scare us."

But hearing Russian jets roaring overhead and the explosions grow closer to her home, and scrolling news sites and social media on her phone, she realized that this was different.

The attacks escalated quickly and Oksana grew concerned about the safety of her children. She lived on the second floor of a small apartment complex with 25 units. It had a basement but it wasn't suitable as a bomb shelter. She worried that if the building were to be hit it would simply collapse and bury them under a pile of rubble. As she thought of what to do, her ex-husband called and suggested they all meet at his parents' apartment building. Built following the Second World War, it had solid walls and a fortified bomb shelter. They grabbed a few personal items amid the explosions and set off.

"We weren't able to take anything with us," Oksana recalled. "I didn't take any clothes. I had no change of underwear, because I didn't count on being away long. I grabbed my purse but forgot my passport in my work bag. We had two bottles of water and a lantern. It was a ten-minute walk. But we ran most of the way."

They spent the next day and a half there. But soon the explosions would be all around them and they felt it was unsafe. They were also running short on supplies. When they heard that people were gathering in a larger bomb shelter beneath the neighborhood's Palace of Culture building, they decided to move.

In the building's underground rooms, Oksana connected with other members of her family, including her 24-year-old niece Daria, a freelance book editor. There were about 60 other people also taking shelter in the cultural center. They didn't know it at the time but they would all spend the next three weeks in the chilly shelter, in the dead of winter, without once stepping foot outside. A few of the men and athletic women were the only ones to leave in search of food and supplies. They darted out in the unsafe open between rounds of heavy shelling, risking their lives. They scoured destroyed pantries and the rubble of buildings and shops for anything that could be eaten, and filled plastic bottles with water from the nearby river. Food and water were scarce the entire time and eventually they'd run out. All they had to eat in the third week of their stay in the shelter were a few boxes of cookies, which they divided up between the children. The adults stomachs' growled with hunger. They clutched them in pain but tried not to show their distress to the children. Fights broke out between some adults who demanded a share.

The situation grew more dire as farther homes and buildings were destroyed and dozens of extra people – nearly 100 – joined them in the shelter. Daria and Oksana's family relied on her grandfather, who had been a military doctor in Soviet times, to bring them bread and whatever else he was able to gather. When there was any lull in the shelling, he would make a fire in the courtyard outside and cook hot soups or whatever meat and vegetables they had stored away.

The family spent the days huddled together for warmth in the darkness, using a flashlight to illuminate the shelter when the electricity went out. Daria's younger sister, Marina, sketched their experience in her diary, illustrating in gray pencil the dark and terrifying situation. She drew pictures of her family, a chair, a light bulb, toys, and strangers. It was her way of documenting what they were going through but also a ritual to pass the time and calm her nerves.

Over the next days, the Palace of Culture's walls were pounded with artillery shells. Daria feared the ceiling would collapse.

"It became clear that this wasn't a safe place. They were actually targeting the building," she said. Daria said the 20 days they spent huddled in a cold, dark bomb shelter were "a nightmare."

But what they would endure next would be unimaginable hell.

On 15 March, after 20 days of hiding in the Mariupol shelter, there was a loud bang on the shelter doors and then a gruff voice shouted for everyone inside to come out. When Daria and Oksana emerged, they found Russian troops waiting for them, the bulky figures of the soldiers silhouetted by the first rays of sunlight that those in the shelter had seen in weeks.

"I don't remember clearly how many soldiers there were, because it was the first time I had seen the sunlight in many days," Daria said. When her eyes finally adjusted to the brightness, she also noticed the destruction around her. "Everything was destroyed," she said.

The soldiers crammed her family with hundreds of other Ukrainians onto rickety buses, deprived them of food, water, and access to toilets, and trafficked them from their home, through a "filtration camp," and across the border into Russia over the course of several days in March. In the chaos, a woman died of a heart attack because the soldiers wouldn't provide her with medical care, Daria recalled. Men were ordered to stay behind. The Russians even separated an older disabled man from his wife. Lyudmila Denisova, Ukraine's human-rights ombudsman for the first months of the war, told me in her Kyiv office that many of the men had been taken to a separate location in Russian-occupied areas, where they were strip-searched and examined by Russian FSB agents and soldiers.

"They look at their tattoos," said Denisova, for anything that might suggest they were part of the Ukrainian military or nationalist organizations. They also checked for calluses and bruises on their arms and index fingers, signs that could indicate they had recently handled a gun. Many of the men were forced to do manual labor, including sorting through the rubble of destroyed buildings, pulling out corpses. One place where they had been put to work, Denisova said, was the site of the destroyed Mariupol Drama Theater, where hundreds of civilians, including women and children, had sheltered until it was hit in a massive Russian airstrike on 16 March.

The buses took Oksana and her children – as well as Daria and her sister Marina and the girls' grandmother – east from Mariupol. The trip took several hours. Outside the windows they could see the devastation wrought by war: shattered buildings, blown-up bridges, missile craters. They stopped at the village of Bezimenne, meaning "Nameless," about 15 miles west of the Russian border. Russian troops, emergency workers, and agents of the FSB, were waiting for them inside a series of tents, the women said.

Adults and children alike were photographed from various angles, fingerprinted and palm-printed like they were being booked for a crime, Daria said. Then everyone was forced to hand over their home addresses and passport information.

They had to unlock and turn over their phones, which were plugged into a computer. All of their data and contacts were then downloaded, Oksana and Daria said. The Russians scanned through photographs and accessed social-media accounts. It was all done to "check" whether they had "connections with the Ukrainian state or with military personnel," Oksana said. Daria said they specifically asked her whether she was affiliated with Right Sector, a marginal right-wing militant group that Russia falsely claims is part of an extremist contingent that controls Ukraine.

Oksana said her children were also interrogated by FSB agents, who were particularly concerned about some photos her teenage daughter had on her phone from an art competition in which she was placed second two years earlier. The competition was sponsored by Ukraine's Ministry of Internal Affairs. "When they found these photographs, the immediate question was, 'How are you related to this structure?'"

All of them were asked about the war. "They asked us, 'Who is to blame? Who's right and who's wrong?'" Oksana said.

The questioning lasted well into the night and long after they were exhausted, the women said. Some people gave answers that the Russians didn't like; they were then taken to a separate area and not seen again. The women believe they were moved to the city of Donetsk or other places where Russia's local separatist proxies had detention centers.

Around midnight, Oksana and her children, along with Daria, Marina, and their grandmother, were put back on the buses and driven farther east, passing through the town of Novoazovsk, in the dark of night. The temperature was well below freezing and they had no blankets with them. They recalled shivering on the cold buses. It was 2:17 a.m. when they arrived at the Russian border.

Another round of interrogations began immediately, this time by Russian border guards. Daria and Oksana were asked loaded questions about what they saw the Ukrainian army destroy, and with which weapons. "Of course, I said that we had been sitting in the bomb shelter all these days, so we didn't see anything, we didn't know anything," Oksana said. After they answered the questions, Daria said, the guards would repeat them in a different order. "The questions were always the same. They were just trying to confuse people and get them to confess something," Oksana said.

Each interrogation lasted between 30 minutes and an hour. There were hundreds of people to get through. The questioning finished around 11 a.m., and then they were put back on the buses. Their next stop was Taganrog, a port city in Rostov Oblast. There, some of the Ukrainians were given a choice: If they had passed the filtration camps and interrogations without raising any red flags and had the means to go on their own, they could do so. Daria and her sister Marina were able to raise some money through friends and a burgeoning network of volunteers in Russia helping Ukrainians taken there. It was enough to get them a train to Moscow and eventually to St Petersburg. From there they made their way to Ivangorod near the border with Estonia, where they were able to cross into Narva following a four-hour document check on 20 March, five days after their forced evacuation east began.

Otherwise, the Ukrainians were taken farther into Russia and placed in temporary housing facilities. Oksana, who had left her passport when she fled her apartment, was separated from her nieces and forced onto a train with her two kids that took them to Moscow and then onward to the city of Vladimir, more than 900 miles north of Mariupol.

When they arrived on 19 March, they were met by a horde of Russian news crews from state-run television channels eager to show how the authorities were helping Ukrainian refugees.

"We were tired, hungry, dirty, and of course unwashed. We had been in a basement for a month, we drove for days, and then we had these cameras and microphones stuck in our faces," Oksana recalled. "I felt like I was in some kind of zoo."

The local authorities gave every family 10,000 rubles, about $150, and told them they should be grateful for the assistance. Then they took Oksana and her children to a tiny room that the family would share for the next month.

During that time, Oksana and her children endured at least four more interrogations. Every week an official from a government agency, including an agent from the FSB, came to grill them with questions about their feelings toward the Russian state and the Ukrainian military, trying to gauge where their allegiances lay. One official told her she must enroll her children in a Russian school, which she did reluctantly and only because she felt they needed some semblance of normalcy after many chaotic weeks.

But at school, Oksana said, her oldest daughter was teased by students for being a refugee and two teachers behaved in a "hostile" manner toward her for being Ukrainian. The curriculum included revisionist history lessons about how Ukraine wasn't a real country but something that was created by Russia, and thus something that could – and should – be taken away.

One day, a group of armed Russian soldiers arrived with a television crew from a state-run propaganda network in tow and pulled Oksana's daughter out of class. They took her and a few other Ukrainians into an office where they pressed them to discuss on camera how the Russian army had saved them.

"My daughter was just hysterical afterward," Oksana said. "She didn't want to be asked those questions and she didn't want to be on camera. Then they used these pictures in their propaganda. After that, after this incident, I just realized that there would be no life here."

On 18 April she told her children to pack their bags. Using a special permission slip she had been given to allow her to find work in the city, she and her children left the housing unit, saying they were going to visit distant relatives nearby.

On 20 April they arrived in Ivangorod and attempted to cross into Narva, following in Daria's tracks. But Russian border guards turned them away because Oksana didn't have her passport. A second attempt the following day also failed. After seeking advice from an acquaintance, they managed to find another way – but it would take four days, two trains, and a taxi to get them safely into Latvia.

By the time we spoke, they were safe. And yet, they longed for Mariupol.

"Home is home," Oksana explained. But recalling the Russian bombing of Mariupol, she sighed. "But what's left of it?"

Over the next several months, Russia would level what was left of Mariupol, including the remains of the Drama Theater. To everyone, it looked like Putin was destroying the city to cover up his crimes.

Both Oksana and Daria were clear about what they believe Russia's goal was in invading Ukraine: "They simply want to get rid of Ukraine and its people," Oksana said. "Genocide."

More than a million Ukrainians in the areas under the control of Russia's invasion forces would be rounded up and sent to camps, where they were separated from their families, stripped of their personal documents and sometimes their clothes, searched and interrogated by troops and security service agents. They were pressured to incriminate their loved ones and smear the Ukrainian military. They were trafficked across the border to guarded compounds in Russia hundreds or sometimes thousands of miles away from their homes. The Ukrainians didn't want to be taken to Russia. But they weren't given a choice. They were threatened with violence if they refused.

I managed to get a hold of documents that had been obtained by Ukraine's intelligence services, which showed that Russia had plans in place for "filtration camps" and resettlement areas weeks before its invasion. One document showed that the deadline for bringing temporary holding centers across Russia to "100% readiness" was 21 February, three days before Putin sent his troops into Ukraine. Another document dated five days later, on 26 February, showed that 36 locations across Russian territory had been prepared to hold at least 33,146 Ukrainians in 377 temporary shelters. The documents detailed shelters located in five of Russia's eight federal districts, including the North Caucasus, Siberia, and the Far East. A handful were as far away as 4,500 miles from Mariupol. Some were even above the Arctic Circle.

By spring, Ukrainian officials as well as President Biden were calling Russia's actions in Ukraine and its filtration camps part of a campaign of genocide.

"It's become clearer and clearer that Putin is just trying to wipe out the idea of being Ukrainian," Biden said. "The evidence is mounting."

44

Summertime in the City

Kyiv, summer 2022

Summer in Kyiv was surreal. After the failed Russian siege of Kyiv, more than a million Ukrainians who had fled had returned to the capital, and so did a semblance of life before the invasion. The central streets were once again clogged with traffic, causing Uber and Uklon (the Ukrainian version of the former) drivers to launch into tirades, especially over the people zipping through on green electric Bolt scooters. Joggers populated the parks and pedestrian bridge over the Dnipro river to Trukhanov Island. Buskers were back on the city's squares, playing renditions of Western pop hits on accordions and violins. Restaurants and shops took down their boarded-up windows and reopened their doors.

There was still a military curfew in place, which meant everyone needed to be home before 11 p.m. But Kyiv's popular Reitarska and Yaroslaviv Val street, and the hipster Podil neighborhood, hummed with activity. The Honey cafe, beloved for their pastries, produced a chocolate tank-trap dessert. Closer, a famed nightclub, shifted hours earlier so that the capital's youngsters could dance their anxiety away to DJs spinning the latest techno jams and still get home in time. We could dine out again on carpaccio and racks of lamb, sushi, and pizza. My favorite cocktail bars, Parovoz and Podil East India Company, opened along with a dozen others, and bartenders poured extra strong drinks.

The tank traps and concrete slabs that blocked the Maidan and marked checkpoints on main streets had been shoved onto sidewalks. And the air-raid sirens still screamed every once in a while. But the atmosphere of the city no longer felt like one of war. Most people didn't scramble to bomb shelters anymore when their iPhone screens lit up with text warnings from the Kyiv authorities. They barely glanced and stayed put at their outdoor tables, sipping cappuccinos and basking in the sun.

This was another form of Ukrainian defiance. They weren't going to live in fear and allow Russia the satisfaction of dictating their lives. Some people pondered whether it was irresponsible or disrespectful to behave this way or to party while soldiers were still fighting and dying on the eastern and southern fronts. But when I spoke to my friends in the army about it, most weren't angry at all.

"This is what we are fighting for," said Ivan, the soldier I met in Avdiivka, over a WhatsApp call. "If we cannot live, they win."

45

The Battle of the Donbas

Donetsk and southern Kharkiv Oblast, summer 2022

With the full force of Russia's military bearing down on the Donbas, I wanted to get to my old stomping grounds to see how the Ukrainians were faring. I hadn't been back since 24 February, the morning of the invasion, when Russian missiles crashed into the Kramatorsk airfield. So in mid-May I picked up the veteran Ukrainian photographer Anatoliy Stepanov and hit the road to report a series of stories for POLITICO. Like me, Anatoliy had covered Russia's war from day one. Between the two of us, there was no place we didn't know or couldn't easily find or get to in the Donbas. Both of us also had great military contacts. On our way, we rung up the 93rd Mechanized Brigade to say we wanted to stop by to say hello and see them at work.

"Come on by," said Iryna Rybakova, a press officer with the brigade. "The boys are waiting."

Ten hours later, we entered Donetsk Oblast. I was behind the wheel and Anatoliy was in the passenger seat, camera in hand and scanning the sky. He was hoping to capture some jets zooming overhead. Along the rough, serpentine roads of the Donbas, there were dozens of convoys hauling in weapons. We saw infantry-fighting vehicles and battle tanks, Soviet-era multiple-launch rocket systems, including Grad, Smerch, and Uragan, as well as Tochka-U short-range ballistic missile systems and an S-300 long-range surface-to-air missile system. Hundreds of soldiers were being transported in buses and military trucks to the front. Dozens of pontoon bridges for river crossings were carried in on large flat-bed trucks. There were vehicles heading in the other direction. Some carried Russian tanks, identifiable by the Zs scrawled on their sides, which the Ukrainians refurbished and then redeployed to be used against their previous operators. Others, marked with crosses and the code *Gruz* 200, were transporting the bodies of Ukrainian troops killed in action.

Anatoliy had just set his camera down to drink his coffee when two Ukrainian SU-25 ground-attack jets flew by.

"Son of a bitch!" he shouted, realizing he'd missed his shot. I laughed and he scolded me. "Chris, it's not funny!"

We checked into the MAN Hotel in Druzhkivka, which had served as lodging for truckers before the war but now had become the preferred boarding house for foreign correspondents. Everyone had followed the fighting from Kyiv and Kharkiv to the Donbas and wanted a piece of the action. The demand was so high to embed with Ukrainian troops that the military began imposing temporary days-long bans on visiting the front line. The next morning, Iryna phoned us to say we'd have to wait a day or two before visiting their positions near Barvinkove, a town just south of Izyum that had become a major staging post for them. She'd been inundated with requests, but also the fighting had grown so intense that the military ordered a brief pause on allowing journalists to visit the front line. So Anatoliy and I decided we'd check out Bakhmut first.

Just two days before, reports showed that an airstrike had destroyed the Horlivka Institute for Foreign Languages and the tallest apartment building in the city, which were situated two blocks north of my old apartment on Sibertseva Street. Another apartment building at the end of my street had also been hit, and a large section of it had caved in. It made me sick to my stomach to think about the lives destroyed there and what sort of shape I'd find my city in when I arrived.

On the way in, we passed through the town of Chasiv Yar, my old swimming hole, so that we could enter Bakhmut on the road where I used to ride my bike. I'd always loved the view of the city skyline as I swooped around a sharp turn near the village of Khromove and plunged into the valley.

Atop the ridge at that turn now we found a fresh Ukrainian checkpoint had been erected. Army soldiers, police, and Territorial Defense Force troops were digging new trenches. These were to be potential fallback positions if they needed to abandon Bakhmut and retreat to higher ground. From that vantage point, I could see black smoke from artillery attacks on eastern Bakhmut across the horizon.

Volodymyr Yelets, a towering 50-year-old volunteer fighter from the city of Toretsk a bit farther south, looked on with concern as he walked me through the new trench system. A human-rights activist before the war, he carried a Kalashnikov rifle with stickers of green marijuana leaves and smoked heavily from the pack of cigarettes he kept in his shirt pocket. I asked if they might be special ones. As much as he said he'd like to light one of those types up, he couldn't right now.

"We need to be vigilant at all times," he said.

By his side was his recently adopted large German Shepherd named Taco. A family had left the dog behind and chained to a post in their haste to flee the fighting. Yelets found him and made the dog a member of his unit. Taco was wary of all people except for Yelets, which made him a good guard dog, he said.

As we spoke, a mortar duel erupted in the distance and smoke billowed from the strikes. But it was far enough away that we didn't need to take cover.

"They're getting closer," Yelets said, adding that Bakhmut had been hit by three missiles just an hour earlier. "Once they're close enough to use artillery, the city is screwed."

With Yelets was another volunteer named Vitaly Koshel. He was 48 but with his boyish looks he didn't look a day over 40. I introduced myself in Russian and he noticed I spoke with a slight accent.

"I'm American," I said.

"Where from?" he asked.

"New York," I said.

"I'm also from New York," he told me. "Not the Big Apple, but the Little Apple."

He meant the Donetsk Oblast town a little farther south.

"I've been there many times. I was there in January," I said. "It's a nice place."

"Well, it was better before the war," he said.

Koshel had joined the 109th Separate Territorial Defense Brigade in March as a rifleman and was dispatched to Bakhmut almost immediately. It had been relatively quiet here when he arrived. Now things were heating up. I asked why he had signed up to fight.

"I don't want to live under the Russians," he told me.

Yelets then walked over and took my phone to take a photograph of us. "Two guys from New York!" he said. "Say tits!"

We stood in the trench and posed. Koshel made me promise that "after our victory" we would meet back up in one New York or the other.

Three months later, I got a message from Yelets. "Vitaly's dead," he wrote. "The terrorists killed him."

Ukraine's military said in a short obituary for Koshel that his brigade "fought its first battle on 31 July. That day, the unit eliminated about 25 enemies. Ten days later, Vitaly fought his last battle." It said that he had been killed on 10 August, "while performing a combat mission near Bakhmut."

"He was fond of fishing, grew grapes and dreamed of breeding new varieties," the obit said, adding that he had left behind a wife and a daughter.

I wasn't prepared to see Bakhmut in the shape it was in when we arrived. Despite being on the edge of the front line for eight years, it had survived without seeing heavy fighting like the cities around it had. Now, though, Bakhmut was being hit harder than most of them.

We turned to the right as we entered the upper district of the city that residents liked to call the *noviy rynok*, or new market, because it was the newer half of the city built up after the Second World War. I wanted to see the MiG monument that Nikolai had first shown me 12 years earlier and if it was still standing. It was. *Phew*. But there were buildings nearby that had been badly damaged by shelling. A factory across the road had partly collapsed and its windows were shattered. Homes on the road toward the center were also damaged. I recognized a cottage where I had spent an evening hanging out with an Afghan War veteran named Andriy. He'd invited me and my friend Andrew who was visiting from Portland over to drink vodka and hang in his *banya*, a steam room with a wood stove. We went through the whole Ukrainian ritual of beating each other's naked bodies with *veniki*, bundles of leafy birch branches, and then dashing outside in the cold to roll around in the snow.

When we reached Vasylya Pershyna Street, the damage to the Horlivka Institute for Foreign Languages building came into view and Anatoliy and I both gasped. The explosion had ripped several upper floors clean off and concrete slabs dangled from rebar like broken teeth. Bricks and twisted metal and other debris were strewn in the street. Power lines were down. Glass was blown out everywhere. In the back courtyard was a 15-foot-deep crater left by the missile. The institute had been relocated from the neighboring city of Horlivka after Russian forces occupied it in 2014. Luckily, faculty and students weren't present when the building was hit. Inside there were remnants of military clothing and MREs. The Ukrainian military had apparently been using its lower floor and basement as a bunkhouse. That must have been why the Russians targeted it.

But the strike also badly damaged an adjacent apartment building, the one I'd always look at from my balcony window. It had these interesting glass corners and I wondered who might live in these penthouse-type rooms. While scanning the debris, I found 55-year-old Yelena, her white hair blowing in the breeze, searching for her potted plant, a little green succulent. Her apartment was among dozens that were destroyed. Yelena was now homeless, along with 38 other residents. Now they all lived in the damaged building's basement.

She led me down to see. It was tight quarters with no ventilation and low ceilings. Mattresses and cots were placed side by side, covered in blankets adorned with floral and animal patterns. There was no toilet; the residents had to go outside to relieve themselves.

"We can be killed just going to take a piss!" grumbled a man named Vitaly, gesturing outside as explosions rumbled in the distance.

Many complained that local authorities had not come to check on their well-being or offer any assistance. They had canned food and preservatives stacked on one side of the room, enough for the next few days. But they were short on water.

Volunteers had started evacuating people from Bakhmut and surrounding towns and villages. Most were taken by car, bus, or ambulance to Pokrovsk, 80 miles to the west, where they boarded an evacuation train carrying them west, away from the fighting. But these people didn't want to leave their home. Many couldn't afford to. Some said they had nowhere to go. A few admitted they were waiting for Russian troops to "liberate" the city.

"Shh," a woman shushed a man echoing Russian propaganda that Kyiv was filled with Nazis. People like him, with that view, certainly didn't make up the majority here or anywhere in Ukraine. But there were some. Ukrainians called them *zhduny* – "the waiting ones" – as in, waiting for the Russians.

A decade ago, all these people had been my neighbors, and some of them still remembered me. "The American, yeah. You taught at School No 11 and in Krasne? You lived right there?" one woman recalled, gesturing to the end of the block. We reminisced about the past – Remember the sinkhole in the street and how deep it was? Remember when the street was being repaved and the asphalt was still wet, but that car drove down it and got stuck? – and forgot for a few minutes about the hell that we were currently in.

After an hour or so, Anatoliy and I made our way a few blocks north to meet Serhiy Haidai, the head of the Luhansk regional military government. We sat on the central park bench near the stadium where Ukraine's Olympians once trained. It was also right beside a children's playground where I had sat countless times before with Igor and other friends, as we sipped coffee or beers in the summer and watched their kids play. Now the situation couldn't have been more different. The stadium had been hit by an airstrike and was mostly destroyed. And instead of the sounds of happy children playing, there were earth-shaking booms from incoming and outgoing mortars and Grad missiles.

Haidai was dressed in full combat gear and had armed guards that followed his every move. I also wore my helmet and vest. I told Haidai the short version of how I'd come to live in Bakhmut and how surreal and heartbreaking it was to be meeting him here like this.

"So you know what it's like to see your home destroyed," he said, sighing.

"Yes, I think I do," I said.

Haidai was tired and in a glum mood. Moscow's forces had entered his home town of Severodonetsk days before, taken up positions inside hotels and residential blocks, and were now fighting with Ukrainian forces in the city's streets.

"They are destroying Severodonetsk, they are shelling it all the time with everything they have. They are destroying everything and then moving through the ruins," Haidai said. "They are carpet-bombing us. The cities they attack are simply being erased from the face of the earth."

He said Russian shelling in Severodonetsk had killed some 1,500 residents and wiped out more than 60 per cent of the city in just a few weeks.

Within days of our conversation, Severodonetsk would be almost completely surrounded. The Ukrainians would be forced to retreat. And the city would fall under Russian control.

The Russians were able to make the type of gains on the ground here that they failed to achieve around Kyiv, albeit at a slower pace than they preferred, because of the sheer amount of resources they had dedicated to the battle and the lack of sufficient firepower on the Ukrainians' side.

President Zelensky said that Russian troops outnumbered Ukrainian soldiers in the Donbas seven to one, and as many as 100 Ukrainian troops were being killed in action daily.

"The situation in Donbas is very difficult. The occupiers are trying to achieve by day 100 of the war the goals they hoped to achieve in the first days after February 24," he said in one of his regular night-time addresses. "So they've concentrated maximum artillery, maximum reserves in the Donbas. There are missile strikes and aircraft attacks – everything."

Before we left Bakhmut, I drove around to all the places I used to spend my time. New York Street Pizza. The sushi restaurant. The amusement park. The Paradise Corner club and cafe. City Hall. They were all in one piece but closed. The central market had taken a couple of hits but wasn't destroyed. My apartment on Sibertseva Street was still standing but appeared mostly empty. A man I didn't recognize was sitting on the bench where the babushkas used to gossip and drinking from a bottle. I asked him if he lived in the building and he said he did. Then I asked if he knew Lyudmila and Oleksandr and any of the other neighbors.

"They're all gone," he told me.

Feelings of disappointment for having missed them and relief that they had already made it out safely washed over me. I looked up at the balcony where I'd spent so many mornings drinking coffee and quiet nights sipping cold beers and looking out over the city.

On Peace Avenue, Igor and Ira's apartment above the gold shop where I'd lived with them for the last six months of my time in Bakhmut was intact on the street side but boarded up. The windows had Xs taped to them. On the backside, however, the apartment had sustained some artillery damage.

The library and School No. 11 across the street had both suffered indirect hits. Their facades were scarred and some of the window frames bent out of shape. But they were standing.

Elsewhere the story was similar. The city center was damaged but not destroyed. The story was different on the east side of the Bakhmutka river, however. That's where much of the fighting was happening. Russian positions were just over the hill and inching closer every day. The winery was still under Ukrainian control, but I wondered how long it would remain so.

Anatoliy and I stopped at my favorite shawarma stand. I couldn't believe it was still open. There were five or six Ukrainian soldiers waiting for their orders when we arrived. Anatoliy and I got the last wraps of the day and ate them on a bench at the adjacent bus stop, still dressed in our protective gear. The sun was hot and I noticed I'd been sweating profusely under my vest. Looking across the street I saw the apartment of someone I once knew and noted the damage to it. The shooting started up again as we ate.

We left via the highway that went past Ivanivske, formerly Krasne, so I decided to drive by the school where I'd taught with Nikolai and to ask if anyone I knew was still around. It was locked up. There were only soldiers present and milling around. Nobody else was on the street. I tried calling Nikolai's number, but a message said it was disconnected. I wondered whether he'd left and where he'd gone. I called Olga Yevgenyevna, but she didn't answer. I made a note to track them later. It was clear the village had emptied out.

Mark Holtsyev knew the window to rescue desperate residents of Lyman before Russian forces razed the town was closing fast. The tall, amateur equestrian turned volunteer paramedic jumped in his ambulance and hurtled down the road, past rocket craters and plumes of black smoke rising from the surrounding fields.

Anatoliy and I had met Holtsyev on the side of the road outside Slovyansk. We pulled over when we saw him smoking beside his ambulance and asked if we could ride with him to Lyman, now one of the hottest spots on the front line. Holtsyev was one of the countless volunteers who had been risking their lives day in and day out, zipping down some of the most treacherous roads to save every life that could be saved. Each dash into a beleaguered town was a serious gamble.

"We managed to rescue 300 people yesterday, 500 the day before. But we've only taken 100 today because the fighting is very intense," an exasperated Holtsyev told me between evacuation runs. "It's terrible. People are afraid to even move."

"Do you really want to go?" he asked us.

"I do," I told him.

"*Davai*," he said. Let's go.

We were off.

The ambulance bounced violently as we sped down the road. More than once I thought we might tip over as it skidded around sharp curves. Artillery exploded on each side of us, sending geyser-like fountains of black dirt into the air.

We pulled over at a shop in Raihorodok, a small town on the outskirts of Lyman, where soldiers and police were gathered. Holtsyev got out and they huddled over coffee and cigarettes to discuss their route and confirm the addresses of people they needed to find. Artillery shells were exploding all around and drawing closer every minute. The soldiers and police said the fighting up the road was dangerous in and around Lyman, and that they were ready to call off the day's rescue operation. But Holtsyev managed to convince the group to make at least one more run. They waited for the next lull in the artillery fire, then Holtsyev and the others jumped back in their cars and raced five miles east toward the city. Anatoliy and I stayed behind so that they would have more space for people who wanted out.

They arrived back in Raihorodok 40 minutes later with a couple of dozen people. They would be the last evacuees from the day.

Several people I spoke to told me they had been living under constant, heavy shelling and mostly in their garden cellars, sleeping beside their potatoes and onions.

Lyman had been a quiet town surrounded by a forested nature reserve and bone-white chalk mountains, and was once home to 20,000 residents – almost half of whom were ethnic Russians, according to local data – until people began spilling out as Russian forces pressed down on the town. It had largely avoided hostilities, save for some street fighting with automatic rifles and grenade launchers in 2014. But now it was a key target of Russia's brutal new military campaign in the Donbas, and another place of demolished homes and shattered lives.

"We can never go back. There is nothing left there for us," cried a woman brought to the Raihorodok staging area carrying several bags of clothing and possessions, her two young children in tow. "They are bombing everything. Our city is dying."

Her husband interjected: "No, the city is already dead."

The family's home had been partially destroyed in mid-May. They spent nearly two weeks living in a neighbor's basement with little food and water, no toilet, electricity, and gas, until Holtsyev and the other rescuers came to pick them up. Everything they had to begin their new lives fit into four duffel bags. I asked about what they would do next and where they would go. The husband tried to speak but no words came out of his mouth. He just shook his head and shrugged.

Ukrainian authorities began urging civilians to leave the Donbas in April when Russia announced it was shifting its focus to the east after running into a wall in northern Ukraine. Hundreds of thousands heeded the warning. But not everyone was convinced that the fighting there would intensify or spread into the places where it had. Many stubborn residents refused to leave their houses and their homeland behind. They argued there was nothing waiting for them west of the Donbas, and they didn't trust that the government in Kyiv would help them rebuild their lives. Some felt abandoned by the capital and sensed more affinity with Moscow. One middle-aged woman who had accompanied her elderly neighbor to the evacuation point was catching a ride with rescuers returning to Lyman. She said she wouldn't flee the town no matter what – her husband was buried in the cemetery there. Others were too fragile to leave under their own power. Many more lacked the means, whether money or a vehicle, to flee.

Among those brought out by Holtsyev was 92-year-old Nina Tykhomirova, with lines drawn into her face like a well-used map. In nearly a century of life, she had endured a lot, including the Second World War. Two large men carried her in a blanket from a van to Holtsyev's ambulance.

Her bright blue eyes and floral-patterned neck scarf betrayed the horrors she said she had witnessed: artillery shells crashing into her neighborhood, homes on fire, people cowering in fear in their vegetable cellars, bodies in the streets.

She was evacuated with nothing but a couple of sweaters wrapped around her fragile frame and a plastic bag with her personal documents that she gripped tightly in her left hand.

"Where am I going?" she asked, trembling.

"Away from here, grandma. You will be safe," Holtsyev said.

Anatoliy and I jumped in with her and Holtsyev shut the ambulance doors. We set off west. I held Nina's hand as we rushed her to safety.

Days later, on 27 May, Russian forces declared that Lyman had been captured. The Ukrainians blew up a bridge between the town and Raihorodok, so that the enemy wouldn't be able to advance easily any farther.

The difference between life and death here was now measured in steps, minutes, and millimeters. In the village of Mykolaivka, opposite Raihorodok and in the shadow of the Slovianska thermal power plant, Nina Strashko found herself on the better side of that grim calculation.

When I found her, she was surveying the remnants of her life. Moments earlier, an artillery attack had destroyed her home. The 83-year-old who walked with a cane had been enjoying a sunny May afternoon on her garden bench when a mortar shell crashed into her cottage just 20 feet from her. Shrapnel sprayed everywhere, ripping apart a child's swing in her neighbor's yard and lashing the branches of the tree hanging over her. Yet somehow the razor-sharp pieces of Russian metal missed her completely. Looking at where they hit, I noticed the marks made almost a perfect horseshoe around her.

Luck or God or maybe both had saved her from death, said her son Ihor as we surveyed the damage together.

"My home is gone. Everything is gone," Nina cried, laying her head on the shoulder of her granddaughter. The family was moving her to their house down the street – still in the line of Russian fire. The family said they couldn't afford to leave and had no one elsewhere to ask for help.

And yet, they were the lucky ones. Four of Nina's neighbors were much less fortunate. Two of them were killed and two more were badly injured by another shell in the same attack.

A few days later, Iryna called us to say we could meet and go together to the front line near Izyum, a city of about 40,000 people that straddles the Siverskyi Donets river in southern Kharkiv Oblast. A critical transportation node, it had been bombed by the Russians throughout March and captured on 1 April. We set off early in the morning for Barvinkove, where we met her. We also found waiting there my friend Roland Oliphant from the *Daily Telegraph* with veteran war photographer Julian Simmonds. Iryna said there were so many requests to visit the 93rd Mechanized Brigade that they couldn't accommodate everyone, so we had to team up. That was fine with all of us. So we piled into a dusty jeep and headed to the front.

On the road, evidence of Russia's destructive reach was everywhere. Homes had been reduced to ruins. Thousands of artillery impact craters dotted the landscape. The tail fins of rockets jutted out from fields of golden sorghum and green barley, like menacing signposts warning of danger ahead. Plumes of black smoke, evidence of active fighting, rose in every direction. We were half a mile from our destination when a call came in from the commander there telling us to hold up. They were under heavy fire. We stopped on the roadside to wait and could hear the explosions up ahead. After thirty minutes or so, Iryna said we'd have to pull back but that she'd phone another commander to take us to a position three miles east.

Andriy Nikolaychuk, deputy commander of the 93rd Mechanized Brigade, said he'd show us the position of his troops. So we stopped by his base and picked him up.

When we finally arrived at the second front-line positions, we found ourselves just ten miles south of the strategic city of Izyum and the target of a large salvo of Russian rockets. They had seen our vehicle kicking up dust on the road and launched an attack. Rockets came crashing down as the soldiers ushered us into a farmhouse cellar for cover. Underground, the dirt-floored room was lined with shelves of pickled vegetables and sprouting potatoes, some of the last vestiges of the former residents.

Oleksiy, a 38-year-old artilleryman from Donetsk, asked how I felt.

"Fine," I said. "This isn't my first time under shelling."

"Then you know," he said, "we're not even safe here in the cellar. They've destroyed our other ones. Our whole position is being subjected to massive artillery attacks every day."

As we waited out the attack, he told me the unit was in charge of several 120mm mortar systems. The enemy was just a mile or so in front of us and bearing down, but had struggled in recent days to advance farther, hence the unrelenting artillery barrages. The Ukrainians were holding them off.

When they weren't fighting, the soldiers spent much of their time in the cellar, hunkering down and waiting for a break in the attacks to respond with their own firepower. While they waited, they drank sugary coffee, cracked crude jokes about their Russian enemies, and played video games on their phones to pass the time. A Starlink system dug into the garden up above and connected to a gas-powered generator provided their link-up and only connection to the outside world.

They also traded stories about close calls they'd had in past rocket attacks. Stas, a young soldier who quipped that the rocket attack was a "welcome message" to me from the Russians, played a video on his phone of a close call he'd had a week ago when Uragan missiles exploded in the garden a few yards away from where we were.

Above ground 20 minutes later, Volodymyr, a 58-year-old soldier from Dnipro, gestured to the remnants of a summer kitchen, a chicken coop and an adjacent cellar that were destroyed days before in a hail of exploding shells.

Nikolaychuk said the barrages were a sign of the Russians' frustration. After pushing through Izyum weeks earlier, their advance had slowed to a crawl.

"We fell back three times since the battle began, but for the past two weeks, the front has been mostly static," he said. Then he corrected himself. "Maybe it was two weeks. Maybe one?"

They all had trouble keeping track of time. The running joke among them and almost every other soldier I met was that 24 February had never ended, and we were all now living in a Groundhog Day-like situation. Oleh, a programmer from western Ukraine who joined the army hours after Putin launched his invasion, professed not to know the date, the day of the week, nor even how old he was.

A little while later, we climbed back into the jeep and set off for another location. Iryna said a group of artillerymen were about to get to work nearby. On our way, we returned Nikolaychuk to his base. There, we all thanked him, shook hands, and parted ways.

On 19 September, Anatoliy texted me to say that Iryna had called him to let us know that Nikolaychuk had been killed the day before. I had two photographs of him. One I had taken while we were in the garden cellar waiting for the artillery attack to stop. He's sitting on a soldier's bunk and exchanging texts with his wife, who was looking after their three children. His rifle is resting on the bunk beside him. It's covered with a blue duvet decorated with gold stars and white kittens. The second photograph I snapped later over my shoulder as we darted through a network of gardens while dodging Russian sniper fire. In it, he's grinning and flashing a peace sign as he passes the tail end of an Uragan rocket jutting from the ground.

The Ukrainian officer's urgent and profanity-laced plea crackled over the radio: "We need artillery support!" His infantry troops were under attack on the front line south of the city of Izyum and they needed help. Could the mechanized troops hit the enemy?

Commander "Topaz," hiding in a cluster of trees a little more than two miles back, responded in the affirmative and shouted to platoon leader "Horizon" to ready the howitzers.

Moments later, crews scrambled among the dense brush onto two self-propelled Ukrainian 2S1 Gvozdikas, or Carnations, threw off the tree branches used to camouflage them, and loaded in 122mm shells. Using a touchscreen device, Horizon checked the coordinates of their Russian targets obtained from satellite images and drone footage, kneeled, and then yelled the order: "Fire!"

The muzzles jutting from turrets poking out of the tree line each belched out a fiery round as clouds of smoke dissipated into the air. Over the next few minutes, the guns fired six more times. There was an uneasy silence between each shot during which I could hear only the wind rustling the grass before the roar of explosions rocked the Russian infantry and armored vehicles in the distance.

"Wasted," Horizon declared, rising triumphantly from the hilltop.

His artillerymen rushed to cover the Soviet-era weapons with tree branches to hide them from Russian drones that would inevitably come looking for their positions before returning fire. "Hurry!" one of the soldiers shouted.

During an artillery duel two days prior, a drone had loitered overhead – a few minutes later Russian shells were raining down on them.

"A whole battery was working on us," Horizon told me. They hadn't been hit since. "I think maybe we already fucked them up," he added, with a grin and the braggadocio of a soldier with several heavy weapons at his disposal. Even so, with Russia's deep reserves, others would soon take their place.

Iryna had brought us here, in the wide expanse of Ukraine's eastern steppe, where heavy weapons had become the defining feature of this new phase of the war. After Russia's failed blitzkrieg near Kyiv, the fight had transformed into a long-range shooting battle across the vast gullies and rolling hills, snaking rivers, and slag heaps that protruded like miniature mountains in this heavily industrialized area. It had always been tricky to advance quickly here in the east, and soldiers on both sides rarely – if ever – saw each other up close. Now the fight was a cat-and-mouse artillery game.

If the Russians succeeded here, Ukrainian forces would be surrounded. But Kyiv hoped the momentum would soon turn in its favor with the arrival of NATO weaponry and munitions.

"If it gets here quickly we can push them back," Topaz said. "In fact, we can win."

It was around this time that Western arms and ammunition from NATO allies began streaming into Ukraine and making its way to the Donbas. President Biden had finally committed to sending new rocket launchers and precision-guided munitions. EU nations were doing the same.

"Western weapons and equipment are helping us to drive the enemy out of our land," said Valery Zaluzhny, commander-in-chief of the Armed Forces of Ukraine. But he said more was still needed to be able to launch counter-offensives against the Russians. "At the same time, we are in dire need of weapons that will be able to hit the enemy at a great distance," he said. "And this cannot be delayed, because the price of the delay is measured by the lives of people who have protected the world from Russian fascism."

With what they already had, the Ukrainians were starting to see results in a few areas along the front line. American M777 howitzers, British FH70 howitzers, and French CAESAR self-propelled howitzers, along with NATO-standard artillery shells, were used by Ukraine's military with great success. "The Russian occupiers are receiving a rebuff they did not expect," defense minister Oleksiy Reznikov announced.

At a roadside shop one hot afternoon, I ran into Anatoliy, commander of a Ukrainian artillery unit that was in possession of two of the 108 M777s that Washington had sent to Ukraine. He was eating a vanilla ice-cream cone in the shade of a truck while his soldiers stocked up on snacks and enjoyed their first rest in days. I asked how he and his men liked their American weapons.

"They work beautifully. They have the precision of a sniper rifle while firing a 155mm shell," he told me, listing three instances when he said the weapon allowed his artillerymen to strike the Russians. "Their range is much greater than our own weapons and we can hit their positions, supply lines, and munitions depots farther away."

The M777 results of their work could be seen weeks earlier in the town of Bilohorivka. There, as Russian forces attempted to cross the Seversky Donets river, the Ukrainians hit them with a devastating artillery barrage that included their own Soviet-era artillery systems and the American howitzers. More than 400 Russian troops and 70 tanks and armored vehicles are believed to have been lost in the attack, according to Serhiy Haidai, head of the Luhansk regional military government.

Indeed, the new weapons were having an effect. Anatoliy said the NATO weapons would allow Ukrainian forces to pivot from defense to offense as they moved to recapture lost ground in the coming months.

"Every day we are getting closer to when our army will surpass the occupiers technologically and by firepower," President Zelensky said in another of his night-time addresses. "Ukraine will take back everything that belongs to it . . . And it's just a matter of time. Every day at this same time, the time until liberation grows shorter."

Haidai, ever the realist, had cautioned it was too soon for that type of talk.

"We need at least a couple more months to prepare our troops, to train them to properly handle Western weapons," he said. "Then we will be able, in principle, to go on the offensive, to capture a village here and there, put a battalion there."

On our way back to Kyiv, we stopped in the city of Pokrovsk. It had become an evacuation point for residents of the embattled towns of the Donbas to catch a train that would take them to Dnipro, and beyond. Charter buses deposited people from Bakhmut, Toretsk, Lyman, New York, Slovyansk, and Kramatorsk. Volunteers from various international and Ukrainian organizations transferred the elderly and infirm in white vans. A group of women in their 70s and 80s were so fragile that they were laid in the back of a van on a pile of blankets and wrapped up. Station workers positioned them onto stretchers and then moved them onto the train cars with a mechanical lift.

I boarded the train to speak with those on board. It was overflowing with people in the most vulnerable state. Kostyantyn, Yulia, and their two children, including two-week-old Artem, were among them. Because the war had paused most local-government services, Yulia said she hadn't even been able to secure a birth certificate for Artem yet. She said Toretsk, the front-line town from which they fled, had been without water for nearly three months and the electricity had been knocked out by shelling – which made giving birth especially difficult.

"We were sitting in our house and everything would just shake," Yulia said. "I would wrap the baby in a blanket and run to the basement every time the shelling started."

Yulia said that a shell had exploded on their doorstep, spraying shrapnel into their home the day before. And that was the final straw. They left with just a few bags and a stroller for their toddler. They had less than $100 between the family and no food.

"We will go to Dnipro," Kostyantyn told me, Ukraine's fourth-largest city that had become a hub for humanitarian aid. "From there, we don't know."

"Could you help us in some way?" Yulia asked. As a journalist, situations like this can be tricky to navigate. Don't we help by exposing these stories? Is that enough? Should we do more? Can't I do more? I gave them a pile of granola bars and some bananas that I had in my pack, then I passed some cash I had in my jacket pocket to them for baby formula and taxi fare. I wanted to do more.

46

"The Terrorists are Destroying Everything"

Bakhmut, August 2022

Mayor Oleksiy Reva wasn't answering his phone, so I sent him a text. Bakhmut was being heavily shelled by Russian troops and mercenaries, he wrote back. He was taking shelter. The once-quiet city where we first met 12 years ago was now subject to the loudest bombing on the front line. I wondered what would be destroyed next. New York Street Pizza, where I spent countless evenings with friends? The *Pobeda* movie theater, where I hosted a monthly American film night? The central market? My school?

While I waited for Mayor Reva to get back to me, I took a walk down my old street in the city, wearing a bulletproof helmet and vest with a medical kit. It was hot and sunny and I sweated profusely under my gear. I could hear the *tat-tat-tat* of assault-rifle fire several hundred meters ahead of me. Moments later, a plane roared overhead and a Russian air-strike hit. The explosion was so close and so loud that my ears rang and the ground shook under my feet. I darted for cover in the basement of the apartment building I'd visited before and found many of the same 38 people cowering in fear. They had been living down here now for nearly four months.

By August, the situation had changed dramatically in the Donbas. That is to say, the fighting had got much worse and Russian troops were razing entire towns and villages to the ground. Mariinka was gone. Putin's troops had erased it from the face of the earth. Videos shared online by Ukrainian and Russian forces showed trees shattered into splinters, buildings pulverized and reduced to dust. Tanks were trundling over the wreckage and opening fire on anything and everything. Roads weren't even visible any longer. Several other places looked similarly devastated and many more faced the same tragic fate.

The Russians were prioritizing Bakhmut as their main offensive effort and were throwing everything at the fight. While the city was not necessarily strategic in and of itself, if the Russians broke through and captured it, this would deal a serious psychological blow to Ukraine and could be a bridgehead from which Putin's forces would be able to launch new attacks on the remaining Ukrainian-controlled areas of the Donbas and bring them a step closer to Kostyantynivka, Kramatorsk, and Slovyansk.

After 20 minutes, I emerged from the basement and moved toward the central squares. There were Czech hedgehog traps and triangular-shaped concrete blocks known as dragons' teeth positioned at key intersections, ready to be dragged out in case of approaching Russian tanks. There were very few people on the streets. I saw a man riding a bicycle with jugs of water strapped to a rack on the back and a woman dragging a cart filled with humanitarian aid she had picked up from a distribution center. Somewhat surprisingly, the meat and cheese shop attached to the Palace of Culture was still open. I walked in to find a woman behind the counter. I stared at her for what felt like forever and she must have thought I was behaving strangely because she snapped at me: "What do you want?" She'd of course seen the PRESS badge stuck to my vest. I just wanted to ask a few questions, I said.

"I don't have anything to say," she told me.

"Can I buy something then?" I asked.

She sold me some slices of sausage and I let her keep the change.

Across the street, I could see the Silpo supermarket and central market behind it had been badly damaged. A gigantic missile crater was smack in the middle of the entrance to the market. I thought about Volodya, my money-exchange guy who Nikolai had introduced me to. Volodya and I had swapped cash years earlier in the very spot where this attack occurred. Behind the market, the footbridge that connected the eastern and western districts of Bakhmut had been blown up by Ukrainian forces to prevent the Russians from accessing the city center. I took several photographs of the area from the same perspectives I had taken snapshots when I lived there. I even printed out several of my old photos and brought them with me to be sure I had the angles and distances just right. I wanted to be able to document how the city had been changed.

Before leaving, I stopped by the hospital a few blocks down the street from the apartment I lived in with Igor and Ira. This was the same hospital I'd visited many times before, including in 2015, when it was the main medical facility for soldiers in Debaltseve, and I found my former student turned military medic Bohdan there. The soldiers didn't let me onto the grounds at first. But after I spoke to the captain of the military medical unit, I was allowed inside.

The air was filled with the metallic smell of blood and the stench of rotting flesh. A young soldier was splashing soapy water onto a dozen bloodied stretchers leaning up against a fence. A group of soldiers stood nearby smoking and talking. The commander tapped my shoulder and told me to follow him inside.

The hallway was filled with soldiers and civilians bandaged up and lying on the floors. Several were wrapped in silver and gold space blankets. Inside the trauma ward, two soldiers were lying on operating tables. Groups of four or five doctors and nurses surrounded each of them. One was naked and unconscious and I could see that he had suffered severe wounds to his abdomen and extremities. Blood was dripping from the table onto the floor beneath him. The second man was awake and half-dressed and screaming in pain. There were injuries to his back and right thigh, which had been torn apart and looked like minced meat. Two nurses held him down as a doctor worked on him and wrapped the leg wound.

"Make a picture," the commander said. "Show the world what is happening here."

I stepped through the operating door and took four photographs. None of them were very good and didn't capture the horror of what it was like to experience in person.

"Come here," the commander then added, grabbing my arm and pulling me back into the hall. He pointed to a box on the floor. It was filled with khaki military boots.

"See this?"

"Yeah."

"It is all the shoes that our guys won't need anymore because they don't have the legs and feet for them."

I asked how many soldiers were being killed and wounded every day. He said the numbers were between 50 and 100 killed and upwards of 200 injured.

Just then, an ambulance pulled up and a soldier with a bloodied arm was rushed in. I saw that his hand was barely connected to his arm by a thin piece of flesh. He was shrieking and writhing on the stretcher. I felt sick and stepped outside.

When Mayor Reva finally called me back, he had the answer about which building would be the next to come down. "The terrorists are destroying everything," he said.

"I know," I said. "I've seen it myself."

47

Missiles

Kyiv, October 2022

I had just returned from a few weeks off at home in New York and was starting my first week at the *Financial Times* when Russia launched the next phase of its war – aerial attacks. It had begun sending waves of cruise missiles fired from planes, warships, and submarines, and Iranian-supplied Shahed kamikaze drones to strike critical infrastructure, as well as civilian targets.

After devastating and embarrassing battlefield losses in Kharkiv and Kherson, where Ukrainian troops shocked the Russians and surprised the rest of the world by storming through miles of occupied territory and routing the enemy forces before they even realized what was happening, Putin had appointed a new commander to oversee his war effort. General Sergei Surovikin, known by the nickname "General Armageddon" and notorious for his terror campaigns in Syria, appeared to want to repeat them in Ukraine. Formerly head of Russia's air force, he knew what type of havoc an aerial bombardment could wreak on a population.

His first attack struck Ukraine on Monday morning, 10 October. A total of 84 cruise missiles pummeled power stations and crashed into neighborhoods. In Kyiv, one exploded into a children's playground in central Shevchenko Park leaving a giant crater, while another struck the busy intersection of Volodymyrska Street and Shevchenko Boulevard 200 feet away, crushing several vehicles during morning rush hour. At least 11 people were killed.

The second wave arrived the next Monday morning, 17 October. I had just returned to Kyiv the day before and was jet-lagged. I hadn't slept most of the night and had just got to sleep when I heard the first explosions around 6 a.m. There were three in a matter of a few minutes and they were so close they shook my apartment building. After sending a quick note to my editors about the attack, I jumped out of bed, threw on my vest and helmet, and dashed outside to see what had been hit.

There was a plume of black smoke to the west near the train station. It was a five-minute walk from my apartment. When I arrived, police were cordoning off Zhylianska Street where it intersected with Vokzalna Street. The top of an energy company building had been partly destroyed and glass from a skyscraper was littered all around. National Guardsmen on the scene told me that the attack was from Shahed drones.

"Fucking mopeds," one National Guardsman said.

The Ukrainians had come to refer to the drones as mopeds or sometimes lawnmowers because their propellers made a loud buzzing sound as they flew in low and slow.

"Was anyone injured?" I asked.

"No," he said.

I snapped photographs and sent them along with a few paragraphs over email to my editors at the *FT* in London, who had begun writing up a report on the attack.

I had just hit 'Send' when I heard a loud buzzing noise.

"Run!" shouted a police officer.

I sprinted around the corner of a building and took cover behind a stairwell. Crouched down, I heard the police and National Guards open fire with machine guns and assault rifles. The drone was hard to see between the surrounding tall buildings. They would fire short bursts and then wait a couple of seconds before opening fire again. Moments later the drone crashed into the street, shaking the earth and igniting a huge fireball. The drone had missed its target, a power station 100 feet away.

The dust hadn't settled before I heard the terrifying *vroom* of another drone. It was coming in from the same direction. This time I peeked around the corner to watch it and that's when I saw the National Guardsmen and police open fire again. One of them stepped into the middle of the street with his machine gun and unleashed hundreds of bullets into the sky. The drone came in low and then made a sudden dive, crashing into an historic residential building. The blast threw the Guardsman to the ground, but he was fine. The building collapsed instantly, burying its occupants. A young husband and wife were later found in an embrace dead under the debris. She had been pregnant with their first child.

The air raids would continue for months. Sirens wailed across the capital every time Ukraine's military detected a new missile launch or drones in the sky, sending people on the streets running for cover in basements and the city's underground metro stations. Residents dragged their mattresses into hallways or slept in their bathtubs where they thought they'd be safe – or at least safer – from the air strikes. "Remember the rule of two walls," people would tell each other – one wall to take the impact of the missile or drone, the second to absorb the shrapnel from it.

As the air strikes picked up, the power situation across the country grew worse. And that was what the Russians hoped for – to freeze Ukrainians in the dead of winter.

President Zelensky urged his people to conserve electricity, especially between 7 a.m. and 11 p.m., and not to use energy-guzzling home appliances like boilers and electric heaters, as planned power rationing began across the country. Around 50 per cent of Ukraine's power stations had been destroyed. The state energy company Ukrenergo said Russian barrages had caused more damage to the power infrastructure in a period of just ten days than in the first seven months of Moscow's full-blown invasion.

It felt a bit like the first days of the invasion, when everyone was in a state of great anxiety. It wasn't full-on panic, but people began buying up the drinking water from supermarkets and shops, as well as non-perishable foods. I bought several five-gallon jugs of water and enough canned food for a week. But I also had a water filter on my kitchen faucet, so I didn't need to lug jugs up my four flights of stairs. Instead, I filled every receptacle I could find with water. When the power was out and my hot-water heater didn't work, I gathered snow on my balcony in two large pots and heated them on my stove top until it was the right temperature for bathing. Then I stepped into my shower and poured one pot over myself. I washed and then rinsed off with the second pot.

There was also a run on power banks and batteries at electronics stores. I purchased a large EcoFlow power bank system that could keep my lights and appliances – and most importantly my internet – running for a few days. I also managed to buy a solar-powered power bank and three more small power banks. Camping equipment became immediately popular. Gorgany, an outdoor store down the street from my Kyiv apartment, overflowed with people. Sleeping bags, camping stoves, and headlamps flew off the shelves. On the day I visited, the manager told me it was their biggest sales day ever.

Authorities announced rolling blackouts to conserve energy. Everyone had at least two four-hour blocks of time each day without power. Some districts, though, were out of power for days.

The streets of the capital were darker than I'd ever seen them. The authorities kept the street lights off after sundown to conserve energy but also so that Russian planes and drones wouldn't be able to make out potential targets on the ground from overhead.

Despite the dangers, Ukrainians remained defiant. And after a few weeks, people became inured to the wail of sirens and attacks that followed them and just carried on. The country's air force got better and better at shooting drones down, and as Western air defenses arrived in the country, most Russian missiles would be shot out of the sky.

Putin claimed he had ordered the missile strikes in retaliation for Ukraine's attack on 8 October on his illegally built Crimea bridge spanning the Kerch Strait. The attack sent two of the bridge's road spans plunging into the sea and ignited a nearby railway shipment of fuel tanks, halting all traffic on the route which the Russian military had relied on to ship military equipment and supplies into the war zone in southern Ukraine. The attack on the bridge was a deeply personal humiliation for the Russian leader, who had opened the $3 billion, 12-mile transport link by driving a Kamaz truck over it in 2018. But Ukrainian military intelligence said that the strikes had long been planned and were part of Moscow's ultimate goal to destroy the will of Ukrainians and their country.

Again, Russia would fail. The Ukrainians would get through the winter without freezing to death. The power grid would stabilize. And the street lights would switch back on.

Perhaps sensing failure and desperately seeking a victory, Putin would double down on his efforts in the Donbas. And the focal point would be Bakhmut.

48

"Fortress Bakhmut"

Bakhmut, December 2022

I returned to Bakhmut in early December despite pleas from my editors and some family and friends to steer clear of the place. I traveled with my friends and sometime fixers Yevheniy and Valeria and photographer Olga. The plan was just to zip in and out, doing just a day of reporting. I knew from speaking to my soldier contacts fighting in the city that the situation had seriously deteriorated.

"We're losing hundreds of guys a day. Killed and wounded," one soldier told me. "The Russians are already in the east and south of Bakhmut. I would advise you not to come right now."

I couldn't stay away, though. I worried that this might be my last opportunity to see the city, whatever was left of it, before it was captured or completely destroyed by the Russians.

We entered through Chasiv Yar and Khromove, down my favorite hill, like I had done countless times before. At the last checkpoint, a Ukrainian soldier waved for us to stop.

"Who are you?" he asked.

"Journalists," we said.

"Where are you going?"

"Bakhmut."

"Shit, guys, you shouldn't go in there. The place is totally fucked. This road was just shelled a few minutes ago. Are you suicidal?"

"We are meeting soldiers in the city center."

"You are sure?"

"Yes."

"Fine. I'll pray for you. And you should pray for yourselves."

Inside the city, we found a group of soldiers who had just returned from the front line. They looked ragged and after they shared what they had seen over the past week, I understood why.

Rockets and mortar rounds rained down on their positions almost every minute, spraying shrapnel and sending troops diving for cover. Then came the Russian infantry, charging across a no man's land of shredded trees and artillery craters. The Ukrainians popped up and mowed down many of them with machine guns and grenade launchers. Moments later the scenes were repeated – although this time the Russian fighters had to navigate their comrades' bodies. Again, many were cut down by Ukrainian bullets.

"It's like a conveyor belt," Kostyantyn, an exhausted Ukrainian machine-gunner, told me. "For what? A fucking meter of our land. They are just meat to Putin," he added, referring to the Russian soldiers, "and Bakhmut is a meat grinder."

We spoke under the cover of fir trees on what used to be Lenin Square. The statue and the plinth were long gone and now it was just a stone plaza without any remarkable features. Nearby, soldiers were digging trenches in flowerbeds that were once filled with fragrant red roses. I told Kostyantyn that I had seen digging in these same flowerbeds once before – when city officials exhumed the bodies of Nazi soldiers from the Second World War. We both just shook our heads.

The city center, which once bustled with a large outdoor market and cafes, had become a fortress. There were now dozens more anti-tank defenses blocking the main avenues than the last time I was here in August. The only traffic consisted of ambulances racing the wounded to the city hospital, and tanks and other military vehicles trundling along chewed-up roads and through tangles of fallen electric tram lines. The signs of all my former local haunts were dangling from wires. Every building I could see was damaged. Some were destroyed. School No. 11 had been annihilated by missile attacks. The historic buildings on Peace Avenue were also scarred and in the coming weeks would be gutted. The Palace of Culture was a shell of its former self. The roof was gone, and its facade was scarred by shrapnel and stained black from the flames that licked its facade after a rocket attack had sparked a massive fire.

It was a gut-wrenching sight, all of it. Back in August, I was still able to see the city I once called home. But now it was harder to make it out.

Over the course of the morning, there was rarely more than five seconds between artillery explosions. The ground shook and the otherwise clear winter sky was hazy from the smoke. Russian drones buzzed overhead, looking for targets.

The battle for Bakhmut had escalated significantly in recent weeks. And yet the front line around it had barely moved in seven months, with both sides fighting for mere inches of territory. Ukrainian soldiers described the intensity of the recent fighting in and around Bakhmut, particularly the artillery barrages, as greater than anything they had experienced anywhere in Ukraine since the start of Russia's full-scale invasion in February.

"A very fierce confrontation is ongoing there, every meter counts," President Zelensky said in one of his nightly addresses.

During a visit to his troops in Bakhmut, he'd called the fighting around the city the "most difficult area that protects not only the east but our entire state." Indeed, it had become Ukraine's own Battle of Verdun, the 1916 fight of attrition on France's western front that ground on for ten months.

"Hell. Just hell," is how Volodymyr, an officer in the 93rd Mechanized Brigade, described the fighting to me. He was with a group of soldiers taking a short rest before returning to the battle. They were leaning on their armored vehicle beside the ATB supermarket in the city center and smoking. One of the men's hands trembled as he lit his cigarette. His face was caked in grime.

Elite Ukrainian units, such as the 93rd Mechanized Brigade and the 58th Motorized Infantry Brigade, were bearing the brunt of the fighting here. But reinforcements, including Special Forces units, Territorial Defence outfits, and International Legion troops had been brought in from elsewhere to support them.

Russia had done the same, moving troops from the Kharkiv and Kherson Oblasts to Bakhmut. But it was members of the notoriously brutal Wagner Group, founded by close Putin ally Evgeny Prigozhin, who were leading the Russian charge here. Prigozhin had recruited fighters on visits to prison colonies in far-flung Russian regions, promising to cancel their sentences if they survived six months of service. Of course, most wouldn't. The rumor was that his men would send the prisoners in the first wave to be mowed down. When the prisoners refused to fight, it is alleged that veteran Wagnerites executed them. Matched with regular troops, including thousands from an autumn mobilization of more than 300,000 men, Russia was able to throw more bodies into the fight.

Some Ukrainian soldiers likened Russia's strategy in Bakhmut to that in Luhansk province farther east earlier that year, where constant artillery barrages had worn down Ukrainian forces and pulverized buildings, making their defense impossible. Others said there seemed to be neither strategy nor logic to the Russian offensive beyond symbolism.

I could barely believe all of this was happening in my Bakhmut, a place that once seemed like the edge of the world when I first arrived 13 years ago. Now it was the flashpoint of Russia's war and a center of the struggle between democracy and autocracy. It had grown to be of great symbolic importance to both Kyiv and Moscow, as they tried to gain the upper hand over one another. Ukrainians had taken to referring to the city as "Fortress Bakhmut," because it remained symbolically standing, even as shelling had reduced it to rubble. And the phrase "Bakhmut Holds!" had become a battle cry for Ukrainian soldiers as well as in President Zelensky's nightly addresses.

Kostyantyn and the other soldiers said they were confident Bakhmut would "hold" through the winter. But that was of little consolation to the residents cowering in the remnants of their homes. Their nerves were frayed, some wore fear on their faces, recoiling with each explosion. Others, hardened by months of fighting, barely flinched as they wandered the streets in a state of shock.

Vitaliy, a man in his 50s, told me he was no longer afraid of dying. As a series of blasts rocked the central square, he sat still on a bench, sifting through a bag of food handed out at a nearby aid center. He didn't want to go home because it had been struck three times by artillery shells and was missing some of its walls. He blamed Ukrainian forces for the damage, saying they had moved into his neighborhood and thus made it a target by bringing the war to his doorstep.

Kostyantyn, who had fought in Bucha near Kyiv in March where Ukrainian liberators had been greeted as heroes, told me such an attitude was common. The "patriots" had all left the city.

"If they want to go to Russia, I'll take them to the front line and show them the way," he said of critics like Vitaliy and the city's *zhduny* – "the waiting ones" – gesturing to the battlefield.

We made one stop in Ivanivske before we departed. I wanted to visit my former school one last time and a field hospital that had been set up in the basement of a house nearby. But just as we pulled off the main highway, the village was hit by a massive artillery barrage. The shells screamed as they flew toward us and then crashed into several cottages and a farm building. We ducked beside a building and waited for the barrage to end. Minutes passed before there was a lull. We then jumped into our jeep and sped off.

As we pulled out of the village and climbed the hill, I turned back and watched Ivanivske burn.

49

"To Peace"

Kyiv and Lviv, December 2021–February 2022

Far from the eastern front where the war was raging lay Lviv, a picturesque western city near the European Union border. It had become a city of sanctuary for many fleeing Ukrainians. Before the invasion, Lviv had symbolized the sophistication and dynamism that a future Ukraine, democratic and fully integrated into the EU, might enjoy. In the Peace Corps recruiting office, a decade and a half ago, I imagined what a relatively luxurious placement it would make, with its old European buildings, cobblestone squares, and cafes. Now, in many ways, it was a picture of how much pain Russia had inflicted by trying to keep that vision of Ukraine from becoming reality.

It was also where Igor and Ira had settled after fleeing Bakhmut on 25 February 2022. They lived in a three-room apartment with their two children, Sasha and Nastya, and Igor's mother, who'd worked for decades as a leading pediatrician in Bakhmut before retiring and leaving the city with them.

I had got in the habit of calling them up whenever I passed through on my way out of Ukraine to visit Bri at home in New York, or back into the country to return to work. We'd meet up at one of Lviv's numerous fashionable cafes and enjoy the food and cocktails.

After my last trip to Bakhmut, I called them up. Ira was away but Igor was home. He invited me over and we sat and sipped beers for hours. He listed the many things he'd left behind in Bakhmut. In their haste to flee, they were only able to take a suitcase each. In them there were coin collections, family photographs, personal documents, and most of their wardrobes.

"I really miss it," Igor said.

But there was a consolation: he had landed his dream job with the United Nations and the family was doing well. The children had adjusted to their new lives, although Sasha being eight years old had memories of the war and sometimes woke up at night from nightmares about it.

I offered to show Igor a few photographs from my latest visit, but he said he didn't want to see them.

"Just tell me, did you see the apartment?"

"Yes, I did."

"How is it?"

"There was artillery damage to the back side, but the front was mostly fine. But some of the windows are broken."

"Hmm," he said. "Do you think we will lose it?"

"I don't know," I said, choking up. "But I know that whatever happens, the place we knew is gone forever."

Our glasses were empty. Igor went to the fridge to open another bottle of beer.

We drank and toasted, "*Za nas!*" – For us!

We drank more and toasted, "*Za vas!*" – For you!

We drank. We toasted. "*Za Donbas!*" – For the Donbas!

And one last time, we drank. Toasting in English, "To peace!"

50

"I. Love. You."

Kyiv, February 2023

I was in Kyiv in February 2023 when the Ukrainian military announced that it would close access to Bakhmut to journalists and aid workers. The same day a soldier in the city with whom I was in contact said they had blown up the bridge on the Bakhmut–Kostyantynivka highway just west of Ivanivske. There was only one road in and out of the city now. I feared that all this might be a precursor of a strategic retreat and thought about the prospect of never being able to return there.

It was a few days before my birthday, which was the day after Nikolai's. I wrote to Olga Yevgenyevna and to Oleksandr, another former teacher at my school in Ivanivske, formerly Krasne, who I knew to be close to Nikolai, and asked whether they knew where he'd ended up. Olga said he'd managed to leave safely and make his way to Germany, where his son and grandchildren lived. But she had some bad news. "Chris, they destroyed our school today," she told me. "I just found out."

My heart sank.

Oleksandr got back to me with a working number for Nikolai. I called him on his birthday the next day, 16 February. He picked up on the first ring.

"*Allo?*"

"Nikolai Georgiovich, it's Chris."

"*Oho!*" I had caught him off guard. "Is it really Chris?"

"Yes, it's really me!"

"*Moy malchik!*" he said.

We spoke for half an hour, reminiscing about Artemivsk and Krasne, now Bakhmut and Ivanivske. He rambled on about watching me play basketball with the students and kicking my ass in table tennis; the events we held in the community; how terrible my Russian was when I first arrived and it felt like the teaching staff was communicating with one of the first-graders. He remembered when I brought Bri to visit and how popular she was with the eighth-grade girls. I told him we'd been married now for a decade.

"Wow-wow!" he exclaimed.

He told me he was having fun with his two grandchildren in Germany. But he ached for home and his school. And he lamented that he hadn't managed to take all of the students' trophies from the awards room before everyone left.

I told him I had been there several times throughout the past year, and that on my last visit I'd seen it in a terrible state. I said the last time I tried to stop by the school I was stopped by heavy shelling. He sighed and told me it was too dangerous and not to go back.

In typical fashion, he spun the conversation toward the positive. He said he'd been learning German and shared a few phrases with me.

"*Danke schön*," he said, before muttering something else I couldn't make out. "It's better than my English," he told me in Russian.

"Do you remember any of the English words I taught you?" I asked him. He paused.

"*Konechno!*" he said, of course. "I. Love. You."

I chuckled and my eyes welled up. He repeated it twice more and laughed.

"That's right," I said. "I love you."

Acknowledgements

This book and the journey it describes would never have been possible without the encouragement, support, trust and patience of dozens of amazing people.

I'm extremely fortunate to have such a loving and generous family, especially considering what I've put them through with my work and time away from home. Bri, my wife and best friend, grounded me and supported me every step of the way. My parents Steve and Cindy are my role models and the most selfless people I've ever known; I can't even begin to list the many ways in which they helped me. My sister, Courtney, and my late brother, Matt, always cared and checked to make sure I was safe. (Matt, I love you and miss you and remember you every day.)

I am immensely grateful to my many brave, brilliant and gracious Ukrainian friends and acquaintances, who enlightened me, guided me, protected me, mourned with me, laughed with me, confided in me and drank with me. Several must be singled out because they were key to me making sense of their incredible country and its multitude of complexities. In the Donbas, thanks to Igor Moroz, Rostislav Sosnovyy, Natasha Zhukova, Nikolai Sokolov, Olga Kazachenko, Roman Stupachenko, Oleksiy Matsuka, Alina Kosse, Ella Ivanova, Alisa Sopova, Volodymyr Kianov, Kateryna Malofieieva, Alisa Kaiser, Anna Dotsenko, the people of Bakhmut and Ivanivske, and the staff and students at Ivanivske village school and School No. 11. In Kyiv, Katya Gorchinskaya, Inna Varenytsia, Kristina Berdynskykh, Zhenya Maloletka, Katya Sergatskova, Roman Stepanovich, Anton Skyba, Liza Bieliavtseva, Tanya Kozyreva, Anna Vlasenko, Oksana Parafeniuk, Alisa Kovalenko, Olga Ivashchenko, Anastasia Magazova, Marichka Varenikova. In Obukhiv, Viktor, Tanya, Lena and Lyosha, who hosted me at their home in Obukhiv for three months when I first arrived in Ukraine and were so understanding with me as I bumbled my way through learning a foreign language and culture.

My publisher Tomasz Hoskins and the wonderful team at Bloomsbury believed in me and my idea for this book from the very start — and before Russia launched its all-out invasion. Nina Jankowicz, a great friend, connected me with Tomasz and cheered me on the whole way.

David Patterson, my agent at Stuart Krichevsky Literary Agency, helped me navigate the publishing world and ensured this book saw the light of day.

My dear friend Paul Hamilos spent countless hours on walks with me through Brooklyn listening to my stories about Ukraine and helping me draw out more for this book before brilliantly shaping early chapters of it.

I am grateful to my editors at the *Financial Times*, who gave me time to write this book in between filing news reports from Kyiv and dispatches from the Donbas. And to those at *Politico*, BuzzFeed News, Radio Free Europe/Radio Liberty, Mashable, *Kyiv Post* and the many others with whom I worked over the years, for backing me and publishing my work. Jim Roberts deserves to be name-checked for giving me my first full-time job as a foreign correspondent. And Louise Roug, too, for teaching me how to do the job properly.

Shout-outs to my foreign correspondent friends and colleagues who were by my side on the front lines of the war between 2014 and 2022, and in a variety of other tough spots, particularly Max Seddon, Noah Snider, Shaun Walker, Roland Oliphant, Mark MacKinnon, Andrew Kramer, Tom Parfitt, Pete Kiehart, Dan Peleschuk, Isobel Koshiw, Brendan Hoffman, Simon Ostrovsky, Stephane Siohan, Gulliver Cragg, Sebastien Gobert, Fabrice Deprez, Isaac Webb and Harriet Salem.

Many thanks to Richard Mason, who copyedited the book with deftness and care. And to my wonderful mother-in-law Rebecca Folz, who proofread my manuscript.

My uncle Craig lent me his home in the woods on an island to have an uninterrupted three weeks to get a strong start on this book.

Thanks to the U.S. Peace Corps for sending me on assignment to Ukraine to do one of the toughest and most rewarding jobs of my life, and setting me on a path that I never before imagined going down.

Respect to the several security teams that backed me up while I was in the trenches over the years, especially the BuzzFeed News squad composed of Tom Namako, Yemile Bucay, Eliot Stempf and Julia Goldberg, who kept me alive in those first unpredictable and dangerous weeks of Russia's full-scale invasion.

To my murdered friends and colleagues, including Maks Levin and Pavel Sheremet, you and your important work will never be forgotten. I'm proud to have a photograph that Maks made during the 2014 Battle of Ilovaisk grace the cover of this book, and I'm grateful to his family for allowing me to honor him in this way.

It would be remiss of me not to thank my cats Tuck and Liza, who Bri and I rescued in Kyiv in 2013, but who have in many ways helped rescue me in stressful times.

Last but not least, thank you to those of you who have read my journalism over the years and cared about Ukraine.

Index

367